MEIR KAHANE

Meir Kahane

THE PUBLIC LIFE AND
POLITICAL THOUGHT OF AN
AMERICAN JEWISH RADICAL

SHAUL MAGID

PRINCETON UNIVERSITY PRESS
PRINCETON & OXFORD

Published by Princeton University Press
41 William Street, Princeton, New Jersey 08540
99 Banbury Road, Oxford OX2 6JX

press.princeton.edu

First paperback printing, 2023

Paper ISBN 978-0-691-25469-2

The Library of Congress has cataloged the cloth edition as follows:

Names: Magid, Shaul, 1958- author.
Title: Meir Kahane : an American Jewish radical / Shaul Magid.
Description: Princeton, New Jersey : Princeton University Press, [2021] |
Includes bibliographical references and index.
Identifiers: LCCN 2021002987 | ISBN 9780691179339 (hardback) |
ISBN 9780691212661 (ebook)
Subjects: LCSH: Kahane, Meir. | Rabbis—New York (State)—New York—Biography |
Political activists—New York (State)—New York—Biography. | Rabbis—
Israel—Biography. | Political activists—Israel—Biography.
Classification: LCC BM755.K254 M34 2021 | DDC 328.5694/092 [B]—dc23
LC record available at https://lccn.loc.gov/2021002987

British Library Cataloging-in-Publication Data is available

Editorial: Fred Appel and James Collier
Production Editorial: Ellen Foos
Jacket/Cover Design: Pamela Schnitter
Production: Erin Suydam
Publicity: Kate Hensley and Kathryn Stevens
Copyeditor: P. David Hornik

Jacket/Cover image: Meir Kahane outside of the New York Board of Rabbis office, 10 East 73rd Street, New York, June 29, 1970. AP Photo / Harry Harris

This book has been composed in Arno

For Aryeh Cohen

חייל של צדק

Warrior for Justice

CONTENTS

ACKNOWLEDGMENTS

IT IS OFTEN difficult to determine when precisely a book project begins. This book arguably began in my office at Indiana University Bloomington in a conversation with a graduate student, Matthew Brittingham, who proposed to write an MA thesis on history and memory in the work of Meir Kahane, an idea that emerged from a brief discussion of Kahane and the Holocaust in my book *American Post-Judaism*. Intrigued by the idea, we set up a few hours a week to read through much of Kahane's written work chronologically, from short newspaper articles in the early 1960s to his published books through the late 1980s. Matt eventually wrote an excellent thesis, but I was also changed by the experience. I came to realize that Kahane was more than a militant rabbi and gadfly in American and later Israeli society; he represented a particular kind of reactionary and radical critique of the liberal establishment of postwar America that has gone largely unexplored. Although the counterculture often claims the moniker of radicalism in that period, I came to see a form of radicalism in Kahane's worldview as well, one that used the tactics of the far left in the service of a right-wing critique of American Jewry.

Thus began a six-year journey in which I took up residence inside Kahane's head as he lived inside mine. I struggled with making intellectual sense of a middlebrow thinker who did not express himself in a register that was easy to analyze and take seriously in an academic study. And yet over time I began to see that Kahane's often rambling, incendiary, and always provocative writing reflected not only a reactionary mood but held together as an intellectual project, a critique of liberalism both in the US and in Israel. Questions of liberalism, radicalism, race, Jewish identity and pride, and the status of Israel stood at the very center of Kahane's writing from the 1960s through the 1980s—issues that remain relevant today fifty years later. Once settling in Israel his attention turned to his nascent political career (which ended in disaster), but he never lifted his gaze from America and continued to weigh in on American Jewry and Judaism, their future and their demise.

In the midst of working on Kahane's published writings I was fortunate to receive an NEH Senior Research Fellowship at the Center for Jewish History in Manhattan, which contained a series of archives that would change the direction of my work. I want to thank my friend and colleague David Myers, who was the director of the center that year. David has been a constant friend and source of support in this and other projects. I also want to thank all the NEH junior fellows and the staff at the center, and particularly the archivists, llya Slavutskiy, Michelle McCarthy-Behler, and Tyi-Kimya Marx, whose patience was invaluable in introducing me to archival work.

During the initial stages of this project I was the Jay and Jeanie Schottenstein Professor at Indiana University in the Department of Religious Studies and the Borns Jewish Studies Program. My colleagues there provided a vibrant and rigorous intellectual community without which all of us could not do our work. Thanks are due in particular to Judah Cohen, Constance Furey, Cooper Harris, Sarah Imhoff, Kevin Jaques, Dov Baer Kehrler, Jason Mokhtarian, Mark Roseman, Lisa Sideris, Winnifred Sullivan, and Jeffrey Veidlinger. The year I left Indiana, J. Kameron Carter arrived. Although we never crossed paths in Bloomington, he has been a tremendous aid, in his writings and in conversation, in helping me understand the complex debates of critical race theory that proved to be indispensable in the chapter on race. In the midst of my work on this book I was fortunate to receive a faculty appointment at Dartmouth College, in large part thanks to the perseverance of Susannah Heschel who has been an exemplary colleague, friend, coauthor, and coconspirator. Her incisive questions and criticisms have made this book sharper and more focused, and her directorship of the Jewish Studies Program at Dartmouth has cultivated an atmosphere of learning and scholarship. I also want to thank the faculty and fellows at the Shalom Hartman Institute of North America, especially Yehuda Kurtzer and Elana Stein Hain, where I have the privilege to serve as a Kogod Senior Research Fellow.

Special thanks are also due to Emily Burack, whom I met at the Center for Jewish History. Emily was working at the center having just graduated from Dartmouth, where she wrote an excellent senior thesis on Kahane's Jewish Defense League. She worked with me as a research assistant that year and also shared with me some of her archival findings, which turned out to be very useful. Along those lines, Menachem Butler continues to be an invaluable colleague, who also has an interest in Kahane and postwar American Orthodoxy. He was a generous interlocutor through the final years of working on the book and shared with me some of his ongoing research on Kahane and American Orthodoxy.

Over the course of these past years I have had the pleasure to have extraordinary interlocutors whose expertise, knowledge, honesty, and friendship have been invaluable. Some have invited me to speak about Kahane in various institutions, podcasts, and so on. Others have read parts of this book and offered suggestions. I am grateful to Lila Corwin-Berman, Martin Kavka, and Eliyahu Stern, each of whom read the entire manuscript and provided valuable criticisms. Others include Sydney Anderson, Leora Batnitzky, Zachary Braiterman, Geoffrey Classen, Hasia Diner, Marc Dollinger, Glenn Dynner, Jeanette Friedman, Pinhas Giller, Aubrey Glazer, Christine Hayes, Hanan Hever, Eric Jacobson, Ari Kelman, Shaul Kelner, Paul Nahme, Eden Pearlstein, Tomer Persico, Steve Peskoff, Riv-Ellen Prell, Joe Schwartz, Naomi Seidman, Joshua Shanes, Ely Stillman, Yossi Turner, and Elliot Wolfson. I also want to thank Yossi Klein Halevi, whose *Memoirs of a Jewish Extremist*, which tells of his complex relationship with Kahane, was very helpful. While we may differ on many things, Yossi and I have known one another since the late 1970s and share a continued interest in the complexity of Kahane. Although we have never met, I must mention Libby Kahane, whose two-volume documentary biography of her late husband *Rabbi Meir Kahane: His Life and Thought* provided invaluable resources for this book. She shared some personal letters in her work that proved significant. She may not like how I have understood her late husband, but I wanted to let her know that I read her work closely and carefully. I also want to thank Avi Weiss and Dov Weiss. Through Dov I was able to obtain copies of all the correspondence between Kahane and Avi Weiss, who was a close confidant in the 1970s and 1980s.

For the past twenty years I have served as the rabbi of the Fire Island Synagogue and I want to thank all of its members for their support, in particular its officers Lisa Alter, Joel Confino, Ed Schechter, and cantor Basya Schechter.

To my children and grandchildren, Yehuda, Chisda, Miriam, Kinneret, Kun, Galil, and Leonard Theodore, your presence is always felt, even from afar. Thanks to my mother Deanna and sister Beth Magid Schwartz for all their support. This book could never have come into existence without my partner in all matters of love and life, Annette Yoshiko Reed. Far from her scholarly interests, Annette spent untold hours talking through my ideas about Kahane and postwar America, reading drafts, and making crucial suggestions. Her keen eye and literary acumen helped bring Kahane to life in these pages. She exemplifies what it means to be a life partner and true beloved interlocutor.

My gratitude goes to Princeton University Press, and especially to Fred Appel, who took an early interest in this project and read every chapter carefully as the final version began to take shape. His editorial hand is much appreciated. And to P. David Hornik for his copyediting and Ellen Foos for her help through the production process.

This book is dedicated to Aryeh Cohen. I first met Aryeh when we were candidate fellows at the Shalom Hartman Institute in Jerusalem in 1985. We then became classmates at Brandeis University and have been talking, arguing, and reading each other's work ever since. Although Aryeh knew Kahane as a young man in the Orthodox world in Brooklyn, he took a very different path. His devotion to social justice, his commitment to painstakingly creating an ethos of nonviolence from the sources of the rabbinic tradition, and his dedication to taking Jewish progressive values to the streets of America are exemplary and a model for future rabbis and scholars. He has been an inspiration to me and to many others. "Whose streets? Our streets!" May it be so.

Shaul Magid
Thetford, VT

ARCHIVES CONSULTED

American Jewish Historical Society—JDL collection
American Jewish Historical Society—Jewish Student Organizations collection
American Jewish Historical Society—Jews for Urban Justice collection
YIVO Archives—JDL collection
YIVO Archives—Peter Novik collection
Rabbi Avi Weiss, private correspondence

MEIR KAHANE

Introduction

WHY KAHANE?

IN THE EARLY SPRING of 2018 I was attending a bat mitzvah in a Jewish suburb of a major American city. The bat mitzvah was at a large Modern Orthodox synagogue. During the Shabbat-day festive meal I was waiting on line at the buffet when I struck up a conversation with a professional-looking man, probably in his mid-fifties. He seemed educated, friendly, and not particularly ideological. He asked me what I did, and I told him that I was at the Center for Jewish History in New York on a research grant. He asked me what I was working on. When I told him I was writing a cultural biography of Meir Kahane, his eyes opened wide and he responded, "If you want my opinion, I agree with everything Kahane said. Everything he predicted came true. He just should have said it in a nicer way." What was so striking to me about his response was its matter-of-factness—his willingness to make that statement to someone he barely knew as if it was uncontroversial. I was wearing a kippah, and as far as he knew, I was a member of the Modern Orthodox "club" that gave him license to voice his positive assessment of Kahane. As we moved on to the buffet I was struck by how Kahane seems on the one hand to be a persona non grata in American Jewry, and yet on the other hand a figure whose presence remains ubiquitous, almost like part of the subconscious of a certain slice of American Judaism, especially Modern Orthodoxy.

More than half a century has passed since Meir Kahane founded the controversial Jewish Defense League (JDL) in New York in May 1968. The JDL was established as a response to the 1968 Ocean Hill–Brownsville school strike that crippled the New York City school system. I tell the story of the role of the strike in Kahane's career in more detail in chapters 1 and 3, but here it suffices to say that anti-Semitic pamphlets were distributed by some African

American PTA members of the school district in part because the president of the United Federation of Teachers, Albert Shanker, was a Jew, and the district had a high percentage of white Jewish teachers among a student population that was over 90 percent black and Hispanic.[1] In addition, liberal mayor John Lindsay, who sided with the teachers' union and Shanker against the parents, was a longtime target for Kahane. Kahane disagreed with Lindsay's liberalism and felt he was not acting in the interest of the Jews of the city.

Through the early 1970s, the JDL flourished and chapters arose in many urban centers in America. The notion of Jewish pride and protecting vulnerable Jews against criminality struck a chord with a new generation of Jews and with older Jews who felt vulnerable in their neighborhoods. JDL activities also included arms smuggling across state lines and illegal transportation of materials to make explosives. They were followed closely by J. Edgar Hoover and the FBI, and by law enforcement. By 1975 the JDL had largely collapsed under local and federal indictments for arms smuggling and possession of explosives. Kahane, for his part, moved to Israel in September 1971 and founded a political party, KACH. After two failed attempts to be elected to the Knesset, he succeeded in 1984. In 1986 KACH was labeled a racist party by the Knesset and Kahane was removed from his parliamentary post. The JDL in America continued without him but never really overcame its legal troubles. And without Kahane as the charismatic leader, it ultimately descended into little more than a street gang.

In Israel, Kahane continued his clandestine activities; by 1972 he had already spent time in Israeli jails. He was arrested over sixty times and found guilty of numerous offenses including incitement to violence. His organization was labeled a terrorist group in Israel, and many of its members spent considerable time in American and Israeli prisons. Nevertheless, even in 2018, a middle-aged Modern Orthodox man at a buffet table might state matter-of-factly to an almost total stranger that "I agree with everything Kahane said. Everything he predicted came true." Many of the ideas Kahane professed continue to resonate today, even in more conventional or mainstream parts of American and Israeli Jewry.

Why write a book about Meir Kahane? Over the past six or seven years, whenever I mention to friends or colleagues that I have been working on such a book, I get one of two reactions. Some scratch their heads and ask, "Why would you want to spend so much time working on such a despicable person, a thug, someone who was an embarrassment to the Jewish people?" But others say, "Oh, that's a great project; I always thought someone should write a serious study of him."[2] The fact that the prospect of a scholarly study of Kahane elicits such starkly opposite reactions is precisely why such a work is needed and where this book begins.

I never met Meir Kahane, although for some years I inhabited a world where he was ubiquitous. In the early 1980s, I once shared a rental in Boro Park, Brooklyn, with a JDL member. He was a young idealistic type. He was very proud to be a Jew and wore a kippah, but he was not very religious; I am not even sure he kept Shabbat. On his bookshelf, next to a Pentateuch and a book of Psalms, was a four-volume softcover set of books entitled *How to Kill*. This series offered details of different ways of murdering someone, including some very graphic photos, instructive diagrams, and lists of weapons. Leaning against the wall were a few baseball bats, brass knuckles, and nunchucks (which were by then illegal in New York State). We remained casual acquaintances. I was a *haredi* yeshiva student at the time, and he was a street Jew, one of Kahane's "chayas" (animals), although he was tall and skinny and not a threatening figure at all. Thinking about him after all these years and after close to a decade of seriously reading Kahane's work, I doubt he had read much of what Kahane wrote. But he was a proud Jew because of what Kahane *represented*. Kahane represented Jewish pride.

By 1980 the JDL was a skeleton of what it once was in the early 1970s, decimated by arrests, indictments, and emigration to Israel. By that time Kahane occasionally visited or wrote to the organization he founded, but he had moved past it, his eyes now set on a political career in Israel. But the JDL nevertheless lived on, and Kahane's image continued to inspire young adherents—as it does to this day.

Who was Meir Kahane? Meir Kahane was an American Jew. He was born in New York City on August 1, 1932, and raised in a middle-class neighborhood in Brooklyn. He spent his adolescence among Jews, many of whom had survived the Holocaust, in a community reeling from the devastating effects of the Nazi genocide. The Holocaust was ever present and at the same time, absent. It surrounded everything but was often hushed up publicly. Kahane's proximate family was not directly affected by the Holocaust; they had emigrated to America or Mandatory Palestine before the Nazi onslaught. After high school, Kahane spent thirteen years attending the Mir Yeshiva in Brooklyn. "The Mir," as it was called, was transplanted from Russia via Kobe, Japan, where many of its students fled after the Nazi invasion of the Soviet Union. Its New York branch opened in 1946 with support from American Jews, one of whom was Kahane's father Charles.

One of the most respected figures at the Mir and the leader of the New York branch was Rabbi Abraham Kalmanowitz (1887–1964). He had been the head of the Telz Yeshiva in Lithuania (which relocated to Cleveland, Ohio) and was elected head of the Mir Yeshiva in 1926 in Belarus. Kalmanowitz led many of its students to Japan sometime before the Nazi liquidation of the Mir Ghetto on August 13, 1942. Kahane had a very close relationship with Kalmanowitz, who officiated at his wedding and gave him rabbinic ordination. During his years at the Mir, Kahane became well versed in classical Jewish texts as well as the method known as musar, which uses Jewish texts to facilitate self-perfection and behavior modification. This will be explored in some detail in chapter 6. Interestingly, while he served as rabbi of a few congregations in Queens and Brooklyn, New York, in the 1950s, his early career and writings do not exhibit his yeshiva training. Among his young JDL constituents he was called "the Reb" (a hip euphemism for "rabbi"), but it isn't until he settles in Israel in the early 1970s that one sees his religious character come to the fore. In chapter 6 I explore in some detail his magnum opus *The Jewish Idea*, a work of over six hundred pages in Hebrew and a thousand pages in English, where Kahane's yeshiva training becomes readily apparent. In general, as will be discussed in chapters 5 and 6, Kahane became a religious figure in Israel in ways he was not in America.

Trained as a rabbi and studying in yeshivot, Kahane also graduated from the NYU School of Law with a law degree specializing in international studies but repeatedly failed to pass the bar exam. An avid baseball fan, he worked as a sports writer for a local newspaper in Brooklyn, as a congregational rabbi, and then as a journalist for the *Jewish Press*, a Brooklyn weekly. Until the mid-1960s it seems Kahane was heading for a middling career as another Modern Orthodox rabbi in New York City. But he clearly had aspirations of grandeur. In 1967 he published a book, *The Jewish Stake in Vietnam*, coauthored with his childhood friend and political operative Joseph Churba, and the same year testified to Congress about Soviet Jewry. But it was really the founding of the JDL in May 1968 that made Kahane a public figure, largely due to the organization's militant activities in New York, Philadelphia, and Boston and its ability to get into the regional and national press.

He rose to national fame through his involvement with Soviet Jewry. While he published a short article called "To Save Soviet Jewry" in 1964, he did not involve himself with them until late 1969; the movement on their behalf was officially established by Yaakov Birnbaum in 1964.[3] By 1970 Kahane became a central figure in the Soviet Jewry movement. He also founded a summer camp,

Camp Jedel, where campers learned martial arts, self-defense, and how to shoot guns.

Kahane emigrated to Israel in September 1971 after he was given a suspended sentence for illegal activities tied to the JDL. In 1975 he returned to America to serve out a sentence for parole violations, spending a year in a federal penitentiary in Allenwood, Pennsylvania, where, among other things, he successfully campaigned for kosher food in the prison. When he returned to Israel, he began a political career, eventually (as noted) founding his own party, and in 1984 he was elected to the Knesset. The controversies surrounding his ideas culminated in 1986 in the "Racism Law" passed to oust him from the Knesset and ban his political party. On November 5, 1990, after a speech at the Marriott Hotel in Manhattan, Kahane was shot in the neck at close range by El Sayyid Nosair, an Egyptian-born Muslim who lived in New Jersey. Nosair was acquitted of the murder. Yet years later, when convicted of charges relating to the first World Trade Center bombing, he admitted to murdering Kahane. Kahane's funeral in Israel was one of the largest in the history of the country.

Kahane's life was colorful and controversial. During his heyday in America (1968–1974) his name was widely known among American Jews and the JDL received donations from various sectors of the Jewish community, religious and secular. But despite his ubiquity during an important era for American Jewry, his life and thought have not been fully integrated into the history of American Jews and Judaism. For example, while researching this book, I was looking up a source in the definitive history of Jews in America, Jonathan Sarna's *American Judaism*—first published in 2004 with a new edition in 2019—and I was struck by the fact that this six-hundred-page study does not contain a single reference to Meir Kahane or the JDL.[4] How could this be, given how influential Kahane was in the United States from the late 1960s through the 1980s? My point here is not to criticize Sarna's monumental work, nor to suggest that a scholar of his stature might have simply forgotten about Kahane or the JDL. My sense is that this omission was intentional and reflects a broader impulse to expunge him—and the radical militancy he represents—from our narratives about American Jewish culture and history. This book makes the case that this history cannot be told without him.

Most studies on the iconoclastic rabbi Meir Kahane view his life and work in reverse. That is, even when they examine his life in America, they often regard it from the lens of his later career in Israel. For example, Daniel Breslauer's book *Meir Kahane: Ideologue, Hero, Thinker* focuses a good deal on his life in

America and yet consistently refers to him as a "fanatic."[5] While I do think "fanatic" captures Kahane's later life and while his program in Israel could easily be deemed "fanatical," I don't think the term quite describes his American career, certainly not in the 1960s and early 1970s. Radicalism, yes; fanaticism, no.[6] Viewing Kahane from back to front may be the reason why Sarna's otherwise comprehensive *American Judaism* completely ignores him. I do not think any history of Israel from 1948 to the present could ever get away with not mentioning Kahane. His rise and fall in Israeli politics and society was a major event in Israel in the 1980s.

I think part of the explanation is that American Jewry and many of its historians are embarrassed by Kahane and refuse to view him as a noteworthy figure even though until the mid- to late 1970s he was ubiquitous on the national stage. I would venture to say that from 1968 to 1973 Kahane was mentioned more frequently in the *New York Times* than any other American rabbi. He gave a feature interview to *Playboy* in 1972 and was the subject of a major article in *Esquire* that same year. Even given that national exposure, many viewed his radical reactionary views as an aberration in the otherwise liberal or progressive climate of postwar America. It is true that his career in America was quite short; he emerged on the scene as a public figure in the late 1960s and by 1971 had left for Israel. While he subsequently divided his time between Israel and the US, one could argue that by the mid-1970s Kahane was no longer part of American Jewish history. This book maintains that such assumptions are mistaken.

Rather than viewing America as Kahane's prehistory and his career in Israel as having significant and lasting impact, I view Kahane and his significance the other way around. America was where his impact was really felt and Israel was a kind of a coda where he ultimately did not succeed, in part because his thinking remained mired in an American discourse. True, there is a significant afterlife of Kahanism in Israel until today, but that afterlife is in large part the product of a homegrown Israeli Kahanism, or neo-Kahanism, that is less about him than we imagine. The Kahanism of Meir Kahane was a dismal failure in Israel. As I will try to show throughout this book, Kahanism was—not in its tactics but in its worldview—far more successful in America than we imagine precisely because he was and remained a product of postwar American Judaism.

His story is not only a Jewish story, nor is it only a Jewish-American story. It is a story of religion and ethnic identity in America in the second half of the twentieth century. Kahane's Jewish radicalism is an untold chapter in the radicalism of race, ethnicity, and identity politics in the 1960s and 1970s. Kahane should be placed alongside Malcolm X and Stokely Carmichael, and the Jewish Defense League should be viewed alongside the Black Panthers and the Young Lords. Can we even imagine a history of black America in the twentieth century without one mention of Malcolm X or the Black Panthers? Even as some historians today may wince at the separatism and militarism of Black Power, they could not justify erasing it from the annals of African American history.

When scholars of American religion today include chapters on Jews and Judaism in their work, these chapters almost never mention Kahane or the JDL. And yet I will argue throughout this book that the shift away from classical liberalism and assimilationism in American Jewry, while it is certainly caused by many factors, also includes the influence of the fairly brief but intense presence of Kahanism as a contestation of cultural and political liberalism. He played a significant role in the emergence of the Jewish counterculture of the baby boomer generation, and he played a part in radical American politics from about 1965 to 1974.

This book is not a biography in any conventional sense. I do not offer a chronological account of Kahane's life nor do I dwell on his background, friendships, or family. For those details one can look at Libby Kahane's very useful, albeit uncritical, two-volume biography *Rabbi Meir Kahane: His Life and Thought*, Robert Friedman's journalistic *False Prophet*, Daniel Breslauer's *Meir Kahane: Ideologue, Hero, and Thinker*, or Yair Kotler's polemical *Heil Kahane*.[7] I am a scholar of Jewish thought and not a social historian. What interests me are the ideas that inform Jewish culture, politics, and religion. This book about Meir Kahane is concerned with the trajectory of his thought in the context of the changing contours of postwar America and later in Israel during the development of right-wing Zionism in the 1970s and 1980s.

As with any public figure, Kahane's life is very much a part of his thought and therefore his life often enters into this study, especially in America. I argue that he is best viewed as a cultural icon who was able to shift the discourse of American Jewry, and later Israeli politics, through sheer will, perseverance, and maniacal certitude. Kahane was a Jewish radical, a militant advocate for Jewish pride, and a destructive force against human decency. But he was also an influential critic of the hypocrisy of 1960s and 1970s American Jewish liberalism and a gadfly to its power.

In Israel, he tapped into the anger and resentment of many who were excluded from the liberally minded Ashkeno-centric circles of power. He was a political jokester, a huckster, and an attention seeker. He was also a powerful critic of hypocrisy, even as his life is itself a study in hypocrisy. Kahane claimed to love all Jews—he often signed personal letters with "for the love of Israel"—yet he spoke derisively about most Jews who disagreed with him. He claimed his fidelity was to Israel and yet he was a quintessential American, even decades after emigrating to Israel. He may have lived in Israel from 1971 until his assassination in 1990 (while spending about half his time in America), but in many ways he remained an American thinker, which is why I argue that his Israeli career was a failure until it struck more indigenous roots among his Israeli followers.

America was where Kahane made his mark, and he made quite a mark—more so, I suggest, than is usually recognized. His militancy has been largely rejected by the American Jewish establishment. Yet many of his basic precepts have been embraced among present-day American Jewry. This is an audacious claim, but I hope that after reading this book it will seem less provocative even if no less alarming. Kahane spoke of Jewish "survival" in a decade when Jewish liberals were still talking about acculturation. Kahane warned of the dangers of intermarriage (e.g., writing a book on the subject in 1974) long before the "intermarriage crisis" became standard fare in American Jewish circles. He was an "Israel right or wrong" advocate before AIPAC and before Israel became the civil religion of American Jewry. He decried the anti-Semitism on the left when most establishment figures were worried about anti-Semitism on the right. And he argued for a Jewish turn toward conservatism a full decade before the rise of neoconservatism. Today much of mainstream American Jewry has become "survivalist," even if we now prefer more genteel terms like "continuity."

More than many others, Kahane understood programmatically the turn in American culture in the era of the New Left. Militarism was a product of the time, and he adopted it toward Jewish ends when most Jews viewed it as something "goyish." When he founded Camp Jedel (which was coed) in 1971 in Wawarsing, New York, in the Catskills, campers learned to shoot guns "as Jews." Today many American Jews send their children for a year in Israel where they take part in Gadna, an Israeli military training program for youth where they learn to shoot guns "as Jews." Militarism has found a comfortable home among many of today's American Jews—so long as it is aimed at the defense of Israel. Kahane wanted to make that true in the Diaspora as well. "Every Jew a .22" was his brand. This is not to say that the American Jewish community is Kahanist. Kahane wanted Jews to embrace the use of violence wherever the lives of Jews are threatened or curtailed, including in the Diaspora, and this is where mainstream American Jewish opinion parts company with him—at least for now. However, many of the structural shifts in questions of Jewish identity, including the issue of anti-Semitism, that have taken root in contemporary American soil were espoused by Kahane long before they were popular.

This book takes Kahane's thought seriously, interweaving accounts of his life, activities, and activism with close analysis of his writings. Not wedded to strict chronology, I return to certain seminal events numerous times throughout the book, examining them from different vantage points depending on the context. Chapters 1 and 2 discuss his critique of liberalism and embrace of radicalism and contextualize it in relation to the political landscape of 1960s America. Chapter 3 turns to the charges of racism against him, drawing out his own discourse about Jews and race and its resonance with the Black Nationalism of his time. Then in chapter 4 I examine his involvement in the Soviet Jewry movement and its relationship to his pro-Vietnam War stance and his writings against communism. In chapters 5 and 6 I consider his Zionism through the lens of his major writings while in Israel. In the process, this book seriously investigates Kahane's "survivalism" in all its facets with an eye to his continued influence even today.

The final two chapters focus on Kahane's career in Israel, and they are based more on his writings than his personal activities. The reason is my surmise that when Kahane begins his rise in the Israeli political world in the 1970s, he becomes a public figure who is known as an ideologue and a voice for a disenfranchised and angry segment of the Israeli population. He writes prodigiously, addressing both the Israeli context and American Judaism. In 1975 he published *The Story of the Jewish Defense League*, which is a kind of retrospective of his American career. In addition, he published a book on intermarriage in America (*Why Be Jewish?*) and one on the failure of American Judaism (*Time to Go Home*) after his *aliyah*. That is, even as he became an "Israeli," he never really left his American roots or his self-appointed role as critic of American Jewry. Most of his Israeli followers know little of those writings.

In the 1980s Kahane focused more on his critique of Israeli society and his increasingly apocalyptic vision of redemption. The last two chapters focus on the trajectory of his thought from an American militant Zionist to an apocalyptic prophet of doom, what I call militant post-Zionism. And yet, as I articulate in the conclusion, even toward the end of his life Kahane still thought very much like an American, which is why he was never quite able to navigate the complex world of Israeli politics; it was only after his death that a homegrown Israeli version of Kahanism that I call neo-Kahanism began to grow. This neo-Kahanism integrates Kookean romantic thinking and the national-religious ideology that emerged among the students of Rabbi Zvi Yehuda Kook. As I show in chapter 5, Kahane had little interest or use for Rabbi Abraham Isaac Kook or his son Zvi Yehuda.

Once he gets his sea legs in Israel in the mid-1970s, and certainly by the early 1980s, his political writings about the future of Israel become his trademark. Personally, he settled into Mattersdorf, a middle-class religious neighborhood in Jerusalem where he lived until his death in 1990, and his domestic life in Israel appears fairly normal. His wife Libby became a librarian and archivist and his children were raised in the religious community in Jerusalem. His son Benjamin was murdered in a terrorist attack in the West Bank in 2000. His short-lived love affair in the mid-1960s with an Italian woman in New York named Gloria Jean D'Argenio aka Estelle Donna Evans, who committed suicide after Kahane broke off the relationship, seems not to have followed him to Israel. There he increasingly adopts a religious persona that serves as the basis of his following.

A note on the organization of the chapters: Since this is not a conventional biography, certain events that happen later are discussed earlier than those that precede them. In fact, the time frame of the entire book is quite short—a mere two decades from Kahane's emergence as a public figure with the founding of the JDL in 1968 to his murder in 1990. In retrospect, it is quite fascinating that what Kahane brought into the world, and what remains thirty years after his death, all occurred in a mere twenty-two years, and the majority of this book, excluding the final two chapters, focuses on little more than a decade, from 1968 until the early 1980s.[8] The chapters are ordered to provide a sense of what is at stake for Kahane and how the key themes impel his activism in both America and Israel. Thus I begin with liberalism and radicalism as these were the issues at play in the late 1960s when Kahane entered the public sphere. Chapter 2 dispels a myth that his reactionary politics were hopelessly at odds with the progressive-left New Jews of the late 1960s and early 1970s. Both were radical critiques of liberalism and expressions of Jewish identity and pride, often using similar methods toward different ends. From there I move to race and violence, which stand at the very center of Kahane's activist project of facing down Jewish assimilation and what he sarcastically called "melting."

The chapter on Vietnam and Soviet Jewry shows that Soviet Jewry was for him merely a piece of a much more complex vision of anticommunism that informs his support for the Vietnam War when most Jews were against it. It is only after a detailed assessment of his American career that we can understand what transpired once he became a political actor in Israel.[9] The last two chapters trace the trajectory of his Zionist "wokeness" in Israel and, after successes and failures, his turn to a dark apocalyptic politics and, in my view, an abandonment of any kind of conventional Zionism. Thus while the venue and context changed, the same basic issues animated his thinking through his short but intense public career.

As a way of keeping a focus not only on Kahane and his thinking but also his afterlife and impact on American Judaism today, exemplified in my Modern Orthodox interlocutor at the buffet table, many of the chapters conclude with a series of observations, often intentionally provocative, about how Kahane's intervention plays out in subsequent decades. These codas are meant to dispel the impression that we are engaged in a purely historical project, and to suggest that we are dealing with a presentist project as well. I argue that by marginalizing or ignoring Kahane we have not seen the way he has, in some way, hypnotized us. That is, we have absorbed more of his worldview than we think.

One of the more vexing challenges of writing a book on such a divisive, problematic, and complex figure is how to do justice to the man and his work in all their outrageousness while at the same time offering a coherent presentation of his ideas. In addition, there are specific challenges involved in writing about a middle-brow thinker. Kahane was not an intellectual; his worldview did not emerge from a deep engagement with the Western philosophical canon. He was a voracious reader of the *New York Times* and topical magazines such as *Time*, *Look*, *Newsweek*, and even *Commentary* and had a fairly lucid understanding of Jewish history as told through an Orthodox lens. The occupational hazard of this project is to make him more intellectually astute than he was. And yet what I have found in the years of delving into Kahane's writings, often outrageous, cynical, comical, and offensive, is that he had an intuitive sense of the how the winds were blowing and had his finger on the pulse of the fears and anxieties of Jews, in America and in Israel. I would not go so far as to say that he was a savant, but he did have an uncanny ability to be in the right place at the right time and express (and also manipulate) the fears of his audience.

The Holocaust stands at the center of Kahane's thought, and he was particularly astute about the anger and challenges of children of survivors who struggled against their parents' often quietistic and fearful approach to the world around them. In a way the Holocaust was the very proof of his ideology. In

Never Again! he writes that most Jews misunderstand the Holocaust. It should not have been a surprise; quite the opposite, it was in a way the inevitable consequence of a world where gentiles simply hate Jews. The Holocaust was simply the instance when Jew-hatred could be implemented in an unfettered manner. According to Kahane, it was not a unique event in Jewish history but, rather, history's logical outcome.

Many of the young men and women who became his base, as it were, were receptive to the notion that anti-Semitism could never be erased, only managed through Jewish strength. In this sense, Kahane was an unadulterated post-Holocaust thinker.[10] He enabled many young Jews to express their frustration and anger, against their parents but also against their surroundings. He became their ticket to express a sense of pride in Jewish power that resembled what many of them saw emerging among Black Nationalists. "Jewish Panthers" was a badge of honor for many JDLers. He gave them an alternative vision of what it meant to be a Diaspora Jew, and for those who emigrated to Israel, to express their anti-Arab sentiment with no guilt.

Kahane and the JDL beg for a serious gender critique.[11] The movement Kahane initiated, while coed, was dominated by young men, and Kahane's worldview incorporated a strong sense of renewed masculinity to erase the effeminate stereotype of Jews that helped feed anti-Semitic tropes for centuries. His use of power and militancy was an attempt, in part, to rebuild the Jewish male in America.[12] Although he often modeled this reconstruction on the "muscle" Zionism of Max Nordau and later Ze'ev Jabotinsky, in many ways Kahane's renewed masculinity was in fact an adaptation of the Protestant masculinity of American religion more generally. As Sarah Imhoff notes in her *Masculinity and the Making of American Judaism*, masculinity was one of the ways Judaism became an American religion.[13] Kahane and the JDL are part of that story.

Thus what Kahane may have thought was an exercise in difference was in fact an exercise in assimilation. Ridding the Jew of the effeminate brand made the Jew more American and, in another sense, more "Protestant."[14] In one regard, then, we can say that the JDL may have been one of the most *assimilated* groups in American Judaism at the time. A serious gender critique of Kahane would then have to explore his marginalization of the feminine as a "mystique" that had damaged the Jew historically in favor of a "new man," a Jew who was both an avid sports fan and physically able and willing to defend himself. Kahane wanted to bury the Jewish "patsy"; but doing so was itself a kind of assimilatory act. The Jew becomes more of a Jew by becoming more of an American.

It is significant to note that while groups like the Black Panthers, whom Kahane both admired and despised, were also dominated by men, there were some important female figures in the Panther movement, for example, Elaine Brown, who took over its leadership in 1974, and Kathleen Cleaver, who was its communications secretary. The JDL had no such prominent women in leadership roles. A serious gender critique, here in terms of Kahane's reconstruction of the Jewish male, would be an important addition to studies of Kahane and his influence. This book does not take on that task but notes the veneration of male strength and the erasure of passivity in numerous places.

While some may argue that Kahane was an incoherent and self-contradictory thinker, I believe his ideas, even as they were presented in provocative and often ugly ways, do in fact cohere with a perspective of Jewish history, religion, and political life. While they may be chauvinistic, racist, and xenophobic, and they may at times offer simplistic and uninformed presentations of the complexities of the ideas he despised, for example, liberalism, Kahane propounds a vision of Jewishness, and later Judaism, that should not be summarily dismissed as incoherent. And the seeds of Kahane's chauvinistic vision indeed constitute a dark side of Judaism more generally. This book argues that he should be treated seriously and critically and the weaknesses of his worldview exposed.

Meir Kahane: The Public Life and Political Thought of an American Jewish Radical is not an apologia of Kahane, even though I sometimes think his critique of the Jewish establishment in America and Israel is quite incisive. Nor is it a diatribe against him.[15] It is an attempt to understand his worldview from his life, activism, and writings as a way to examine his influence, both in his time and today. And it is an attempt to see his influence today, especially in unpredictable places.

This book has two objectives. The first is to critically examine the outlook of one of the most divisive Jewish figures of the second half of the twentieth century. The second is to explore the way some of Kahane's ideas, which were shunned and rejected by much of the Jewish world, inadvertently seeped into the Jewish mainstream, certainly in Israel but also in America. One can see that in the snapshot of my Modern Orthodox friend at the bat mitzvah buffet that began this chapter.

In order to make the second case, I need to offer a coherent rendering of those ideas, both as they emerge from the Jewish tradition but also in the social and political context of postwar America and in an American Judaism that was struggling to both assimilate yet maintain a sense of difference in the tumultuous countercultural years from about 1960 to 1980. In particular, I suggest that Kahane's ideas resonated with a young population, some of whom had been radicalized by New Left politics and found their way back to Judaism in light of the New Left's critique of Israel after 1967.

My argument is thus counterintuitive in the sense that I maintain that the figure who is one of the most shunned and maligned in recent Jewish history may unwittingly stand at the very center of Jews' continuing struggle to understand their place in history. In this sense, Kahane is to me what Sabbatai Zevi was for Gershom Scholem: the heretic who played a central role behind the scenes in defining a messianically infused normative Judaism, or in Kahane's case, Jewish identity.[16]

By any measure, his life and thought form a fascinating chapter in Jewish history. But there must be more. My contention is that he is not just a curious footnote to that history and should not be marginalized from our narratives about American Jews and Judaism in the twentieth century. Rather, Kahane's ideas remain very much alive, even where we might not expect to see them. We erase Kahane from our imagination and our history at our own peril.

This book is thus an intervention into contemporary Judaism and Jewishness as much as it is a book about Meir Kahane. Kahane makes most Jews uncomfortable, and rightfully so, and yet without that discomfort it is too easy to miss crucial fissures and gaping holes in understanding the Jewish experience today. Kahane is the Jew whom Jews would like to forget, and yet he keeps coming back to haunt us. The reason, I suggest, is that he remains very much inside the Jewish psyche, as the gentleman at the buffet readily acknowledged. The wager in this book is that there is no getting beyond Kahane except through him.

Meir Kahane: The Public Life and Political Thought of an American Jewish Radical is thus more than the story of one man. It is the story of a time through the lens of one man who was ubiquitous in that time—loved, hated, followed, rejected, imprisoned, lionized, politicized, and eventually martyred. Few Jewish individuals in the twentieth century evoked such visceral responses. And few have been so misunderstood.

1

Liberalism

MEIR KAHANE'S AMERICAN PEDIGREE: RADICALISM AND LIBERALISM IN 1960S AMERICAN JEWRY

"Indeed the JDL was the most fully American of any Jewish organization, for it tested, without anxiety, the limits of American tolerance toward Jews."

"No Jewish leader spoke as incessantly of love for the Jewish people as Kahane did, and none so despised his fellow Jews."

YOSSI KLEIN HALEVI, *MEMOIRS OF A JEWISH EXTREMIST*

"We have done nothing less than revolutionize American Jewish thinking and radically change the views and activities of the American Jewish community."

MEIR KAHANE, "A DECADE ENDS—AND BEGINS," *JEWISH PRESS*, 1978 (REFLECTING ON THE TENTH ANNIVERSARY OF THE JDL)

Kahane's American Agenda

This book is not really about Meir Kahane, a Jew born in prewar Brooklyn who studied in the Mir Yeshiva, became a rabbi, graduated from Brooklyn College and then the NYU School of Law, had a wife and three children, and became a journalist. Rather, it is about Meir Kahane the public figure, who only really enters the scene in the spring of 1968 when New York City was reeling from a contentious public school strike in the Ocean Hill–Brownsville neighborhood of Brooklyn that brought to the surface anti-Semitic sentiments among some of the black parents and administrators.[1] The strike inspired this struggling young rabbi to found the Jewish Defense League. From that point, Kahane developed a systemic and public critique of the American Jewish establishment whose impact reached far beyond his small band of Jewish vigilantes.

There were three issues that drove Kahane's ideological agenda in America: racism, communism, and assimilation. These were also central to the American Jewish postwar experience more generally. In each case, Kahane frames his critique as an attack on liberalism. By liberalism I do not mean the more formal definition made popular by John Locke of a political ideology that, in opposition to republicanism's notion of "the common good" and "the public sphere," argues for "individual liberties" and "private happiness."[2] This classical liberal ideology is the foundation of America and in general Kahane would agree with it. More contemporary forms of liberalism and conservatism are really different and convergent iterations of America's liberal-democratic ethos. When radicals disparaged liberalism in the 1960s, they were referring to a system that viewed incremental correction as preferable to revolutionary change. From that viewpoint, the inequities and injustices that existed in the present form of government could be mended while retaining the basic capitalist and imperialist system, for example, by implementing President Johnson's Great Society program. For these radicals, the evil of liberalism was that it perpetuated injustice in the name of justice. The Black Nationalist critique of liberalism was essentially that civil rights and desegregation eventually came up against the forces of white hegemony and the structural inequalities that the liberal civil rights movement could not eradicate. The legislative successes of civil rights (e.g., the Civil Rights Act of 1964 and the Voting Rights Act of 1965) left in place the hegemony of white society and structural racism that no legislation could eradicate. Scholars have argued that Martin Luther King became increasingly aware of that reality as well and moved closer to Black Nationalism and issues of entrenched poverty in the last year of his life.[3]

Liberalism was, for Kahane, the great challenge of American Judaism, and later, the factor that was undermining the legitimacy of Zionism in Israel. But while Zionism played a role in Kahane's early work, it is marginal in contrast to the three pillars of his American agenda. His breakout book *Never Again!* has only one chapter on Zionism, and it isn't until the 1970s that Kahane gives up on America and calls for mass *aliyah* (which never got off the ground). On this reading, Israel for Kahane was a solution to what he viewed as the failure of the American Jewish dream, the dream that stood at the very center of his early career. And as we will see, Israel fails for him precisely because it absorbs too much of American liberalism to maintain its assertive claim to Jewish power. Even when he lived in Israel, he continued to write books in English to and about American Jews. In some way, then, Kahane's American and Israeli careers overlap. That which makes Jewish flourishing in America impossible, liberalism, also robs Israel of its destiny as a truly *Jewish* state. In a feature article and interview in the Sunday *New York Times Magazine* in 1971, the year he emigrated to Israel, Kahane said, "When people think of Jewish defense, they automatically think of physical assault. And that's not all we meant when we spoke of Jewish defense." If anti-Semitism disappeared tomorrow, he said, "Jews of this country would still face decimation through assimilation, intermarriage, alienation from their background and heritage. . . . I don't think there is an ethnic group in this country that is more alienated from its background and heritage than Jews are."

I think we err if we see Kahane's program as solely about Jewish militancy, although it was also about that.[4] He sought to save the American dream for young American Jews. What I think he meant by that is that Jews could rise up and succeed while also retaining their distinct identity as Jews.[5] And the true enemy of the Jews for him was not the black militants or white supremacists. Those enemies could be dealt with rather easily; the real enemy for Kahane was Jewish liberalism.[6]

To understand the overarching project of Meir Kahane, one must move beyond his call for renewed Jewish pride and fighting anti-Semitism with a fist. One must understand his radicalism and the deep and searing rift that existed between radicalism and liberalism in Jewish America, and in America more generally in the postwar era.[7] The period examined in this chapter runs from 1965 to 1974, a time in which the mainstream liberal American Jewish community was facing challenges on numerous fronts. The chapter will focus on Kahane as a radical antiliberal American Jewish thinker at a time when almost all radical antiliberalism was coming from the far left.[8] I will expand on my understanding of Kahane as a "radical" in the next chapter. Suffice it to say here that he was an anti-incrementalist in the sense that he did not believe the liberal system could be mended enough to protect Jews. To survive, the Jews had to sever their ties with the liberal mindset that empowered them as that liberalism would eventually destroy them, not by persecution but by winnowing away any reason to remain a Jew.[9] Ironically, Kahane emerges from liberal America, not in the mode of an impoverished black man from Oakland, but as a middle-class Jew from Brooklyn who had benefited from postwar liberalism.

Here we can see the stark incongruity of Kahane's worldview. Liberalism made Kahane possible. His antiliberal radicalism was in a way an act of self-immolation, which he seemed to understand. The liberalism that made *him* possible, he surmises, could not sustain Jewish survival in a generation that had a more diluted memory of persecution. Here again the Holocaust serves as a marker. In his view, the more distant the Holocaust becomes the more liberalism threatens the American Jew. The reason is that a liberal society as he envisions it enables at least two things to occur in relation to Jews. First, the rise of ethnic minorities such as African Americans who protest discrimination, a stance he tacitly supported, will invariably produce anti-Semitism, as anti-Semitism for Kahane is an ontological reality ("Esau hates Jacob") and not simply a product of historical circumstance. Second, liberalism increasingly offered Jews the ability to become absorbed into American society at the price of erasing their Jewishness. Without a palpable and proximate memory of the Holocaust and the liberal Weimar Republic that preceded it, Jews would easily be seduced into believing America would ultimately accept them.

While one could make a similar critique of middle-class blacks who were radicalized in the 1960s, those blacks were inheritors of centuries of slavery and racism in America while Jews were mostly protected from anti-Semitism by the liberal system Kahane derides. But we need to keep in mind that for Kahane anti-Semitism and toleration are simply two edges of the same sword that will destroy the Jews. His critique of liberalism as he understood it was in part an adaptation of the mindset of Black Nationalism, combining anti-integrationism and Malcom X's famous adage "by any means necessary" that was born from disempowerment and persecution. And in part this reflected his fantasy of the Irgun terrorist/freedom fighter who refused to succumb to the dictates of British rule in Palestine. Liberalism gave Jews freedom. But to survive, the Jews needed power.

Kahane contributed a number of things to what would later become part of the Jewish mainstream in the following decades: first, the popularization of the idea that anti-Semitism was pervasive in America; second, the use of religion as a tool of pride;[10] and third, the breaking of the bond between liberalism and Jews that had persisted since the beginning of the twentieth century. Pervasive anti-Semitism helped with the popularization of Israel in the American imagination; Zionizing American Jewry was a way to keep anti-Semitism in play. We can see that today in the debate about anti-Zionism and anti-Semitism and the voices that claim anti-Zionism is simply another form of anti-Semitism. Religion helped launch the *kiruv* (Orthodox Jewish outreach) movement; and the questioning of the linkage between Jews and liberalism (which was also happening at around the same time with the New York Intellectuals and *Commentary*) emerged a bit later in the role of Jews in neoconservatism.

This is not to suggest that mainstream American Jewry was directly influenced by Kahane in all these ways, although I will argue that the influences were far greater than usually considered. Rather, it is to say that Kahane's real influence came from his American context and what he determined were the three things that most threatened Jews in America. The question of violence is important and played a prominent role in Kahane's thinking for a variety of reasons; I examine that subject in another chapter. Here I will just say that Kahane adopted violence as a tactic in America (even if in Israel it morphed into something else) and that he largely absorbed the general violent tenor of the radicalism of that period, much of which he borrowed, often with proper attribution.

Kahane was adept at the exercise of power and identity—or power through identity—that was once the province of ethnic minorities. The works of white nationalists such as Jared Taylor, Kevin MacDonald, Richard Spencer, and even arguably Steve Bannon and the alt-right are expressions of the first pangs of anxiety in white Christian America over its coming minority status.[11] Advocating separatist and ethnocentric political solutions was common among anxious ethnic groups, including Jews. Kahane was a major representative of that tendency among Jews to the consternation of the Jewish establishment, who largely remained committed to the liberal state's role in protecting Jews from ethnic animus and violence. But even liberals such as Leonard Fine began to see the limits of liberal solutions. In 1972 he wrote, "The last decade of cacophony has effectively destroyed the simple, somewhat simple-minded, liberal myth of this first half of this century. . . . Among many lessons we are now beginning to learn is that even with the best of will and the mostly amply funded of government programs, group conflict persists."[12]

Charles Liebman, in his 1973 book *The Ambivalent American Jew*, offers a slightly different take on Jews and liberalism in postwar America. Far from being a gesture to the universal, Liebman argues that liberalism for Jews in America was a way for them, largely *as* Jews and *with other* Jews, to unite and champion non-Jewish causes. "Jews prefer to get together with other Jews to promote ostensibly non-Jewish enterprises (which assist Jewish acceptance) and then to pretend the whole matter has nothing to do with being Jewish."[13] For Liebman, Jewish liberalism is the expression of the ongoing tension between survival and integration that informs the American Jewish experience; it enables the Jew to express universalism while doing so as an exercise in survival. And yet, in his conclusion, Liebman maintains that the project is doomed to failure because the tension cannot be sustained, or because what Jews would need to do "to redefine [their] religion and the nature of [their] commitment . . . and the extent to which the Jew perceives anti-Semitism from the Left" would push the survival option to the fore. In large part, I think his prediction was correct. For many American Jews, sustaining Jewish liberalism for the Jew who is committed to Jewish survival has proved to be just too difficult. Kahane, who had a much simpler view of liberalism and its defects, intuitively understood quite early on the dangers Liebman described.

As one committed to the survival of the group at all costs, Kahane regarded liberalism as the enemy of the Jews. The Jews' commitment to liberalism, against their own collective interest, was in his view an act of repugnant self-hatred that was rooted in anxiety but sparked resentment. Liberalism sought to ameliorate resentment by claiming that the social and political system should not focus on *groups* but *individuals* when it came to rights, goods, and services. Yet when group identities feel threatened and unstable, when power shifts from one group to another, when a group feels disenfranchised and ignored, and when communities feel under siege, very often liberalism itself is attacked because its focus on the individual is assumed (rightly or not) to be the very source of these social changes.

In viewing Kahane as a broadside response to liberalism, I offer a case study that can hopefully contribute to the history of American radicalism in its relationship to ethnic stability and safety, identity, and the struggle to survive. I begin by exploring Kahane's critique of liberalism in general and Jewish liberalism in particular as a way to situate his story in the broader frame of the religion of minorities in postwar America. What emerges is not a fanatical program but a radical one that addresses the very challenges of Jewish survival that were matters of concern for American Jews more generally.[14]

"I Want a Radical Jew"

"I want a radical Jew. But I want the Jew to have something to be radical about." Meir Kahane spoke those words in a television interview, likely sometime in the 1980s, that appeared in a short film by Noam Osband, *Radical Jew*, about one of Kahane's students, Baruch Marzel.[15] The moniker "radical" has a complicated history. While it was often viewed negatively, from the 1920s to the early 1970s it was sometimes used as a badge of honor for many Jews in America such as Emma Goldman (1920s and 1930s) and Abbie Hoffman (1960s), and for others in Europe such as Gustav Landauer and Martin Buber in Germany and Hillel Zeitlin in Poland.[16] Zionism itself was often viewed as a "radical" ideology, certainly among some of its literary figures such as Micha Yosef Berdyczewski and Yosef Hayyim Brenner.[17] In a similar vein, in 1971 Kahane said, "There is a tremendous alienation of young Jews from Jewishness. It's not because, as most Jewish parents think, the kids don't want to be Jewish. That's nonsense. The kids would very much like to be Jewish if they could find Jewish roots that were worthwhile. But the kind of Jewishness they were raised in is a sham, a fraud, and a hypocrisy."[18]

Kahane used his form of radicalism to respond to that "sham." The term "radical" is used in many different ways. For Jews in America, "radical" often referred to socialism or communism as in Tony Michael's history of American Jewish socialism entitled *Jewish Radicals*.[19] In the 1960s radicalism often referred to Marxist-inflected critiques of American liberalism (Herbert Marcuse, a German immigrant associated with the Frankfurt School, was a leading influence here, counting Angela Davis and Abbie Hoffman among his students at Brandeis University in the 1960s), which held that the problems of American capitalist society were systemic and thus could be resolved only through a political and cultural revolution based, in large part, on wealth redistribution.[20]

Thus figures such as Mao or Che Guevara were often viewed as models for 1960s radicals and were later ironically commodified on posters and T-shirts. The term "radicalism" is often a synecdoche for "political radicalism" that implies a revolutionary shift in the political reality of a collective or country. Among Jews this often applied to Zionism, which indeed had strong radical or revolutionary strains, certainly in its early phases, but it could also be applied to Jewish culture—that is, in America the move away from assimilation and accommodation and toward more constructive, positive, and overtly public displays of Jewish pride through ethnic, cultural, and religious identity. When asked in a 1971 interview about the main accomplishments of the JDL, Kahane responded, "By far the most important things we've done is [*sic*] to instill the Jews of this country with a sense of *schtolz*—pride. Particularly the youth. We've given them something Jewish to be proud of."[21] In this regard Gabriel Ross's description seems apt: "A Jewish movement must be concerned with the problems of insuring a continued Jewish existence. But a *radical* Jewish movement must go beyond this; it must be concerned with the quality of

Jewish life. It must strive for the conditions which will allow for the actualization of positive Jewish aspirations; a real possibility only in a liberated world."[22]

Calling Kahane "radical," even though he self-identified as such, requires some explanation. If we look at earlier forms of radicalism such as those of Emma Goldman or Gustav Landauer, we usually find a commitment to some form of anarchism, a belief in the abolition of all government in favor of a purely voluntaristic structuring of society.[23] By the time we get to postwar radicalism, the most common critical template is Marxism in one form or another, from Trotskyism to Maoism to various forms of socialism. Marxism becomes the tool most young radicals used to systemically criticize American imperialism, liberalism, capitalism, and consumerism and to argue that American exceptionalism, the notion that the American liberal system of democracy was unlike others, a break from other Western patterns of racism and colonialism, was bogus.[24] Kahane viewed Marx as precisely the problem, calling him "the most bitter and famous of all Jewish anti-Semites."[25]

When I refer to Kahane as a Jewish radical in this book I mean to suggest that he was waging a systemic critique of American liberal society as it related to Jews, and an equally systemic critique of liberal American Jewry in its accommodation to the American (liberal) establishment. His radical critique of liberalism did not apply only to the political liberal ideology of the time (e.g., Johnson's Great Society or the New Left) but equally to the American Jewish program of assimilation, or "Americanization" that he felt was robbing a generation of Jews of any positive sense of Jewishness or pride in being Jewish.[26] He believed American Jewry was being threatened from within (through assimilation) and from without (through the ever-present anti-Semitism that he believed would invariably raise its head). By the early 1970s Kahane had ostensibly given up on America, believing that Israel was the only possible solution for Jewish survival. Before that, and even after his *aliyah*, Kahane waged a radical battle against American liberalism and American Jewish liberalism in particular, arguing that the American Jew had to become a "New Jew," one who defended himself with a fist and was unafraid, as an American and a Jew, to express his Jewishness openly, and radically.

It should thus be noted that the radical militancy Kahane espoused was in his view in the service of the American dream. Writing about radicalism more generally, Ben Halpern notes regarding minorities, "There is a confidence that the radical militancy of the aroused minorities is, in the final analysis, fundamentally attuned to the American Way."[27] The very notion that to be a Jew in postwar America, and even beforehand, was to be a liberal, that liberalism was almost a given for American Jews, was something Kahane was devoted to contesting in a radical fashion. Jewish neoconservatism arose later to argue similarly but did so in a more restrained, more secular, and more effective way.[28]

It is somewhat ironic that Kahane was as adamantly opposed to Marxism as he was because in some way, structurally at least, he was guilty of "Marxist" tendencies.[29] Although to my knowledge he had no serious economic theory, he often viewed social conflict in "class" terms that pitted many of his child-of-immigrant underclass followers—his *lumpenproletariat*—against the bourgeois American establishment. He often mocked the assimilated Jews from "Great Neck" and "Scarsdale" (upper-class New York suburbs with large Jewish populations) and the materialistic Judaism of their suburban lives.[30] Responding to criticism from the ADL and Rabbi Maurice Eisendrath, president of the Union of American Hebrew Congregations, Kahane replied, "How can a rich Jew or a non-Jew criticize an organization of lower- and middle-class Jews who daily live in terror? The establishment Jew is scandalized by us, but our support comes from the grass roots."[31] He castigated American Jews for their lavish and opulent bar mitzvahs and white "Jewish" flight to the suburbs that left their elderly relatives to fend for themselves in changing neighborhoods.[32] While serving his one-year sentence in Allenwood Prison in Pennsylvania in 1975, he formed a "Union for Jewish Prisoners" to obtain kosher food. Responding to his request for Jewish items, Emanuel Rackman, who was then provost of Yeshiva University, a onetime supporter of Kahane who turned against him, remarked, "How come Rabbi Kahane turns to the 'fat and contented' when he needs them," to which Kahane replied, "Of course, the fact [is] that I need nothing from the corruptors of religion, the fat and contented, for I have my own siddur and Bible and kosher food and all the things I won in my own battle."[33]

In Israel he claimed to speak for the impoverished Mizrachi Jews marginalized by the wealthy Ashkeno-centric ruling class. In almost every instance Kahane played into the very Marxist categories utilized by his New Left and Black Nationalist adversaries. While he is often accused of fascism, and rightly so, especially in Israel, Kahane's "Marxist" or at least classist approach to society is often overlooked by those who take him seriously. One of the most interesting things I find about Kahane is the way he enables us to see that his apparent contradictions are illustrations of the way right and left, reactionary and progressive, sometimes fold in on one another, especially when they take radical forms. Kahane was a figure many did not know how to define. One reason, I suggest, is that he defied conventional categories and in doing so, unsettled our understanding of how to navigate complex shifts in social and cultural norms.

His approach sought to subvert the entire system of American Jewish liberalism through revolutionary (including violent) means, to change and refashion the very notion of what it meant to be a Jew.[34] He did not intend to overthrow the American system, which he viewed largely in functional terms of enabling Jewish survival. But in line with many radicals on the left, he was an anti-incrementalist and often viewed compromise and moderation as signs of weakness. Once he emigrated to Israel and became involved in the political process there, his stridency took an even more pernicious turn.[35] There he set his sights on overthrowing the liberal Zionist establishment through the political process so as to usher in what he believed was the true Zionist vision of a Judeo-centric, one might say a Judeo-chauvinist, state ruled in large part by Torah laws and not by liberal-democratic principles.[36]

The radical critique of liberalism at this time is captured in James Sleeper's "The Case for Religious Radicalism," first published in the journal *Genesis II* in 1970 and reprinted in the book *The New Jews* in 1971. "The liberal's faith in the democratic workings of the system is no longer satisfying, because politics within the established processes are merely ways of seeing that everyone—regardless of race, religion, or creed—received his 'fair share' of the American social pie. But what if the pie is poisonous? One begins to become a radical when one discovers that liberals can handle quantitative demands for a redistribution of the pie but not qualitative demands for a change in its recipe." Sleeper later cites Genesis 12:1: "*Get yourself up, from out of your land, and from your roots and kin, and from your father's house, to the place that I will show you*. . . . The radical break is there—as far reaching as you can get. . . . In the survival of the Jew lies the crystallization of a radical message that alone has outlasted empires. It says that even more radical than 'turning on' is the attempt to respond to the statement 'You shall be holy.'"[37] One can find many such comments coming from the radical Jewish left in those days, but here Sleeper turns radicalism toward Judaism—attempting to make Judaism *itself* radical—by juxtaposing the radical mandate coined by Timothy Leary of "turning on" with the biblical mandate "You shall be holy." What is intriguing in Sleeper's statement is the merging of radicalism and Judaism, or at least the appropriation of Jewish motifs toward radical ends, which can be seen elsewhere as well as Jewish radicals began moving away from the New Left in the late 1960s. Rabbi Arthur Waskow's "Freedom Seder" in 1969, examined in the next chapter, as well as Waskow's 1971 book *The Bush Is Burning! Radical*

Judaism Faces the Pharaohs of the Modern Superstate, illustrate the way radicalized Jews were adopting Judaism as the template of their protest against liberalism.[38] Kahane's program was also an attempt to construct a radical Judaism opposing liberalism, not toward progressive causes but toward survivalist ends.

I choose to focus in this chapter on the years 1965–1974 for a variety of reasons. Malcolm X was assassinated on February 21, 1965, only a month before the famous March on Selma. This helped give birth to the Black Panthers and the Black Power movement a year later. The March on Selma in 1965, with the iconic photo of Abraham Joshua Heschel marching with Ralph Abernathy and Martin Luther King, sparked a liberal upsurge among young American Jews in regard to civil rights. The signing of the Voting Rights Act also took place in the summer of 1965, as did the Watts riots. In October 1965 the Clergy and Laymen Concerned about Vietnam, which became a major religious organization opposing the war, was founded. In 1965 the US also saw a significant escalation of the Vietnam War including the extensive bombing in Operation Rolling Thunder and the first direct confrontation between US and North Vietnamese forces in the Battle of la Drang. In addition, on April 17, 1965, more than twenty thousand young men and women converged in Washington in the largest antiwar demonstration in the history of the city.[39] Sponsored by SDS (Students for a Democratic Society), in many ways it sparked the antiwar movement. The escalation of the draft that year prompted an increase in student antiwar protests. The Free Speech movement in Berkeley also began during the 1964–65 academic year. The Student Society for Soviet Jewry (SSSJ) was founded by Yaakov Birnbaum in 1964 and began more vocal activities in 1965.

The year 1974 saw the impeachment of Richard Nixon, which symbolically marked the end of an era in American politics. It was also the year the JDL began to truly fall apart, plagued by court cases and indictments. Kahane had emigrated to Israel a few years earlier; although he returned often, by 1974 he began to focus more on founding an Israeli political party than on the JDL's activities. In 1974 Kahane published *Our Challenge: The Chosen Land*, which was his first book-length study of his vision for Israel and indicated that his focus would be primarily on his fledging Israeli political career.[40] That year, 1974, also marked the diminished influence of the Black Panther Party with Huey Newton going into exile in Cuba. While the party lasted until at least 1977, its power began to decline for various reasons around 1974.

As Jack Nusan Porter and Peter Dreier note in 1971, "The American Jewish community now finds itself under attack by both Jewish radicals and radical Jews—each group a small but outspoken minority among Jewish college students and young adults. In both the political and ethnic arenas, Jewish parents and the Jewish establishment spokesmen are increasingly at odds with their sons and daughters."[41] Porter and Dreier were speaking about two groups: Jews who had remained in the New Left and Jews who had abandoned the New Left and become the New Jews, radical advocates for Jewish causes or those, like Waskow, who initially used Judaism as the template for radical-left politics.[42]

Porter and Dreier likely did not have in mind Meir Kahane and his Jewish Defense League established in 1968.[43] I have argued that Kahane is a missing piece in understanding the Jewish-radicalism protest against liberalism, and understanding his impact requires placing him squarely in the "attack" Porter and Dreier describe above. Kahane's early disciples were mostly not those who attended elite universities or the wealthier Jews of the Upper East or West Side of Manhattan or the suburbs, but the lower-middle-class youth of Brooklyn, Queens, and the Bronx; many were children of Holocaust survivors who lived in troubled and racially mixed neighborhoods and often suffered from latent and overt anti-Semitism.[44] In a 1970 article "Jewish Vigilantes," Kahane is quoted as saying, "Our organization is made up of the unhealthy, the people who feel the pain."[45] As Shlomo Russ puts it, "Those who joined the League were much more parochial in their approach to the American Scene. They identified more with their neighborhood than with American society in its entirety. When they looked beyond their neighborhood, it was toward the fate of their fellow Jews rather than towards members of other ethnic groups."[46] The disparity between those in the more traditional and (as they were called) "frontier" neighborhoods and those in the establishment, who lived in upscale urban neighborhoods or in the suburbs, is stark.[47] For example, in a 1970 article "The JDL: Heroes or Hooligans?" we read: "To the residents of the Boston suburb of Mattapan the JDL members are heroes. To the residents of the Brooklyn Crown Heights area they are heroes. To the leaders of the Jewish establishment they are 'a bunch of vigilantes,' or 'the Jewish Panthers.'" Kahane is quoted as saying, "We don't care what other Jews think of us. It is the non-Jew whose attention we are seeking. Nor do we care what names people call us. . . . Let them leave their comfortable homes in Scarsdale and come live in areas of Brooklyn that we patrol, and then let them give us their opinion."[48]

For Kahane's JDL, Brooklyn was like Oakland for the Black Panthers. Jewish Brooklyn, made up mostly of children of immigrant working-class Jews, and North and West Oakland, a neighborhood of mostly poor blacks next to the prosperous San Francisco and the increasingly New Left Berkeley, were locales that were receptive audiences to the message of revolution and radical change founded on ethnic identity.[49] Kahane's JDL certainly drew from a different social class than many of the Jews on the left. Stokely Carmichael once said, "Man, every cat's politics come from what he sees when he gets up in the morning. The liberals see Central Park and we see sharecropper shacks."[50] When many JDLers woke up in their "frontier" neighborhoods in Brooklyn, they saw groups of black and Puerto Rican kids hanging out beside the Bodega (a Latino convenience store) ready to knock kippahs off Jewish kids' heads.[51]

The angst and anger of many of these young Jews from Brooklyn, Queens, and the Bronx was not very different from that of the more privileged kids of the New Left except that young Jews attracted to Kahane were often fighting a double battle: against the liberalism that denied their Jewishness through the call to assimilate, and against the quietism of their Holocaust-surviving relatives whose psychological wounds did not permit resistance to the injustices they suffered. Many of the parents of the New Left Jews were assimilated, some deeply so. The parents of many young JDL members, some Holocaust survivors, just wanted to live out their lives apart from dangers of assimilation and overexposure to a world that was erupting with interracial and interethnic strife.[52] Whereas the trauma of the Holocaust was still very palpable for the parents, in whom it often yielded a more quietistic response, the children of that Holocaust generation were more American, often more easily radicalized by their parents' experience, and more comfortable expressing the angst that it produced.[53]

In an August 1970 article on the JDL in *Esquire* entitled "Superjew," Kahane is quoted as saying, "Even some of those who went through the Nazi hell refuse to think. They are tired of suffering. They do not want to believe that it can happen again."[54] Those survivors were not his audience; rather, they were the tool he used to attract his audience. In some grotesque way, Kahane used the survivors as the countermodel to his New Jew. The survivors were remnants of Jewish failure; they represented what Jews should cease to be. This was not new with Kahane; Ben-Gurion made similar remarks about survivors when visiting displaced persons camps after the war.[55] The survivor as the witness of Jewish failure resonates throughout this period of Kahane's career, while at the same time he warns his readers that it will happen again, and this time Jews need to be ready to fight and resist.

Kahane made it his mission to convince the children and relatives of those survivors that it could indeed happen again. And it could happen in America. Yossi Klein Halevi notes of his early exposure to Kahane, "Kahane promised to resolve the contradiction between my internal life as a surrogate Holocaust survivor and my objective life as an American. Kahane was telling us, young American Jews, that our comfortable lives were an aberration, a meaningless interlude between times of persecution."[56] Radicalism here was thus a response to the lure of postwar America (both the desire to be fully American and to remain tied to a traditional past) as well as a rebellion against parents who were advocating either assimilation or quietist separatism. Klein Halevi continues, "Even more than trying to free Jews from the Soviet Union, I loved Kahane for trying to free us from America."[57] In my view, he did not free them from America but, rather, showed them one radical way to be American and Jewish at the same time.

But perhaps there is something else going on here. Kahane attracted not only Orthodox children of survivors but also some refugees from the New Left who felt abandoned by the movement after the critique of Israel as "Zionist colonialism" at the New Politics Convention in Chicago in September 1967. Some of these young men and women, radicalized against the "quietism" of liberalism in regard to systemic change, were taken by Kahane's call to action against liberal America. Here we have an interesting amalgam of two kinds of quietism: that of Holocaust survivors who wanted to live out their lives in peace and that of liberal acquiescence and commitment to incremental change. Thus angry children of survivors often met New Left refugees in the JDL.

One of the fundamental dimensions of postwar American radical critiques of liberalism, from SDS to the Black Panthers, was their commitment to internationalism; they believed that the inequality and injustices of the Third World were in large part promulgated or at least enabled by the West. Mao's call for the Third World to rebel against the West resonated very strongly with many of these radicals. One example of this is Roger Williams's book *Negroes with Guns*. Williams was one of the key forerunners of Black Nationalism and Third World internationalism. He called for blacks in the South to arm themselves to defend their families from the Klan and other white supremacists. [58] As we will see in subsequent chapters, this internationalism, in some way the precursor to contemporary notions of intersectionality, is at least partly behind the anti-Israel sentiment that emerges after the Six-Day War and the beginning of the occupation. The story was more complicated and broader than the question of Third Worldism or internationalism.[59] As James Loeffler notes, "With its sudden victory in the Six-Day War, Israel had switched roles in the mind of the emerging global human rights community." Human rights suddenly became a liability for Israel and its supporters.[60] Kahane will label this garden-variety anti-Semitism, and some of it certainly was, but it was also the left's commitment to global politics, especially in the Third World, that contributed to the New Left's siding with the Palestinians and against Israel.[61] Many viewed post-1967 Israel as increasingly an appendage of American imperialism.[62]

Kahane was a vocal and vehement critic of communism even before he became involved with the Soviet Jewry movement. His 1967 book *The Jewish Stake in Vietnam* supported the war by arguing that communism was a major force of anti-Semitism in the world that needed to be contained.[63] And while he often criticized American Jewish consumerism he certainly was not a critic of capitalism. As a product of middle-class America, he very much lived its bourgeois ethos. The real center of Kahane's social and not economic critique of liberalism, but for reasons different from those of other (left-wing) radicals of his time, was liberalism's lack of a cogent argument for fighting anti-Semitism. Jewish liberalism was based, rather, on the belief that Jewish integration into American society would decrease the depiction of the Jew as "other" and thus dismantle anti-Semitic stereotypes. Kahane held that liberal Jews were fooling themselves into believing that anti-Semitism was not a constitutive part of gentile society. It could never be eradicated, only controlled.

Kahane's war against liberalism, and in particular American Jewish liberalism, which he referred to as "the American Jewish establishment," was of a different sort, although he shared the radical call for systemic rather than incremental change. He too believed in the limits of American liberalism but also acknowledged the extent to which Jews had largely benefited from it.[64] In *Never Again!* we read: "The liberalism of Jewish organizations was born in the hope that it would save Jews from anti-Semitism. In certain cases, however, it is this liberalism which leads the Jew down the path of inaction that can destroy him."[65] For Kahane anti-Semitism is endemic to gentile society. The danger of liberalism for him is not recognizing this; through assimilation it makes the Jew vulnerable to anti-Semitic attack, not necessarily as the result of liberalism but simply as a societal inevitability.

One striking, if ironic, illustration of this is Kahane's boasting that when a group of Jewish radicals and liberals in Rochdale Village, Queens (where he had once served as a rabbi) invited the black militant Leslie Campbell to speak—though he had expressed anti-Semitic views in connection to the Ocean Hill–Brownsville school strike in 1968—JDL members broke into the meeting and proceeded to beat up the Jews in the audience while Campbell stood on the stage and watched.[66]

With many others at that time, Kahane believed the Jews were caught in the middle between the white aristocracy and the black underclass; they served as pawns to maintain white hegemony thus evoking black hatred while simultaneously being excluded from white privilege. And within the Jewish community, besides inaction, liberalism and its focus on individualism served as a substitute for tradition, collective identity, and fidelity to Jewish peoplehood that threatened the Jews spiritually. In some way Kahane's anger at the American Jewish establishment is similar to young radicals' anger at the Great Society with accusations of hypocrisy and perpetuating rather than resolving injustice. As Jack Newfield wrote, "The adjectives the SDSers invoke most frequently to condemn Johnson's Great Society are not 'reactionary' or 'militaristic' but 'ethically corrupt' and 'hypocritical.'"[67]

In his above-cited 1971 interview to the *New York Times*, after decrying Jewish assimilation and alienation from Judaism, Kahane further remarked, "The Jewish Defense League came into being to physically defend Jews. It also came into being to go out among Jews and instill within them a feeling of Jewish pride, to defend the Jews from simply fading out."[68]

In an essay on Kahane and terrorism, Judith Tydor Baumel makes a distinction regarding his use of terrorism that may help us understand the critique of liberalism I am describing. She argues that there were two main forms of terrorism in the US in the late 1960s and early 1970s. The first came from marginal ethnic groups such as the Black Panthers; the second came from social and ideological protest groups such as the Weather Underground. Each viewed violence as a way to systemically undermine the stability of the society and bring about radical change. She writes, "The underlying hypothesis [of this essay] views Kahane and the JDL as boundary crossers: using tactics from both of these categories, they fell into neither of them, creating instead a hybrid terror organization which mobilized an American-born ethnic constituency in order to better the status of co-religionists elsewhere—in this case behind the Iron Curtain."[69]

While that is certainly true up to a point, Kahane also used violence for other reasons as I discuss later in this book. I have two quibbles with Baumel's reading. First, violence as it was used by groups like the Black Panthers, while focused on the plight of American blacks, also had a more global reach than she suggests. Second, Kahane's use of violence did not begin with the Soviet Jewry movement but, very much like the Panthers in Oakland, with civil patrols to protect Jews at risk. In the case of the Panthers it was aimed at police brutality (an issue that continues in the black community to this day) and in the case of Kahane at local groups, black and white, who threatened Jews in New York City.

But Baumel's larger point rings true. Suffice it to say here that Kahane's radicalism also borrows from both the ethnic radicals (the Black Panthers) and the ideological radicals (the Weather Underground). In fact Kahane's radicalism is a merging of the ethnic and the political. Yet the way in which it differs from both is that Kahane had no program to overthrow America or even cause large-scale national havoc. He was not interested, as were the Panthers, in radical societal change of the American system. And unlike the Weather Underground, Kahane was not interested in punishing American civilians with the same violence the US was perpetrating in Vietnam. Nor did the JDL ever view the police as their enemy, although Kahane did view many political figures such as liberal mayor Lindsay of New York as the enemy. In the case of tactics against anti-Semitism (mostly black anti-Semitism) his goals were defensive, aimed at making the black anti-Semite think twice about acting violently against innocent Jews (although I argue in my discussion of Kahane's views of violence that violence served other purposes for him as well).[70] In the case of Soviet Jewry his tactics focused on influencing the US administration about a foreign policy matter.[71] More pointedly, he used violence to bring the Soviet Jewry issue into the national media, which he largely succeeded in doing; he believed he could thereby exert more leverage on the US government to pressure the Soviets. In this one sense, Kahane's strategy was similar to the Weather Underground;[72] he wanted to make Soviets residing in the US suffer for their government's oppression of Jewish dissidents. In Weathermen fashion Kahane said, "Let the world know that when the Jews are on trial in Russia, the Soviet Union will be on trial [in America]."[73]

Kahane offered a systemic, and not occasional, critique of American Jewish liberalism, which in my view makes him a radical. His critique was identarian in nature. He believed that the American Jew had lost any substantive sense of Jewishness as a result of decades of liberalism that promoted both assimilation and cosmopolitanism. If the Black Panthers and Black Nationalists wanted to construct a new Black Man (and woman) through "Black is Beautiful" aesthetics and politics, "Black Power" in opposition to the Uncle Tom stereotype, and through bypassing the limits of the liberal civil rights movement that fought largely for desegregation and civil recognition, Kahane wanted to create a "New Jew" in opposition to what he called the "Uncle Irvings" who were satisfied simply not to be too exposed.[74] To him the American Jewish liberal mantra was "Shah schtil" (Be quiet).[75] And yet unlike the Panthers, the political component did not involve transforming America.[76] Both the Panthers and the JDL had national and international interests. Kahane's politics were focused on the Jewish community in America but extended outward to Soviet Jewry, Jews in Syria, and eventually to Israel.[77] In this sense he had an international reach not unlike New Left radicals, but for him the international subjects were only Jews, whether in Russia, Israel, Syria, Iraq, and so on.[78] Injustice was only injustice toward Jews; he totally particularized the radical internationalist agenda. In fact, part of his criticism of the American Jewish establishment was that while focusing so much effort on Israel it had largely ignored Jews in those other places. Although, after emigrating to Israel in 1971, his focus primarily becomes Israel, in his early career he spoke out against Jews who did not heed the cries of Jews who were oppressed in other countries.

In this sense Kahane also differed from right-wing radical groups such as Joseph Colombo's Italian-American Civil Rights League, founded in 1970, even though Colombo and Kahane had close ties.[79] Colombo's group was largely geared toward civilian violence against blacks and others who threatened his community.[80] Kahane explained his alliance with Colombo at the 1971 Convention of the International JDL by stating, "My alliance is not with Joe Colombo but with the tens of thousands and hundreds of thousands of Italians. . . . I'll match with anyone if I think I can help a Jew. . . . I want to help Jews and they [the Civil Rights League] can help us and I will use them."[81] Kahane justified his ties with Colombo by stating that Colombo had publicly expressed support for helping the Jews in the Soviet Union. "I'd take help from anybody. If the State of Israel took help from Joseph Stalin, then I could take help from Joe Colombo. That's all there is to my relationship with the Mafia. You can't really call it 'links.'"[82] But Kahane's agenda was not limited to America; it just began there. That was why he wanted to create an International JDL in Jerusalem, though it never materialized.

Kahane had a much broader social, cultural, and religious critique of American Jewry; protecting Jewish civilians was only one aspect. In this early period, he wanted to rebuild the Diaspora Jew. In Kahane's *Manifesto* for the JDL we read: "The Jewish Defense League was created because we think that the American dream is worth saving and can be saved."[83] In the document called "Jewish Defense League: Aims and Purposes," we similarly read that the JDL "is committed to the American dream of a democratic consensus. It is behind the prophetic social justice the Bible proclaimed."[84] In the famous advertisement Kahane published in the *New York Times* on June 24, 1969, which began,

"Is This Any Way for Nice Jewish Boys to Behave?," the copy of the ad ended with: "We are speaking of the American dream."[85]

Kahane's deeply held belief in America is often overlooked, certainly by those who read only his later writings from Israel. In general, his books about American Jewry, culminating with *Time to Go Home*, focused on the future of the American Diaspora. He emerges on the scene as a Jewish expositor of the very possibility of the Diaspora. It isn't until the early 1970s, after moving to Israel, that Kahane decides the American Diaspora cannot be saved or at least that it does not hold a future for Jews. The irony is that he continues to write books for and about the American Diaspora and spends half his time there. In fact, one finds his writing about the American Diaspora more cogent, and in many ways more effective, than his assessments of Israel. Of course, irony filters through Kahane's entire life—for example, his proposed legislation against Jewish-Arab dating in Israel even though he had a non-Jewish mistress for a short time in the US. Once militancy subsides in America after the end of the Vietnam War, Kahane's message abates even as his broader worldview of perennial anti-Semitism and program of survivalism continue to seep into the collective American Jewish psyche.

In 1975 Kahane wrote, "The total absence of Hadar Yisroel, pride in Jewishness, finds its bleakest expression in the failure of the young Jew in the Galut, in the Diaspora, to have self-pride, any pride in his people, in his heritage, in his future." This sentiment is not presented as pride only in the state of Israel, though that too, but more directly, pride in the Jew in America. Kahane's JDL was founded as an attempt to refashion the diasporic Jew. In Camp Jedel there was an *American* flag that flew from a flagpole. Before he gave up on America in the early 1970s, Kahane's program was an American one. In this sense he had a great deal in common with the Black Panthers; even though Black Nationalism had a strong "Back to Africa" contingency, the Panthers were still primarily an American organization.

Kahane's ideological battle also was not waged against the American system per se; he was a firm believer in American democracy as he makes clear in *Time to Go Home*. The aim was to fight for Jewish interests from within the system, sometimes acting against its legal parameters, but always to influence it, never to replace it. If he viewed America as the greatest country for the Jews (except Israel), that is, if he exuded a kind of American patriotism, then what is the nature of his radicalism? His radical critique, as noted, was against the American Jewish establishment.[86] In his 1971 interview to the *New York Times* he said, "I don't think that Jews have ever lived in any country outside Israel which has given them more than this country has. I don't think that a society in human history has ever arisen that has been as good and as decent as the society that was built up painfully and pragmatically in this country . . . despite what the radical left says in its inanities."[87] In *A Manifesto* Kahane writes, "America has been good to the Jew and the Jew has been good to America. A land founded on the principles of democracy and freedom has given unprecedented opportunities to a people devoted to these ideas."[88] Here, then, Kahane was a radical only in regard to the Jewish world and not America.[89] This changes when he moves to Israel and transplants his critique of liberalism to a place where he is part of the majority. At that point his systemic critique is directed toward the government itself, and thus in Israel his radicalism actually represents other ideological groups in America in that his intent is to radically transform, and even arguably overthrow, the Israeli political system itself. Like other American radicals in the US—for example, Eldridge Cleaver's 1968 presidential run under the banner of the Peace and Freedom Party, or Black Panther Bobby Seale's campaign for mayor of Oakland in 1973—Kahane sought political power in the Israeli system (never in the American one), eventually becoming an elected official in the Israeli parliament.

Even given these parallels with leftism, in general Kahane had little affinity for New Left radicalism, and one would think the same was true regarding the radicalism of the New Jews who turned from the New Left toward a positive Jewish identity. In fact, he was diametrically opposed to the radicalism of the left as he believed that its secularism was corrosive; its values, including drugs and free love, were hedonistic; and that the New Left, certainly after the rise of the Black Power movement in 1965–66, was anti-Israel and anti-Semitic (a distinction he believed was essentially nonexistent).[90] There is indeed some merit to radical writer Jack Newfield's observation that "the beat's [countercultural artists, musicians, writers, and political activists in the 1950s] mysticism, anarchy, anti-intellectualism, sexual and drug experimentation, hostility to middle-class values, and idealization of the Negro, and of voluntary poverty, all have clear parallels in the New Left."[91] An Orthodox Jew from postwar Brooklyn would have little inclination to accept these attitudes as productive for Jews or Judaism in America.

And yet Kahane was surprisingly open to the radical-left Jews he encountered. In a winter 1971 interview published in a little-circulated newspaper called *The Flame*, Kahane said, "When I speak in synagogues and temples out in the suburbs, the adults come there expecting me to agree with them and someone gets up and attacks the Jewish new left youth as lousy kids with long hair, and so on. They're usually very stunned when I say—and all our people [the JDLers] say that, on the contrary, our great hope is not so much with apathetic youth but with radical leftists who at least march for something and feel something . . . and now of course we have to change them to the right way."[92] In "Jewish Defense League: Aims and Purposes," Kahane makes this quite clear: "It is possible for JDL to wean many [young radical-left Jews] away from Marxism and back to Jewish and democratic thinking and the JDL is committed to this very thing."[93] One cannot underestimate Kahane's talent for creating a mood that would evoke a passion for action among his young listeners; it was one of his greatest assets.

According to the JDL, "if young Jews are participating in the SDS they obviously lack Jewish pride."[94] And yet Kahane sometimes seemed to contradict himself. In "Superjew" he is quoted as saying, "The average student whose Jewishness is only marginal, and who is drawn to radicalism, seeking excitement or escape, does not know what the Jewish Defense League is talking about." Instead the JDL wanted to attract the other side: "It's these people—who make up the silent majority, the silent middle—who must be won over to forge a common democratic front." Yet Kahane still felt a certain affinity for Jewish radicals, and he certainly aped the militant tactics of the radical left more generally, often calling the JDL "Jewish Panthers."[95] Although he more openly claimed his militarism was derived from Jewish terrorist organizations such as Irgun and Lehi (the Stern Gang), in practice he was more a child of postwar American radicalism of the left than the maximalist Zionist Revisionism.[96] In some way, the militant heroes of Revisionism such as Ze'ev Jabotinsky, Avraham Stern, and Menachem Begin gave him the Jewish "cover" he needed to exercise his American radicalism.[97] At times he made the left a model the Jews were unfortunately unwilling to follow. In one of the segments of his serial "Communism vs. Judaism" articles, published in the *Jewish Press* in 1967, he addresses the compromising and largely ineffectual tactics of the Jewish mainstream. Asking why the Jews continued to protest for Soviet Jewry a block from the Soviet Mission and not in front of it (a New York City ordinance forbade them from doing so), he wrote, "Every leftist and Negro group is willing to challenge a law it considers unconstitutional. What prevents Jews from doing the same."[98] Kahane was not only a product of his time but just as much a product of his place. And his place was urban America.

In any case, radicalism as a form of protest, as a posture toward upending the status quo and confronting the failures of liberalism to effect real, sustained change in society, was something Kahane not only shared with leftist radicals; he also respected them for it and learned from them.

It is true that Kahane's politics were right-wing and reactionary; he advocated for law and order (even though he broke the law often and was arrested many times), supported the Vietnam War, was a vociferous critic of communism, and backed Israeli militarism toward its Arab minority.[99] But those and other political positions and the culture wars they helped promulgate are girded by a commitment to radicalism as a posture and as the preferred approach to remedying the contemporary challenges of the American Jew, even if that required breaking the law. As Shlomo Russ notes, Kahane's distinctive contribution is that he developed "a leftist style for causes of the right."[100] In full radical mode that acknowledges the law and also the right, or need, to break it in extenuating circumstances, when questioned about illegal activities in regard to Soviet Jewry, Kahane responded, "We respect the right and the obligation of the American government to prosecute us and send us to jail. No one gripes about that."[101] The liberal will often argue that her protest is part of the system, at least in spirit, even if it is illegal. The radical acknowledges that her protest is *against* the system and illegal and thus the illegality is an integral part of the protest.

"New Jews" Rising

The move toward radical-left positions among many young Jews in the late 1960s is coupled with a move to the right among many middle-aged Jews at the same time. In a 1972 article "Why Jews Turn Conservative" in the *Wall Street Journal*, Irving Kristol, who would become a patriarch of neoconservatism, wrote, "One can sum up the matter in this way: Jews are perceiving an identity of interests between (a) the preservation of Jewish values and institutions, and (b) Jewish survival. Jews were attracted to the Left so long as it seemed to incorporate liberal values in a wider vision. They are now experiencing a revulsion against the left that wishes to negate liberal values. For these values are indispensible to Jews."[102]

Kristol's argument is that the Jews didn't abandon the left but the New Left abandoned the leftist values of the Old Left that were so crucial for Jewish survival. Jews (like him) turned rightward because the New Left did not represent their values and could not assure their survival (think of the New Left's negative attitude toward Israel after 1967 and the growing animosity toward Jews in the Black Nationalist movement). But just as many middle-aged Jews felt that their liberalism was taken away from them by the New Left, younger Jews felt that the continued liberalism of the Jewish establishment ignored the systemic problems of inequality and growing imperialism that they were devoted to eradicating. It was they and their friends who were being drafted to fight and die in Vietnam. And so there was a kind of Jewish generational parting of the ways; older Jews turned right toward conservatism while many younger Jews turned radical, even as that radicalism increasingly became an expression of their Jewishness.

Kahane is an interesting case that does not fit either mold. He advocated a radicalism that manifested what we could call a "rightist" position (he was staunchly anticommunist and backed the Vietnam War) while doing so in a decidedly antiestablishment way, mimicking some of the radical-left movements of this period. He was thus an idiosyncratic Jewish radical of the 1960s who favored survival as the only, or certainly primary, Jewish value, and thought it could be assured only through radical-activist tactics such as violence against anyone or any group that he believed threatened Jews' security. His radicalism was not intended to salvage the Old Left ideals Kristol writes about but precisely to show that even those ideals could not assure the Jews' survival. In this sense Kahane's radicalism was not only in opposition to the New Left but also to the Old Left liberalism Kristol espoused.

Locating the genesis of postwar Jewish radicalism in America is difficult. In general one might say that the Port Huron Statement of 1962, the document that founded SDS, gave birth to what would become New Left radicalism.[103] Among American Jews it is plausible to suggest that the group of young activists who called themselves "Jews for Urban Justice" and, on Yom Kippur 1967, demonstrated outside a prestigious Washington synagogue against Jewish insensitivity to major social problems of impoverished classes in America, were the first to enact New Left *Jewish* radicalism.[104] Seven or eight months later Kahane founded his JDL in the wake of the New York City teachers' strike, responding, as noted, to the anti-Semitic literature distributed by some of the black parents in the Ocean Hill–Brownsville school district.[105]

More relevant to the comparison with Jews for Urban Justice, one of the JDL's breakout acts occurred on Friday, May 9, 1969, when members showed up with baseball bats and chains at Temple Emanu-El, the largest Reform temple in Manhattan, to make sure black militant James Forman, who had been invited to speak by Rabbi Maurice Eisendrath, would not easily enter the synagogue. Kahane was opposed to Forman's suggesting that Jews should bear any responsibility for American slavery in the form of reparations.[106] Forman, in churches in the New York area, had been publicly demanding reparations to blacks for slavery, and he intended to do so at the synagogue that evening. Kahane and the JDL threatened to break his bones if he showed up. Forman never did, and the police broke up the protest; but it was covered by three separate articles in the *New York Times*.[107] Kahane saw this as a great public relations victory.

As mentioned previously, a year earlier on June 24, 1968, Kahane took out an ad in the *Times* introducing the JDL. It showed six tough-looking Jews in sunglasses and holding weapons with the caption "Is This Any Way for Nice Jewish Boys to Behave?"[108] Two years later the same photo appeared in a local Philadelphia newspaper, the *Distant Drummer,* but now the caption read, in light of the Temple Emanu-El event: "The Jewish Defense League Answering a Demand of Reparations from Synagogues from an Ad in the New York Times."[109] It should not go unnoticed that, whereas one of the first acts of New Jew radicalism took place at a synagogue when Jews for Urban Justice accused those inside of inattentiveness to global concerns of social injustice, Kahane's breakout act was to protest a synagogue's choice to invite a black militant, implying that Jews should *not* enable black claims of social injustice to fall on their shoulders. In both cases the establishment is being challenged, in the former to reach beyond the Jewish community and in the latter to protect it against claims from outside.

Whatever one feels about reparations, Kahane was making a very strong, and radical, statement that Jews have no real responsibility, and certainly no obligation, to the African American struggle for justice. Thus, while in substance Kahane's move may be the inverse of the Jews for Urban Justice protest, it shows the similar ways that both understood "the street," including acts of civil disobedience, as the place where Jews could best express their concerns. This is a good example of where the New Left and Kahane actually agreed and of how such agreement may have been a product of their radicalism. Part of the New Left's critique of the Jews was that their interests did not extend beyond themselves, even as some, even many, committed themselves to a New Left agenda. Yet many Jews did so in those years at the expense of any positive Jewish identity.

Kahane's radical Jewish agenda actually illustrates the New Left's critique of the Jews: that when they live as proud Jews, they feel little obligation to the wider world.[110] In an article in *Commentary,* Clement Greenberg called these Jewish radicals "negative" Jews.[111] As Jews become more invested in their identity, so the argument goes, they become less invested in the world outside the

Jewish community. Nathan Glazer, for example, believed this was simply a false assessment by the New Left.[112] What mattered for Kahane was Jewish interest alone; if their interests coincided with the interests of others, fine, but only if the interests of the Jews and their community took precedent. In this sense Kahane's radicalism squares nicely with black radicalism of the same period, and it is not a coincidence that before 1967 some black militants called their movement "Black Zionism," a throwback to an earlier movement among American blacks.[113]

Kahane's radical program was to create what he called a "New Jew" of a different order. Whether that was a play on the New Jews of the radical left I do not know; it was more likely inspired by the "New Jews" of the early Zionist movement. Kahane's New Jew was meant to undo the "Old Jew," which for him was not the Eastern European traditional Jew but the Old Left liberal Jew who dominated the establishment and maintained that the right path for the Jew in turbulent times was to lay low and not make trouble. Kahane often told the joke about two Jews being taken out by anti-Semites to be shot. As blindfolds were put on their eyes, one cried out "The blindfold is too tight!" The other one then frantically whispered to him, "Quiet, don't make trouble. . . ."[114] This, for Kahane, was the Old Jew he was trying to erase.[115] And it could be done only by subverting the ethos of Jewish acquiescence by means of a radical revision of how the Jew is viewed by society and how Jews viewed themselves in society. This is why for Kahane the moniker "Jewish Panther" was a good thing. If the white man is afraid of the Panthers, all the more so will the anti-Semite be afraid of the Jewish Panthers. In addition, the Jewish Panthers would challenge the Black Panthers at their own game. In his 1972 *Playboy* interview Kahane said, "We're happy when people call us Panthers, because we know a Panther doesn't mess with a Panther." [116] In an interview to the doctoral student Stanley Clawar he said, "If we think we are Jewish panthers, that's okay too. We'll probably get what we want."[117]

In his 1971 interview to the *New York Times,* Kahane offered an anecdote about the time he and fifteen JDLers entered a meeting where black militant Sonny Carson was haranguing some Jews from the Crown Heights Jewish Corporation, a civic group of Crown Heights (Brooklyn) residents. When Carson saw them he stopped and said, "Now man, now sit down, and talk. Now we understand. Now we're speaking Panther to Panther."[118] The article "Superjew" quotes Kahane as saying, in regard to a Jew who gets beaten up "because he wears a yarmulke," "Well baby, there's a new Jew. The Yiddish word is *skotzim,* that is, not nice Jewish boys. The Jewish Defense League was formed to change an image, and frankly we don't give a damn what you think." Finally, in a television interview to NBC on November 6, 1971, Kahane said concerning his Camp Jedel, the militant summer camp he founded, "We Jews have an image; we don't hit back. We came and decided to change that Jewish image. . . . This effort to change the Jewish image will not only save people's lives in Crown Heights and East Flatbush and other ghetto Jewish areas, but will hopefully save lives of Jews in wealthy areas, who at the moment are safe."

The real issue was the radical reconstruction of the Diaspora Jew in line with the model of the "muscle Jew" that Max Nordau used to describe the Zionist. While Nordau was an avid secularist and religion played almost no role in his thinking, Kahane, an Orthodox Jew living in the American Diaspora, used religion not primarily as a spiritual lifestyle but as a means toward identarian ends, that is, toward the eradication of the acquiescent liberal Jew. The Berkeley Free Speech movement had a saying "The issue is not the issue," which meant that free speech, while important, was simply the occasion for a more radical subversion and reconstruction of society. "The issue is not the issue" is a usable phrase to describe radical-left politics in general and captures Kahane's program as well. For Kahane protest, violence, anti-Semitism, the Soviet Jewry movement, even Zionism was "not the issue."

Kahane didn't want his constituency to merely be Zionists: he wanted them to be radical Jews like the Revisionist Zionists; he wanted them to fight (literally and metaphorically) for their right to be an unassimilated Jew in America. On this reading, before he abandoned America as a home for the Jews in the early to mid-1970s (and arguably even after), he wanted the Diaspora Jew to emulate the Revisionist Zionist while living in the Diaspora.[119] As Kahane made clear in a 1971 essay "Galut in Israel," exile was a state of mind and not a physical place.[120] After his early attempt to make the Diaspora Jew into a "muscle Jew" he abandons that goal as hopeless, largely because it failed to stem the tide of Jewish liberalism, and advocates mass *aliyah* as the only solution for the Jews in America.

Just as the early Revisionists such as Jabotinsky, Begin, and others observed nationalist and even fascistic movements in Poland and Italy to construct their Revisionist Zionism, Kahane used the tactics and methods of radical-left movements in America to further his nationalist goals.[121] Kahane wanted the American Jew to feel that his diasporic experience, even though protected by the American Constitution, was not unique but as precarious and fragile as any other. Leon Wieseltier put it quite well when he wrote in 1985, "The climate in Brooklyn was clement for Kahane's message, which was essentially that we, the Jews of Brooklyn, were as besieged as our ancestors, and as our brothers and sisters in Israel. We, too, were fighting for our lives. He seemed to move our uneventful history to the calamitous center of Jewish history, to enlist us in the great Jewish melodrama."[122] The "New Jew" of Zionism that saved Jews from total annihilation in Europe and was modeled after the warrior Jew of Israel's ancient past should be transplanted to Coney Island Avenue and Eastern Parkway. The deracinated liberal Jew should be replaced by the Jew with a fist and the will to use it. Survival.

Admittedly, Kahane's "New Jew" moniker is a bit more nuanced. As a person with strong ties to tradition, he often claimed that his New Jew was really the authentic "Old Jew" in the mold of Bar Kokhba, an Israelite general who revolted against the Romans in 135 CE, or Shimon bar Giora, a militant rebel in the Jerusalem-centered First Jewish-Roman War in 66–73 CE. He wanted to "return the crown to its proper place" (to borrow a rabbinic phase), in some sense remasculinizing Diaspora Jewry.[123] The inheritors of these ancient militants were the Revisionist Zionists who waged a terrorist battle against the British Mandate in the early twentieth century. Kahane wanted to create a Diaspora Jew like the militant Jew of antiquity and the nationalist Jew of Zionism.[124] His was a case of radical Jewish Diasporism opposing liberal assimilationism, rejecting the way in which the combination of the Diaspora and liberalism made the Jew effeminate and incapable of standing up for oneself against interethnic urban belligerence. Of course, his mimicking the Black Panthers, or in some way white nationalism, was its own form of assimilation. Thus Kahane wasn't so much antiassimilationist as opposed to any form of assimilation that would yield the erasure of Jewish identity.

It is often overlooked that Kahane was initially very much a Diaspora Jew and his radical project was a diasporic one. For a variety of reasons I will go into elsewhere, in the early 1970s, as we have seen, he gave up on the American project and changed his program to one of collective *aliyah*. This is the subject of his 1972 book *Time to Go Home* and is reiterated in a chapter called "Aliyah: Time to Go Home" in his 1975 book *The Story of the Jewish Defense League*.[125] His radicalism, I suggest, is not born from Revisionist Zionism but rather an extreme reaction to the radicalism he encountered in the New Left as a young rabbi in the 1960s coupled with a disdain for the way liberalism had, in his view, emasculated the American Jew.

It is perhaps best not to compare Kahane's radicalism with the Free Speech movement or even SDS, both of which were by and large nonviolent in principle even if they occupied university offices as a form of protest (most notably at Columbia in 1968). Both were primarily ideological movements. From 1968 to 1969 some in SDS became more radicalized, resulting in the formation of the Weather Underground for which violence became a necessary and accepted tactic. Mike James, who served on the SDS National Council in Chicago in 1969, said, "The time will come when we'll have to use guns. Don't let it hang you up. Some of you guys say violence isn't human. Violence, when directed at the oppressor is human as well as necessary. Struggle sometimes means violence, but struggle is necessary because it is through collective struggle that liberation comes."[126] This is fairly classic Fanonian logic that Kahane, for his part, expresses in numerous ways, especially in *The Story of the Jewish Defense League*. I will discuss Kahane's theories of violence in subsequent chapters. Suffice it to say here that while his radical early thinking envisaged violence as a last resort, by the early 1970s it became a dominant theme that turned the JDL from civilian guardians to bomb makers and arms smugglers.[127]

This espousal of violence occurs fairly early in Kahane's radical turn. Take, for example, his response to a question about justifying the JDL's violence in his *Playboy* interview: "As a general principle, if there is no need for violence, then even a little bit is bad. But if a crisis arises in which nothing can work but a great deal of violence, then *not* to use it is a tragedy. Was it more merciful not to go to war with the Nazis in 1935? Was it more moral, more ethical, more decent, more humane? I think it would have been a lot more humane for a lot of innocent people if we had gone to war then." The interviewer states that many Jewish leaders claim that violence contradicts the principles of Judaism.[128] Kahane responds, "Gandhi, a pacifist, was not a Jew. Moses *was* a Jew—and he smote the Egyptian."[129] A year earlier in *Never Again!* he states it more emphatically: "[Moses] saw an Egyptian beating a Jew . . . and he acted in a manner that should be a lesson for the Jew in how to behave toward his oppressors . . . the Bible tells us, in simple and unsophisticated terms, *And he smote the Egyptian*."[130] I will have more to say on Kahane's *Playboy* interview below; here it is worth noting that when asked about the JDL's advocacy of violence, Kahane brings up America's mistake in not going to war against the Nazis in 1935—with a specific intent.

The title of Kahane's book *Never Again!*, published only a year before this interview, conveys that Jews will never allow themselves to be endangered without striking back. While he is not comparing American anti-Semitism to the Nazi regime, his point is that what Jews should learn from the Holocaust is that sometimes violence can prevent more serious violence, not unlike the Maoist popular adage that "sometimes you have to pick up the gun to put the gun down," which was used often by Malcolm X. Kahane writes, "We were no fools. None of us expected that, in the advent of another Hitler, the JDL could save American Jewry. Not one and not a hundred JDLs could do that. But it was the local Hitlers who could be dealt with speedily and well if Jews knew how."[131] Preemptive violence was moral in his eyes because it prevented violence that spun out of control. And Hitler was not, for him, categorically exceptional but more of a horrific manifestation of something that underlay much of gentile society;[132] "local Hitlers" were ubiquitous. Elsewhere, in writing about the 1968 New York City school strike, he refers to blacks as "Nazis whose will is imposing numerous clauses on a city while the Board of Education officialdom sits in timid fear."[133] He quite often mixes the Jew-Nazi, black-white dichotomies in his writing; for example, "The Jew will not stand for the violence and bigotry shown by the Black Nazis anymore than he would stand for another white Hitler."[134] In another article Kahane described the teachers' strike in Ocean Hill–Brownsville as "the battle for Black Nazism in Brownsville."[135]

Referring to Moses and the Egyptian as he often did is quite apt.[136] Seeing his fellow Hebrew in danger, Moses struck the Egyptian and killed him; he did not try to negotiate with him. This resulted in Moses's life as a fugitive and also his subsequent vocation as the redeemer of Israel (Kahane saw himself as both). Like many of the New Jews but in a different register, Kahane is claiming that Judaism is a radical and not a liberal religion.[137] The question, of course, is how one assesses when violence is necessary, and what ends besides defense it serves. Kahane's thoughts on this issue changed over time, especially after he emigrated to Israel and became more situated there.[138] But the very liberal notion that violence contradicts Judaism is something he had little tolerance for, a theme he developed further in his revision of Zionism in *Listen World, Listen Jew*.

The *Playboy* Interview

While I have cited the *Playboy* interview earlier, I return to it now because it serves as an important primary text of Kahane's early career, especially as a venue to propound his radical politics to a liberal readership. Launched in 1953, by the late 1960s and early 1970s *Playboy* magazine was in its heyday. Originally dedicated to opening up the closed and "uptight" sexual world of 1950s America, *Playboy* soon became the home of some of the great literary, political, and entertainment figures in the United States.[139]

Authors such as Norman Mailer, James Baldwin, and Joyce Carol Oates published articles and interviews in *Playboy*. Extensive interviews with Muhammad Ali, Fidel Castro, Bertrand Russell, Jean-Paul Sartre, Martin Luther King, Jimmy Carter, and many others occupied its pages. In its October 1972 issue, *Playboy* published a long interview with Meir Kahane. While I do not know the details of how *Playboy* came to Kahane or why he agreed to be interviewed, the interview suggests a couple of things: first, that Kahane was enough of a national figure by 1972 that *Playboy* deemed it appropriate to feature him; second, that Kahane, while an Orthodox Jew, did not see himself barred by what one might call the etiquette of Orthodoxy from appearing in a magazine whose raison d'être was the relaxation of sexual mores by featuring naked women under the subtitle "Entertainment for Men." Kahane knew that, having no official affiliation, his only path forward was self-promotion. *Playboy* gave him a national audience; he could make his case for Jewish pride to many readers who had never heard of him. This was simply an opportunity he could not pass up, even given the venue.

In the 1960s and 1970s Kahane was the only Jewish figure who represented a Jewish movement of any kind, religious or otherwise, who was interviewed by *Playboy*. Along with post-Holocaust theologian Richard Rubenstein, Kahane was likely the most "Jewish" interviewee in the magazine's history.[140]

The preamble to the interview states, "Nearly every reader of a news magazine has heard of the Jewish Defense League and seen pictures of its tough-looking youths 'patrolling' inner-city neighborhoods, trained in karate, standing armed guard before the doors of synagogues." The impetus for the interview, implied in the rather lengthy but not uncharacteristic preamble, was that Kahane was a radical Jew (remember, this was 1972) who was as much at war with his liberal Jewish community as with the world around him. While nothing Kahane said in this interview was new, it encapsulates a particular moment in the self-fashioning of his radicalization. That makes it a significant historical document, in part because the questions were pointed and Kahane knew he was speaking to a readership far beyond his Jewish audience. We find moments of stark honesty that illustrate a radical personality, one who is unapologetic about his commitments. For example, in a discussion about how far Kahane was willing to go in his use of violence, the interviewer remarks, "Then the only difference between you and, say, the American Nazi Party is that they're wrong and you're right," to which Kahane replies, "I can't put it better than that."[141] There is no attempt to create a moral hierarchy that would justify this action and not that one. In some sense, the radical is willing to acknowledge the extent to which his or her position cannot easily be justified outside of itself; it does not require rationalization. Radicalism is, to some degree, a zero-sum game that is founded on the sheer strength of resolve to accurately assess the situation and the necessary solution. In that sense Kahane has more in common with other radicals who opposed him than with liberals who opposed him.

This stance emerges later in the interview when Kahane turns from his assessment of black anti-Semitism, the use of violence, and the danger in contemporary America to the vacuity of the liberal American Jewish establishment. It is here that he articulates the larger dimensions of his early project. There is an odd exchange where Kahane is asked about his feelings toward the emphasis on ethnic identity in America and responds that he is bothered by it. When then told that he seems to be advocating something similar, he answers that the issue for him is not so much ethnic identity but an ideological foundation for any identity at all. "All forms of life become things to be enjoyed. . . . Nobody built a Conservative temple because of ideology; they built it because they wanted something a little more modern, a little easier. When it filtered down to people that the Conservative rabbi would let them ride to synagogue instead of walk, that's what created a Conservative temple. There's no ideology in any of it."[142]

This remark deserves some attention. Part of Kahane's critique of American Jewry, and American Judaism more generally (I would include here Modern Orthodoxy), is that it is largely about convenience, that for most American Jews religion is void of ideology. Although he does not say so here explicitly, this is also part of his critique of liberalism in general and liberal religion in particular. The moderation built into a liberal approach to society or religion produces a kind of mediocrity under the guise of moderation that stands in opposition to radicalism and thus real lasting change, collective or personal. It is an approach close to the Musar tradition in which he was trained that I will discuss in another chapter. Thus he cynically pushes aside any claim that Conservative Judaism, for example, is built on an ideological foundation of tradition and change. While this may be true for its architects, for the average Jew in the pew, Kahane argues, the attraction of a Conservative synagogue is mostly convenience. While certainly overly dismissive here, in terms of the average Jew who frequented a Conservative synagogue in America in the early 1970s, he is not far off target. And at the time of this interview, Conservative Judaism was in its heyday in terms of synagogue membership and impact.

It seems clear that in fact Kahane is advocating for Jewish ethnic identity—what else does "Jewish pride" (*hadar*) actually mean—but he focuses on ideology and not ethnos because in some way liberal Judaism, what he and others called "bagel and lox Judaism," is precisely an ethnic identity void of ideology.[143] Or, if it has an ideology, for example, liberalism, it is not a Jewish one. Citing Kahane, journalist Mel Ziegler wrote, "As far as the Jews in Scarsdale were concerned, hell with them. What did they know anyway, those country-club going, martini-drinking, self-hating Jews, if you could even call them Jews with their Reform churches.[144] Hell with them and most of their pals, the *goyim*, and what they thought."[145] The question for Kahane was not to be or not to be an identifiable Jew, but a *reason* to be Jewish, and more specifically a *Jewish* reason to be Jewish. There is a distinction he seems to be making between ethnicity void of ideology and ethnic identity born from ideology. Judaism of pride (*hadar*) is the option he offers, a combination of religious nostalgia, muscular nationalism, and Jewish assertiveness.[146]

Notwithstanding Kahane's very packaged and caricatured American Orthodox critique of non-Orthodox Judaism (Kahane was once a pulpit rabbi of a Conservative synagogue in Howard Beach, Queens, that he claimed to have restored to Orthodoxy after which he was summarily fired), his point was to subvert the substitution of Judaism with liberalism that he believed had infected American Judaism.[147] When asked, "Are you saying that the kind of Judaism widely practiced in this country isn't really Judaism?" Kahane replied, "Right. It may be nonviolent principles of Tolstoy; it may be the liberal principles of Americans for Democratic Action; but it's not Judaism. . . . When a Reform rabbi talks about the morals of Judaism and the ethics of Judaism, I think that's wonderful; I'm all for morals and ethics, only what he is talking about isn't particularly Jewish. . . . Ethics aren't enough. Everybody's ethical. . . . I don't mock the values. I only mock the people who think that these [liberal] values will solve the Jewish problem in this country."[148] This is unremarkable and could be said by many Modern Orthodox rabbis, or Jews, in America at that time or now.

What is interesting, in my view, is only how this view is then used to promote Kahane's radical project. Daniel Bell wrote that whereas ethics is concerned with justice, politics is "a power struggle between organized groups to determine the allocation of privilege."[149] On Bell's definition, Kahane's project was political from start to finish and thus he remained tone-deaf to the religious case for ethics so common to the liberal Jewish circles of his time. He certainly contested the liberal Jewish notion that Judaism was essentially about ethics, but more to the point, Kahane was concerned with power and privilege above theoretical notions of justice.

Asked in the *Playboy* interview if his radical activities are "consistent with Jewish law," Kahane responds, "That's what we're trying for. When a young Jew who has never felt much for his Jewish past participates in one of our protests, he experiences for the first time the feeling that he's doing something for the Jews. It's the first step back to Judaism." He continues, "JDL isn't a religious organization. We're not interested in drawing them back to Orthodox Judaism. We want to get rid of their ignorance about what Judaism is, and then if they choose to practice it, fine."[150] There is something *kiruv*-like (missionizing) about the way Kahane viewed the JDL, but not in any conventional sense. For Kahane it was a Judaism for which the street was more important than the synagogue, for which protests were religious rituals. In Kahane's mind there was something "religious" about the organization.[151]

What is striking here is the extent to which, for Kahane, his radical Jewish agenda of pride through political activism and militarism is what will undermine the substitution of liberalism for Judaism in America. This resembles certain statements by Black Panthers that their black consciousness was aroused, or in today's parlance, they were "woke" through the activism they experienced in Panther protests. The way to Judaism for Kahane is not through study but a feeling of "doing something for Jews." Orthodoxy is not the goal; rather, the goal is a sense of ethnic pride and fidelity through ideology. It is likely that when he expressed concern about the move to ethnic identity (thinking, presumably, of the Black Nationalist movement), he envisioned the JDL as reshaping Jewish identity toward more familial rather than ethnic terms. He openly denied Jews were a race and thus claimed he was not a racist. His belief in the superiority of the Jew, determined by a theological precept of chosenness, deeply informs his radicalism. Later in his career, after his move to Israel, he does say, "I'm not a nationalist. I'm a religious Jew." But as we will see later on, his use of religion as a tool for his identarian project is a complex matter.[152]

In any case, for Kahane liberalism, especially disguised as Judaism, makes Judaism into something that can never serve particularistic ends; liberalism will inevitably take the Jews' concerns beyond the Jewish community and, in a free democratic country like America, erase the Jewishness of the Jew.[153] The liberal, he posits, will almost always end up a universalist or an internationalist (perhaps today we can say intersectionalist), and even if he or she still cares for the Jews, that will not be the primary, and certainly not exclusive, concern. For the Jews to adequately fight the battles necessary to ensure the safety of the Jews in America, they must first *become* Jews, which, for Kahane, meant fidelity to Jewish survival by rejecting liberalism as a substitute for Judaism.

They must have something to be "radically Jewish" about. As discussed above, this does not necessarily mean a return to Orthodoxy;[154] it means a return to primal fidelity to Jews. Religion for Kahane is a means toward that ideological end. Janet Dolgin captured this when she wrote, "The fact that JDL subsumed certain religious laws and assumptions into its ideology became the point of significance. The primacy of religious authority was replaced by the superordinance of JDL Ideology . . . for the JDL the stress was not on the relation between man and divinity; it was the relation between the Jewish people and anti-Semitism."[155]

These comments exhibit the extent to which Kahane's project is founded on a deep and radical critique of liberalism, not so much as a political ideology but more pressingly as a template for American Judaism, as a substitute for religion. The liberal Jew, he argues, is not enough of a Jew to fight the battle for Jewish survival, certainly not in America; it is only the radical Jew, the one who may not necessarily understand Judaism very deeply but understands, and feels, a primal fidelity to the Jews, who will stand up when Jews are challenged and protect them from harm. Thus Kahane divides up the JDL between what he calls "scholars" and "chayas" (literally, animals). The scholar educates, the chaya acts. Both serve one another, like the rabbinic Yesachar and Zevulun, to construct a society that has the ideology to move it forward and the practical application to fulfill its goals.[156] The "chayas" in the JDL served a similar function to the *lumpenproletariat* in Malcolm X's vision of the Black Nationalist movement. The *lumpenproletariat*, a term coined by Karl Marx to define the underclass and uneducated masses who had no real understanding of the revolution but were happy to take part in it, became for Kahane the "chayas" whose job it was to engage in disobedient and often criminal behavior for the sake of the movement.

A similar sentiment could be seen in his critique of Israeli society in the 1980s when he argued that Israelis had become liberal like Americans and thus could never defeat the Arabs who knew nothing of liberalism. Ironically, in the 1980s Kahane suggests that for Israel to survive it has to become less American and more like the Arab enemy.[157] In the late 1960s and early 1970s in America, this same notion is expressed through his call for Jews to become "Jewish Panthers" so as to dissuade the enemy from confronting Jews. Of course, Israel is a much more complex problem because Jews are the majority and hold political and military power. But on both shores, his project is not about any specific issue but rather remaking the Jew, moving him or her from a liberal mindset to a radical one; away from compromise and toward an overarching ideology of survival.

A Final Word on Liberalism and the Jewish Radical

In the assessment of many New Jews, Kahane was not as much a radical as he thought. In fact, in Jack Nusan Porter and Peter Dreier's "Introduction" to *Jewish Radicalism*, they describe him as "nonradical": "Yet we should not overlook a decidedly nonradical approach which has attracted growing numbers of young Jews, particularly in working-class areas of New York. This is the other side of the ideological coin, the right-wing Zionism of the Jewish Defense League and Betar, and their own hero Ze'ev Jabotinsky. . . . The Jewish left is ambivalent toward Meir Kahane and his followers. Most radical Jews are critical of the JDL's strategy. . . . The Jewish left's confusion over the JDL is reflected in a comment by one of its activists: 'I like their style, but abhor their politics.'"[158]

Porter and Dreier refer to the differences between the Radical Zionist Alliance, a product of New Jew radicalism, and the JDL, whose politics are reactionary and not progressive. But as we will see in the next chapter, the sympathy for and even symmetry between late-1960s Jewish radical groups and Kahane's JDL was not occasional. In their methods (or, as the above activist states, "style") they had at least something in common, and more important, they had a common enemy, and at least to some degree common goals, in regard to Jewish identity and the centrality of Israel. New Jew David Mandel in his critique of the JDL notes, "JDL's attacks on the Jewish Establishment in America are almost totally valid."[159] While many New Jew radicals drew their radicalism from Marx, and Kahane from the hypernationalism of Jabotinsky, both viewed the current situation as requiring systemic and not incremental change. And both understood effects of liberalism in regard to Jewish identity and fidelity to the Jewish people and Jewish causes.

Porter and Dreier, however, are too wedded to "politics" as the defining factor of radicalism and ignore the dimension of radicalism as a critique of liberalism, either from the right or the left. For example, it is common in Israel today to use the term "radical" to define right-wing settler Zionism as much as far-left post-Zionism. When Abbie Hoffman purportedly said of Kahane "I agree with his methods but not his goals" (see in chapter 2), Hoffman appears to have understood Kahane as a radical of a certain type. Thus, while Kahane did have sympathy for Colombo's Italian-American Civil Rights League, which was not a radical organization, he may have been closer to the Radical Zionist Alliance and the Black Panthers in terms of how he viewed the world around him and what he believed needed to be done.[160]

In Bill Novak's requiem for Jewish radicalism in 1971, he mentions Kahane as well:

> There were, in the beginning, attempts to synthesize "Jewish" action and "American" action. But now there seems to be a feeling that we have to choose, that it is an either-or proposition. And so we find ourselves tolerating the Jewish Defense League, because they are Jews, or because the cause they claim to speak for is beyond reproach, or because they are "raising the consciousness" of the community or because we dislike their enemies or because, as it sometimes seems, "at least they are doing something!" And we keep silent about our moral outrage and their open cowardice, and worse, we do nothing ourselves.[161]

Novak's rhetorical comment "at least they are doing something!" in regard to the JDL is strikingly similar to Kahane's answer to those who want him to join them in condemning the young leftist Jews mentioned earlier. For Novak, action with the wrong politics should not merit support, while for Kahane action with the wrong politics is better than apathy because at least it shows concern. Novak's lament that the New Jews have lost their commitment both to America and to the world notwithstanding, he is descriptively correct in noting that over time the "Jewish" aspects of the New Jews began to overshadow the larger frame of leftist politics as some moved toward a "radical" particularism (in opposition to what Arthur Waskow called "multi-particularism") that made Kahane more attractive. And even more so, Novak is correct that this move to the right often took the form of a survivalism whereby ideology became driven by a tribalism that undermined the left's cosmopolitan and universal commitments.[162] In a similar register Waskow notes, "Inaction by radical Jews would feed the growth of the Jewish Defense League and similar rightward 'defensive' organizations which cannot be answered by conventional Jewish liberalism, and would allow the formerly liberal Jewish community to become a permanent enemy of the liberation of American society."[163] Here Waskow interestingly suggests that the radicalism of Kahane's program could only be countered by a radical, and not a liberal, alternative. Kahane said as much in a synagogue in Columbus, Ohio: "There is no other alternative than to be a militant."[164] Waskow might have responded that there was no alternative than to be a radical nonviolent actor.

Novak concludes his essay with the proclamation: "For we must assert it loudly: Mere existence for Jews, *even in the wake of Hitler,* is simply not enough."[165] But it is still the case that the failure Novak describes is a failure *within* radicalism and not *of* radicalism. Kahane was attractive in part because he embodied a similar mindset with different goals, because he too was a radical: not a Jewish radical or a radical Jew as much as a radical *for* the Jews. At least for some New Jews whose Jewishness was aroused through the turn toward Israel (the Radical Jewish Alliance) or Jewish activism (Jews for Urban Justice), this resonated quite strongly. In his 1971 *New York Times* interview Kahane said, "We've turned them on. Hundreds of young people who were active in the radical left have now joined us. I think there was a pathetic yearning for something Jewish. . . . We come and we're non-establishment. We're radical. And, above all, they look and they say, 'They didn't just talk. They've even gone to jail.'"[166]

Kahane himself was quite aware of the symmetry between his movement and the New Jews. In an interview to Zvi Lowenthal and Jonathan Braun in the leftist student organ *The Flame* in 1971, Kahane said, "I believe that there are only two meaningful Jewish trends at this moment on campus. They are the JDL and the radical Zionist trends. They are the two groups which offer sacrifices, which offer substance, not form. I feel very close in many ways to the Radical Jewish Alliance though I differ with them strongly on certain issues. But I know there is substance there, and meaning and sincerity which young Jews sense both in them and in us."[167]

The tension between liberalism (the Old Left) and radicalism (the New Left) defined the 1960s, especially after 1965.[168] As radicalism became more popular toward the end of the decade with the escalation of the war alongside the protests against it—perhaps culminating at Kent State in May 1970 when National Guards fired sixty-seven rounds into a crowd of unarmed protesters killing four and wounding nine others—the country seemed to be in a kind of free fall. In the small corner of the Jewish world, young Jews were rediscovering their Jewish roots through various forms of activism that included the Soviet Jewry movement and a renewed sense of radical religiosity. The House of Love and Prayer was founded in San Francisco in 1967, Havurat Shalom in Somerville, Massachusetts, in 1968, the progressive minyan Farbrengan in Washington in 1971, and the Aquarian Minyan in Berkeley in 1974. The other side of this radical renaissance was Meir Kahane's Jewish Defense League founded in 1968. Understanding Kahane and his impact on American Jewry requires us to view him in the larger context of radicalism's critique of liberalism in the late 1960s and early 1970s.

While his politics were reactionary and racist, some of his goals were not that distinct from those of radical Jewish groups on the left. As noted, this changes somewhat when he emigrates to Israel in 1971 and turns his attention to the Israeli scene, where his radicalism becomes more fascistic and his advocacy of violence more vindictive and even apocalyptic. But in the early days of the JDL, and even before, Kahane is best viewed as a Jewish radical of his time convinced that liberalism endangered the American Jew. About a decade later neoconservatives would make a similar argument. Kahane was, despite his Zionism, quintessentially American, believing that he could "save the American dream."

Kahane's solution was not a return to Orthodoxy or traditionalism, nor was it a secular turn to conservative politics. Unlike the *Commentary* crowd at the time, for example, he did not poke holes in liberalism from the confines of the high-rise offices of high-minded journals but instead took Judaism to the street (he certainly would have appreciated the popular call "Whose streets? Our streets!"). His program was to create a New Jew in the American Diaspora, a radical Jew who would be unafraid, assertive and, if necessary, violent, in order to ensure the survival of the Jews at a time when Kahane felt they were threatened by the radicalism of Black Nationalism and the lure of American assimilation. It is from this context that the importance of his life can best be understood.

2

Radicalism

RADICAL BEDFELLOWS: MEIR KAHANE AND THE "NEW JEWS" IN THE LATE 1960S

"We're the marching liberals
And we march for all the others,
But we're much, too much, too busy,
For the causes of our brothers."

JERRY KIRSCHEN, *JEWISH LIBERATION JOURNAL*

"If you want to get busted then get busted for a Jewish cause."

NEIL ROTHENBERG, NATIONAL COORDINATOR OF THE JDL YOUTH MOVEMENT, EARLY 1970S

Kahane and the New Jews

As discussed in chapter 1, Kahane's attack on liberalism was at the center of his project, both in America and later in Israel. He shared this disdain for liberalism with many participants in Jewish leftist movements who, returning to Judaism in the late 1960s, carried with them their antiliberal views from their days with the New Left.

One introductory example relevant to our discussion will suffice. Such disdain was on display in a variation on the book of Esther that Kahane, who was adept in the populism of theatrics and comedic parody, composed in the late 1960s. This parody was called "Megillat (Scroll of) Heyman" and targeted George C. Heyman Jr., then president of the Federation of Jewish Philanthropies, for mockery. Heyman, whose name is phonetically identical to the villain of the book of Esther, Haman, appears as the great villain of contemporary

Jews. Kahane's scroll opens with the words: "And it came to pass in the days of Heyman who ruled from Westchester to Long Island over a hundred and thirty agencies."[1] This derisive depiction of the vacuity of American Jewish liberalism could have easily appeared in any number of New Left publications such as *Ramparts*, or New Jewish outlets such as *Brooklyn Bridge* or the *Jewish Liberation Journal*.[2] This type of performative style can also be seen in various adaptations of guerrilla theater common among the New Left Yippies, a group founded by Abbie Hoffman and Jerry Rubin (both Jews) and influenced by the Jewish comedian Lenny Bruce.[3] Both Kahane and the New Jewish radicals were antiliberal, albeit from different perspectives.

Kahane was strongly influenced by the sort of "law and order" politics typically associated with American conservatives and Nixon supporters, while the countercultural New Jews were influenced by Marxists such as Herbert Marcuse and by the Kulturkampf that overtook the civil rights movement as it morphed into Black Nationalism and the antiwar movement. It was a shared commitment to radicalism and a critique of liberalism that brought them into close proximity. In particular, it was their shared view of the Jewish establishment as the crux of the problem facing Jews in postwar America that allowed for their convergence.[4]

I use the term "radical" to define Kahane in part because he used it to define himself. But what did Kahane mean by it? He viewed biblical figures such as Abraham and Moses as radicals, individuals who were iconoclasts, willing to risk everything to change the social dynamic so as to achieve their ends—epitomized, in the case of Abraham, by the midrash about him breaking the idols in his father's idol shop for the sake of monotheism, and in the case of Moses, by first killing an Egyptian taskmaster and then speaking truth to power against Pharaoh so as to liberate the Israelites. Kahane also seems to have defined himself as "radical" in the way Malcolm X or Stokely Carmichael did. He believed in a full inversion of an exilic Jewish identity, from passive *golus* (exilic) acquiescence to Jews as carriers of power that would deter violence against them by threatening violence in return. Just as the Black Nationalists held that fighting racism required threatening violence against blacks with violence against whites, Kahane believed that anti-Semitism, which could only be managed and never eradicated, needed to be dealt with through deterrence. This newfound power would refashion the American Jew as a force to be reckoned with as opposed to manipulated.

The point of this chapter is to show how radicalism is often an approach to social critique that unites radicals from opposite ends of the political spectrum. Left radicals and right radicals often use one another's tactics and borrow one another's brand to express their rejection of the moderate middle both are seeking to undermine. One clear example is how the JDL used the clenched fist as an emblem, almost identical to the clenched fist of the Black Panthers. And here I reach back to the anecdote in the introduction about my Modern Orthodox interlocutor at the bat mitzvah buffet table who spoke so positively about Kahane. How would he react to knowing that Kahane's reactionary radicalism and far-left radicalism shared a great deal? How would he respond to Kahane's remark that the New Left radical Jews were better than the nonideological Jews who filled American synagogues because "at least they believed in something"? Indeed, how would he react to the fact that Kahane would critique his bourgeois lifestyle in the suburbs that did not include any activism whatsoever? That Kahane respected Jews in the street more than he did Jews in the synagogue? Kahane's radicalism was not only aimed at liberalism but also at the complacency of affluent American Jews, observant or not, who lived in the comforts of what he called "the gilded suburbs of Great Neck and Scarsdale."

In 1971 the left-leaning Baltimore-Washington Union of Jewish Students published an advertisement that Kahane would have admired: "To be a Jew on America's terms is to trade in historical and religious ethics of social justice for a $60,000 house in Silver Springs or Stevenson. . . . To be a Jew in America is to forget 2000 years of oppression because of 20 years of prosperity." The ad concluded: "TO BE A JEW ON AMERICA'S TERMS IS NOT TO BE A JEW AT ALL."[5]

Kahane was no less American in his activism than Abbie Hoffman, and the JDL no less American than the Yippies or SDS. All were protest movements out to undo the establishment by testing the elasticity of the American liberal system, even as both transgressed the norms of that system in order to make their voices known. Kenneth Braiterman's 1970 assessment rings true: "If the debate between the JDL and the liberal Jewish establishment reduces itself to mere questions of tactics, young American Jews in the 1970s will probably find anti-establishment militancy more attractive than bureaucratic moderation."[6]

The Jewish counterculture, or as many of its members called themselves, the New Jews, arose as a protest against both the postwar American liberalism (beginning with the "Old Left" or "New Deal" liberalism of the 1930s and 1940s) that had dominated the American Jewish establishment, and the radical New Left that had taken root among young Americans in the mid-1960s.[7] By

"New Jews" I refer to those young Jewish activists coming of age in the late 1960s whose inclinations were generally aligned with the New Left including its radicalism but who, after 1967, began to rethink their associations with their Jewish identity largely as a result of the anti-Zionism and sometimes anti-Semitism in some of the New Left's political positions beginning in 1965.[8] These New Jews believed that the Jewish establishment was the enemy and the only way to effect change was through extreme pressure, protest, and in many cases civil disobedience. As a cohort they were disorganized, with no shared, or at least no unified sense of what they wanted to build. They were composed of disparate groups with very different perspectives and agendas. As one contemporary observer and critic, Benjamin Ross, noted in a 1970 essay, "The 'Jewish radicals' see a crying need for radical change in the Jewish community. But they are quite fuzzy when it comes to saying what kind of change is needed."

Ross went on to note, "The largest 'new, creative, and experimental' project in the Jewish community today is the Jewish Defense League" but then pointedly observed that "the Jewish students of Boston are *not* demanding support for the Jewish Defense League."[9] While it is true that many of the New Jewish radicals were not supportive of the JDL, which had established a strong chapter in Boston that included civil patrols in the "frontier" neighborhoods of Mattapan and Dorchester, we saw earlier that the protest against the liberal establishment was something both sides, from opposite perspectives, had in common.[10] Reflecting on the tenth anniversary of the JDL's founding, Kahane noted, likely with the New Jews in mind, "Today, tens of thousands of ordinary Jews have become radicalized and dynamic Jews. They have become disenchanted with the Jewish Establishment that was so responsible, through their silence and inaction, for the tragic Holocaust . . . that is so much to blame for the cancer of Jewish assimilation and alienation of young Jews. . . . These people cannot find their place within the Establishment but at the same time, are not prepared to join a group that is openly violent, regardless of their sympathy with it."[11]

By then, 1978, Kahane had already left the JDL and had published a book-length history of it in *The Story of the Jewish Defense League* (1975). In this 1978 article he reflects on the ways in which the JDL had "revolutionized American Jewish thinking and radically changed the views and activities of the American Jewish community."[12] While this is perhaps exaggerated and certainly self-aggrandizing, what Kahane initiated in the late 1960s and early 1970s had an impact not only on right-leaning Jewish reactionaries and Orthodox Jews but also on some New Jews who had abandoned the New Left and rediscovered their Jewishness while retaining radical political views.

It is noteworthy that these Jewish refugees from the New Left embraced the term "New Jews," which Kahane often used to describe what he was trying to create with the JDL. Many took the New Left's attack on corporate America and America's military complex and turned it against the Old Left liberalism and accommodationism of the Jewish establishment that they claimed prevented a free and "radical" expression of their newly discovered Jewish identity.[13] Increasing numbers of young Jews in the late 1960s and early 1970s were contesting the New Left's rejection of Jewish particularity and, in some cases, Zionism.[14]

One watershed event in this distancing of these leftist Jewish radicals from New Left radicalism was their response to the platform of the leftist New Politics Convention in Chicago in September 1967. A press release by the conference organizers designated this gathering as "nothing less than the nation's rebirth." The New Left journal *Ramparts* trumpeted the event as "the biggest and most representative gathering of America's Left opposition in over two decades."[15] Aside from adopting an anti-Zionist platform, the organizing committee's black caucus urged the whites in attendance to leave the black movement to blacks and "organize among your own." This hostility toward white activists, some of whom were Jews, led to the formation of what was called the Jewish Liberation Movement, which lasted from 1968 until around 1974. Bill Novak, an active participant in this transient group, noted that "it was a loose confederation of many autonomous groups that more or less shared a variety of ideas and interests."[16] The general sentiment, sparked by the New Politics Convention in Chicago, was expressed by a young New Leftist, Steven Plaut, in a 1971 article "My Evolution as a Radical Zionist": "Today I am no longer an American new leftist. Today, my place is in my Jewish community. I still maintain my progressive politics, but the New Left and I are on the opposite sides of the barricade."[17]

In the Jewish world, the Six-Day War played a constitutive role in awakening young American Jews, many of whom had been educated (or, not educated) in suburban synagogues across America, to a sense of Jewish pride and an activism that melded Zionism and radical-left politics.[18] In the words of Shlomo Russ, "The Six-Day War enabled Jews to become parochial again."[19] The abovementioned Rabbi Arthur Waskow, political activist and one of the founders of the still loosely defined Jewish Renewal movement born during this period, wrote about this sentiment in the following comment about a

Freedom Seder he took part in at Cornell University on April 7, 1970, with radical Catholic clerics Fathers Dan and Phil Berrigan: "That night I faced the choice between the Woodstock Nation and the Jewish People, and I learned that 3,500 years of struggle . . . had more to teach me than the plunge into the Now. In that night, and a few weeks following, I crossed the frontier from being a committed Jewish radical, to being a committed radical Jew."[20]

While 1967 was a watershed year for many, including Kahane, it should be noted that for him the war merely affirmed what he already believed and was more of an occasion to publicize his radical views than the event that sparked them.

Although the summer of 1967 (which was also the Summer of Love) may have brought Israel into focus for young Jews negotiating their relationship with the New Left, 1968 was truly the year of seismic change in American Jewish identity. One significant event often overlooked in this tumultuous year is Kahane's founding of the JDL. It was created not in response to anything in Israel but rather to a local event, the Ocean Hill–Brownsville Brooklyn school strike that, as noted, saw expressions of anti-Semitism among some of the African American parents who protested against the Jewish president of the United Federation of Teachers, Albert Shanker, and his defense of the predominantly white Jewish teachers in the district.[21] Shanker was an unlikely target of African American anger. He was an ardent civil rights supporter and in 1965, just three years before the strike put him in the center of the controversy, marched with Martin Luther King in Selma.[22] But as UFT head he could not support the program put forth by the parents of the school district. His stated reason was that he was committed to protecting the teachers under his aegis, most of them white, who were being asked to leave their teaching positions by the parent board of the school district.

One of the JDL's earliest documents, the aforementioned "Jewish Defense League: Aims and Purposes" (1968), portrays the Jewish establishment as the main impetus for forming the organization: "When Jewish rights are eroded to an unprecedented degree and when the establishment's apathy and indifference grow, we are faced with a unique problem which calls for a unique solution. That solution is the JDL."[23] This description offers a more general reason for the JDL that extends beyond the school strike, which was the initial stimulus for its founding. In addition, an advertisement the JDL took out in the *New York Times* on October 20, 1969, stated, "Do not listen to the soothing anesthesia of the 'Establishment.' They walk in the paths of those whose timidity helped to bury our brothers and sisters less than thirty years ago [referring to the Holocaust]."[24]

While by the early 1970s almost every major American Jewish organization had denounced the JDL—from the ADL, which even provided information on JDL activities to the FBI, to the American Jewish Congress, the American Jewish Committee, and the Jewish War Veterans—the JDL gained real traction among Jews for whom Kahane's crusade against anti-Semitism and assimilation, and promotion of Jewish pride, spoke to their sense of anxiety about the future of American Jewry in the turbulent days of the late 1960s and early 1970s.[25] Emanuel Rackman, who was initially quite sympathetic to the JDL before turning against it, said in 1971, "My guess is that the Jewish Defense League has more sympathizers than the combined membership of all the established organizations."[26]

Jews in the Street: Kahane's Protest Rituals

Kahane attracted young progressive American Jews to his movement by taking Judaism to the streets and using Jewish rituals as a form of political protest. Describing the Soviet Jewry movement, which Kahane took part in, Shaul Kelner observed that "through activities like Passover marches and 'Freedom Seders,' which brought Jewish rituals out into the streets, and 'Matzoh of Hope' rituals, which brought Jewish political protest into the home, Jews enacted and thereby advocated the idea that an authentic religious Judaism was one that was engaged in 'redemptive' political action in support of other Jews."[27] This captured not only the Soviet Jewry movement but the Radical Zionist Alliance and the JDL as well, even though the JDL also advocated violence while other groups did not. The concern about violence was evident in a letter written by the JDL to youth-group directors about the 1966 New York Youth Conference march for Soviet Jewry, in which the authors stated, "It cannot be stressed too strongly that with large numbers involved, it is most important that students conduct themselves with utmost propriety."[28]

Kahane's use of religious ritual as a form of political protest was thus characteristic of many Jewish groups at this time who were turning away from the universalism of the New Left to more Jewish causes. Concerning the general phenomenon Kelner states quite cogently, "Ultimately, [the Soviet Jewry movement] was the creation of a new understanding of ritual that made the proliferation of its movement-based innovative application possible. The reason was simple: the ability to put ritual to political use depended first and foremost on the ability to conceive of it as a thing to be put to political use. Although we might take this for granted today, it is precisely the generation of this knowledge that needs to be examined, for the 'discovery' of ritual as an instrument represented an innovation in its time."[29]

Taking Jewish ritual to the streets—in fact, taking *Judaism* to the streets, thereby upending the modern Jewish adage coined by the poet Yehuda Leib Gordon (1831-1882), "Be a Jew in your home and a person [*mensch*] in the street"—was one of the great turns in American Jewry at this time.[30]

Waskow's "Freedom Seder: A New Haggadah for Passover," produced for the Passover Freedom Seder in 1969 that was sparked by Martin Luther King's assassination in 1968, is arguably one of the most influential Jewish ritual innovations of that same era. Waskow, who was part of the Washington-based radical group Jews for Urban Justice, wanted the Haggadah for the Freedom Seder "to assert a unity—in the form of a Haggadah—between the historic imperatives of Jewish liberation and the urgency of today's black rebellion."[31] In many ways the Haggadah illustrates the Jewish Liberation Project's position that being Jewish necessitated being involved in revolutionary struggles for all peoples. The Jewish Liberation Project was a diffuse organization of New Left Jews in the late 1960s and early 1970s who had been radicalized by the New Left and in many ways returned to their Jewish roots while critiquing the liberal Jewish establishment. In Waskow's case this involvement was manifested in formalized Jewish ritual, reinvented to express that solidarity.[32] As Waskow wrote, "The Freedom Seder tried to develop a liturgy in ways that asserted the liberation of the Jewish People alongside the liberation of the other peoples, not theirs against ours, or ours against theirs. Thus it celebrated the Warsaw Ghetto Uprising in 1943 (Ringelblum) alongside the Black Uprisings of the 1960s (King and Cleaver)."[33]

Kahane certainly knew about Waskow. In fact, in a 1972 lecture at the Leadership Training Center he established in Jerusalem, Kahane talked openly about him, citing both an article Waskow published in the University of Maryland's Jewish student newspaper *Doreinu* and Waskow's activities in Jews for Urban Justice.[34] Further evidence of his awareness of Waskow, and specifically of Waskow's "Freedom Seder," is found in his own JDL's "Liberation Seder" of 1970, a clear imitation of Waskow.[35] Kahane's "Liberation Seder," which was later replicated by many in the Student Society for Soviet Jewry (SSSJ), is introduced with the following preamble in the *Jewish Defense League Newsletter* (April–August 1970): "In Russia, it is a crime to celebrate Passover and hold a seder. Therefore, JDL decided to have the first public seder to be held on Russian soil. In April 1970 on the Sunday before Passover, JDL set up a table, wine and matzohs for the seder. Several JDL members chained themselves to the gates of the Soviet Mission"—thus making it officially "on Russian soil."

Kahane's "Liberation Seder" then continues with his rewrite of the Four Questions. It asks:

> Why is the Soviet Jew different from all free Jews? In all other lands, we are permitted to practice our religion, but in the Soviet Union we cannot.
>
> In all other lands our children may study the Jewish heritage many times over but in the Soviet Union they may not study it even once.
>
> In all other lands our people are permitted to leave and join their relatives but in the Soviet Union Jews must remain against their will.

Kahane then answers the theoretical son in the Haggadah:

> *Avadim Hayinu*—we were slaves unto Pharaoh in Egypt even as today our brothers are slaves unto Brezhnev in the Soviet Union. . . . For their sakes we rise and exclaim: Pour out Thy wrath on the Soviets that know Thee not. Stretch out Thy hand to redeem Thy people and bring them home from their Soviet exile.

The preamble concludes: "Ten of us, including Rabbi Kahane, were arrested for participation in this religious service for our Jewish brethren."

In many respects Kahane's "Liberation Seder" and Waskow's "Freedom Seder" are quite similar. Both use this Jewish ritual of redemption and liberation as a template for the oppressed and as a protest against injustice. While it is true that Kahane makes this a wholly internal Jewish message about Soviet Jewry and Waskow extends it outside the Jewish orbit, even to include those who were not considered friends of the Jews such as the Black Panthers, the sentiment was similar. Both were appropriating, and revising, a traditional Jewish ritual as a response to a series of contemporary events.

And perhaps it is here that we have an illustration of what the radical left and radical right shared and the center, or liberals, did not: the willingness to subvert convention and uproot normative behavior for the sake of undermining a system each felt was corrosive. What Waskow and Kahane shared was a commitment to radicalism even as each understood the situation very differently. Kahane and Norman Podhoretz, editor of *Commentary*, may have made a similar diagnosis of the American Jewish scene, and Robert Alter and Waskow may have shared core liberal values of freedom and justice, but what this comparison between Waskow's "Freedom Seder" and Kahane's "Liberation Seder" shows is that common radicalism enabled each to enact his protest in ways that, while differing on substance, shared the value of cultural subversion.

This brief comparison of left and right radicalism in the work of activists like Waskow and Kahane highlights a moment in American Jewish history where the "center"—in both Waskow's and Kahane's estimation, "liberalism"—was threatening the expression of Jewish pride and self-assertiveness. While the term "radical" more often applies to the left in this period, Kahane's use of similar tactics and a similar attack on the dangers of liberalism, obviously toward different ends, reflects an affinity among many Jews in this tumultuous period when it came to waging war against an establishment that, in their view, imperiled Jewish survival.

Kahane vs. the Jewish New Left

Kahane and Jewish radicals affiliated with the New Left were certainly aware of each other and positioned themselves in part against each other. As I mentioned earlier, when asked what he thought of Kahane, radical (Jewish) activist Abbie Hoffman purportedly said, "I agree with his methods but not his goals."[36] Kahane's radicalism was built on extreme exceptionalism, insularity, and a religious sentiment that secular leftists, even those with a partiality toward religion through the discovery of their identity after 1967, could not stomach. Yet many JDL members and supporters were not precisely Orthodox but rather, as one scholar suggested, "folk" Orthodox Jews, who supported the insular, communal way of life Orthodoxy espoused but were not very scrupulous in practice.[37]

The suspicion was mutual, as Kahane made clear in a 1971 interview to *The Flame*. In it he asserts, among other things (see later in this chapter), that "it is quite possible for JDL to wean many of [the Jewish radicals] away from Marxism back to Jewish and democratic thinking. JDL is committed to this very thing."[38]

The definitive break between the JDL and the Jewish radicals of the anti-Vietnam War movement occurred over three issues. The first was the war itself. Whereas the New Jewish radicals were stridently antiwar, Kahane saw the conflict as a necessary bulwark against the spread of communism and Jew-hatred. At one point he claimed that Jewish antiwar groups were more dangerous to Israel than the Arabs.[39] The second concerned the Arab-Israeli conflict and specifically the cause of the Palestinians. Once Vietnam played itself out, Palestine increasingly came into focus for the left as the major social-justice cause of the era. Many of the New Jewish radicals saw Palestinians not as enemies but as potential partners in creating a humanistic, and oftentimes socialist, society in Israel. The third area of principled disagreement between Kahane's movement and the leftist American Jewish radicals concerned the phenomenon of Black Nationalism.

The New Jewish radicals largely viewed themselves in solidarity with the Black Nationalist movement (even if many contested its anti-Semitism). For example, in 1969 student activist Hillel Levine was quoted in *Newsweek* saying, "The black awakening reminded us that the melting pot was a fool's fantasy, and that racial and religious differences are legitimate. For many of us, this means turning our concerns inward toward the Jewish community."[40] In some cases Zionism was openly equated with Black Nationalism. For example, Dov Peretz Elkins wrote in 1971, "Black Power is nothing more or less than Negro Zionism."[41] Kahane, by contrast, saw the movement as an enemy of the Jews. He was unwilling to wed Jewish identity politics with those of other minorities, especially blacks. He told reporters, "Most Jews came here in galleys long after blacks were freed. Blacks deserve nothing from us and that is what they will get."[42]

The constellation of Jewish radical views that Kahane found anathema is well captured in an article by M. Jay Rosenberg, "My Evolution as a Jew," that was quite popular in its time: "What we say is this: We are radicals. We actively oppose the war in Vietnam. We support the black liberation movement as we endorse all genuine movements of liberation. As thus, first and foremost we support our own. We will march with our brothers on the left. . . . Our position in support of black, Vietnamese, African, and other national movements is a natural outgrowth of our identification with Israel. So is our recognition of a new Palestinian Arab nationalism which exists and must be considered."[43]

Jewish Protest Culture

Both Kahane and the radical Jewish groups were oriented toward protest, in some cases guerrilla-style, to further their cause. "Over and over," as Michael Staub observed about this period in his book *Torn at the Roots*, "activists not only adopted a physically confrontational style but also expressly emphasized their own Jewishness as a weapon against members of the Jewish establishment perceived to be too accommodationist to gentile society."[44]

Three examples from this era of the Jewish radicals' penchant for protest-oriented action will suffice. In November 1969 a group of young radical Jews took over the Jewish Federation Council in Los Angeles, breaking and entering illegally and affixing 200 mezuzahs to the doorposts in protest against what they saw as the federation's assimilationist agenda. While not violent, this was certainly disruptive (and illegal). A second example occurred in May 1970 when three members of the Radical Jewish Union (RJU) of Columbia University disrupted services on Friday night at Temple Emanu-El, one of the largest Reform synagogues in New York City, because its rabbi Nathan Perilman had denied a request by the RJU to have one of its members speak out against the Vietnam War. Entering the temple shouting "Remember Kent State," Rabbi Bruce Goldman, Victor Levin, and Anne Rosen made their way to the pulpit and took the microphone before being arrested by plainclothes policemen.[45] A third example transpired in Washington in 1968 when the Poor People's Campaign, which had constructed a "Resurrection City" on the National Mall, called a nearby Jewish Community Center and asked if they could use their showers for a new group that had arrived. The Jewish Community Center said no. A group of young radical Jews attending a meeting of the Urban Affairs Subcommittee of the Jewish community received an emergency phone call explaining the events and had to decide how to respond. Arthur Waskow, who was at that meeting, tells what happened: "We decided to call our friends—we thought we could easily turn out about fifty people—and show up at the Center at five o'clock. We would give the Center until five-thirty to turn on the showers. If they didn't, we would take over the building in the name of the Jewish tradition and the Jewish community, invite the Poor People's campaign to send its people over, and turn on the showers ourselves. The message was received and by mid-afternoon the center had reversed its decision in order to prevent the take-over."[46]

The JDL shared this penchant for direct action, as illustrated by the episode recounted in the previous chapter when JDL militants came to Temple Emanu-El in May 1969 to prevent Black Nationalist James Forman from speaking about black reparations. Kahane had organized a group of his followers to show up early for Friday-night services armed with baseball bats, chains, and other homemade weapons to make sure Forman did not enter the synagogue.[47] Kahane notified the media that if Forman came anywhere near it his men "would break his legs, or worse." Forman never showed up but the event garnered a lot of media coverage. After the incident Rabbi Maurice Eisendrath, who was president of the Union of American Hebrew Congregations and had invited Forman to speak, told the *New York Times* that "the so-called Jewish Defense League violates every ethic and tradition of Judaism and every concept of civil liberties and democratic process in American life."[48]

In February 1970 a two-day conference was held at Camp Ramah in Palmer, Massachusetts, called "Jewish Radicalism: A Search for a Renewed Zionist Ideology." The venue for the conference is significant. That summer (1969) the camp's director Ray Arzt, a Conservative rabbi and disciple of Mordecai Kaplan, had allowed students to stage an antiwar demonstration on the camp grounds that included burning the American flag. Arzt was also known to be lenient on the smoking of marijuana by the staff. The events that summer sparked such an uproar among the parents that the camp decided to close the next summer for one year to let things settle down.[49] The conference in February brought together various radical Jewish student groups from around the country; the result was the manifesto of the Radical Jewish Alliance, which rejected assimilation and called for "a liberation movement of the Jewish people."[50]

This document, called the "Radical Zionist Manifesto," is important here because it exhibits the two sides of this movement: first, a strong sense of a kind of Jewish liberation theology drawing heavily from the Black Nationalist movement, with Israel as the centerpiece; second, an equally strong commitment to the New Left's agenda of radical equality, participatory democracy, and civil disruption. It states, "To this end, we see Israel as central to the liberation of the Jewish people. The Jewish state, Israel, is a modern expression of a people's right to national life in its own land." And, further: "We are committed to the creation of a socialist society in Israel. We look toward mutual recognition of the national rights of the Jews and Palestinian Arabs, and the cooperation of all people in the area toward the realization of socialism and human justice."[51]

The use of the term "liberation" in regard to Zionism (as opposed to, say, "redemption" or "self-determination" or "safe haven") reflects New Left radicalism, as does the manifesto's commitment to socialism. In addition, 1970 was quite early to be speaking positively of the "Palestinian Arabs" and certainly to be calling for their equality in Israel's socialist state. A few years later, in 1973, the Breira group (which likely included some of those at the Camp Ramah conference) called for equality and two states and was summarily denigrated by the Jewish establishment as far too radical.[52]

Jewish radicalism of this period was not, of course, limited to Zionist groups. The Brooklyn Bridge Collective, which produced the newspaper

Brooklyn Bridge, had much in common with the radical Zionist groups that produced the *Jewish Liberation Journal.* Yet, while decrying the liberal Jewish establishment and the "assimilationist mentality of Amerika," the collective was not only non-Zionist but also criticized some of the radical Zionists for being too close to the JDL. They openly denounced Kahane—which many of the radical Zionists did not quite do, at least not in any programmatic way at that time—and remained committed to fighting anti-Semitism but equally committed to fighting the oppression of blacks in America. One issue of *Brooklyn Bridge* provocatively linked anti-Semitism and racism—something that made American Jews very nervous—with a poster-size spread that read: "Kaddish—For Our Sisters and Brothers who fought and died in Warsaw and Attica."[53] That association was quite common among the New Left. For example, Mark Rudd, one of the founders of SDS, remarked in a public address in 2005, "World War II and the Holocaust were our fixed reference points. We often talked about the moral imperative not to be Good Germans. We saw American racism as akin to German racism toward the Jew."[54] In light of the fact that the first two SDS chapters grew out of the Zionist youth movement Habonim in 1965, this should come as no surprise.[55] In addition, Waskow, in a 1967 address entitled "How to Prevent Pogroms," called the 1965 Watts riots a "pogrom" against blacks by the police.

The Brooklyn Bridge Collective is an interesting case of a group of self-identified New Left Jews who were resisting the cosmopolitanism of the New Left while basically furthering its agenda on identifiably Jewish secular terms. Yet, as non-Zionists, they did not wed their Jewish identity to Israel as did the *Jewish Liberation Journal* and thus were able to draw a categorical distinction between their program and that of the JDL, even as they too supported strong protest tactics. Their criticism of the JDL and the New Jewish left's proximity to Kahane reflects the symbiosis between Kahane and some of the radical New Jew groups that arose at the time.

Renewing the American Bar Mitzvah

Part of an Orthodox community not known for ritual innovation, in one instance Kahane deployed his critique of American liberalism through the prism of reinventing a Jewish ritual: the American bar mitzvah.[56] It is noteworthy that both Waskow and Kahane chose rituals that are loosely articulated in the halakhah yet had both become ubiquitous to the American Jewish experience: the Passover seder and the bar mitzvah. They also are both public rituals that are open to various forms of innovation. The bar mitzvah is a ritual that has few, if any, halakhic criteria. At the age of thirteen Jewish males (females were added in non-Orthodox communities in the early twentieth century) become full members of the religious community (e.g., they can be included in a minyan, or prayer quorum). Traditionally, communities mark this event by calling the bar or bat mitzvah to the Torah, delivering a Torah lesson, or some other symbolic act. Nothing more is required and customs vary from one community to the next.

In America the bar mitzvah had become, by the 1960s, mostly an occasion for lavish parties accompanied by nominal synagogue performance. In most instances it did not mark the beginning of the young boy or girl's journey into Judaism but its conclusion. By the early 1970s the New Jews had launched their attack on the American bar mitzvah. A 1971 experimental film *Thirteen Years,* which began as a student project, mocked the American bar mitzvah and juxtaposed it with a hippie-inflected countercultural one.[57] It exemplified the critique of affluence common in New Jew appraisals of the Jewish establishment and shared a great deal with Kahane's critique. For Kahane the American bar mitzvah represented everything that was wrong with American Jewry and thus needed radical revision; as he used to say, "All bar and no mitzvah."[58]

The Passover seder is a ritual whose halakhic parameters are quite minimal, requiring the consumption of four cups of wine, eating matzah and bitter herbs, and telling the story of the exodus from Egypt. The Passover Haggadah serves more as a guide than a sacred text, and Haggadah and seder innovations have long been part of Jewish history. These two rituals were thus great occasions for political revision in the thought of both Waskow and Kahane. Both were activists who sought to take Judaism into the street as a means of protest against Jewish apathy. In one case, protest served to contest Jews' apathy in regard to human rights and justice. In the other case, protest served to contest apathy about Jewish causes and expressions of Jewish solidarity and pride.

Here Waskow expresses a view Kahane may have agreed with, at least in part:

> No seriously radical Jewish movement can ignore these areas in which Jews are oppressed, along with other people, which focuses solely on areas in which Jews are oppressed as Jews or in special "Jewish" ways. To do so would not only leave Jews unliberated in crucial aspects of their lives, but would mean adopting for our own movement a new version of the slogan "Jews at home citizens outside." We utterly reject any such idea, believing as we do that Jewishness is adequately expressed only through wholeness,

> and therefore that our movement—as well as fully liberated individual Jews—must be Jewish both "at home" and "outside": both on "Jewish" and on "general" problems.[59]

Kahane would likely have sympathized with Waskow's "utter rejection" of Yehuda Leib Gordon's earlier-quoted adage "Be a Jew in your home and a person (*mensch*) in the street." Both wanted to collapse that binary such that being a Jew would be holistic, equally requiring internal fidelity to tradition and to public action. Where they differed was that for Kahane Jewish concerns were paramount, even exclusive, whereas Waskow held that the prophetic spirit of fighting injustice everywhere was an essential component of Judaism. Kahane was a survivalist through and through while Waskow was a renewalist who wanted Judaism to have a global reach as part of a messianic project. One could perhaps put it otherwise, though not without caveats, by saying Kahane viewed Judaism through a biblical/rabbinic lens while Waskow viewed it through a prophetic one.

In his 1971 book *Never Again!* Kahane takes on the American bar mitzvah with a vengeance, calling it "the unique temple rite" facilitated by the caterer, that is, "the American Jewish god." He writes, "It is the Bar Mitzvah that drives his parents to educate him; it is the Bar Mitzvah that will end his thirst for Jewish knowledge.... The new American Jewish temple; the new American Jewish religion of convenience; the new American Jewish education of Scott, son of Abraham . . . All part of the American Jewish way of death, and the young Jew is its primary victim."[60] For Kahane the very center of American Judaism is that which makes Jewish pride impossible, killing such pride by making Jewishness a parody of itself and thus preventing the young Jew from being Jewish in any authentic way. The bar mitzvah had become a soul-killing ritual, a form of banal idolatry.[61]

Kahane often states that the entire purpose of the JDL was to recreate the American Jew, to refashion his or her image, to make Jewishness alive through the performance of protest through ritual. But Kahane also used ritual to critique American Jewry. For much of suburban non-Orthodox American Jewry, the American bar mitzvah in the 1960s had become a symbol of lavishness largely void of content, perhaps captured succinctly in the Coen brothers' film *A Serious Man*. It was largely a synagogue-based event followed by a caterer's dream of "schmorgesborgs" and Viennese desert tables.

Kahane poked fun at the bar mitzvah as the exit for many young American Jews rather than an initiation into Jewish adulthood, and he used the event as a call to political rebellion.[62] The initiation into Kahane's version of social action was his new "bar mitzvah." In March 1971, speaking about a JDL demonstration for Soviet Jewry in Washington that resulted in mass arrests of JDL participants,[63] he proclaimed, "You should have seen the shining faces of the JDL members in the streets of Washington waiting to be arrested. Then you would have known what it means to be proud of being Jewish. *For those kids that was a Bar Mitzvah*" (emphasis added).[64] This remark about the JDL "bar mitzvah" reappears in Kahane's writings.

What is really happening here aside from a rhetorical flourish? The bar mitzvah is an act of initiation, a proactive and public assertion of one's presence as a Jew. For Kahane the moribund American synagogue can no longer house that Jewishness; it is the place (especially the non-Orthodox synagogue) where Judaism died, serving as the cemetery. Authentic Jewishness is now lived in the street, and the demonstration for Jewish causes is the JDL bar mitzvah;[65] going to jail for speaking truth to power is the bar mitzvah party. Janet Dolgin writes, "JDL's evoking the Bar Mitzvah as analogous to political activism turned accepted custom on its head in a way that, if it came to it, could be justified through Talmudic reference and Biblical verse. JDL reasserted its central position as a modern counterpart to 'Moses' through the Bar Mitzvah, and the Bar Mitzvah emerged through the JDL in an entirely new form, but as authentic as ever. The present was parodied, the past hallowed; and the JDL represented the second in the language of the first."[66] By saying the JDL "reasserted its central position as a modern counterpart to 'Moses' through the Bar Mitzvah" in the form of street protest, Dolgin appears to be suggesting that "Moses" comes to his "Jewishness" precisely through an act of protest, a violent one, killing the Egyptian taskmaster and having to flee for his life. Authentic Jewishness is forged in the street, not in the study house; the bar mitzvah is initiation through asserting Jewish power. Such a reversal is more common in regard to the "muscle Jew" of Zionism, replacing Rabbi Akiva as martyr with Bar Kokhba as warrior. Kahane brings that Zionist reversal to the American Diaspora as a template for the flourishing of the Jew in America.

On this reading, Kahane's bar mitzvah and Waskow's Freedom Seder share a radical revision of ritual toward purposes that each believed embodied the authentic Jewish tradition. For Waskow in the battle for universal justice that made Thoreau, King, Arendt, Dylan, even Cleaver rabbis and prophets, and for Kahane who viewed the exercise of Jewish pride as embodying the very roots of the Mosaic tradition and civil disobedience as an act of initiation into an elite group, the "New Jew" was the Jew on the street fighting anti-Semitism.[67] Each had different, in some ways opposite goals, Waskow taking Judaism *to* the world and Kahane constructing the Jew to fight *against* the world, but both used traditional ritual, radically revised, as a means to achieve those ends. And both viewed those ends as leading toward justice, even as they had very different understandings of what that term meant.

Amerika! and Uncle Irvings

This section touches briefly on two documents that illustrate the ways in which the radical Jewish movements of the late 1960s, emerging from the New Left even as they are critical of it, come quite close to Kahane's right-wing form of Jewish chauvinism. The first is the 1970 essay "Oppression of Amerika's Jews" by Aviva Cantor Zuckoff, then editor of the *Jewish Liberation Journal*. The second is M. Jay Rosenberg's "To Jewish Uncle Toms," published in 1969 when Rosenberg was a student at the State University of New York at Albany.[68]

Cantor Zuckoff begins her essay in a vein very similar to Kahane and to Frantz Fanon.[69] The fact that Jews in America don't *think* they are oppressed, she asserts, is only a sign of their assimilation, which itself constitutes a form of oppression. They are oppressed, she argues, because they are led to believe they cannot "act to gain control of [their] destiny . . . they are programmed for and forced into certain roles for his [Amerika's] benefit." In other words, they may seem to be free but they are oppressed. In what may be a response to the rising anti-Semitism in the Black Nationalist movement in the late 1960s, Cantor Zuckoff claims, "The Jews are constantly forced into the dangerous position of being trapped between the peasants and the nobles, the ruling elite and other oppressed groups. In the role of oppressor surrogate, and otherwise, the Jew functions as society's 'lightning rod' for absorbing and deflecting the rage of oppressed groups that might otherwise be turned on the ruling elite."[70]

Kahane offers a more simple, or simplistic, assessment of this phenomenon, calling it a reified anti-Semitism "tucked away in the corner of the brain, waiting for the proper stimulus to bring it, full-blown, to life."[71] But not unlike Kahane, Cantor Zuckoff describes the American (or Amerikan) Jewish dilemma as a kind of colonialism even though she never uses that term. "It [oppression] means being exploited and used in the interest of the oppressor and against your own, and being programmed for and forced into certain roles for his benefit."[72] Similar language was used by the blacks in Brooklyn who described Jews as "colonial exploiters."[73]

Although Cantor Zuckoff views the Jewish plight in Amerika as more situational, the oppression she describes is close to Kahane's balder-faced description. And for both, this is all in the service of a severe chastisement of the Jewish establishment that both claim is self-hating by design because it deflects its rage against its oppressor to anyone who openly expresses his or her Jewishness. In classic postcolonial fashion, Cantor Zuckoff ends her essay by stating, "The process of liberation begins with the consciousness of oppression. What Jews in Amerika lack most is this consciousness; that keeps them paralyzed in a state of ethnic amnesia. It is to raising the Jewish consciousness of Amerikan Jewry, that our efforts should be directed."[74]

Cantor Zuckoff's essay calls for nothing less than a revolution in American Jewry and there is little that Kahane would disagree with.[75] Both waged a war against the establishment, the folly of freedom, the liberal elite that internalizes the oppressor's hostility toward those in its purview who are too "Jewish." This is all vintage Kahane. And yet we can see from Cantor Zuckoff's use of the *k* in "Amerika" that, as Michael Staub suggests, she may be closer to Jews for Urban Justice and even the New Left than to Kahane, and her call to arms may be closer to Richard Rubenstein's notion of power. But here I am not sure there is much of a difference as some of Rubenstein's essays on power come quite close to Kahane's thinking.[76] In any event, there is something performative in Cantor Zuckoff's essay, something rhetorical that her radicalism illustrates in ways that Rubenstein's more cerebral approach does not.[77] If Rubenstein's essays on Jewish power call for reorientation, Cantor Zuckoff's essay is a call for revolution. And it is precisely there where she and Kahane meet even as Kahane's call for open violence may extend beyond where Cantor Zuckoff wanted to go.[78]

This is even more evident in Rosenberg's "Jewish Uncle Toms" as the title itself appears to borrow from Kahane's coinage of the terms "Uncle Jakes" and "Uncle Irvings" in *Never Again!*, which Rosenberg (and Cantor Zuckoff) most likely read.[79] In fact, the *Jewish Defense League Newsletter* reprinted Rosenberg's article as "To Uncle Tom and Other Such Jews." And in January 1971 Rosenberg published an article "The Self-Destruction of Judaism in the American 'Jewish' Community" where he argued that the only solution for American Jewry was emigration to Israel, something Kahane began to advocate the following year.[80]

Rosenberg decries "the self-hating Jew," the naive "liberal" Jew who cannot openly come out in favor of Israel against its Arab enemies. He begins by stating, "It has become fashionable in some liberal (and predominately Jewish) circles to scoff at anything that smacks of Jewishness."[81] Rosenberg then claims that the black in America had come to realize by 1968 what the American Jew cannot avoid: "the inherent lie in the concept of the melting-pot. . . . [The American Jew] desperately craves assimilation; the very idea of Jewishness embarrasses him. . . . The concept of Jewish nationalism, Israel notwithstanding, he finds laughable. The leftist Jewish student . . . is today's 'Uncle Tom.'"[82] Black Nationalism has made the Uncle Toms obsolete or at least illegitimate, and that has been replaced by the liberal Jew, what Kahane calls the "Uncle Jakes."

Here Rosenberg sounds very much like Kahane at that time. In fact, Kahane quotes Rosenberg and offers a largely positive assessment of him in his 1977 book *Why Be Jewish?*[83] But whereas Kahane calls for the end of Black Nationalism because it is mired in anti-Semitism, Rosenberg uses his similar critique of the Jewish liberal to offer his Jewish radical (left) alternative: "The Jew can be an ally of the black liberation movement and should be. But first he must find himself."[84] He takes this even further: "Therefore it is as a Jew that I must accept Black Nationalism. The blacks may or may not be the equivalents of the militants of the early Zionist organizations, and Malcolm X may or may not be a black Vladimir Jabotinsky, but surely the parallel is there."[85] Yet he too recognizes that the black community has learned to use the Jew as the scapegoat: "Thus when some black nationalist calls us 'racist Zionists' . . . we must see him for what he is; just another *goy* . . . we must fight against him with all we have. That's the way it has to be; we must scrape for no one."[86]

What Rosenberg articulates here, perhaps in somewhat adolescent prose, is a radical Jewish agenda that remains solidly on the left yet whose radicalism moves toward a more Judeo-centric worldview that puts him close to what Kahane was espousing at the same time on the right. In a later article Rosenberg declares, "What we say is this. We are radicals. We actively oppose the war in Vietnam. We support the black liberation movement as we endorse all genuine movements of liberation. And thus, first and foremost, we support our own. We will march with our brother on the left. We will support them."[87] It is worth noting that from today's perspective, the radical nature of Rosenberg's words is blunted by multiculturalism (which would begin only in the 1980s). For example, for today's American Jew to be a proud Jew, supporter of Israel, and also an activist in Blacks Lives Matter is simply twenty-first-century American Jewish liberalism.[88]

But at that time what Rosenberg had to say was indeed radical. And part, though not all, of that radicalism was being espoused by Kahane. Thus it is important to note that liberalism today could also include some of what Kahane was advocating in the late 1960s: Jewish pride, zero tolerance for anti-Semitism (however inchoate), ardent support for Israel, anti-assimilationism, and Jewish exceptionalism.

There are obviously many things in Kahane's repertoire that today's Jewish liberal would reject—violence, racism, xenophobia, Islamophobia, and so on. But I suggest that we view Kahane's work in this early period as an adaptation of New Left radicalism for the purposes of Jewish pride. And the radical New Jews discussed here were resisting New Left cosmopolitanism and American liberal assimilationism by adopting parts of the New Left's radical agenda combined with a return to Jewish identity that was also espoused by Kahane, even if that identity formation required tactics of civil disruption or even violence. Kahane and many of the New Jews had a similar enemy (the American Jewish establishment), derived tactics from similar sources (New Left radicals), and had similar goals (Jewish pride and Jewish identity formation). They certainly differed on what those goals would look like if achieved, but what they shared was arguably greater than their differences.

The Ebbing of Jewish Radicalism in the Post-Nixon Era

After Nixon's resignation in 1974, political radicalism began to dissipate in America on the left more generally and on the Jewish left in particular. Alternatively, some of the radical strains began to become more mainstream and less jarring. For example, environmental activism and the anti–nuclear power movement that arose in the late 1970s and early 1980s did not have the radical edge that the antiwar movement had had only a decade before. In addition, what began to emerge was New Age religion and a move toward a new spiritualization of American youth. Robert Fuller's *Spiritual but Not Religious* traces the roots of this form of spiritual experimentation at that time and the way it changed America.[89]

To cite one example of the deradicalization of the New Jews in regard to politics, a look at the *Jewish Catalog* published in three volumes from 1973 to 1980 shows a trajectory from a more edgy call-to-arms of Jewish identity in the first volume (subtitled *A Do-It-Yourself Kit*) to a much less radical return to liberalism in the third one (subtitled *Creating Community*). Only that volume offers a long section on Zionism and Israel,[90] and it tells the story in fairly conventional, even romanticized terms: the ancient Jewish precedent for love of the land, the development of Jewish messianism, the "miraculous" nature of the founding of the state, the Six-Day War, and so on. It traffics in the heroism of the Jewish solider, the kibbutznik, and a countercultural Jewish Orientalism in a myriad of photos of Hasidic and Yemenite male Jews in beards and traditional garb. Published three years after the Likud Party led by Menachem Begin came to power in 1977, the volume contains very little about the occupation, very little about settlements, very little about the plight of the Palestinians, very little politics in general.

There is mention of supporting, or tolerating, a constructive critique of Israel's policies but only if it is very mild. I do not intend to make a political, or polemical, point here; rather to say that by 1980, and even before, the radicalism of 1967 to 1974, fueled by inequality and injustice, had all but disappeared among many countercultural Jews. New Age religion, with its largely spiritualist apolitical sentiment, had almost fully eclipsed the radical political agenda of late-1960s New Jews. Many New Jews went on to become rabbis, journalists, scholars, and Jewish educators. The political remnants of the New Jews had folded back into mainstream American liberal Zionism (reemerging momentarily perhaps in events like the Sukkot gathering at Occupy Wall Street in 2011). There are certainly exceptions, such as Arthur Waskow's Shalom Center and Michael Lerner's *Tikkun* magazine. But these are indeed exceptions. More recently, new forms of radical Judaism and Jewishness are emerging around groups like IfNotNow, Bend the Arc, JFREJ, and the magazine *Jewish Currents*.

But around 1968 when the world seemed to be undergoing a seismic shift, the coming of age of the baby boomers yielded new forms of Jewish radicalism such as the Jewish Liberation Project, Jewish street militias, the non-Zionist Brooklyn Bridge Collective, Jews for Urban Justice, the Freedom Seder, and the proto-neocon journal *Ideas*. The radicals among the Jewish baby boomers had different goals but often shared sympathies for subverting authority, disturbing the peace, and forcing change through participatory democracy. Kahane and the JDL were certainly among them, and he and the JDL had more in common with many of those radicals on the left than we think.[91]

3

Race and Racism

KAHANE ON RACE AND JUDEO-PESSIMISM

"A race without authority and power is a race without respect."

MARCUS GARVEY

"It [the JDL] grew out of a sick reaction to the Black Revolution."

JOACHIM PRINZ, *LOOK MAGAZINE*, APRIL 20, 1971

"JDL has never and never will be a racist group."

MEIR KAHANE, "FROM A JEWISH FATHER," *NEW YORK TIMES*, OCTOBER 20, 1969

Race and Kahane's Politics

The issue of race and racism begins Kahane's career in 1968 with the founding of the JDL as a response to black anti-Semitism, and ends his career with the "Racism Law" that ousted him from the Knesset in 1986. Accusations that Kahane was a racist flowed through his entire public life and he addressed those accusations in a variety of ways, both in America in regard to blacks and in Israel in regard to Arabs. This chapter will explore in detail the role of race and racism in Kahane's thought within the broader context of race politics in postwar America and to a lesser extent, in Israel.

I use the term "grammar of racism" that I adopt from critical race theorists rather than simply calling Kahane a "racist," which I believe he was, because the latter term is not an analytical category but a judgment of character. In addition, Kahane was not distinctive in holding racist views among many who lived in his Orthodox community in those years, and sadly, even today. When he often stated "I say what people think," meaning on the question of race, he was arguably not far off. If one simply begins an assessment of one's subject by labeling him a racist, then understanding the underlying mechanisms of that racism, and the structures that perpetuate it, seems less pertinent. My goal is to explore *how* race is used by Kahane, *how* he negotiates his own whiteness and Jewishness in response to the racialized world in which he lived, and in what ways we can understand his responses denying his racism. Put otherwise, I am less concerned here *that* Kahane was a racist than about *how* he used race to promote his ideas. The "grammar of racism" is in my view the best tool to do this.[1]

One final prefatory note. The first two chapters showed the ways in which Kahane's radicalism against the liberalism of his time put him in proximity to Jewish radicals on the left who were waging their own battles against Jewish quiescence, assimilation, and materialism. I noted there that radicalism as a stance can often bring together strange bedfellows and that shared tactics can foster alliances. In this chapter I illustrate how such alliances against a common enemy, in this case liberalism, have their limits. Radical Jews on the left saw themselves engaged in fighting injustice in general, fighting *as* Jews, *for* Jews, but also for all who suffer from social ills. Here the transition suggested by Arthur Waskow in his book *The Bush Is Burning* from "Jewish radicals to radical Jews" is instructive. When the Jewish radicals became radical Jews, they did not abandon their project but only altered their position in relation to their radicalism and their identity as Jews. They stood now not as New Leftists who happened to be Jewish, but as American Jews whose radicalism came from their Jewishness.

On the race question, Kahane does not share a common cause with these radical Jews but, in fact, opposes them on two grounds: first, their claim that commitment to fighting societal injustice in general is a Jewish value; and second, what he considered their misguided belief that in the end most gentiles are not anti-Semites. On these two points Kahane's Orthodox orientation comes through—not that all Orthodox Jews think this way but that these perspectives are not uncommon in the Orthodox world where Kahane was raised. Kahane certainly weaponized and politicized these notions in ways that made many Orthodox Jews uncomfortable, but the core values he espoused were not strange to the world of postwar Orthodoxy in America.

Here then we can ask whether the race issue shows that Kahane's radicalism was faulty, even false, because it denied a universalist component that much of radicalism shared—although Black Nationalism also shared Kahane's focus on one group, even as it focused on Third Worldism more generally. In Israel it may play out differently in that radicalism there, from the Revisionists to the settler movement, is often expressed by insularity and not expansiveness, by exclusivity and not inclusion. If I am correct, then the "Racism Law" that removed Kahane from the Knesset was not necessarily an indictment of his call for Jewish power and exclusivity but reflected the fact that he had gone too far and framed those attitudes in a way that most Israeli Jews felt was unacceptable. In a sense, Kahane introduced the race issue to Israel/Palestine very forcefully; the conflict had often been framed as purely nationalist, and Kahane's assertions of racialization made many Israelis uncomfortable. Put otherwise, Kahane overly Americanized the Israel/Palestine conflict.

In 1984, after two failed attempts to win a seat in the Knesset, Meir Kahane was elected to the Israeli parliament as leader of his KACH Party. His election sent shock waves through the Israeli political world.[2] His political platform of expelling the Arabs, and his provocative argument that it was "schizophrenic" to claim that Israel could be "both Jewish and democratic," rattled a country that had been struggling to come to terms with its almost twenty-year occupation of the West Bank and the Gaza Strip and growing Israeli Arab and Palestinian resistance.[3] Even then-prime minister Yitzhak Shamir, who had been a member of a terrorist organization in his youth, announced he would not allow KACH into a Likud-led coalition, a sign that the Israeli right, as well as the left, were afraid of what Kahane's political power would generate.[4]

What Kahane and his allies would do with political power had been made clear three years earlier when in May 1981 he took out a full-page ad in the Israeli daily *Maariv*. Entitled "She Is a Daughter of Israel. Perhaps Your Sister, Your Daughter or Granddaughter,"[5] the ad spelled out some of Kahane's proposals for the upcoming Knesset election. These included (1) a law forbidding the "abomination of assimilation and communion with goyim" (in this case, Arabs), (2) a mandatory prison sentence for any Arab who had sexual relations with a Jewish girl or woman, and (3) a law restricting United Nations forces from engaging in any type of relations with the Jewish population. In addition, Kahane later declared that if elected he would strip all Israeli Arabs of their citizenship and work toward expelling any who refused to relinquish it. Kahane actually submitted such a bill—called the "three tolls bill"—to the Knesset in late 1985.[6]

Fearing significant repercussions from Kahane's newfound platform and sensing its popularity among sections of the electorate, Israeli legislators took the drastic action of amending the country's Basic Laws to bar "racist parties and candidates" from running in Israeli elections. Known as article 7a of the Basic Laws, this amendment rendered KACH illegal, and Kahane and his party were removed from the Knesset.

The reason given by the Knesset was that Kahane and his followers were "inciting racism and endangering security."[7] This law was clearly legislated for Kahane and KACH alone; it was never successfully invoked again.[8] In many ways it was a final blow to Kahane's political career in Israel.[9] He appealed the ruling to Israel's Supreme Court, and the court upheld the Central Elections Committee's decision thereby barring him from running in the 1988 and 1992 elections. Although Kahane remained popular, he knew his political career would be a zero-sum game: either he would take over the direction of the country or he would be rejected by it.[10]

Given how central issues of race were throughout Kahane's public career—including its beginnings two decades earlier in America—it is fitting that his political career ended with this official Israeli designation of him as a racist political actor. Not only did he found the JDL in response to black anti-Semitism connected to the New York City school strike in the spring of 1968, but most of his early programs of civil patrols to protect elderly Jews focused on those living in what the media then called, as noted, "frontier" neighborhoods, meaning black and Latino neighborhoods in New York, Boston, and Philadelphia.[11] The JDL's first real action took place on Halloween night in 1968 when a group of young JDLers went armed with bats and man-made weapons to the Montefiore Jewish cemetery in the Bronx where in years past black youths had desecrated tombstones. Black youths indeed showed up that night but were scared off by this ragged bunch of Jewish teenagers ready to physically confront them. Kahane viewed this as a tremendous victory for the fledging and ramshackle organization.[12]

Engagement with what Kahane called "black anti-Semitism" was central to the JDL's efforts to attract press attention.[13] When accused of racism himself, Kahane often countered that he and the JDL "are not against any race, creed, or color. We are against anyone who is against the Jews."[14] The disingenuousness of this comment will be explored below. Yet the question of race swirled around Kahane's entire career. He did not quite identify Jews as white, although Jews certainly benefited from white privilege, and he undoubtedly resisted the idea that "white" Jews were part of the same "club" as John Birch Society members. Yet the whiteness of Jews, and what that meant, stood at the forefront of his concept of race. James Baldwin called this the "American pattern," aptly described by Keith Feldman as "the spatially stratified structure of whiteness."[15]

Much of Kahane's American career focused on what he perceived as black anti-Semitism and the responses of many urban blacks to Jews, famously described at the time in James Baldwin's celebrated essay "Negroes Are Anti-Semitic Because They're Anti-White."[16] Kahane's ethos of self-defense and Jewish pride was a response to what he considered the liberal establishment's weak-kneed approach to these matters. He explicitly contested, for example, the stance of Dore Schary, then president of the ADL, who "cautioned the American Jewish community not to exaggerate fears of Negro anti-Semitism" even in the context of the 1968 Ocean Hill–Brownsville school strike.[17]

Kahane himself, moreover, made statements about race and racism that upended liberal Jewish assumptions, not least in relation to Jewish chauvinism and claims of superiority. In a 1987 essay "I Hate Racism," he proposed that "racism is the very essence of the secular Jew," suggesting that if one does not identify as a Jew through accepting the biblical notion of divine election, and instead identifies Jewishness as an ethnos,[18] a secular, purely ethnic identity, that identity is in fact racist. Kahane thereby implicated liberal secular Jews and secular-leaning Reform rabbis in racism, while claiming that accusations of racism launched at him by these parties were forms of hypocrisy and projection. In his 1987 book *Uncomfortable Questions for Comfortable Jews*, where he writes extensively about the racism charge, he goes even further, arguing that if he is a racist, Zionism is racist because "Zionism is Kahanism."

The question of race is crucial to understanding Kahane's entire life and work, from the time he entered the public stage in the mid-1960s to his later career in Israel. It stands at the very center of his political and cultural agenda.

From Rights to Power: The Black-Jewish Parting of the Ways

In *The Story of the Jewish Defense League* Kahane wrote, "Ugly, open and unabashed anti-Semitism began to manifest itself and for the Jewish Establishment and liberals it came from a totally unexpected and decidedly ungrateful source. The Negro—now insisting on being called black—community turned on its 'noble and generous' benefactors with a hatred and rage that horrified all the Jews."[19] This depiction of the blacks, accused of ingratitude for all the Jews had done for them in the civil rights movement, illustrates a common sentiment at the time among American Jews across the religious and ideological spectrum. Jewish contributions to the civil rights movement and Jewish participation in the Freedom Rides, in which integrated interstate buses entered segregated black neighborhoods from 1961 to 1964 to oppose segregation, are well-known. Moreover, a Jew, Kivi Kaplan, served as president of the NAACP from 1966 until his death in 1975.[20] But black leaders such as Stokely Carmichael called for the removal of whites, including Jews, from core black organizations. Such calls were amplified in his famous speech in Greenwood, Mississippi, in 1966, in the SNCC (Student Nonviolent Coordinating Committee) "Position Paper: The Basis of Black Power" the same year, and with the founding of the Black Panthers on October 15, 1966. In the wake of the Six-Day War in June 1967, Black Nationalists of the era viewed Palestine as part of the global cohort of people of color in need of liberation.

This atmosphere, combined with the urban uprisings and riots in the mid-1960s, which ravaged many Jewish businesses in majority–African American urban districts, pushed relations between the black and Jewish communities into a state of acute tension.[21] Carmichael claimed that the attack on Jewish shops and properties was sparked by outrages perpetrated by Jewish landlords and merchants, not black resentment toward Judaism or Jews as a whole.[22] Just months after the outbreak of the Six-Day War, at the New Left's New Politics Convention in Chicago, black delegates proposed a motion condemning "Zionist imperialists"; white delegates agreed to it in large part to keep the black caucus in the movement. Kahane takes note of this convention in his writings and in one place cites Dick Gregory who said at the event, "Every Jew in America over thirty years old knows another Jew that hates Negroes and if we hate Jews, that's just even, baby."[23]

At this point in his career—from the mid-1960s through the early 1970s—Kahane claimed he was fighting for the American Jewish dream and that those who were undermining that dream were Jewish liberals. Understanding the debates about Jewish-Negro relations thus situates Kahane's thoughts and actions in this period and gives it the necessary texture and nuance.[24]

In February 1965, the very month Malcolm X was assassinated, civil rights leader Bayard Rustin published an article in *Commentary*, "From Protest to Politics," that articulated a shift in the civil rights movement. Rustin was at the time one of the preeminent black intellectuals and a leading tactician of the movement; he had organized the March on Washington in 1963. It was his first contribution to *Commentary*, which at the time was a vanguard intellectual venue that was prominently represented by members of a loose group known as the New York Intellectuals, many of whom were Jews. *Commentary* had published numerous other articles on black America and on black-Jewish relations; perhaps the best-known were Hannah Arendt's controversial "Reflections on Little Rock" (1959) about school desegregation and Norman Podhoretz's "My Negro Problem—and Ours" (1963), a personal reflection on growing up as a Jew in a mixed neighborhood in Brooklyn. Rustin begins "From Protest to Politics" by suggesting that the turn from rights to equality in the wake of the Civil Rights Act meant that "no longer were Negroes satisfied with integrated lunch counters. They now sought advances in employment, housing, school integration, police protection, and so forth. . . . A conscious bid for political power is being made, and in the course of that effort a tactical shift is being effected: direct-action techniques are being subordinated to a strategy calling for the building of community institutions or power bases. . . . What began as a protest movement is being challenged to translate itself into a political movement."[25]

The move beyond integration and the dismantling of Jim Crow brought civil rights more deeply into the urban north, where many blacks were living in ghettos and did not witness the sea change that many blacks did see in the south. But the energy of protest did generate a sense of power that began to turn to militancy, Malcolm X becoming its major expositor. The call for "moderation" among many white liberals was viewed by many blacks as hypocritical. Rustin writes, "The more effectively the moderates argue their case, the more they convince Negroes that American society will not or cannot be reorganized for full racial equality." Rustin is not calling for militarism, but he is calling for radicalism: "I believe that the Negro's struggle for equality in America is essentially revolutionary. While most Negroes—in their hearts—unquestionably seek only to enjoy the fruits of American society as it now exists, their question cannot be objectively satisfied within the frameworks of existing political and economic relations. . . . The term revolutionary, as I am using it, does not connote violence; its refers to the qualitative transformation of fundamental institutions, more or less rapidly, to the point where the social and economic structure which they comprised can no longer be said to be the same."[26]

The political power to which Rustin refers came in many forms, from elected officials to community and school boards, organizations for economic justice, and tacit discrimination. Rustin remarks, "If there was anything positive in the spread of the ghetto, it is the potential power base thus created, and to realize this potential is one of the most challenging and urgent tasks of the civil rights movement."[27] The successes of such a transformation from rights to power are plain enough: economic growth, educational opportunities, better health care. The failures lie mostly in the creeping militancy that was ever present in these years.

Rustin's article captures much of the conditions in which Kahane weighed in on race in America. Rustin, not known as a radical, freely used the term "revolutionary" to describe the move of blacks from rights to power. Kahane entered the fray in the midst of this transition, and his tactics, mirroring some of those used in black circles, appeared to be a response to what he thought was growing antipathy of blacks toward Jews. In many ways Kahane emerges as a public figure, certainly an influential one, after the civil rights movement, which, as Rustin suggests, reached its apex with the 1964 Civil Rights Act and the 1965 Voting Rights Act. This is not to say these legislative victories ended the need for civil rights activism; rather, the ostensible destruction of the legal foundations of racism and the dismantling of segregation enabled blacks to think more reflectively on the deficiencies of those victories and thus move toward a desire for power and equality as opposed to "rights." This is crucial because Kahane's issue with black America was not about civil rights per se. Rather, it was the way the morphing of the movement from rights to equality, and ultimately power, began to affect the Jews—their status and their safety in America. And here Kahane was far from the only American Jewish leader to weigh in on the rise of Black Power and its impact on the Jews. Most of the others were intellectuals and rabbis, whereas Kahane, also a rabbi, was essentially a "street Jew" and thus his response was in direct relation to what was happening on the ground. For this reason he preferred to engage the likes of Sonny Carson (a local Brooklyn head of CORE [Congress of Racial Equality]), James Forman, and Stokely Carmichael rather than debate with black intellectuals such as Bayard Rustin and James Baldwin. Kahane presumably knew he didn't have the intellectual firepower to go head-to-head with the likes of those two.

Kahane emerged on the scene just as the shift from civil rights to Black Power was unfolding, and I argue that his views on race are best characterized as a negative reaction to the way blacks were challenging Jews as "white" and, in some way, laying claim to the most-victimized status. It is not accidental that he takes aim at what he sees as "black anti-Semitism" in particular, calling it "racism." The Jew as the most-victimized victim is a foundation of Kahane's view of the world and of Jewish history. Whether that victimization manifests as open hatred and exclusion, as in Europe, or tacit acceptance and integration, as in America, there can be no replacement for anti-Semitism as the only true racism that matters for the Jew. And the ostensibly endemic nature of anti-Semitism meant that even though Kahane did acknowledge the immoral practices of some Jewish landlords in black ghettos, he never understood those actions as the cause of black anti-Semitism, only the occasion for its expression.[28]

Kahane's attitude toward race, that is, blacks, was not simply pragmatic in regard to the physical safety of Jews; it also reflected the way the transition from rights to power (and the way Jews were implicated as oppressors) countered his understanding of the world. As Baldwin maintained, it is arguably the case that the underlying assumption of black anti-Semitism was that Jews were white, and that was not lost on Kahane. Ironically, his contestation of Black Power was exercised by mirroring its tactics; thus "Jewish Power" and "Jewish Panthers" put Jews and blacks on an equal footing as to who was oppressing whom and what to do about it.[29] In a talk he gave in the Mattapan neighborhood of Boston in 1969, Kahane was quoted as stating, "We have a reputation, spread by our enemies, that we are Jewish Panthers. Never deny it!"[30]

As a radical thinker, Kahane understood the anger that pushed many in the black community toward militancy. One could say he even sympathized with it. And he also understood, as did others, that the Jews were situated in the middle between the white wealthy class and the black underclass. This did not go unnoticed by many black figures as well. For example, Baldwin wrote, "[The Jew] is playing in Harlem the role assigned him by Christians long ago. He is doing their dirty work."[31] While many young Jews succeeded in digging themselves out of poverty in the 1960s through hard work and education, the success came at a high price: assimilation and the desire to live the life of their gentile neighbor.[32] The notion that the solution to the Jewish problem in America was for the Jews to become "the same as Gentiles in everything outside the synagogue" for Kahane, a primary principle of Jewish liberalism as well as the most destructive aspect of the American Jewish experience.[33] This is one of the reasons Kahane had such an animus toward the Jewish "white flight" to the gilded suburbs of Great Neck and Scarsdale while abandoning their less fortunate relatives to live in proximity to black ghettos. And yet Kahane had his own dalliance with such a desire, sometimes even posing as a non-Jew and using the name Michael King in his early days with his friend Joseph Churba, and, as noted, having a gentile mistress named Estelle Evans whom he secretly supported and in whose name, after her suicide, he dedicated a foundation.[34]

The question of race and racism in Kahane's thought is integrally bound to the question of Jewish whiteness. In the 1960s, when Jews were living in closer proximity to their gentile neighbors, entering white organizations that were off-limits to them a decade earlier, and improving their own and their children's economic prospects, they began to benefit from white privilege.[35] Jews, from the perspective of African Americans of the 1960s, became part of "whitey."

The whitening of American Jews meant that they were being seen less and less as an ethnic—as opposed to a religious—minority in the United States. President Lyndon Johnson's Great Society initiative, a broad-based platform of social and economic reform launched in 1963 to address systemic inequality, focused largely on ethnic minorities. Jews were excluded from that status on account of being considered white. Most American Jews embraced Johnson's initiative even though their exclusion from ethnic-minority status in his legislation meant that they were not among the intended beneficiaries of the new program. Jews were in a state of upward mobility in the 1960s and largely held to a liberal mindset that supported civil rights and programs to help less fortunate ethnic minorities.[36]

The shift in the black movement gave pause to many whites, including Jews. As David Danzig wrote in *Commentary* in 1966, "If the civil-rights movement is losing its idealism and becoming a movement 'merely' to advance Negro interests, does it deserve liberal support?"[37] Jewish liberals found this shift from "color blindness" to black racial self-assertion aberrant. Kahane, by contrast, did not. While he opposed it because he associated it with the anti-Semitism that it allegedly expressed, he fully understood why ethnic minorities rose to challenge the hegemony of a dominant culture.

What Kahane did not accept was the extent to which American Jews were already part of the majority-white hegemonic culture. Kahane saw the American Jewish identification with this majority culture as the greatest and most damaging form of anti-Semitism (even if—presumably without that intention—espoused by Jews themselves), more so than the neo-Nazi anti-Semitism that, while demonizing the Jew, viewed the Jew as a distinctly non-Aryan "other." The kind of anti-Semitism that "others" the Jews into an entirely separate—and supposedly inferior—ethnic or racial category is what Jews have dealt with for centuries.[38] Kahane, however, was mistaken insofar as white anti-Semitism is in many cases built not on the alleged inferiority of the Jews but on fear of their "superiority." This first becomes evident in Houston Stewart Chamberlain's *Foundations of the Nineteenth Century* and is then popularized in *The Protocols of the Elders of Zion*. In any case, this more traditional anti-Semitism—whether viewing Jews as "superior" or inferior—usually does not view the Jews as white, or does so in a limited way. For Kahane black anti-Semitism, by contrast, does the opposite. Insofar as it places the Jew with the white majority, the Jew (also) becomes the oppressor of the black, even if the Jew is also oppressed by other whites. The Jews becomes a party to white hegemony.[39]

Whatever Kahane's personal attitudes toward African Americans or Arabs may have been, he was adept at using the grammar of racism to weaponize race so as to accomplish his intended goals of fashioning a diasporic form of the "New Jew" in America and defending a Jewish state in Israel.

The Encounter with Afro-Pessimism

Recent critical race theory that focuses on structural rather than personal dimensions of race in America can help explain what might otherwise seem paradoxical in Kahane's thought—such as why he had such a vexed relationship with Black Power and Black Nationalism, which he opposed, while simultaneously advocating something quite similar for Jews. Critical race theory draws from postcolonial thinkers such as Frantz Fanon, who contested the liberal integrationist model favored by the mainstream civil rights movement and Martin Luther King. In the 1960s Malcolm X became the standard-bearer for Fanonian thinking in America. The African American social critic Harold Cruse captured the dilemma of integration when he wrote in 1967 that "one of the great traps of racial integrationism [is that] one must accept all the values (positive and negative) of the dominant society into which one struggles to integrate."[40] The Afro-pessimist view was founded on the black person's lack of agency in a society such as America founded on the enslavement of the Negro as part of its white hegemony.

As African American film critic and dramatist Frank Wilderson III explains, "Afro-pessimists are theorists of Black positionality who share Fanon's insistence that, though Blacks are indeed sentient beings, the structure of the entire world's semantic field—regardless of cultural and national discrepancies . . . is sutured by anti-Black solidarity. . . . Afro-pessimism explores the meaning of Blackness not—in the first instance—as a variously and unconsciously interpellated identity or as a conscious social actor, but as a structural position of noncommunicability in the face of all other positions; this meaning is noncommunicable because, again, as a position, Blackness is predicated on modalities of accumulation and fungibility, not exploitation and alienation."[41]

Wilderson argues further that being black is to be constituted by violence and what he calls "social death" or the negation of being human. Black identity is something created by violence inflicted on blacks by a hegemonic white class. Unlike Jews, who, as Fanon put it, "went into Auschwitz and came out as Jews," Africans "went into the ships and came out as Blacks. The former is a Human holocaust; the latter is a Human *and* a metaphysical holocaust. This is why it makes little sense to attempt an analogy: the Jews have the Dead (the *Muselmann*) among them; the Dead have the Blacks among them."[42] Wilderson and others distinguish between racism and antiblackness. The first exists among many groups and it is often situational and can be remedied. Antiblackness, however, is structural, even ontological (Afro-pessimists prefer the term "political ontology"), such that it can never be undone. Wilderson writes, "Afropessimism is premised on a comprehensive and iconoclastic claim: that Blackness is coterminous with Slaveness: Blackness *is* social death: which is to say that there was never a prior metaphysical moment of plenitude, never equilibrium; never a moment of social life."[43]

Although without any comparison to Jews and without Wilderson's ontological claim, sociologist E. Franklin Frazier made a similar assessment when he maintained that blacks did not take their culture and religion with them from Africa, or more precisely that it did not survive, and that Christianity became a new bond of cohesion for a slave collective whose culture had been erased by the Middle Passage.[44] The Middle Passage was an act of erasure, not only enslavement. By contrast, some Afro-pessimists argue in Fanon's vein that although six million Jews were murdered in the Holocaust, Judaism indeed survived. One point of the Middle Passage, however, was to replace the past with new names, a new religion, and a new subservient status.

Afro-pessimists do not deny the existence and depth of anti-Semitism but instead consider that the racism directed at black people in America inflicted a form of violence that is qualitatively different, and more catastrophic, than the violence that has accompanied anti-Semitism. Put otherwise, Auschwitz cannot be likened to the Middle Passage. For Wilderson, anti-Semitism is a form of racism, but antiblackness is the very structure of white civilization without which it cannot survive.

Afro-pessimists thus do not diminish the Jewish experience of anti-Semitism but rather push back against its claim of uniqueness and perhaps also against the special ontological status it is often given. For those who hold such a view, racism is an endemic and structural part of American society that cannot be resolved through civil rights. Separatism—meaning, in some cases, physical separation from the US, as exemplified by Marcus Garvey and (for a time) Malcolm X—and expressions of Black Power are the only ways to move beyond the racism of white hegemony. Talk of integration only serves to dilute rather than concentrate Black Power. Blacks thus needed a new curriculum to teach their children how to be black outside the orbit of white society (hence the emergence of Pan-African schools in the late 1960s). Even black culture, as the Afro-pessimists argue, is produced primarily for a white audience (think of jazz or Motown or the adage that rock and roll was nothing more than "white folks playing black people's music"). From this standpoint reparations are not only legitimate but a right, not to resolve slavery but simply to institute some sort of justice in a continuing unjust system.

Kahane and the Afro-pessimists would certainly have deep disagreements over the nature and status of anti-Semitism. For Kahane, alongside many others, anti-Semitism is a sui generis and ontological hatred of the Jews that outweighs other forms of racism. But he too thought about race structurally and rejected liberal notions of integration and peaceful coexistence in a multicultural society.

What is so suggestive in juxtaposing Afro-pessimism with Kahane's view of anti-Semitism is that while Kahane did not have the intellectual skills to make a more sophisticated argument, and certainly knew nothing of Afro-pessimism that emerged decades later, for him anti-Semitism is quite similar to how some critical race theorists understand Afro-pessimism. For Kahane, while racism exists, it is categorically different from anti-Semitism, which is a metaphysical maxim captured in the rabbinic adage "Esau hates Jacob." And for Afro-pessimists like Wilderson, following Fanon, anti-Semitism certainly exists, but it is mostly a "family feud" between white people whereas antiblackness is categorically different.

By making claims such as that anti-Semitism is in the DNA of the gentile, Kahane openly suggests that there is no solution to anti-Semitism. This is simply the way the world is constructed; all there is is management. Here Kahane espouses a kind of Judeo-pessimism, positing the perennial and unfathomable persistence of what Holocaust historian Robert Wistrich called a "lethal obsession."[45] What many scholars of anti-Semitism refuse to acknowledge, while it seems to come through in some of their work, is an ontological claim of anti-Semitism that Kahane propounds openly, and that Afro-pessimism theorizes in relation to antiblackness.[46]

Racial Activism in the Schools and Synagogues

To explore Kahane's view of race in greater depth, we need to return to two events recounted earlier, the 1968 Ocean Hill–Brownsville, New York, school strike that was the impetus for his founding of the JDL, and the JDL protest against black militant James Forman, whose abortive speech at Temple Emanu-El in Manhattan in 1969 first put Kahane and the JDL in the headlines.

The Ocean Hill–Brownsville strike in Brooklyn in the spring of 1968 was a watershed moment for race relations in New York City and generated numerous book-length studies and dozens, perhaps hundreds, of articles and essays.[47] None of these studies, however, make any mention of Meir Kahane or the JDL.[48] Kahane took action in response to one aspect of the strike: the anti-Semitic rhetoric of some of its organizers such as Sonny Carson, Rhody McCoy, Leslie Campbell, and others, including some of the parents of the children in the school district. It should be noted here that Kahane was a local political animal at this time and a voracious reader of the New York City–area press. His interests were driven by local issues including the mayoral campaign of John Lindsay, Leonard and Felicia Bernstein's parlor meeting for the Black Panthers in May 1970, black militancy on college campuses in the area (e.g., Brooklyn College), and patrolling inner-city neighborhoods to protect elderly Jews.[49]

The Ocean Hill–Brownsville case was perhaps the most volatile example of an amalgamation of issues that came to fruition in the late 1960s.[50] The Ford Foundation helped set up three experimental school districts, of which Ocean Hill–Brownsville was one, that would try out decentralization and community control of the public schools in an attempt to grant parents in ethnic-minority communities more control of their children's education. Community control in the public schools was "a mass-based, grassroots campaign, one that helped stimulate the less visible and more enduring black independent school movement of the 1960s and '70s."[51] The black community was trying to give its young an alternative to inferior schools and an education that did not prepare them for the realities of the world.

Kahane was convinced that this decentralization project would lead to the expansion of Black Power and black separatism and to increased hatred of Jews and whites more generally. In his view it would teach revenge: "What will happen is that schools will produce children taught to hate the white man so that robbery, looting, rape and murder will be looked upon not as evil but as legitimate means of revenging oneself on 'oppressors.'"[52] The legitimate claims of blacks became for Kahane a mere excuse for antiwhite and anti-Semitic hatred. That was why he so adamantly opposed this policy into the early 1970s, by which time most Jewish children in New York City public schools were no longer attending troubled schools like those in Ocean Hill–Brownsville.

By the late 1960s majority-black New York City public school districts like Ocean Hill–Brownsville were receiving far fewer resources than white districts. At the same time, many of the public school teachers in these mostly black and Hispanic districts were white—and many of these white teachers were Jews, a legacy of the large entry of New York–area Jews into the public-education field in the 1960s, many having benefited from the GI Bill. Albert Shanker, who, as mentioned earlier, had taken an active role in the civil rights movement in the south, was president of the UFT (United Federation of Teachers) and a major player in the debate over the decentralizing project for the Ocean Hill–Brownsville district that began in July 1967. Shanker opposed decentralization because he felt it threatened the autonomy of the teachers in his organization.

Opposing Shanker was an African American educational administrator named Rhody McCoy, a Howard University graduate who had spent almost twenty years in public education and had served as principal in various schools. He was not a radical militant; he took the job "because he saw it as a way to do something about the educational catastrophe he saw developing in the city's black community."[53] On May 9, 1968, a month after the assassination of Martin Luther King, McCoy and the local board sent out notifications to thirteen teachers, five assistant principals, and one principal in the Ocean Hill–Brownsville district that their contracts were terminated, effective immediately. The letters stated that they should report to the headquarters of the New York City schools for reassignment.[54] The governing board, or at least McCoy, wanted to replace these teachers and administrators as part of its attempt to revamp the district and its curriculum. It is significant that the replacements appointed by McCoy included whites, both Jews and gentiles, as well as African Americans.

Shanker rejected McCoy's terminations and instructed his teachers to report for work as usual. The teachers and administrators tried to enter the schools but were stopped by protesting parents and community members. At Shanker's request, Mayor Lindsay provided a police escort for the teachers who successfully entered the schools. In protest, the local board closed all the schools in its district; Shanker and the UFT responded by pulling out all of its 350 members in Ocean Hill–Brownsville, prompting a massive strike that would last to the end of the school year.[55] Shanker, a veteran administrator and a liberal white Jew, and McCoy, a powerful African American educator, brought the New York City public school system, one of the largest in the country, to a screeching halt.

Writing in the *New York Review of Books* in 1969, Jason Epstein warned that "the urgent crisis is the outrageous and heartbreaking and potentially dangerous hostility between the city's blacks and its Jews that followed in the wake of the strike."[56] Shanker openly suggested that anti-Semitism was at play in the parent council, though he also understood that the local community's grievances could not be reduced to it. (The initial complaint of McCoy and the parents against the UFT concerned the lack of representation of blacks in leadership positions.) Activist Todd Gitlin, a sympathizer of McCoy and his decentralization initiative, dismissed at the time the charge of black anti-Semitism as overblown, asserting that "if black anti-Semitism didn't exist it would have to be invented" and suggesting that the charge was used to clothe the strike "in a holy crusade."[57] Accusations of Jewish racism were also bandied about; Shanker was accused of using the term Nazis to describe his black opponents (a description Kahane used many times).[58]

On December 27, 1968, Julius Lester, a black militant who later converted to Judaism and became a professor of Jewish Studies at the University of Massachusetts in Amherst, invited a group of leaders of the AATA (African American Teachers Association) to his radio program on WBAI-FM in New York City, *The Great Proletarian Cultural Revolution*, and during it conducted an interview with local black leader Lester Campbell. Also during the show Campbell read out a poem by a student named Thea Behran, directed at Albert Shanker, and it began: "Hey, Jew boy, with that yarmulke on your head, You pale-faced Jew boy—I wish you were dead."[59] This public broadcast of anti-Semitism compelled Lester and the chairman of WBAI, Harold Taylor, to publicly apologize. Taylor said, "The anti-Semitic views expressed on WBAI . . . are deeply repugnant to all of us connected with the station." But the damage had been done, and provided further impetus for the JDL. Kahane sprang into action,[60] organizing a JDL protest outside the WBAI studios. That same month the Metropolitan Museum of Art in Manhattan presented an exhibit *Harlem on My Mind* that similarly featured verse from young blacks that disparaged Jews.[61] In response, the JDL staged a public protest in front of the Met.

In the broader New York City–area Jewish community, the complexities of the school strike and the legitimate complaints of many district parents that blacks were not sufficiently represented among the teachers and administrators all but disappeared in the wake of these anti-Semitic incidents. Kahane brilliantly exploited the situation to maximum advantage. His adept knowledge of the grammar of racism was now deployed to expand his goals beyond the strike and into the Jewish community at large. He had now entered the race wars of the late 1960s and in doing so, brought Jews along with him—because once the JDL became a news story the Jewish establishment had to respond.

The Jews became the focus of black parents' animus in Ocean Hill–Brownsville in large part because of their overrepresentation among teachers and administrators, which itself was the product, in part, of the GI Bill and other opportunities afforded Jews, among other less affluent communities, after World War II. While the GI Bill was officially "color-blind," Kathleen Frydl notes that blacks were often excluded from various aspects of the bill due to various issues in the Veterans Administration, including legally encoded racism. Fewer blacks were able to benefit from the bill and enter white-collar professions. Thus, while the black parents in Ocean Hill–Brownsville likely did not know it, the large representation of Jewish teachers was in part *because* Jews made use of white privilege to attain educational opportunities that many could not afford without government aid.[62] Why exactly the parents of Ocean Hill–Brownsville decided to focus on the Jews (other than the fact that Shanker was openly a Jew as were many of the white teachers) is open to debate and, as discussed above, speaks to the more complicated relationship between blacks and Jews in this period. But it is safe to say that at least in part, Jews played such a prominent role in the public school system at that time as a result of white privilege.

A second episode of alleged black anti-Semitism that galvanized Kahane and his fledgling JDL occurred on Friday, May 9, 1969. That evening black militant James Forman was slated to speak at Temple Emanu-El, one of the premier Reform synagogues in Manhattan. Forman had been making the circuit of churches preaching about reparations for Negroes for the ravages of slavery.[63] He planned to address Emanu-El with the same message. For Kahane this was yet another instance of black anti-Semitism identifying the white Jew as among the parties responsible for slavery. Kahane was especially irked by the fact that Forman had chosen to make his case in a synagogue, implying that American Jews were white enough, or had benefited from their whiteness enough, to be included in the community culpable for racism. On reparations Kahane made himself quite clear: "Our position is that it might very well be that Eisendrath [Maurice Eisendrath, the aforementioned Reform rabbi, civil rights activist, and Vietnam War critic who was president of the Union of

American Hebrew Congregations, headquartered next to Temple Emanu-El] had had Baptist slave-owners for ancestors, but as I told the press, 'Most Jews came here in galleys long after the blacks were freed. Blacks deserve nothing from us, and that is what they will get. . . . If anyone is talking about reparations and if anyone deserves it, we Jews are first in line.'"[64] The Crusades, the Inquisition, and both the Catholic and Martin Luther's massacres of Jews were difficult memories to erase. Setting aside that most Jews did not arrive on American shores in "galleys," certainly not like those of the Middle Passage that brought African slaves to the New World, and Luther, though he turned out to be quite anti-Semitic, did not physically massacre Jews, the issue of reparations and what it implies is worth exploring in greater detail.

Kahane organized a protest against Forman, stationing JDL members with bats, clubs, and chains in front of Emanu-El who threatened to prevent Forman from entering (using Malcolm X's dictum) "by any means necessary."[65] Kahane devoted three pages to this incident in *The Story of the Jewish Defense League*, proudly describing his JDL compatriots as "the most unlikely group of Jews imaginable; indeed, had they remained in front of the temple a few more days property values on East 65th Street along Central Park would have plummeted. Some had baseball bats, some had iron pipes, none smiled; all waited, waiting for Forman."[66] In the end, Forman never showed but the press did and the story was quickly reported in the *New York Times*. Kahane had achieved his goal of notoriety.[67] Apart from Forman, Kahane's target at the Emanu-El event was the aforementioned Rabbi Eisendrath, who represented for him the privileged and assimilated Jewish establishment Kahane despised and referred to as WASHs (White Anglo-Saxon Hebrews), who, Kahane wrote, lived "in the gilded ghettos surrounded by unseen walls that nurtured the illusion that the gentile loved them."[68] Kahane explained this action as follows:

> Let it be understood why we did all this. To begin with, the Forman incident had to be seen against a background of years of growing violence and Jew-hatred that had erupted among a significant section of the Black community. This had manifested itself in a bitter teachers' school strike that had unleashed open and blatant anti-Semitism. . . . We were not interested in whether Temple Emanu-El was willing to capitulate. We couldn't care less whether Temple Emanu-El wanted us there or not for in reality we were not there to defend Temple Emanu-El. To be perfectly frank, I was not overly worried about what happened to the assimilated Jews who had turned their backs on both Judaism and Jews decades earlier. . . . We were not there to

defend Temple Emanu-El as such but rather the *synagogue* as a concept. Forman did not know the difference between Emanu-El or any other synagogue and he did not care. He chose it because it was famous, prestigious, and wealthy.[69]

Kahane's claim against Jewish reparations for black slavery was that Jews were by and large not in America at that time and those who were there generally weren't slave owners.[70] Setting aside the falsity of that claim, it is true that the large majority of Jews arrived on American shores from 1880 to 1920 after the abolition of slavery, but Jews certainly lived in America before the emancipation of slaves.[71] But more to the point, as Ta-Nehisi Coates argues in "The Case for Reparations," the question of reparations, and certainly the responsibility of various parties, is not limited to the reality of slavery. Coates depicts how the ethos of slavery continues to plague the black experience in a myriad of ways. America, for Coates and other Afro-pessimists, is a "white supremacist" society. "Liberals today mostly view racism not as an active, distinct evil but as a relative of white poverty and inequality. They ignore the long tradition of this country actively punishing black success—and the elevation of that punishment, in the mid-twentieth century, to federal policy."[72] In Coates's view, the case for reparations is not *for* slavery. Instead slavery was one, certainly the most egregious, aspect of a white-supremacist nation that continues to exist in the very contours of American liberalism. Reparations are due to the black community for enduring the continued racist framework of American society.

This is all relevant to Kahane's rejection of Forman's call for reparations, with at least three operative issues at play. The first is America itself and Kahane's professed love for it; the second is the claim of systemic racism and how it effaces Kahane's belief in endemic anti-Semitism; and the third is the fact that Forman chose to make his case in a synagogue, implying that American Jews were white enough, or had benefited from their whiteness enough, to be included in the community responsible for racism notwithstanding—or on Coates's reading, perhaps precisely because of—their liberalism.

From Afro-Pessimism to Judeo-Pessimism

In his 1972 book *Time to Go Home*, published a year after his emigration to Israel, Kahane declares that America cannot protect its Jews from anti-Semitism. He sees anti-Semitism as a ubiquitous part of the human condition, sometimes dormant but never absent: "When times are good, people dislike Jews quietly; when things are not so good, they dislike them loudly; and when things are critical they hate them violently—and act on their hate."[73] It is part of the hardware of human civilization and part of the divine plan not to enable Jews to become too comfortable while living among the gentiles. In this sense Kahane was a Judeo-pessimist.

Kahane's Judeo-pessimism echoes an Afro-pessimism that only really emerged after him but had its roots in the Black Nationalism of his time. Indeed, in a chapter of *Time to Go Home* entitled "The Great Racial Crisis," Kahane acknowledges the plight of the American Negro and even offers a kind of Afro-pessimist response that "the white man has always feared blacks and does so still"; what the black wants stems from a "natural desire," yet the white man will never give it to him. The reason? "Huge numbers of whites do not want to live with blacks, and they demonstrate their feelings by fleeing both city and neighborhood."[74] The battle of race is an ongoing one and the black will never get the upper hand. But Kahane's apparent Afro-pessimism here is really a veil for Judeo-pessimism. Who will lose in the ongoing battle? The blacks will never get what they rightfully deserve, but their lot will continue to improve over time. The Jew, by contrast, whose passing-as-white status has enabled him or her to greatly benefit from America, will lose in the end. Whereas in medieval and early modern Europe the Jew suffered as the middleman between the rulers and the peasants, in America the Jew will once again be squeezed as a middleman in the coming race wars, viewed by each side as collaborating with the other, being simultaneously not white enough and too white.[75] For conservative white Americans the Jew becomes the liberal champion of civil rights, a collaborator or even instigator of the black cause. "It is the Jew who is held up by the haters as the man behind the successful civil rights movements and black demands. It is the Jew who is portrayed as the evil genius behind the scenes. It is the Jew who uses the Negro to destroy America so he can take it over."[76] For the American Negro, by contrast, the Jew is now "whitey." And American Jews are caught in this pincer movement, in Kahane's view, because of the liberal Jewish agenda, which Kahane associates with the abandonment of tradition and assimilation.

It seems to me there are two operative issues for Kahane in this matter. The first is the black claim, made decades before by Fanon and reiterated by Afro-pessimists like Wilderson, that the victimization of the Negro—antiblackness—is categorically different from the victimization of the Jew ("Jews went into Auschwitz and came out as Jews. Africans went into the ships and came out as Blacks"). The ontological distinction between the Jew and the black regarding suffering reinforces Kahane's belief that, as opposed to racism, anti-Semitism is not circumstantial but itself ontological. Kahane can have sympathy for the plight of blacks in America, but black suffering can never equal the suffering of the Jews. The request for reparations takes Jews out of the status of most-victimized victim and puts them on the side of the oppressor.

Second, both the school strike and reparations remove the special status of the Jew by making him white enough to be viewed as part of the problem. This draws us back to Baldwin's argument about anti-Semitism. Kahane might say the Jews had become too white for their own good and this was now turning against them. And it was because of their liberalism, because they had abandoned their traditions, because they had succumbed to the embrace of assimilation. When Jews assimilate, what do they assimilate to? For Kahane, they assimilate to whiteness (the "Scarsdales" and "Great Necks" that dot the American landscape, as he liked to say). Or, as landlords and shopkeepers, they take advantage of the ghetto dweller because, being white, they can. They become targets of black animus because they are viewed through their whiteness, through their ability to be an ethnic minority that can pass.[77] This, for Kahane, was why black racism against Jews was worse than white anti-Semitism, even if possibly not as threatening. In fact, he comes quite close to agreeing wth Baldwin. Blacks were anti-Semitic because Jews became too white.

Kahane saw white anti-Semitism as ontological, exacerbated by the Jews' adaptation of whiteness: he imagined the (white) gentile saying, "The Jews are foreign, they are different, they threaten to undermine, or take over, our society. They are *not* like us, they are *not really* white. The gentile, when given the opportunity and the power, will resent and hate Jews."[78] Black anti-Semitism, by contrast, seems to attribute more blame to the Jews: even worse than being born white, they *became* white. This variety of Jew-hatred came from a posture of victimhood, a position historically occupied by the Jews. All this is not to argue that this is an accurate assessment of a very complex set of circumstances between blacks and Jews in postwar America. It is only to argue that it describes Kahane's obsession with race. Again, the question of racism proper is not the issue. In my view, it is rather clear that Kahane was a racist. Instead I try here to explore the contours of his racism, the motivations for his use of the grammar of racism, and why he thought black racism against Jews posed such a challenge to the Jews in America. Also noteworthy is the way he used the grammar of racism to make his case against liberal Jews, or secular Zionists, who he argued were the real racists. Asserting the racism inherent in liberalism, Jewish and gentile, Kahane aligned himself with similar sentiments in Black Nationalism that morphed into Afro-pessimism against liberal America.

In the late-1960s urban ghetto, Jews were seen as the landlords and shop owners (sometimes referred to by ghetto dwellers as "Goldbergs") wholly complicit in what many in the black communities called "economic rape" or "colonial exploitation."[79] The Jews were resented for being able to "pass" as white whereas blacks knew they could not.[80] Kahane was inclined neither to empathize with this resentment nor to acknowledge any Jewish complicity in white oppression of African Americans. He did not believe the Jews had any obligation whatsoever to blacks or anyone else, unlike many Jewish liberals and progressives of the time who believed that black anti-Semitism was circumstantial, the result of a variety of social conditions that put the Jew, as white, in close proximity to the ghetto-dwelling black. Jewish liberals understood black anti-Semitism largely as a reaction to such conditions, and in some cases they even acknowledged that Jews played a role in fostering them.[81] They argued in different ways, and to a limited degree, that black anti-Semitism could not be totally divorced from Jewish racism.[82] Kahane vehemently disagreed. In 1970 he claimed that, unlike Jewish militancy, black militancy had no basis or justification because "there has been enormous change for the blacks and incredible progress achieved."[83]

This blindness to the continuing struggles of low-income blacks in the urban ghetto, combined with an unwillingness to recognize the extent to which Jews benefited from white privilege, was foundational to Kahane's racism. And Kahane was far from the only American Jew to hold such views. Many in the Jewish community, especially Holocaust survivors and children of immigrants with a more traditional leaning, especially those who lived in mixed neighborhoods in the urban north, were more sympathetic to Kahane's easy diagnosis. And coupled with a latent suspicion that many of these Jews held toward blacks before Black Power, the rise of black violence against Jews only strengthened Kahane's argument.

Flipping the Race Card

Kahane certainly trafficked in racist language and was adept at the grammar of racism, referring to black neighborhoods in Brooklyn as "jungles" and calling blacks "natives," and his statements about Arabs in Israel were racist in rhetoric, character, and style.[84] There is also little doubt that he took advantage of the overtly racist attitudes of many of his followers in both locales.[85] Perhaps a better way to frame this is to suggest that, Kahane's racism aside, the more interesting issue is how he utilized the grammar of racism to push his agenda of Jewish pride and assertiveness. I borrow this term "grammar" from the abovementioned film theorist Frank Wilderson III who writes, "Semiotics and linguistics teach us that when we speak, our grammar goes unspoken. Our grammar is assumed. It is the structure through which the labor of speech is possible."[86] Kahane knew how to use racist language; how to turn it against his adversaries, blacks and Jews alike; how to weaponize race (while denying it); and how to tap into the racist attitudes of his followers in ways that would increase his base.

Like Black Nationalists, who contested the accusation that they were practicing "reverse racism," Kahane claimed that he was not being racist at all in his battle against black racism/anti-Semitism or against Arabs in Israel. He described his militancy in terms of a fight against discrimination and as a form of self-defense, with one vulnerable minority protecting itself against another, black minority that had become increasingly militant and violent.[87] That was precisely Kahane's defense of the JDL's activities in its early civil patrols that initially gained acceptance among many Jews. There is little doubt that Kahane held negative opinions about blacks. But he claimed that these views arose not because of any distaste for their skin color but because they were threatening Jews.

In the JDL's founding document "Jewish Defense League: Aims and Purposes," Kahane addresses the question of racism and proclaims, "The JDL is not a racist group. Unlike Panthers or the American Nazi Party it does not impute any racial or ethnic group with evil qualities of some of its individuals *and that is the definition of racism.* If there appears to be an inordinate emphasis on black anti-Semitism that is because . . . many black militants have become a clear and present danger to the Jews. . . . JDL has never practiced hatred or contempt for others. Panther weapons are for offense. JDL is truly a defensive group" (emphasis added).[88] Kahane must not have known, or have chosen to ignore, that the original name of the Black Panther Party was the Black Panther Party for Self-Defense.

Of course, having to deny racism is itself a sign of its proximity to one's agenda. Of interest here is not so much the dubious accuracy or falsity of these claims but what underlies them. Here Kahane associates the radical left (the Black Panthers) and the radical right (the American Nazi Party) with the nefarious tendency to ascribe to individuals "evil qualities" on the basis of dark skin color or ethnic attributes. This is not, insists Kahane, something he or his fellows in the JDL do. He elaborates on his ostensible antiracism in a short essay written in 1969 entitled "Brother David"; the title refers to a black convert to Judaism named David Solomon. In this essay Kahane viewed Solomon as one who had heroically rejected his affiliation with the black community and entered a new community of believers, becoming part of the "chosen people." In so doing he had turned his back on what Kahane saw as the pathologies of that community, first and foremost anti-Semitism. By saying he accepted black Jews who, as part of their conversion, rejected their blackness, Kahane attempted to reject the racism label precisely by affirming racism. One could be a black Jew, but one could not be both a Jew and black. "The persecuted minority rarely learns from his agony much about the milk of human kindness. Unhappily, he looks forward to his opportunity to become the aggressive oppressor, and freedom, too often, means the chance to be as brutal as the colonizer. But my brother has transcended this and, in doing so, achieved a greatness that I—unashamedly—am jealous of. . . . Those whose skins are white must go far to feel the agony of the black man, and whose skins are black find it immensely difficulty to rise above the passion of revenge."[89] David Solomon became Kahane's "brother" (one of his people, to paraphrase Ruth's comment to Naomi in the book of Ruth), and thus no different from any other Jew. His conversion was the fruit of a choice against the oppressive mindset and practices of black anti-Semitism. In Kahane's words, "His [Solomon's] goodness stands in stark contrast to their own sickness." In becoming a Jew, this black man repudiated his "negritude" or "Afrikanity," "the impervious domain of a cultural 'blackness' itself," and thus ceased to be the enemy of the Jew.[90] This treatment of a case like Solomon's provides a ground for Kahane to rebuff the charge of racism; yet it really only affirms it. In his denial of biological racism Kahane at the same time affirms a cultural hierarchy—with Judaism and Jewish culture decidedly above black "Afrikanity"—that is difficult to see as anything but racist.

Almost two decades later, in a 1987 essay entitled "I Hate Racism," Kahane revisits the topic.[91] The context for this essay is crucial. As noted above, in 1986 the Israeli Knesset passed its "Racism Law" prohibiting anyone deemed racist from assuming a seat in that parliamentary assembly. The law was promulgated solely with Kahane in mind, and after its passage he was ousted from the Knesset and his KACH Party was disqualified from participating in future elections. Kahane appealed to the Israeli Supreme Court, which upheld the law in 1987. In "I Hate Racism," Kahane once again deflects the charges of racism against him by claiming that his positions are wholly in line with Jewish law. A "religious Jew," he notes, believes that Jewish distinction is founded on one thing only: divine election.[92] There is nothing inherently distinct, certainly not unique, about the Jews other than the fact that God chose them.[93] And divine election assumes, for him, a belief in a transcendent deity who communicates its will to the Jews at Sinai. "Of course, for the religious Jew—who believes that Torah is derived from the divine source at Sinai—this declares his Jewishness, and this is clearly understandable. For assuming that Torah is G-d's Law, then it is the perfect truth." Those Jews who are not religious in Kahane's eyes—and here he names in this piece the left-wing Knesset member Yossi Sarid, Reform Rabbis Alexander Schindler, Balfour Brickner, and Morris Adams, the Canadian Jewish businessman Edgar Bronfman Sr., the right-wing Israeli politician Geula Cohen, and the neoconservative editor of *Commentary* magazine Norman Podhoretz—allegedly repudiate the traditional Jewish understanding of election and associate it with racism:[94]

> The secular Jewish leaders, the ones who trumpet the "need" to be Jewish and then call for humanism and the equality of all human beings, the ones who condemn racism and oppose intermarriage, wallow in their schizophrenia and drown in their dichotomy and agonize in their dilemma. Let us pity them, *those who call me racist, but who are the real Jewish racists, the ones who—deep in their hearts—know that their "Jewishness" their "Zionism" their "cultural tradition," their insistence about being a part of a separate group, is sterile and barren tribalism, at best, noxious and obnoxious racism at worst.*[95] (emphasis in original)

As Kahane sees it, Jewish liberal secularists want to cling to the idea of Jewish difference but refuse to embrace it in terms of divine election because they do not believe in the divine nature of Torah. In light of this, Kahane asks, what is the basis of Jewish difference? What sets the Jew apart that would justify a "Jewish" state on land where others already reside? For Kahane the secular Jew can find a ground for Jewish exceptionalism only in ethnic or racial factors. Kahane thus turns the charge of racism back on those he sees as embodiments of the liberal Jewish establishment. They are racists because they have no definition of Jewish exceptionalism other than ethnic difference. And that ethnic difference justifies chauvinism toward another minority; what can be more racist than that?

The substance of the challenge is less important than its rhetorical punch. The accusation of the liberal as (also) "racist" is not new to Kahane. Black Nationalism, and later Afro-pessimists, have also argued that liberals aid and abet the continuation of structural "white supremacy" even as they fight for black "rights."

Kahane goes on to say, "To be Jewish is to have truth and holiness and sacredness and to climb the mountain of spiritual greatness. IF there is a G-d, and Torah, and truth. But if there is not, then 'Jewishness' is a cheap, illogical, reactionary form of racism, practiced by Brickners, Bronfmans, Geula Cohen and Hashomer Ha-Tzair, progressive Zionist types who lack either the intellect or the courage to reject this blackest kind of abomination—racism."[96] Kahane's inclusion of the right-wing Zionist Geula Cohen in this list is noteworthy. Cohen (1925–2019) was a longtime Knesset member and founder of the secular right-wing Tehiya Party. At one time she favored legislation that would transfer West Bank Arabs out of the West Bank so that Israel could safely annex the territory. Although she and Kahane were not very far apart politically, she opposed the KACH platform and supported his ouster from the Knesset. But fidelity to a right-wing stream of Zionism does not spare Cohen from Kahane's ire, since her Zionism is not founded on a belief in God and Torah. For Kahane Cohen is no less a racist, and no more a Zionist, than her left-wing Israeli counterparts.

This definition of Jewish difference in a purely theological register represents a shift from Kahane's earlier work. In his writings of the late 1960s and early 1970s he sought to instill pride in the Jew qua Jew, what he called *hadar*. Later in Israel he deployed theological claims to counter political attacks against him and sought to expose what he saw as a hypocritical thread in Jewish secularism, a theme that he turned to repeatedly in mocking statements such as the following: "You who think you are not racist because of your liberalism? What exactly is the basis of your understanding of Jewish difference that would be against inter-marriage and in favor of Israel as a 'Jewish' state?"[97] Such questions were aimed at eliciting discomfort in those who were ostensibly committed to equality while pouring tons of resources into retaining difference and survival based purely on notions of Jewish ethnicity.

Kahane's *Uncomfortable Questions for Comfortable Jews* intensified his attack on his secular Jewish opponents. Here he addressed their condemnation of UN Resolution 3379 of November 10, 1975, which deemed Zionism akin to racism: "How droll. For it is the same indignant Jews—indignant that anyone could ever dare to paint Zionism as 'racism'—who are in the process of doing just that, proving to their enemies that they are, indeed correct."

"The very same infuriated, fuming Jews of indignation who have spent the last two years in an unbridled attempt to paint Meir Kahane as a racist for declaring that Zionism, a Jewish state, and Judaism are incompatible with

Western democracy, and that there must be a legal and political differentiation between Jew and non-Jew so that Israel should remain a Jewish state—these same Jews proceed by this very obsession down the mad road of 'proving' that Zionism is 'racism.'"[98]

Here Kahane defends Israel's Law of Return, which grants Jews the right to immigrate to the country, as "not racism but self-preservation" and Zionism itself as not racism but "*havdala*, separation . . . that is not biological but ideological."[99] He also claims that in Israel democracy must give way if Zionism is to endure. "For if you define what Meir Kahane says as 'racist,' and then ban it, you will legitimize the U.N. resolution that delegitimizes Zionism."[100] Kahane equates his own views with Zionism rightly understood. If Israel is to remain true to its core principles, it is identical to Kahanism. Its rejection of Kahanism is tantamount to its own self-abnegation. This is another example of the grammar of racism that Kahane wielded so successfully. The equation of Zionism with racism was so shocking to Jews in part because it associated their national movement with something (racism/anti-Semitism) they had been victims of for centuries. Kahane claims that the attempt to counter this equation by asserting Israel's "Jewish and democratic" character is incoherent, dishonest, and undergirded by a racism that Jewish liberal secularists claim to abhor. He unwittingly echoes Black Nationalists and Afro-pessimists in accusing liberalism of covering up the racism that it perpetuates, even while ameliorating its effects through the according of "rights" to its victims. Although Kahane is clumsy in his argumentation, he inadvertently stumbles upon an important aspect that hides under the rug of liberalism and is exposed through the Afro-pessimism that Ta-Nehisi Coates translates for a popular audience: we live in a white-supremacist (or, I would add, in Israel, a Judeo-supremacist) society.[101]

When applied to Israel, Kahane's point is sobering. It suggests that a true democracy is impossible in a Jewish state, which must, to ensure its own survival, assign non-Jewish individuals and communities, that is, Arabs, a second-class status. Kahane suggests that even if Arabs are treated fairly in Israel they can never be treated equally, a view that echoes the arguments of Black Power theorists that civil rights laws and regulations do not erase the structural, underlying racism of a society based on white supremacy.

Conclusion

I want to raise two remaining issues related to Kahane and race. The first concerns the similarities between his own antiassimilationist aims and the Black Nationalist agenda against integration. The second is how all this plays out in

Israel for Kahane with two distinct constituencies: Arabs and Mizrachi (non-white) Jews.

Above I mentioned that the fight against integration by Malcolm X and later by Black Nationalism can be likened to the fight against assimilation among some Jews in America, both liberal and traditional. For many Black Nationalists, integration, arguably one of the mainstays of King's civil rights agenda, would undermine black people's ability to fully achieve their potential. Thus Carmichael, for instance, argued that black liberation had to be achieved by black people alone; this was a main tenet of Black Power. It was articulated comically but potently in Malcolm X's "coffee and cream" speech responding to the abovementioned March on Washington. For Malcolm and his followers, a colorless society meant a white society. The 2017 film *Black Panther* (its title a double entendre referring to a utopian all-black society and also to the Black Panthers) offers a powerful fictitious depiction of this approach. And the film's release on the fiftieth anniversary of the Black Panthers' founding in Oakland is significant. Numerous articles in the Jewish media have discussed the film's relationship, or lack thereof, to Zionism, which only illustrates some of the parallels I have explored in this chapter.[102]

For Jews in postwar America, assimilation was increasingly becoming a major problem. As Jonathan Woocher discusses in his 1983 book *Sacred Survival: The Civil Religion of American Jews*, at this time survival became the sine qua non of American Judaism.[103] Jewish organizations began pouring money and resources into programs meant to ensure that assimilation would not cause the erasure of Jewishness in America. Elsewhere Woocher wrote:

> Assuming that "Jewish survivalism" has become the ideology of American Jewish leadership, how is it expressed concretely in that leadership's perceptions of communal problems, its priorities for the allocation of communal resources and energies, and its definitions of what it means to be a Jew on a personal behavioral level? Does "survivalism" have clear and constant implications in these areas which will enable us to speak not only in broad terms of a "turning inward," but to define the specific patterns of concern likely to shape the communal agenda and of Jewish identity likely to be reflected among community leaders?[104]

A decade earlier in 1973, Charles Liebman put it this way: "The majority of Jews [are] torn between two forces: the desire for acceptance by the gentile society and the attraction of non-Jewish values and attitudes, and the desire for group identity and survival as a distinct community. This phenomenon is, of course, not distinct to Jews, but the intensity of both forces is probably more pronounced among the Jews than in any other group in American society."[105]

Black America had different challenges but a similar agenda. For them assimilation was not possible as they were not white. As Black Nationalist Julius Lester asserted, "There is no need for black people to wear yellow Stars of David on their sleeves; the Star of David is all over us."[106] Hannah Arendt put it more boldly: "While audibility is a temporary phenomenon, rarely persisting beyond one generation, the Negroes' visibility is unalterable and permanent."[107] Frank Wilderson puts it even more starkly: "Blackness and Slaveness are inextricably bound in such a way that whereas Slaveness can be separated from Blackness, Blackness cannot exist other than Slaveness. There is no world without Blacks, but there are no Blacks who are in the world."[108]

But for many integration was certainly possible and, as Martin Luther King argued, the goal. It is no accident that Kahane adopted many of the Black Panthers' anti-integrationist tactics, but less well-known was their shared ideological project. And this project of fighting for difference was not only Kahane's but one he also shared with some of the American Jewish leadership he contested. Whether Jews could assimilate yet remain different was an ongoing internal battle of American Jewry at that time, and remains so today. The battle lines were thus drawn less on the program itself and more on its implementation. Kahane largely translated antiassimilationism into anti-integrationism (thus in line with Malcolm X) while many others in the Jewish community believed that difference could survive integration, more along the lines of King. What Marc Dollinger shows in his book *Black Power, Jewish Politics* is how many liberal Jews in the 1960s also identified, or at least sympathized, with Black Power, both for the black community itself and as a model for Jewish survival.[109]

The rise of black anti-Semitism on the left, now more focused on Israel, is becoming a double-edged sword for American Jewry in ways that Kahane predicted. As a firm anti-integrationist, he shared basic sentiments with Afropessimists that structural anti-Semitism would never allow the Jew to integrate without disappearing (which the Jew, compared to the black, could more easily do). And if the Jew remained separate, and support of Israel was part of that separatism, segments of society would turn against the Jew. It is certainly the case that parts of white America, especially evangelical America, have newly fallen in love with the Jew *because* of Israel.[110] But this love is contingent and, as Kahane noted in the 1970s and others note today, could easily evaporate the moment Israel does not serve America's interest. Be that as it may, for Kahane the whiteness of the Jews and their assimilation would threaten them from one side, and the whiteness of the Jews, again resulting from assimilation, would threaten them from the other. Therefore, he concluded, as did many in the "Back to Africa" movement, it was "time to go home."

What happened when Kahane "went home" to Israel is quite interesting. One of his first acts was to contest the Black Hebrews of the town of Dimona, thus taking with him the identity politics of his country of birth and transplanting it on Israeli soil. But most Israelis had little interest in battling a small and largely benign group of American blacks who thought they were part of the lost tribes and had settled in Israel; they did not share Kahane's prebaked animus toward blacks.

Failing to gain much of an audience against the Black Hebrews, Kahane quickly turned his attention to the Arab as the enemy, except now he was in a Jewish majority and not a competing, albeit white, minority. All this was predictable. What was unpredictable was how he ingeniously used the grammar of racism to build his base with the Mizrachi community, who were nonwhite Jews. In the 1970s a small group of Mizrachi Jews formed a movement called the Black Panthers, modeling themselves on the American original; the white enemy was now the "white" Ashkenazi elite. Kahane played up discrimination against the Mizrachim by the white Jewish liberal elite, whom he often referred to as "Hebrew-speaking goyim" or "Jewish Hellenists." While the Israeli Black Panthers may have served Kahane's attack on the Ashkenazi elite, they were also openly supportive of the Arab minority, even recognizing the PLO, and thus became his adversary.[111] In fact, the Israeli Panthers clashed with Kahane and his group, in some way reinventing the "Panther-JDL" clashes in America in the streets of Jerusalem.[112]

Kahane was shaken by the extent to which this group of Mizrachi Jews, who should, he thought, have been his allies, attacked him. They too, perhaps, viewed him as white, now part of the white Ashkenazi hegemony they were subverting. Hence the Black Panthers' protest against white Ashkenazi hegemony did not translate into Kahane's racial paradigm.[113] As Sami Shalom Chetrit notes in his study of the Israeli Black Panthers, "Kahane was profoundly scared by the Panthers' direct attack against him, and having realized he could not drive them out of the Mizrachi theater under the threat of his American strongmen, he initiated a reconciliation meeting with the *HaPanterim HaSh'horim* leaders, where he asked that the clashes between the movements cease."[114]

It is quite interesting how this played out on the race question. The Israeli Black Panthers were, as noted, founded on an internal racial battle against the Ashkenazi (white) elite and, for some, Israeli Arabs. Kahane, now in Israel, turned his attention to the disenfranchised Mizrachi (nonwhite) community, and now some in that community (the Panthers) viewed him as part of the white hegemony they were fighting against. Because many of the Israeli Panthers identified as part of the political left, some of them included the disenfranchised Arab population as part of their struggle. In April 1972 Kochavi Shemesh, an Israeli Black Panther, spoke at a gathering in Beit She'an (near Tiberias) and said, "We must reach a situation in which we will fight together with the fucking Arabs against the establishment. We are the only ones who can constitute a bridge of peace with the Arabs in the context of a struggle with the establishment." On this Michael Fischbach wrote, "The Panthers in Israel actually believed that Mizrachi/Sephardic Jews and Palestinians were culturally part of the same people. All that separated them was religion; other than that, the Panthers argued, they and the Palestinians shared a common Middle Eastern/North African cultural heritage."[115] In fact, two of the Black Panthers' founders, Sa'adia Marciano and Charlie Biton, later served in the Knesset in left-wing parties. This is quite different from the second iteration of Mizrachi pride in the founding of the religious Shas Party in 1984.

In Israel at this time, Kahane reset the dichotomy between black and white in two ways: the Jews (white) against the Arabs (nonwhite), and the Ashkenazim (white) against the Mizrachim (nonwhite). He cleverly navigated between identification with the people of color when they were Jews, and then with the white Jews against the Arabs. He was also acutely aware that most Mizrachi Jews generally were less favorable toward the Arabs than the liberal white Ashkenazi Jews. The white Zionist elites thus became, for him, a version of the liberal American Jewish establishment while the Mizrachim became a version of the American blacks (except in Israel he supported their cause). The Arabs became the enemy of both. In this way he tried to use the growing Ashkenazi-Mizrachi "race war" in the 1970s to his advantage. He all but accused the white Ashkenazi elite of racism against the Mizrachim, an accusation Mizrachim had been making long before Kahane arrived. Kahane, however, utilized it in a particularly adept political manner. A bit later the Mizrachi Shas Party did the same, although unlike the Israeli Black Panthers, Shas was religious in its platform and did not find common cause with the Arab minority. But similar in sentiment to the American Black Panthers, Shas too aspired to "racial" purity and so Kahane was, for them, an outsider.

Thus in Israel as much as in the US, race was at the center of Kahane's program, not just between Jews and Arabs but also between white Jews and nonwhite Jews. The racial intonations of Kahane's program truly began to catch the attention of Israeli legislators when he was elected to the Knesset in 1984 with a platform against the Arab minority that was uncompromising, antiliberal, and openly antidemocratic. The Knesset and the Supreme Court acted swiftly to prevent this from spinning out of control. But the racial fires Kahane helped stoke were not easily extinguished and continue to burn in many corners of Israel and the Diaspora Jewish communities today.

In a sense, the situation with the Israeli Black Panthers in the 1970s exhibits the falsity of Kahane's use of race. In Israel he presents himself as the underdog who wants to undermine the "white" Ashkenazi elite by evoking the ire of the nonwhite Mizrachi Jews. Yet the Black Panthers view him as no less white than the Ashkenazi rulers and view their plight at least in part in solidarity with the nonwhite Arabs. In short, Kahane gets entangled in his own confused machinations. American racial politics cannot be easily transferred to a country with two nonwhite populations (Mizrachi Jews and Arabs) both of whom are oppressed by a white elite; yet for Kahane only one of these groups (the Arabs) constitutes the enemy. In seeking to divide the two nonwhite populations in Israel, he tries to pit them against each other but practically pits both of them against him. It is true that many Mizrachim supported Kahane for two reasons: their hatred of the Ashkenazi elite and their hatred of the Arabs. But the Israeli Black Panthers present him, and us, with a more interesting dilemma: the racialization of Israel potentially creates an alliance between Mizrachim and Arabs that makes Kahane's grammar of racism untenable.

4

Communism

VIETNAM AND SOVIET JEWRY: KAHANE'S BATTLE AGAINST COMMUNISM

"This was our generation's messianic message; to violate sealed borders."

YOSSI KLEIN HALEVI, *MEMOIRS OF A JEWISH EXTREMIST*

"Let the world know that while Jews are on trial in Russia, the Soviet Union will be on trial."

MEIR KAHANE, *THE STORY OF THE JEWISH DEFENSE LEAGUE*

Kahane and the Cold War

Born in 1932, Kahane was a young twenty-something yeshiva and college student during the heyday of Cold War anxieties about the Sino-Soviet communist bloc. The Red Scare, the HUAC (House Un-American Activities Committee, founded in 1938 in response to Roosevelt's New Deal policies and the fear of communism at home), and the blacklisting that transpired in Hollywood and in American literary circles all took aim not only at ostensible communist activities but also at American leftist movements and policies more generally. Kahane was reared in such a climate, and it shaped him as much as having grown up among Holocaust survivors and their children in Brooklyn. Thus the Cold War–obsessed 1950s had as much influence on Kahane's mature political outlook as the political radicalism of the 1960s.

Given this combination of pervasive anticommunism and a post-Holocaust American Jewish upbringing, it is not surprising that advocacy for the plight of the Jews of the Soviet Union became a signature issue for Kahane and his JDL in the late 1960s. And yet this issue was neither in the forefront of Kahane's earliest political writings nor part of the JDL's initial activities (which, as we saw in the previous chapter, arose out of a perceived Jewish vulnerability to anti-Semitism from African American communities in the New York area). Rather, what paved the way for Kahane's embrace of the cause of Soviet Jewry in the late 1960s and early 1970s was a decade-long preoccupation with the dangers of communism and a concern about rising American political opposition to the Vietnam War, an opposition that he saw, ultimately, as bad for the Jews and for Israel. For Kahane, Soviet Jewry was part of a much more complicated American project.

Kahane's Anticommunism

The early 1960s were trying years for Kahane. Working as a part-time Orthodox rabbi and youth leader in Brooklyn and Queens, he was looking for something bigger where his voice could be heard. Kahane's childhood and later college friend Joseph Churba, a fellow Brooklynite born to a large Syrian Jewish family, became his connection to the greater political world he sought. Churba, a wily character with strong politically conservative leanings, was the worldlier of the two. After college he started a Washington-based political consulting firm aimed at supporting American involvement in the conflict in Vietnam. Churba made Kahane a partner in the firm, introducing him to both the Washington nightlife and its policy scene in the early 1960s. Through his work with Churba, Kahane began to present himself as an expert on communism and anti-Semitism and learned his way around the corridors of power in Washington.[1]

Through Churba, Kahane made professional contacts with the FBI in 1963, when he apparently was asked by the bureau to obtain intelligence from the right-wing anticommunist John Birch Society.[2] Around the same time, Churba and Kahane's consulting firm opened a branch office on the Upper East Side of Manhattan, but it doesn't appear that the firm actually operated from that address. As Kahane later confided, "What we wanted was an East Side address that could impress prospective clients."[3] In 1965 Churba and Kahane, who by then was occasionally acting under the pseudonym Michael King, turned to political militancy, setting up the "Fourth of July Movement," a short-lived attempt to create small cells on college campuses that would support the war at a time when the antiwar movement was gaining momentum.[4]

None of these organizations made much headway, and soon afterward Kahane and Churba went their separate ways. Churba went on to have a successful career in Republican politics, eventually becoming the air force's top Middle East intelligence expert and president of the International Security Council, a Washington-based institute; he also was a campaign adviser to Ronald Reagan. Perhaps more consequential than Kahane and Churba's efforts at political consultancy and militancy was their intellectual collaboration on the abovementioned 1967 book *The Jewish Stake in Vietnam,* on which Kahane's pseudonymous name Michael King appears. This book, which stressed the dangers of communism to both America and the Jews, set the stage for Kahane's eventual transition into a fervent activist for Soviet Jewry. These early forays into public policy, with an emphasis on support for the Vietnam War effort, facilitated in part through Churba, give us a sense of Kahane's trajectory from Orthodox rabbi to political activist that would blossom with the founding of the JDL in 1968 and gain international attention with his Soviet Jewry activism from 1969 through 1973. During the early 1960s he was learning the ropes of government activity, navigating the shadowy worlds of the FBI and the CIA, and discovering ways to move through, and around, the political halls of power. With Churba as his guide, these lessons would serve him well when Kahane himself became the subject of FBI surveillance and an actor on the margins of the law. This experience would also help him when he launched his political career in Israel in 1973.[5]

Kahane's contribution to *The Jewish Stake in Vietnam* was an amalgam of previously published pieces from the *Jewish Press* entitled "Communism vs. Judaism." As Kahane's widow and biographer Libby Kahane later noted, the chapters dealing with Vietnam's foreign relations were clearly authored by Churba and drew on his expertise in Southeast Asia, while Kahane contributed the chapters on the dangers of communism for Israel and the Jews.[6]

Kahane's chapters featured the ideological argument that Jewish support for US military involvement in Vietnam would counteract anti-Semitism in America and help Israel. The choppy nature of the book confirms Libby Kahane's assessment. Even as the title suggests that it is a book about Vietnam, the book is divided between a statistical and wonky assessment of the communist takeover of Vietnam and the role of China in the conflict and, as noted, a more ideological assessment of the dangers of communism specifically to Jews, focusing mostly on the Soviet Union and the Middle East.

Kahane was especially keen in this book to link the Cold War with the Arab-Israeli conflict and to persuade readers that this regional conflict was reflective of the broader global struggle against communism. This seems to be Kahane's central thesis, which he deployed both on behalf of Soviet Jewry and to build his Zionist base. In the book he points out that both the USSR and China viewed Israel as an appendage of American imperialism and thus an enemy of communism, even though at that time Israel was essentially a democratic-socialist state and had a functioning communist party. Here he was largely correct. From the Sino-Soviet point of view, then, Vietnam becomes the catalyst for a "war of liberation" being fought by the Viet Cong that mirrors the "war of liberation" being fought by the PLO, which was founded a few years earlier in 1964.[7]

In this book and in the earlier articles related to it, Kahane accuses well-meaning liberal-minded American Jewish groups of failing to understand these connections. American Jewish liberals, he argues, have been duped by communist-sympathizing leftists. "Behind the protests and bewilderment concerning U.S. involvement in Vietnam lies a terrible and almost fantastic ignorance and confusion. . . . Because never before have so many known so little about so much, we find the leftists groups . . . able to manipulate a great many liberals and other decent people. . . . Because of this immense ignorance . . . many well-meaning groups have been sucked into the general protest movement under the misconception that they are fighters for peace."[8] Kahane calls out in particular the American Jewish Congress and the Reform movement's Union of American Hebrew Congregations, both of which had already come out against the war. In doing so, he suggests, such groups echoed the words of the Jewish head of the Students for a Democratic Society, who proclaimed that "our people do not believe that the U.S. should be the policeman in the Middle East or the Far East." "Naturally," Kahane writes, "the Arabs answered with a loud Amen."[9] He continues by arguing that "to begin to understand what would be [if the Viet Cong prevailed] for free people and for the United States, for Jewry, Judaism and Israel, and to begin to dispel the false illusions and understand the truth about Vietnam, we must begin to understand the origins of the conflict."[10] Kahane then goes on to offer a thumbnail sketch of the history of Vietnam.

For Kahane, then, there was a clear affinity between anti–Vietnam War sentiment and the view that Israel was the aggressor in the Six-Day War. Many left-leaning, pro-Israel American Jews of this era felt obliged to contest this alleged affinity, to defend their positions as both anti–Vietnam War militants and Israel supporters. For example, Michael Walzer's *Just and Unjust Wars* (1977) was in large part driven by this need to reconcile those two positions.[11]

Kahane, however, was having none of it, declaring it "astonishing" and absurd that so many leftist and liberal American Jews attempted to metamorphose from "timid Vietnamese doves" into "audacious Middle East hawks."[12] He found the efforts to carve out an anti–Vietnam War, pro-Zionist position unsustainable in the face of a communist propaganda machine determined to treat Israel and Vietnam as part of the same conflict. Kahane wanted to show that communism, whether in the Sino-Soviet bloc or in the US, collapsed Israel and Vietnam as two examples of an American imperialism determined to crush any popular liberation movement—whether it be the Viet Cong or the Palestinians—that stood in its way. In Kahane's Manichean view, to be pro-Israel meant to be in favor of the US intervention in Vietnam because structurally the Viet Cong and the PLO were the same, or at least they were viewed as such by America's enemies, the communists and their supporters.

Kahane, then, frames communism in terms of two major challenges to the survival of Jews and Judaism: the erasure of Jewish religious difference and the endangerment of Jewish national aspirations. Communism threatens both religion and nationalism, which, as we have seen, Kahane regarded as two central and overlapping (if not identical) tenets of Jewish existence.[13] This was a common view of the left among traditionalists, and Kahane made great use of that conventional thinking to his advantage.

The Jewish Stake in Vietnam was likely not written for those who shared his reactionary mindset (we can see how various spin-off articles in the *Jewish Press* catered to his own community) but primarily for a liberal, largely American Jewish audience that was increasingly sympathetic to an antiwar movement that was gaining steam. New Left and radical activists such as Lee Webb and Gar Alperovitz had organized Vietnam Summer in 1967, mobilizing student protests in favor of a larger radical program.[14] Martin Luther King added his voice to the growing antiwar movement, and in October 1967 the biggest antiwar rally thus far, numbering over a hundred thousand, took place in Washington. Kahane was acutely aware of leftist activism and responded with it in mind.

His message to liberal, mostly young American Jews was that they were endangering themselves and Israel by joining the antiwar movement. He was not so much warning about a communist takeover of the US as about an elimination of Jewish difference and the possible end of a Jewish state. By succumbing to a Marxist-Maoist ideology that disdained religion and applauded a form of assimilation, Jews were digging their own graves in America. Jewish identity in America, Kahane argued, could not survive participation in progressive causes. Those intuitions arguably resonate in the American Jewish mainstream to this day, certainly among many in the Orthodox community.

Kahane notes that the international communist rejection of Israel extended even to a refusal to engage with Maki, the Israeli Communist Party. No fan of Maki, Kahane dismissed it as made up of "only a handful of Jewish renegades and basically an Arab group."[15] He recounted how the party was barred from participating in large leftist conferences such as the First Afro-Asian–Latin American People's Solidarity Conference in Havana on January 15, 1966, which featured delegates from eighty-two other countries (including the PLO). Clearly, as Kahane pointed out, communist international solidarity had its limits; it could not extend to a communist party based in a country deemed to be a US puppet regime. Even though communism played a role in Zionism and the Jewish state, the communist bloc refused to recognize the existence of a Jewish communist party.

It is certainly true that the conference had a pro-Arab agenda. And it is true that the conference members were committed to all "national liberation" movements including the Viet Cong and the PLO but *not* Zionism. And it is true that the conference viewed Zionism as imperialist or colonialist. None of this is new. What Kahane wanted to emphasize, however, was the alignment of two disparate conflicts, the Vietnam War and the Arab-Israeli conflict, as requiring the attention of liberal Jewish protesters of the former. As the Chinese delegate to the 1966 Havana conference, speaking for Mao, declared, "The Chinese people salute the Arab people's just struggle against the American imperialist tool of Israel and for the restoration to the Palestinian people of their legitimate rights"—a connection that Kahane takes care to note in *The Jewish Stake in Vietnam*.[16] In a *Jewish Press* article right after the Six-Day War, Kahane similarly points out how "May 18th ('Palestine Day') led the official Chinese organ *Renmin Ribao* to exclaim, 'As long as the Palestinian people and the other people persist in the struggle they will finally defeat . . . U.S. imperialism and its tool for aggression, Israel.'"[17] On this Kahane writes elsewhere, "Here the Arabs and the Communists joined in a definite plan to destroy, not only Israel, but all vestiges of Western and democratic influence in the Middle East."[18]

The point Kahane is trying to make here is not simply a geopolitical one describing the Sino-Soviet-Arab network. It is, rather, a specific claim about the dangers that communism poses to Jewish national aspirations. While China openly aligned itself with the PLO as a "liberation movement," it was the Soviet Union where millions of Jews were trapped behind the Iron Curtain and Jewish lives were most vulnerable, and that is where he turned his attention. Thus in the section of *The Jewish Stake in Vietnam* entitled "The Death of Jewishness," Kahane makes his case that communism writ large, including both the Sovet Union and China, endangers Jewish survival.

Kahane was no philosopher and did not engage with philosophical ideas in any serious way. He generally preferred to attack the local or regional activists who translate those ideas into action. We saw previously how he did so with Black Nationalists. Nevertheless, in *The Jewish Stake in Vietnam* he uncharacteristically quotes excerpts from Karl Marx's essay "On the Jewish Question," not to offer any detailed analysis of Marx's argument but to use it to reinforce his own conviction that for Marx and for all of his leftist and communist followers, "the only answer to the Jewish problem was assimilation. . . . The word was loud and clear. Judaism as a religion, was a mortal enemy of Marxism and would be strangled and Jewishness as a national concept was a falsehood. The alternative was assimilation, forcibly aided and abetted by the Communist State—the goal the disappearance of the Jew."[19] And not only Judaism but religion in general—"the opiate of the masses"—was threatened by Marxism. Again, this was conventional wisdom that Kahane deployed for his own purposes. In words that echoed those of American Cold Warrior religious leaders such as Billy Graham, Kahane predicted that the political victory of communism would result in "the general onslaught of religion: the clear goal of destroying God; the past and present persecutions of Judaism, the attempt to eradicate Jewish identity. All clearly indicate what kind of future Jewry would expect to have under the benevolent rule of autocratic Communism."[20]

Against this backdrop, Kahane urges his target audience of young, left-leaning American Jews to drop their anti-imperialist agenda and cast their lot with the American project. He does not deny the reality of American imperialism as much as try to argue for its merits given the Sino-Soviet alternative. For Kahane it was a price worth paying to prevent the erasure of Judaism and Jewishness. The relative freedom America provided its population, and certainly its Jews, was worth saving if only for the sake of Jewish survival. Writing in 1967, Kahane asserted that "communism is to the Jewish soul what Nazism was to its body. The Marxist-Leninists are the deadly enemies of Jews and Judaism, seeking spiritual and national genocide. Let us remember this the next time we feel constrained to protest United States defense of Vietnam and remember that, there but for the grace of God and the United States military, go we."[21] America, in this view, is the protector of the Jews and the defender of freedom against the Marxist-Leninist project, thereby preventing the erasure of the Jew though assimilation or national destruction. But America is not immune to communism and can protect its citizens, including its Jewish citizens, from it only if it is able to exercise its imperialist muscle. In 1967 that effort was most prominently focused on the war in Vietnam.[22] "Somewhere it [communism] must be stopped and the symbol of the Free World's stand today is the pain-wracked land of Vietnam. It is there where American Jewry pins its hopes and its prayers that it will be spared the cry of that forlorn, elderly Russian Jew: 'Help me so that my Volodenka will remain a Jew.'"[23] In short, for Kahane Eisenhower's "domino theory" became the guarantor of Jewish survival.

Kahane contra Soviet Communism

On June 9, 1968, Kahane testified before the House Un-American Activities Committee on communism and Soviet anti-Semitism. In the synopsis of the testimony we read that Kahane said he had made "a 15-year study of communism and Soviet anti-Semitism." He did study international relations at the NYU School of Law, but that would hardly have made him expert enough for congressional testimony. And the only thing Kahane had to show for his fifteen-year study was *The Jewish Stake in Vietnam* and the earlier series of articles "Communism vs. Judaism" in the *Jewish Press*, which Kahane claimed in his testimony was "the largest Anglo-Jewish newspaper in the country."[24] The likelihood is that his name was given to Congress by Joseph Churba.

In his testimony Kahane defined the JDL as an organization "to defend the Jewish people against anti-Semitism and to defend this country against various extremist groups such as the Communists and the black nationalists."[25] He did so without making any mention of Soviet Jewry and the movement to emancipate it. And while Kahane invokes Israel in his remarks, it is not a focus.

Kahane's goal was to inform the committee about communism in America and in the Soviet Union but also about the Jewish plight in Russia in historical perspective.[26] He also stressed communism's negation not just of Judaism but of all religions: "All faiths in the Soviet Union are persecuted. The *Jewish Press* has come out time and again calling for the American Jew to stand up in protest against the persecution of the Baptists in the Soviet Union."[27] Kahane wanted to impress on the committee the alleged connection between the Jewish plight in the Soviet Union and America's battle against communism in Southeast Asia, as well as the idea of an inherent link between America and Israel. Regarding Israel, Kahane draws some of these threads together in his testimony: "Unfortunately, very, very few people know or realize how closely linked American foreign policy is to American security, the American future, is linked to that of freedom-loving nations such as Israel, and I would like to make a comment right here that I believe my newspaper believes that the majority of American Jews believe, that the war in Vietnam and the war in the Middle East were part of the same war, same enemies. . . . Communism is an entity, a unity. The Israeli troops fought for America. American troops in Vietnam fight for Israel."[28]

Kahane's perception here was out of step with majority American Jewish public opinion. Most American Jews by 1968 were opposed to the war in Vietnam. In almost every poll taken in the late 1960s, Jewish opposition to the war was among the strongest of any American group. In its report on a giant antiwar demonstration in Washington in November 1969, the Jewish Telegraphic Agency noted the huge Jewish participation in the rally and in antiwar activities more generally.[29] This antiwar cast of mind of most American Jews at the time, while acknowledged in the Jewish press, was ignored not just by Kahane and his allies but by the Israeli government itself, which was keen to solidify Israel's bond with the US by amplifying this Kahanist theme of a unified Cold War front against communism. Then-Israeli prime minister Golda Meir, for example, who took a positive view of President Nixon's prowar "Silent Majority" speech of November 3, 1969. Given this insistence on the Soviet Union-Vietnam-Israel triangle and the Cold War message, it is understandable why Kahane's testimony was filled with criticisms of American Jewish leaders and organizations that refused to follow this script. Mindful that the congressional committee was not well-informed about the various factions of the American Jewish community, he stressed that the left-wing Jewish position of being both anti–Vietnam War and pro-Israel was untenable. If one was against the war one could not be a bona fide supporter of Israel and vice versa. For Kahane, as he stated emphatically in his testimony regarding the Middle East and Vietnam, "it is one war."[30]

Kahane and the Soviet Jewish Crusade

Shortly after this June 1968 testimony, Kahane and his JDL—as we have seen—turned their attention to the issues of race and black anti-Semitism in America. By late 1969 the JDL would change course yet again and become the militant arm of the Soviet Jewry movement. The activist turn to Soviet Jewry officially began on December 29, 1969, when JDL members vandalized the New York offices of the Soviet press agency TASS, the Soviet tour operator

Intourist, and the Soviet airline Aeroflot and leapt aboard a Soviet jet at Kennedy Airport. The next day the JDL broke through police barriers at the Soviet Mission in Manhattan in an illegal protest.

The JDL's harassment of Soviet diplomats—following them in cars, jeering at them in the streets, and cursing them in Russian—took a violent turn very quickly. On January 8, 1971, a bomb went off in the Soviet cultural building in Washington. This was the JDL's first official operation in the nation's capital and part of Kahane's campaign to tie the cause of Soviet Jewry to militant anticommunism.[31] After the bombing news agencies received anonymous calls saying, "This is a sample of things to come. Let our people go. Never again." It was a shot across the bow. JDL spokesperson Bertram Zweibon denied the JDL had anything to do with the bombing but applauded it nonetheless—a classic JDL tactic. The incident immediately raised the ire of the Soviet government, and Foreign Minister Andrei Gromyko registered a formal complaint.[32]

Kahane knew that harassment and even bombing would only rattle the Soviets and not facilitate a change in policy. To have a deeper impact he needed more widespread support. He knew there was sympathy for the JDL's position on Soviet Jewry, yet he also knew many who were reluctant to sign on because of the violence and the recent bombing.[33] He knew Washington's desire for détente would prevent it from pushing the Soviets too hard on an issue that was largely a Jewish cause. He understood he had to make it worthwhile for both the US and the Soviet Union to act. All this drove his call for civil disobedience.

About a year later, when in court for instigating the 1969 riot at the Soviet Mission by ignoring police barricades, Kahane cynically claimed that he was simply trying to pray at the Park East Synagogue located directly across the street from the mission. The jury threw out the charge of resisting arrest but found him guilty of disorderly conduct. After the conviction Kahane held a brief news conference outside the courthouse. When asked about the trial he said, "It was a fair trial, a fair jury, a fair judge, and a lousy verdict."[34] But even if "lousy," the verdict served the purpose of giving him "street cred" as a militant on the Soviet Jewry issue; he had achieved his aim. This, however, was just the beginning; immediately after the news conference he raced to Kennedy Airport to catch a flight to Brussels so as to "crash" an international conference on Soviet Jewry that would begin the following day.

The international conference held in the Palais des Congrès in Brussels on February 23-25, 1971, was intended to give public voice to Soviet Jewry's plight.[35] It included a major delegation of 250 Americans as well as strong delegations from Europe and Israel. Attending were some of the great Jewish leaders and intellectuals of the time, including film director Otto Preminger, screenwriter Paddy Chayefsky, writers Elie Wiesel and Saul Bellow, scholar Gershom Scholem, American rabbi Alexander Schindler, head of the Herut Party Menachem Begin, and Labor Party leader Golda Meir. An elderly and ailing David Ben-Gurion was also in attendance. By choosing to attend the conference after his initial request for an invitation was rejected by the committee, Kahane gained an international setting in which to publicly accuse the Jewish establishment of being complacent and ineffectual in defending Jewish interests—charges similar to those he had launched in New York during the school strike a few years before. After successfully avoiding serious punishment for his actions, he was taking his "street cred" to the establishment.

The moment, for Kahane, was propitious. By 1971 the race wars had died down; the Vietnam War was widely unpopular; and he needed a new cause to breathe life into his movement. Kahane was particularly eager for this opportunity specifically after his formal request to speak there had been denied. After arriving in Brussels and being met by JDL members who had arrived a few days earlier, he strode with his small group into the conference uninvited and sent a personal note to the chairman requesting to speak. Reflecting on the conference some years later in 1975, Kahane summarized his reasons for attending: "I went to Brussels because I feared that the conference would content itself with platitudes. It did. I went to Brussels because I sensed that concrete programs would not even be on the agenda. They were not. I went to Brussels because, if playwrights and producers and authors and architects who have little or no share in the struggle for Soviet Jewry were allowed entry, representatives that had literally spilled their blood on barricades and gone to prison for our oppressed brethren had a moral and natural right to speak."[36]

The ten-point platform that Kahane wished to present was not in keeping with the outlook of most of the conference speakers, who were calling for quiet diplomacy with the Kremlin on behalf of Soviet Jews. This was the tack taken by Yaakov Birnbaum, founder of the Student Society for Soviet Jewry (SSSJ) in 1964. Among other things, Kahane called for an immediate cessation of talks with the USSR on disarmament, space, culture, and trade, as well as a full trade embargo, a ban of Soviet athletes from the Olympics, nonviolent civil disobedience, and nonstop daily demonstrations at all official Soviet installations. Basically Kahane was demanding that the US launch a boycott of the Soviet Union until Jews were free to emigrate. It was an unrealistic plan with little chance of official US support, which Kahane knew. But he also knew that public patience for unavailing diplomacy was growing short. He knew many American Jewish youth had been radicalized. And his presence at the conference gave him the international notoriety he craved and launched his new career as the self-proclaimed militant arm of the Soviet Jewry movement. The issue itself had widespread support among American Jews, and this shift would gain him prominence and popularity. But it would also lead to his downfall in America and that of the JDL as well.

Kahane attained this notoriety despite being denied access to the conference podium, and maybe even because of it. It is unclear whether the conference organizers called the Belgian police, who arrested Kahane and removed him from the premises. In the end, no formal charges were filed. But Kahane certainly benefited from the rumors circulating at the gathering that its organizers had called on the local police to arrest and eject him. Menachem Begin, the only one in the closed session who voted in favor of allowing Kahane to speak, accused the organizers of an "un-Jewish act" in turning him over to the police.[37] Delegate Morris Brafman, a Holocaust survivor, supporter of Ze'ev Jabotinsky's Revisionist Zionism, and wealthy Manhattan entrepreneur, jumped onto the stage, grabbed the microphone, and began yelling "Meir Kahane has been arrested! I demand to know who ordered Meir Kahane arrested!"[38] Otto Preminger went even further in his public address that evening, saying Kahane had been treated "exactly as contemptible [*sic*] and wrong as what the Nazis and the Soviet Communists have done."[39] The *New York Times* story on the conference featured Kahane's ousting more prominently than Golda Meir's summation speech. The episode made the front pages of newspapers worldwide—in Vienna, Amsterdam, Antwerp, Paris, London, Hamburg, Rome, and even in South America.[40]

Essentially Kahane turned the conference on its head. Its leaders were now being accused by participants of the same discriminatory practices they claimed to be protesting against. It was similar to the guerrilla theater in which Yippies Jerry Rubin and Abbie Hoffman threw five-dollar bills onto Wall Street and then photographed grown men in suits diving in the streets, fighting for the money. And such accusations against the conference organizers dovetailed with Kahane's own general critique of liberalism: its claim to openness was really a disguise for the exclusion of more radical views. For Kahane Brussels aptly illustrated precisely what was wrong with the Jewish establishment on numerous fronts.

In sum, the Brussels conference was a coup for Kahane. The proceedings themselves were largely ignored, and his protest became the main event. As Gal Beckerman noted, "It was Kahane's moment and he grabbed it. In the weeks leading up to and following the Brussels conference, he brought unprecedented attention to Soviet Jewry"—and I would add, to the JDL as well.[41] Kahane won in Brussels on two fronts: first, he succeeded in getting Soviet Jewry on the front pages of newspapers worldwide; second, he succeeded in getting people to pay attention to *him* while bringing embarrassment to the liberal establishment. Being denied the podium allowed him to play the martyr, which he did to perfection when he returned to the US.

On the heels of the Brussels coup de théâtre, Kahane furthered his campaign in the US to capture the headlines and overshadow moderate-liberal Jewish voices on the Soviet Jewish cause. To those ends he organized a large rally in Washington a month after Brussels, on March 21, 1971.

The 1971 Washington Rally

In 1971 Kahane watched closely as antiwar sentiment among young Americans eroded support for the war with large protests. He knew of the October 1967 rally in Washington that attracted over a hundred thousand people and had a strong impact on the antiwar movement. Kahane also knew he could not fall into the trap of being labeled simply a "terrorist," even as he was convinced that in speaking truth to power as he saw it, violence always had to be an option. Like many others in his time, he claimed to be a militant for a just cause. And yet he still tried to navigate the narrow path between acts of violence and nonviolent protest.

He also knew he needed the JDL to work with the SSSJ and not in opposition to it. To that end he cosponsored a rally at Hunter College in Manhattan on February 14, 1971, with a group called Student Activists, a front for the JDL modeled after the SSSJ. Having the ear of more moderate Soviet Jewry advocates, he used that rally to reinstate his policy of harassment. Kahane was trying to play both sides—advocating violence and nonviolence—in such a way that each would strengthen the other.

In preparation for the Washington rally on March 21 that year, Kahane called for the JDL to hold smaller rallies in state capitals. These took place in Providence, Albany, and Philadelphia. Kahane spent considerable resources publicizing the Washington rally, including a paid advertisement in the *New York*

Times that drew a connection between Soviet Jewry and Auschwitz: "This is the price of silence. . . . [In] 1943 . . . we knew that 12,000 Jews were daily being shipped to Auschwitz . . . because of that silence 6,000,000 died. . . . Come with us to the White House, Sunday. . . . You can help free Soviet Jewry if you get off your apathy."[42] Linking the present to the Holocaust past was a common trope for Kahane dating back to his early writings, especially *Never Again!* Even though the Soviet Union was not Nazi Germany, he knew this was a successful way to evoke the interest of his audience and the angst of the Jewish youth.

The Washington rally was a great success and arguably overshadowed the SSSJ's local activities at the time. Over five thousand people showed up in Washington for Kahane's event, mostly young and very passionate Jews from both the right and the left. Protesters sat down and refused to move from the streets they were blocking, knowing they were going to be arrested. In the end more than 1,300 were arrested, at the time the largest arrest total for civil disobedience in Washington's history. The rally was covered extensively in the national press. Many heartfelt stories were told about Jewish teenagers calling their parents to ask permission to be arrested. An oft-cited *Washington Post* article by Carl Bernstein of Watergate fame reported on the event: "As he led the young man away to be arrested, the patrolman turned to his sergeant, then whispered, 'I kind of hate to do it; these kids are different.' Indeed aside from their youth, the determined army of Jews who sat down in the streets near the Soviet Embassy yesterday bear few resemblances with those with whom Washington's police are more accustomed to dealing."[43] The protesters heeded Kahane's call during the rally not to engage in violence or resist arrest. "If a policeman touches you," he exhorted, "stand up and go with him, and tomorrow morning the papers will say 5,000 Jews got arrested for Soviet Jewry."[44] The rally showed that Kahane could work the more nonviolent side of the movement successfully, even as he justified acts of violence for the cause in other settings.

More than drawing attention to the cause, Kahane viewed the rally as proving that Jews, even those on the left, could fight for Jewish issues. In April 1971 he wrote, "Here were Jews marching and being arrested, not for Vietnam or Laos or Mozambique, or Antarctica. Here were Jews defying all the laws of the 1960s and crying out for their own people."[45]

With the Brussels conference in February 1971 and the Washington rally in March, Kahane engaged in two nonviolent initiatives that brought him large-scale recognition. He was poised to become a major Jewish activist. The March 1971 rally represented the high-water mark of Kahane's American popularity. In the wake of his triumphs in Brussels and Washington, a *Newsweek* poll in 1971 showed that one in four Americans had a positive view of the JDL. But this moment in the sun would be short-lived. Kahane's dalliance with violence persisted, overshadowing his public calls for nonviolent civil disobedience and soon leading to the death of an innocent woman.

The Beginning of the End of Kahane's American Project: The Sol Hurok Bombing

As the 1960s moved into the 1970s, violence was very much part of legitimate political discourse among radicals. Activists were seriously reading Frantz Fanon's *Wretched of the Earth*. In 1970 the Weather Underground broke from the more politically moderate Students for a Democratic Society over the issue of violence. The Weathermen argued that the only way to get Nixon and the "American war machine" to end the war was to "bring it home"—that is, to commit acts of public violence so as to inflict pain on American citizens. Kahane's attitude was similar to the Weathermen except that to "bring it home" meant to the Soviet Union. He believed that where Soviet Jews were concerned, the only way to effect change in Soviet policy was to inflict pain on the Soviet diplomatic corps and Russian citizens taking part in Soviet state-sponsored missions in the US. This was not easily accomplished.

Acts of low-level harassment and violence were difficult to organize against Soviet diplomats who were protected by security. It was much easier to attack softer targets: Soviet cultural groups such as musical, theatrical, orchestral, and dance contingents who visited the US on cultural exchange programs, attracting large audiences, making large sums of money, and spreading Soviet culture to Americans during a Nixon-administration program of US-Soviet détente. Kahane knew that targeting such groups would attract more media attention than harassing Soviet diplomats on their way home from work. Throughout 1971 young JDLers at Kahane's instigation disrupted Bolshoi Ballet performances and other Soviet cultural events numerous times in multiple cities. These acts resulted in a few arrests for disrupting the peace and were generally treated as no more than a nuisance.[46] But that would change in the following year.

Aside from the Soviet artists, the JDL also set its sights on the American impresarios who booked Soviet acts. Once such impresario was Sol Hurok, a Jewish talent agent with an office in midtown Manhattan. A little after 9:00 a.m. on January 27, 1972, a bomb went off in the offices of his Sol Hurok Enterprises, causing a fire that injured thirteen employees and killed a twenty-seven-year-old Jewish employee, Iris Kones, who died of smoke inhalation.[47]

Five days before the bombing, Kahane's son Baruch became a bar mitzvah, with the ceremony taking place in Jerusalem.[48] When contacted about the incident in Israel, where he was living by that time, Kahane called it "an insane act" and denied any prior knowledge or connection to the bombing. However, he offered help and moral support for JDL members who were arrested for it.[49] That spring Kahane went on a speaking tour in the US, including an appearance on the *Dick Cavett Show* on June 7, 1972. On Sunday, June 11, he went to take part in an annual convention of the North American Jewish Students Network. It was there that he found out on June 16 that three JDL members had been arrested for the Hurok bombing. He extended his stay in the US to try and help them; but charges were eventually dropped due to insufficient evidence. Living in Israel, Kahane indeed may not have known about the Hurok bombing beforehand, but he certainly condoned and encouraged the purchase of weapons and the building of explosives, which ultimately led to the attack. By this time Kahane's day-to-day control of the JDL had waned. And yet, while JDL sympathizers or militants may have instigated it alone, Kahane had lit a fuse and then escaped across the ocean without extinguishing it.

It was well-known that Kahane hated Hurok for supporting Soviet cultural projects as much as he hated Leonard and Felicia Bernstein for holding a fundraiser for the Black Panthers.[50] But this bombing of a Jewish business and murder of an innocent Jew weighed on his conscience. This became clearer in September 1974, when, in an internal letter to JDL members, he wrote: "I say this with great sadness, into the JDL has [*sic*] come certain elements whose conduct, language, and character were the antithesis of everything that HADAR, Jewish pride, was meant to be. Threats of physical violence against Jews, filthy language and the concept of the JDL as some kind of street gang will never be things that the JDL was meant to contain AND THEY NEVER WILL BE."[51] Clearly Kahane felt that these JDL members, left to their own devices and rudderless after his family's emigration to Israel late in 1971, had crossed a red line.[52] As Alan Rocoff, a Kahane supporter, wrote to Libby Kahane, "After the death of the Hurok employee, Meir was subconsciously closing down the JDL."[53]

By 1974 Kahane had long since turned his attention to his new Israeli life and political career. The JDL he had abandoned had by then lost any real sense of purpose and indeed devolved into a kind of street gang. The race wars of the late 1960s were over; America's role in the Vietnam War was over. The Soviet

Jewry movement had a life of its own and progress was being made along diplomatic channels, with the Israeli government becoming more involved. The JDL no longer had any real ideological purpose; it became mostly an outlet for Jewish rage. Those who remained after Kahane left included many young Jews who probably had never even read his earlier articles on communism or his book on the war in Vietnam. They likely were unfamiliar with the triangle he had constructed between Soviet Jews, Russian aid to the Arab world, and the affinity between the Viet Cong and the PLO.

It is often lost on many who knew Kahane, or knew of him, in those days and thereafter that before he adopted the activism that would lead from a highly successful Washington rally in March 1971 that was nonviolent in accordance with his demand, to the disastrous Hurok bombing in January 1972, he had crafted a theoretical foundation for his program. One may not agree with it, and it surely stretched credibility, but it was a justification for militancy not unlike what was espoused by the Black Panthers or some factions of SDS.

I think historians often look at Kahane's contribution to the Soviet Jewry movement in reverse, but doing so gives a skewed picture of how this fits into his larger project. That is, they view it as an exercise of violence and rage. That is because by about 1972 and thereafter his approach mostly involved violence and wreaking havoc. But if we look at its prehistory in *The Jewish Stake in Vietnam* (1967), his anticommunist work with the FBI, and his articles on "Communism vs. Judaism" in the *Jewish Press*, we get a different picture. His shift to Soviet Jewry in late 1969 appears to have been aimed partly at bolstering his organization, which was losing momentum in its race-related activism. And once he latched onto Soviet Jewry he had to define himself against the establishment, which had already set up an infrastructure of diplomacy he could never agree with. The Jewish liberals he confronted in the Soviet Jewry movement were not unlike the gentile liberals he confronted in the aftermath of the 1968 school strike. Liberalism, for Kahane, would always lean toward socialism. And socialism would always threaten Jewish survival, and certainly the survival of Judaism.

But Kahane's move to the Soviet Jewry issue is more complex than that. Soviet Jewry was not simply an exercise in opportunism for Kahane. To think so misses something important in understanding him on everything from race to Zionism. It is true that Kahane was a reactive thinker and often seemed to have only short-term goals in mind. But when we place Soviet Jewry in the larger perspective, we can see it as an integral part of a program of Jewish identity politics, pride (*hadar*), and a post-Holocaust attempt to rebuild Jewish existence through a critique of liberalism and assimilation.

One of the tragedies of Kahane's role in the Soviet Jewry movement is that the adaptation of militancy from his antiblack period to the Soviet Jewry issue never worked. Contesting a world power is not like contesting a persecuted minority; the stakes were much higher. Kahane did not seem to understand that when he entered the international arena, he was in the big leagues and the rules were different. His JDL, filled with confidence at the prospect of real power and popularity after the Brussels conference and the Washington rally, went into a tailspin after the Hurok-bombing debacle. Kahane's career was subsequently destroyed in America, and having already moved to Israel, he had a chance to start over. But he seemed to keep making the same mistake.[54]

5

Zionism

KAHANE'S ZIONISM: THE POLITICAL EXPERIMENT OF ABNORMALITY AND ITS TRAGIC DEMISE

"There will be no peace between Jews and Arabs as long as there remains a Jewish state of *any* kind, no matter how small."

MEIR KAHANE, *OUR CHALLENGE* (1974), 26

"From a magnificent miracle, a State of the Jewish People, we have turned into a state of anarchy, a state of confusion, a state of despair."

MEIR KAHANE, DEBATE WITH ALAN DERSHOWITZ, NEW YORK, NOVEMBER 10, 1984

"I don't hate Arabs. I love Jews."

MEIR KAHANE, *UNCOMFORTABLE QUESTIONS FOR COMFORTABLE JEWS* (1987), 319

Prelude

The previous chapters presented Kahane's early thought as manifested in his writings—mostly journalistic—and his public activities, drawing from published and archival materials. While Kahane wrote prodigiously in those early years, the only two books he published were *The Jewish Stake in Vietnam* in 1967, coauthored with Joseph Churba, and *Never Again!* in 1971, released just as he was emigrating to Israel.

Once he settled in Israel he began a more sustained writing endeavor, publishing books in English and Hebrew both about Israel and America. While he remained an activist in Israel, spending ample time in its prisons, Kahane rose to political prominence through his public persona while also producing a body of written work that laid out his Zionist vision for the future of the country. This culminated in his *The Jewish Idea*, which is the subject of the final chapter of this study.

To convey a nuanced sense of Kahane's Israeli career and his idiosyncratic Zionist vision, this chapter traces the development of his writings from the early 1970s through the late 1980s. What seems more important to me than his public activities in Israel is his developing Zionist ideology, which began to take root both in Israel and America. Thus, these final two chapters focus primarily on his writings so as to examine more closely a vision of the Jewish future that was eventually rejected by the Israeli political establishment but remains popular in certain circles to this day. This was illustrated by the anecdote about the encounter with a Modern Orthodox Jew at a bat mitzvah buffet that framed the introduction. While Kahane's early career in America was primarily as an activist and gadfly, in Israel he became an ideologue and political force. A close examination of his writings is the best way to explore that phenomenon.

Although, as he turns to Israel, Kahane's radicalism takes a somewhat different form than it did in America, the basic elements of his Israeli career are rooted in his Americanness. In America his radicalism was aimed at the assimilatory liberalism of what he called the "establishment," and his larger critique was (1) that anti-Semitism would rise whenever there was a social crisis (such as America's defeat in Vietnam) and (2) that tolerance would serve as the "kiss of death" for American Jewry through assimilation. What might remain was what later became known as JINO (Jews in name only), but any substantive Jewishness would disappear.

In Israel, Kahane's radicalism is expressed through his rejection of Zionism as "normalcy"—that is, to be "like all the other nations." He believed this was a trap that had plagued the entire Zionist project and would ultimately cause its collapse. This, in his view, was manifested in numerous ways, but Kahane's focus was on Zionism's alleged veneration of democracy above the value of Jewish exclusivity, dominance, and power. By promoting the equality of Jewish and non-Jewish citizens, he considered, Israeli democracy could undermine the survival of a true Jewish state. Kahane believed in democracy everywhere but in Israel. Israel had a different calling, and to fulfill its destiny it had to be "abnormal," an interesting inversion of the anti-Semitic trope of Jews as an abnormal people. The coherence of Israel as both a democracy and a Jewish state has been the topic of ongoing conversations among Zionists and Israeli legal experts for decades. Kahane was one of the early voices, certainly on the right, to argue that Israel as a democracy *and* a Jewish state was simply incoherent.[1]

The similarity to the American context is that for Kahane "normalcy" was a kind of political assimilation. By creating a society where all citizens were assured equality, Israel could never be a Jewish state but would merely reproduce a diasporic framework under the aegis of autonomy. The failure of Zionism for Kahane was that it could not free itself from the shackles of diasporic thinking.[2] Zionism, or at least the Zionism that came to reject him, became for him the great failure of Jewish resolve to substantiate abnormality through political sovereignty. It became, in his words, "Jewish Hellenism."

While Kahane's focus on Israel took him away from the American context, one of the often overlooked aspects of his provisional Zionism was how American it was. The racial categorizations (in the early 1970s, as noted, he went after the Black Hebrews of Dimona) and the fear of assimilation (one of his first political proposals in Israel was to outlaw Jewish-Arab dating) were all American ideas, or fears, that Kahane transplanted onto Israeli soil. Why should a majority society like the Jewish Israelis fear that a small number of them might marry Arabs? What dangers would that portend? Interestingly, then, while Kahane was accusing mainstream Israelis of "Americanness" when it came to democracy and equality, he was just as guilty of Americanness in his call for separatism and injecting race into Israeli discourse.

Finally, this chapter is more than a descriptive analysis of Kahane's Zionism. It shows that the components of his Zionism include the Revisionism of Jabotinsky, the adaptation of religion as a vehicle of power, American ideas about race, revolutionary separatism, a critique of false aspirations to equality, and a messianism that indeed seems to pervade Zionism even in its more moderate forms. This results in a Zionism that deconstructs itself and becomes its opposite, in Kahane's case a kind of militant and apocalyptic post-Zionism. Kahane moves to Israel to realize that the Zionism that rules the state, like the liberal American Judaism he left behind, fails to achieve precisely what modernity offered the Jews: a state in which to maintain their categorical abnormality while protecting it from physical harm.

Beginnings

> Meir [Kahane] was a soloist at the memorial service for Ze'ev Jabotinsky's widow. *Tel Hai* [the Betar movement's newsletter] reported: "On December 24, 1949, a Betar misdar [assembly] honored the recent death of the 'Mother of Betar' Madam Hannah Jabotinsky. As the Betar members stood at attention, Meir Kahane chanted the beautiful and deeply moving 'El Malei Rahamim'" [a prayer of remembrance].[3]

> Some former Betar members I interviewed said that Meir left Betar after the February 1951 convention because he was not elected *naziv* [head of American Betar]. It seems more likely however that the influence of his friends Avraham Silbert and Baruch Gefand with whom he studied at the Mirrer Yeshiva and Brooklyn College, moved him to Bnei Akiva. Meir told me that with the establishment of the State of Israel, Betar's main goal—supporting the Irgun—was no longer relevant. Now the challenge was to ensure the state's religious character.[4]

These two anecdotes convey two pillars of Kahane's Zionism. From the first, we see that Ze'ev Jabotinsky, the right-wing Revisionist Zionist thinker and politician, and mentor to Menachem Begin, was a mythic figure for him. Jabotinsky was a friend of Kahane's father Charles Kahane and would sometimes stay at the Kahane home in Brooklyn when visiting America. Kahane was born in 1932 and Jabotinsky died in upstate New York in 1940, so Kahane could have remembered him only as a young child. But those memories certainly remained a crucial part of his self-fashioning. Much of what he wrote early on about Zionism seems to be paraphrasing Jabotinsky with a religious flavor baked in.[5] Kahane would become one of Jabotinsky's most influential—and radical—interpreters.

The second anecdote, also told by Libby Kahane, is a useful window into Kahane's Zionism. In his youth, the notion of Jewish survival and religious life in Israel were separate. Survival took priority over religious life. Jabotinsky and the Revisionists were not religious, and they conceived of Israel as a secular state. Kahane, by contrast, was raised Orthodox and was a member of the Bnei Akiva religious youth movement as a teenager, and he was influenced by religious Zionism. For Kahane, once survival was assured through a state and an army, the religious nature of the state became more of a focus.[6] Like most other things about him, his Zionism is complicated and idiosyncratic, incorporating numerous countervailing forces.[7]

The core of Kahane's Zionism was that Israel's right to the land should be viewed as a divine mandate, and conquering it as a religious obligation rather than a secular solution to a modern Jewish problem. The establishment of the state owed nothing to the nations of the world—the so-called international community—since the "state of Israel," for him, had always existed; it was not a creation of the United Nations. He argued for an unabashed and unashamed theo-political justification of the state, based on a biblical promise: "This is Zionism and this is the Jewish claim to the Land of Israel. Not a nationalist one, not simply because 'we once lived there,' not because of a Balfour, a League of Nations or United ones. Not a request or a plea but a proud claim, based on a Divine grant."[8]

In his 1978 book *Listen World, Listen Jew* Kahane writes, "The sovereignty of the Jewish people over the entirety of the Land of Israel must be proclaimed by virtue of the promise of the Almighty and the historical fact of tenure and unbroken hope of return based on that promise."[9] As an assertion this is not as unprecedented in the history of Zionist thought as one might think.[10] In his address to the World Zionist Conference in August 1957, David Ben-Gurion stated that there were three components of Zionism: attachment to the ancient homeland, the Hebrew language, and the messianic promise of redemption. For Kahane, however, Ben-Gurion's secular Zionism was a wrong-headed and destructive force. It may have had its use in persuading Jews to settle in the land of Israel, but it was incapable of sustaining Jewish life in the Holy Land over the long term. Thus Kahane's Zionism was at war against the Zionism upon which the state was founded.

Separating from the past is an occupational hazard of autonomy, and for Kahane many secular Zionists, including many native-born Israeli Jews (sabras), fall into this trap. They see themselves as free of the past—as "New Jews"—but for Kahane this is an odious kind of Jewish novelty. With no deep connection to Jewish history and to their God, sabras have no sense of Jewish national destiny and purpose. For Kahane, ironically, what one needs in order to have this sense is the painful experience of the Diaspora Jew: the experience of exile. As he writes, "The sabra does not know the Galut, never had the anti-Semite give him a beating and a negative reason for being a Jew."[11]

The Zionism of Ben-Gurion, for Kahane, produces "Hebrew-speaking *goyim*," "gentilized Hebrews," and a liberal Hellenistic state of the Jews. A state run by such Jews is a tragic missed opportunity.[12] Against the Ben-Gurion project Kahane espouses a very different understanding of Zionism, one that is the fulfillment of Judaism *itself* and that represents the telos of Jewish history. It is a Judaism that is unafraid, "abnormal," and harbors no guilt.[13] (As Kahane wrote in the 1980s, "The AIDS of the Jewish people in our time is guilt.")[14] And it is the antithesis of a secular project. This line of thinking, as we will see, leads Kahane away from the position of an immanent critic of the Zionist project to that of a post-Zionist thinker.

Kahane maintained that something had gone wrong with the Zionist endeavor. The native Israelis were losing their connection to the divine nature of their history. They were increasingly seeing themselves as free of the past as New Jews yet, for Kahane, a false kind of New Jew. As he saw it, this marked the death of Zionism from another direction: not that of absorbing the liberal ethos of the West, but that of losing a sense of national mission.[15] The Zionism of Ben-Gurion was "a product of environmental nostalgia," an exilic mentality that combined rights founded on secular principles and fear of the gentile. Such Jews merely brought diasporic thinking to the Holy Land. In short, the Zionist establishment had failed to shed itself of exile and failed to see itself as the fulfillment of Judaism (and not simply as the telos of Jewish history). By the late 1980s Kahane believed that the state of Israel was becoming a travesty and a tragedy.[16]

It is noteworthy here that this chapter is based primarily on his Zionist writings and less on their reception. *Never Again!* sold over a hundred thousand copies and was a publishing bonanza for its time, but its audience was mainly American. *Our Challenge*, his first book written in Israel, and exclusively on Zionism, was an utter failure both in English and Hebrew. His other works gained a larger following. Books like *Forty Years*, *They Must Go*, and *A Thorn in Our Sides* (first published in Hebrew), all written in the mid-1980s, were widely read in Israel, less so in America. Finally, *The Jewish Idea*, Kahane's summa, remains his most widely read book. His books' reception seemed to follow his rise in prominence. When he was elected to the Knesset in 1984 his readership, both among those who loved him and those who hated him, rose precipitously.

Early Writings on Zionism: Zionism as Pride (*Hadar*)

Never Again!, released in 1971, was Kahane's most popular book, selling ten thousand hardcover and a hundred thousand softcover copies. It was the idea of Edward L. Nash, a young Jewish advertising executive from New York who started a publishing company in Los Angeles called Nash Publishing. Nash knew of the JDL and was sympathetic to its program. In an email to Libby Kahane in July 2000 he wrote, "JDL was of special interest to me because of boyhood memories of running a gauntlet of anti-Semitic bullies (in the Bronx) who gathered around our Hebrew school."[17] This was a common sentiment among many of Nash's generation (born 1936), perhaps most famously articulated by Norman Podhoretz in his 1963 *Commentary* article "My Negro Problem—and Ours."[18] Nash had the idea for Kahane's book and also came up with the title. Kahane began writing it, according to Libby Kahane, in April 1971 and submitted the manuscript in June. Upon receiving it Nash telegrammed him, "Manuscript received, better than anything we could have hoped for. It's a beautiful as well as an important book."[19]

In the one chapter on Zionism in *Never Again!*, Israel functions largely as a source of pride for the Diaspora Jew rather than as a place to live. At this stage in his career, Kahane was still committed to advocating heightened ethnic self-assertion and mobilization of American Jews within the US rather than mass emigration to the Holy Land. His views of America, and its continued viability as a home for Jews, pervade *Never Again!* and also make an appearance in the above-cited private JDL publication *A Manifesto*, likely published in late 1968: "America has been good to the Jews and the Jew has been good to America. A land founded on the principles of democracy and freedom has given unprecedented opportunities to a people devoted to those ideals. . . . The dream that is America . . . is in immense danger today, and all the citizens of these United States face the consequences of the collapse of that dream." In the late 1960s and early 1970s, Kahane had yet to give up on the Jewish Diaspora; Zionism remained for him a functional tool of Jewish pride. Thus he portrays Israel, at this time, less as a country in which to live than a place that allows American Jews to hold their heads high with a sense of Jewish might. Kahane's telling of Jewish history in *Never Again!* provides his intended audience—in particular, young American Jews tempted by the New Left but put off by the demonization of Israel by most progressive groups of the day—with a cadre of heroes they can relate to. "There are, of course," he remarks, "no Jewish heroes of note and the Jewish Nationalist Liberation Movement is surely a My Miami Beach night club routine." He follows this, however, with an exhortation: "Sit down, Grandson of a stubborn zeyde [grandfather] and learn something about your people."[20]

Instead of telling his readers how the kibbutzim made the desert green—Otto Preminger's 1961 film depiction of Leon Uris's 1958 book *Exodus* having strongly influenced how many American Jews saw Israel—Kahane's *Never Again!* gives an alternative history. Its Jewish heroes are not the pioneers farming in malaria-infested swamps and hot deserts but instead people like Shlomo Ben-Yosef. A member of the Irgun terrorist group found guilty of attacking an Arab bus in April 1938 and hanged by the British, he was the first Jew to be hung for terrorism in the Mandate period.[21] Or Eliyahu Hakim and Eliyahu Bet-Zuri, the assassins of Lord Moyne (the anti-Zionist British politician

Walter Edward Guinness) in Cairo in 1944.[22] Kahane presents the Ben-Yosefs and Eliyahu Hakims of history as the heroic revolutionaries of the Jews—like Jewish Eldridge Cleavers and Che Guevaras, except that they also fulfill the dream of the hapless *zeyde* who bore the weight of exile on his shoulders. It is telling that throughout this early work, Kahane refers to Zionism as the "Jewish National Liberation Movement" (sometimes the "Jewish NLM")—an obvious gesture to the various liberation movements that were attracting the attention of the young idealists of the period.

Kahane pursued two contradictory aims in his early writings on Zionism. The first was to argue that Zionism was not a modern phenomenon but the fulfillment of an age-old central tenet of Judaism, an idea he later elaborated in *Listen World, Listen Jew*; the second was to frame Zionism as a contemporary Jewish-liberation movement.

> Israel came into being because it never came out of being. Israel came back to life because it never died. It was the Jewish State in the days of Joshua, it was a Jewish State when there were Pharoahs. . . . Do you think Theodor Herzl created Zionism? Not so! Zionism came into being the day that the Jews went into exile and was nurtured by every religious law and custom. . . . Had there been no Balfour Declaration—here would still have risen the State of Israel. Had there been no United Nations—there still would have come into being a Jewish State. . . . The stubbornness of Jewish zeydes can be denied for only so long.[23]

Absent is any mention of messianic redemption. Rather, in this early phase of Kahane's thinking, Jewish power achieves a state simply because the hope of return was so strong and persistent as to be irresistible. There is no such thing for Kahane as "modern Zionism"; it was not Theodor Herzl who created Zionism. Yet at the same time Kahane presented the "Jewish National Liberation Movement" as aligned with many of the liberation movements of the time, each one a new form of resistance against colonial and imperialist power. Although the mix of old and new is common in Zionist ideology more generally, Kahane articulates it in a very specific way. What is old is the persistent hope of return and the very notion of a state (which went back to the days of Joshua, the time of the Pharoahs). But what is new is overcoming the passive mentality of exile and the false belief that the Jew can trust anyone. What is new is the willingness of the Jew—the New Jew who is really the ancient one—to bear arms to fight for his or her liberation.[24] It is something the young Jew can relate to and be proud of—in the Diaspora.

The Maturation of Kahane's Zionism and the Quest for an Abnormal State

Kahane emigrated to Israel in September 1971 under the cloud of a five-year suspended sentence and a $5,000 fine from the US District Court in New York.[25] Getting a family settled in Israel took time, and Kahane subsisted those first few years on a salary for writing for the *Jewish Press* in Brooklyn, to which he continued to contribute weekly articles. This kept him very involved in the events unfolding in America.

One might think that as a Zionist and new immigrant, Kahane would fulfill his dream by settling in Israel and working within the system to find his place. But that was not what happened. From the outset, Kahane's Zionism did not cohere with the reality of a secular democratic state with deep roots in socialism. In fact, it was its polar opposite. For Kahane's Zionism to be fulfilled, the state would have to be transformed and the society transvalued. And he believed he was the only one who could do it. Thus he began his Israeli career as just as much, or perhaps even more, of a revolutionary than he had been in the US.

Kahane did not waste any time in pursuing a political career in Israel. In the fall of 1972 he announced his intention to run for the Knesset. He began writing *Our Challenge* as his political platform (he wrote it in English as his Hebrew was not yet good enough for that purpose). Kahane never had an easy time finding people to publish his books and often turned to a few stalwart supporters to help him. One was Benton Arnowitz, who worked for Macmillan in the early 1970s, then moved to the Chilton publishing firm, and would later become director of academic publications for the US Holocaust Memorial Museum. Arnowitz liked Kahane's ideas and agreed to publish *Our Challenge*. Even with Arnowitz's support, though, the book was a publishing failure—quite unlike Kahane's 1971 *Never Again!*—and soon fell into oblivion. Yet for our purposes it is quite useful in that it succinctly expresses Kahane's first real case for Israel as he articulated it in the 1970s, largely without the bile and bitterness that would permeate his later work. And in this slim and largely optimistic volume we can also see the seeds of many of the ideas that would emerge in the coming fifteen years, culminating in his frontal attack on the entire Zionist project in *Uncomfortable Questions*.

In 1973, while *Our Challenge* was being written, Israel was in a state of transition. The victory in the 1967 Six-Day War resulted in a tremendous problem of occupying territory and assuming responsibility for hundreds of thousands of Palestinians, many of whom lived in abject poverty in refugee camps and could not be absorbed into Israeli democracy without threatening the Jewish character of the state. Only in 1965 had Israel lifted the military rule of the Arab Triangle in the northern part of Israel proper, enabling Israel Arabs to live under civilian law, and at the outbreak of the Six-Day War the country was just beginning to absorb this population. The war also sparked the beginnings of a religious-nationalist brand of messianic Zionism. Led by the students of Rabbi Zvi Yehuda Kook, who viewed the events of 1967 as the advent of the messianic era, it would develop into a full-blown movement after the Yom Kippur War of 1973. Yet despite all these changes, Israeli society in the early 1970s still remained a product of classical Zionism, socialist and secular, a hard-fought experiment in Jewish normalization built on the foundations of modern nationalism and the right of collective self-determination.[26]

Kahane's *Our Challenge* (and the Hebrew version *Ha-Etgar: Eretz Segulah*) struck at the very heart of Zionism's claims of normalization, criticizing its dream of peaceful coexistence with its neighbors and its vision of a secularity that could embrace religion while not being overcome by it. *Our Challenge* combined the maximalist tenor of Jabotinsky's Revisionism and a nationalism rooted in religion that was neither romantic nor metaphysical in the way envisaged by the Kooks.

In this book Kahane argued that contemporary Israel had not yet disabused itself of the exilic mentality—a mentality that Kahane associated with the notion that Israel could coexist with its Arab neighbors:

> It is time for the Jew in Israel to throw away those negative attitudes that he retains from the Galut, the Exile. Chief among these is the unwillingness to look at bitter reality. . . . We may not enjoy hearing it, but the truth is that there will not be a sincere de jure peace with the Arabs. . . . It is against this enemy that we must struggle . . . a struggle for Jewish existence and a Jewish state that will never cease to be a struggle; a realization that between us and the Arabs stands a massive barrier that may never be breached; a determination by two peoples to live in a land that at least one will never compromise on. . . . The Arabs intend to wipe us out; we must be strong enough to stop them.[27]

The Machiavellian model was operative in Kahane's Zionism throughout. Zionism, for him, was about conquest, power, and the establishment of a state that did not require adherence to geopolitical dictates or secular policies: "The cornerstone of Jewish foreign policy must be the knowledge and faith that the

Jewish people have a divine destiny that cannot be denied and that the State of Israel is the culmination of that destiny."[28] These and similar assertions undermine the classical Zionist goal of normalcy—the establishment of Israel as a normal nation-state that becomes part of the family of nations. Just as Jews are a chosen people, the Jewish state is also divinely chosen. As chosen and thus exceptional, the state cannot and should not follow the dictates of the unchosen gentiles: "Israel came into being on behalf of Jews, all the world's Jews, and not to worry over 'What will the nations say?'"[29] Its raison d'être was a literal reading of the Hebrew Bible in its most warring vein of divine sanction supporting unapologetic militancy.[30] "The state of Israel is not a western one or an eastern one; it is not a 'secular state'; it is not one to be modeled after 'the nations.' It is a *Jewish* state with all the uniqueness that this implies. It is a state whose personality, character, behavior, and structure must be the reflection of Jewishness and Judaism."[31] Any idea that a Jewish state must be dependent on non-Jewish allies is an error in understanding the core of Zionism: "Indeed, there are no allies and the United States itself will cut its bonds to Israel as its interests dictate. In the end, Zion and Zionism stand alone with the Almighty G-d who created them."[32] Kahane's point here is to challenge the very normalcy of the state as an aspiration.

For Kahane the classical Zionist program of normalization of the Jewish people through membership in the community of nations is a ruse. Isolation was, for him, not a sign of failure but of success: "To be isolated is not to be alone. The greater the isolation of the Jew, the greater the awe of G-d's ultimate victory. The more we stand 'alone' and the less who stand with us, the more astonishing is G-d's majesty."[33] As elsewhere, Kahane subverts previous articulations of Zionism by celebrating the isolation and abnormality of the Jews. Under the guise of modern nationhood, Zionism makes possible not power with global responsibility, but power with responsibility only to fellow Jews. To be fully abnormal, one has to have the power to self-isolate. Kahane acknowledges that the Jewish people have had plenty of experience of isolation in their history—in the form of enforced segregation in ghettos. But this was isolation without power. In Israel, by contrast, the Jews can self-isolate from a position of power. And the assertion of Jewish power through the Jewish state is simply the fulfillment of that covenantal promise. In Kahane's Zionist vision there is no distinction between religion and state. "Religion and state constitute one entity, and there is no Jew who is not simultaneously part of the same religion and nation."[34] The state of Israel provides the opportunity of structural isolation that is embedded in the covenant: "The wisdom of the Torah, and . . .

the divine destiny of the Jewish people was to realize its greatness and its exclusiveness, to remain separate from the nations lest it assimilate and lose its divine uniqueness, and to return to the homeland of Erez Yisroel, there to rebuild an independent, truly Jewish state that would be a model society for mankind."[35] The classical Zionist notion of normalcy, in Kahane's view, is the result of wrong-headed ideas that were born in the long centuries of diasporic life in exile and have no roots in Torah.

Kahane also takes issue with the prevalent view, shared by Israel's founders and by liberal American Jews, that Arab citizens of the young Jewish state would agree to live peacefully under Jewish jurisdiction. Such a view, he maintains, fails to recognize the fact that the Arabs, too, have national feelings no less pervasive and legitimate than Jewish nationalism. In *Our Challenge* Kahane writes: "The fact is that the Arab in Israel may be a citizen, he may be given equal opportunities in education and employment, but he is doomed to a minority role because he is an Arab in a Jewish state. And from this flows the inescapable resentment on the part of any minority, which is compounded by the Arab's belief that the state is really his, and that he should be the majority."[36] It is common both for supporters and critics of Kahane to say that he believed liberals did not understand the Arabs. That may be true, but Kahane's position was more nuanced than is often thought. Early in his Israeli political career in the 1970s, he made a serious claim about the realities of Arab nationalism and its threat to the Jewish state. The claim that Arab equality is not feasible if Israel is to remain a Jewish state is made by many Zionists. Kahane goes further to argue that democracy is not feasible either because democracy would require full Arab equality. This would be laid out more explicitly in *Uncomfortable Questions for Comfortable Jews*. But even as early as 1974, Kahane maintained that "the best partial solution, the most humane in the long run, and the safest for Jews is an effort to separate the Arab minority from the Jewish majority by a planned and well-funded emigration of Arabs from Israel. I speak here of the idea of an urgent creation of an Emigration Fund for Peace and I immediately point out that I refer only to a voluntary one, through the free choice and determination of individual Arabs."[37]

Kahane's understanding of Arab nationalism is articulated in many places in his writings, and it occupies a crucial plank of his early political platform in *Our Challenge*. In this book he takes to task the complacent assumption that the loyalty of Arab Israeli citizens could be bought with increased economic prosperity:

> No nationalist was ever bought by an indoor toilet and electricity in his home. And that is exactly what those who preach *peace through materialism* are doing. They are buying, or attempting to buy, the Arab nationalist and his love and pride in nationhood and state. Such an attempt is immoral and self-defeating. What the "moderates" and "compromisers" do not realize is that the Arab nationalist is as committed to his own people and to what he considers his own land as the Jews of Israel are to theirs. The Western colonialists who sincerely and honestly believed that they were benefiting the Asians and Africans whom they ruled, found that their arguments fell on deaf ears of native peoples who preferred poverty with independence to high living standards under foreign rule. Why should we expect Arabs to be different? Why should they not have the same pride that Israelis expect their children to have?[38] (emphasis added)

The gesture to colonialism here is revealing. Kahane is essentially accusing Israel's (secular) political leaders and the Zionist establishment of behaving as colonialists in their unwillingness to take Arab-nationalist claims seriously, while cynically believing that economic incentives would dissolve Palestinian desires for self-determination.[39] He borrows this idea from Jabotinsky, who in his famous essay "The Iron Wall" wrote, "The childish fantasies of our 'Arabophiles' is [*sic*] rooted in a kind of prejudiced contempt of the Arab people, in a kind of groundless perception of this race, which sees it as a corrupt mob that would surrender its homeland for a good railway system."[40] Jabotinsky, like Kahane, claimed the Arabs understood and respected him because he recognized and gave credence to their nationalist aspirations.[41]

But this avowed respect for Arab—or Palestinian—nationalism is not accompanied by any concession to the political demands that come with it. Rather, Kahane simply claims to know the force of nationalism as an ideology. "It is because we—more than the Jewish leftists and liberals—understand and respect the reality of Arab nationalism, that we realize the futility of expecting the nationalist to give up his dream."[42] This pragmatism leads directly to the dilemma that exists at the heart of the Zionist project: How can Jews justify enacting their nationalist aspirations on their ancestral land where another collective with similar nationalist claims to this same land already resides? Zionism has provided many answers, from denying the peoplehood of Palestinians to making a claim of indigenousness founded on historical evidence to acknowledging Palestinian national claims and arguing for two states living side by side.[43] Kahane, for his part, insists that the predicament is a zero-sum game. Any claim to the land is meaningless and carries no weight if it is not accompanied by divine sanction. The land has been given to the Jews by God, and this subverts any competitive claims based on indigenousness.[44] For Kahane secular Zionism has no basis of legitimacy whatsoever. This is at the root of Kahane's assertion of Israel's "abnormality": its national project is founded on a theological claim not subject to the rules of normal states. In a sense Kahane triangulates secular Jewish nationalism, religious nationalism that agrees to work with the secular state, and Arab nationalism, criticizing each from his theological position of Jewish ownership of the land via divine election.[45]

> If we are chosen, then we are a certain kind of people with a certain kind of role and a certain kind of state. There is a Chosen People, a chosen land, a chosen state, and a chosen destiny. The normal rules of nationhood and statehood do not apply; the normal logic of foreign policy is not ours. If we obey the call of the Jewish destiny, the command of the Almighty, we shall endure and live, both in this world and the next. If we do not return to the Jewish role, we will pay a terrible price before the ultimate redemption comes, wiping away our sins with the suffering of pain and war.[46]

The apocalyptic tenor that ends this passage becomes more prominent in books like *Forty Years* and *Thorn in Our Sides* in the mid-1980s. An interesting politicization of chosenness is at play in Kahane's Zionism; it underlies his literalness when it comes to viewing Zionism *as* Judaism through the lens of the Hebrew Bible thus eschewing any role for the secular in the Zionist project. If, as Kahane argues, Zionism *is* Judaism, then the foundational ideas of Judaism, such as chosenness, must play a central role in the formation and behavior of the state if the state is to be "Jewish."[47]

On this reading, secular Zionism is as much an anathema to him as Reform Judaism; both trade in the fundamentals of Judaism for accommodation to the larger world. Cognizant of the apparent contradiction between the "Zionism *is* Judaism" equation and secular Zionism's transgression of that equation, Kookean Zionists had to present the secular in a way that served the larger redemptive vision of religious Zionism as taught by Abraham Isaac Kook.[48] Kahane had no need for such a dialectical claim.

Our Challenge is Kahane's first sustained statement on Zionism.[49] What he advocates here is not religious Zionism in any conventional sense. It was the divine promise, not as rhetoric but as substance, that made Israel necessarily abnormal in the family of nations. And he wanted his constituency to embrace that abnormality as an instantiation of chosenness. He wanted to convey that "to be religious *is* to be a nationalist" and drive home that "all the secular nationalism in the world will not suffice to justify Jewish exclusiveness. It is only religion that justifies nationalism and indeed, it is impossible to speak of Judaism without connecting the two. Judaism is religio-nationalism."[50] This merging of religion and nationalism, loosely conceived, would become the central thesis of Kahane's sweeping revision of Zionist ideology in *Listen World, Listen Jew*, first published in 1978.

The book has an interesting backstory. It was initially framed as a response to an Oscar acceptance speech by actress Vanessa Redgrave at the 1978 Academy Awards in which she took a swipe at Kahane and the JDL. Redgrave had long been an outspoken activist on many global issues, including the Palestinian cause. In 1977 she produced and narrated a documentary called *The Palestinian*, which portrayed the lives of Palestinians under Israeli occupation and included a discussion about the PLO and its leader Yasser Arafat. That same year she starred in the film *Julia*, for which she won the 1978 Academy Award for best actress, concerning a woman who was murdered by the Nazis for her antifascist activities. Kahane and the JDL had been after Redgrave for some time. Her open activism for the Palestinians, as well as other progressive causes, was widely known. Kahane and the JDL unsuccessfully lobbied the Academy of Motion Pictures to deny her an Oscar for *Julia* because of her work on *The Palestinian*. Fully aware of Kahane's campaign, Redgrave referred to it in her Oscar acceptance speech:

> My dear colleagues, I thank you very much for this tribute to my work. I think that Jane Fonda and I have done the best work of our lives, and I think this is in part due to our director, Fred Zinnemann. . . . And I also think it's in part because we believed and we believe in what we were expressing—two out of millions who gave their lives and were prepared to sacrifice everything in the fight against fascist and racist Nazi Germany. . . . And I salute you, and I pay tribute to you, and I think you should be very proud that in the last few weeks you've stood firm, *and you have refused to be intimidated by the threats of a small bunch of Zionist hoodlums whose behavior is an insult to the stature of Jews all over the world* and their great and heroic record of struggle against fascism and oppression. (emphasis added)

Redgrave's remarks prompted some jeers and boos, and later that night Paddy Chayefsky, a noted playwright and novelist who was also active in Jewish causes, responded to her when presenting another award: "I would like to say—personal opinion, of course—that I'm sick and tired of people exploiting the occasion of the Academy Awards for the propagation of their own personal political propaganda. I would like to suggest to Miss Redgrave that her winning an Academy Award is not a pivotal moment in history, does not require a proclamation and a simple 'thank you' would have sufficed." Chayefsky was cheered for his statement. He was not an unbiased player here; having been in attendance at the Brussels conference on Soviet Jewry where Kahane tried unsuccessfully to speak to the delegation, he knew very well who Kahane was and what the JDL was up to.

Kahane did not intend to let Redgrave's televised swipe at him go unanswered. In a letter to his wife on May 9, 1978, he wrote, "The incident involving Vanessa Redgrave gave me an idea. I have a manuscript lying around for years, *Listen World, I Am a Zionist,* I changed 'world' to 'Vanessa' and have given it to three book publishers."[51] The resulting book, first published in 1978 and reprinted in 1980 by Kahane's own press, the Jerusalem-based Institute for the Jewish Idea,[52] became a sweeping revision of Jewish history that places Kahane's version of militant Zionism at the very center of Judaism.

Some early religious Zionists generally viewed Zionism similarly as a manifestation of the unfolding divine promise, a leap from exile to redemption as part of the final act of the covenantal drama.[53] For Abraham Isaac Kook especially, the Jews were being swept up unawares in a cosmic movement, and thus Kook with his religious worldview could affirm secularist Zionists (and even secular Zionism) as taking part in that tectonic spiritual shift.[54] Kahane, by contrast, did not view Judaism in cosmic terms but in material ones. Judaism—that is, God's promise forged at Sinai and interpreted by the rabbis—gives the Jews the religious and political right to the land, and the Jews' desire to return to the land is the central tenet of historical Judaism. This enabled him to lay claim to that land to the exclusion of all of its other inhabitants, not as some kind of unfolding mystical drama but, more in line with a biblical worldview, as a mandate for conquest. Kahane was not spiritually minded enough to think that divine intervention would convince anyone of this, at least not in the 1970s. Rather, the implementation of this right must occur through human force; divine fiat has no role in this version of Zionism except perhaps to generate its beginnings.

Kahane was very aware that a convincing revision of Jewish history centering on his militant version of Zionism would require a recalibration of history, in many cases rehabilitating figures marginalized due to their beliefs and actions. This process of recanonization would be necessary to convince his readers that his Judaism/Zionism was an extension of, rather than a deviation from, Zionism per se. If Zionism is, as he argued, "a national liberation movement," its radical leaders need to be foregrounded. Kahane viewed Zionism in revolutionary terms, not as a case of normalizing a nation but rather of abnormalizing it. Normalization for him suggests a kind of integration on a collective scale, to be like the others, to relinquish part of the Jews' uniqueness, to fit in. This, he argues, is the Zionism of modernity that not only will fail miserably but will have sold Judaism's birthright to the world at large. Antinormalization stands at the very center of Kahane's Zionist vision in *Listen World*. "It is incumbent upon us to stop our made gentilization of ourselves and failure to know who we are. . . . If it is true that we are like all nations and that only through leaning upon men, compromising, retreating, and betraying will we survive, then know that *we will not survive*. If there is no Divine guarantee and if we must depend on allies and the good will or change of heart of our enemies—*there is no hope*."[55] How does one convince a reader that Zionism means antinormalization? Of course, by citing scriptural references that support this claim, and there are many. But many of Kahane's readers at this point were not religious and Scripture would not convince them. And Scripture alone would not successfully counter the secular-Zionist narrative. Kahane needed to revise the canon of heroes since, on his terms, many of the existing Zionist heroes were compromisers.[56]

In *Listen World, Listen Jew* Kahane constructs his revision in three ways. First, he retells the story of ancient Israel from the perspective of Jewish violent revolutionaries such as Samson, Bar Kokhba, Bar Giora, the Maccabees, and others. "The Zionists. Jeftah and Gideon and Deborah and Ehud. They are what the fighters for Jewish freedom, the Zionists of the year 135, remembered as they marched from their homeland into Exile that was to stretch to two millennia."[57] His anachronistic use of "Zionism" here is intentional; it may be a modern term but it is an ancient idea. These and other figures are well-known in Jewish history but are considered marginal to some degree, in part because the rabbis of the Talmud, products of exile, viewed them as such.[58] For Kahane they are central because they embody his Zionist idea. Ben-Gurion also attempted to revise Jewish history, incorporating the books of the Maccabees into the Israeli curriculum, but Kahane's revision is much more strident and exclusivist.

Second, Kahane offers a schematic rendering of medieval Judaism in what Salo Baron would call a highly lachrymose tone, decrying Jewish marginalization, oppression, and victimhood in the spirit of Jewish historian Benzion Netanyahu, who in turn drew much from Jabotinsky.[59] This is all really a setup for Kahane's broadside against Jewish emancipation, for it was only Jewish emancipation in his view that introduced liberalism, accommodation, and reform, and thus anti-Zionism, to Judaism.[60] Third, this seduction into normalization, which included both socialism and nationalism (i.e., secular Zionism), had in his view eroded the Zionism of old, marginalizing the revolutionary figures Kahane sought to bring back to life. Figures such as Moses Mendelssohn, his student David Friedlander, Yehuda Leib Gordon, "salon Jews" such as Henriette Herz and Rahel Levin (better known as Rahel Varnhagen), and of course Jewish socialists are all, for him, "Fleers of Zion," presumably a play on the term Hovevei Zion (Lovers of Zion).[61]

Kahane suggests that without Zionism, modernity would have destroyed the Jews. Not the Zionism of Herzl or Ben-Gurion, but the Zionism of names few of us know: David Raziel, Shlomo Ben-Yosef, Abraham and Shalom Djuravin, Israel Kimhi, Mordecai Dresner, Eliezer Kashani, Dov Gruner. These and others are Kahane's unsung heroes of Zionism, members of the Irgun, the Stern Gang, or Betar, Jewish terrorists who fought violently against British "occupation" and in many cases paid with their lives. These, and not the accommodationists such as Chaim Weizmann, were the true inheritors of the "Zionism" of the biblical figures Samson, Deborah, and Yael, or the rabbinic ones like Bar Kokhba and Bar Giora. These were the Zionists of true Judaism (even as many were secular); they embodied the revolutionary spirit of liberation that was embedded in the divine covenant of the Jewish people. These and not the Zionist "negotiators" knew that "we are not like other people and the norms and realities of the world are not for us."[62]

The iteration of Zionism in modernity is legitimate only to the extent that it espouses the ancient Zionism of uncompromising rebellion founded on the unequivocal mandate of the divine decree.[63] In Kahane's view, many Zionists might gesture to the divine decree but few are willing to take it literally. Instead Zionism has chosen the path of conciliatory modernity that includes liberalism, democracy, and equality for the Arab in Israel. Kahane's revision, extending from Bar Kokhba to Shlomo Ben-Yosef—as noted, the first Jew to be hung by the British in Palestine for terrorism—is an attempt both to counter Redgrave's "Zionist hoodlums" remark and at the same time give warning to the Israeli political establishment that Kahane intends to revive an ancient civilization.

If we step back from Kahane's presentation here, we see that during his early years in Israel he was envisioning a new political program. While *Our Challenge* was its public face, *Listen World* was its underbelly. *Listen World* remained in manuscript until Redgrave's speech gave Kahane the impetus to organize and publish it as a response to the world's misunderstanding of Zionism, a misunderstanding that Zionism itself had fostered. More than a political program, *Listen World* represented a new national narrative. In America, Kahane frequently used the image of the "New Jew" to counter the "Old Jew" of the ghetto who was afraid to fight. But in Israel Kahane counters the Zionist "New Jew" by advocating for the Old Jew—not the Old Jew of the ghetto but the *very* Old Jew as warrior, supplanted by the weakened Jew of the Diaspora. It was the image of this "Old Jew" that Kahane took to the street to promote his new KACH program. Finally, on his third try, he was elected to the Knesset in 1984. It was there that his Zionism really began to die, as we see in *Uncomfortable Questions for Comfortable Jews* (1987) and the events leading up to it.

Zionism contra Democracy

In the 1984 Israeli elections Kahane's KACH party finally succeeded, on its third attempt, to secure representation in the Knesset. KACH received 25,907 votes spread out among 545 localities in Israel, enough for one Knesset seat. Kahane was now a part of the very legislative body he had fought against for the preceding decade. This modest but significant electoral success was likely a response to a growing vacuum in the Israeli right after the signing of the Camp David Accords between Israel and Egypt and the rise of an Israeli peace movement—manifested by the founding of Peace Now in 1978, which was perceived as threatening by many ultranationalist voters. Their fear was that Camp David and the evacuation of Yamit, a Jewish settlement in Sinai, were the first steps in a "land for peace" initiative that right-wing voters strongly opposed. A poll conducted one year after the 1984 elections by the Modi'in Ezrachi research institute found that support for Kahane's party was no aberration. The data suggested that if another vote were to have been held at that point, Kahane's party would have won eleven Knesset seats.[64]

The reaction to his election was swift and it came from both sides of the political spectrum. The Knesset voted on December 25, 1984, to restrict Kahane's parliamentary privileges. Lawmakers were understandably worried, in part, that Kahane's freedom of movement in Arab villages would spark riots and violence both from Jewish settlers and Arab villagers. Even right-wing Knesset member Geula Cohen of the Tehiya Party averred that "every one of us wants as little Kahane as possible."[65]

The opposition to Kahane in the Knesset culminated in a 1985 amendment to Israel's Basic Laws that became known as the "Racism Law." It expelled him and his party from the Israeli parliament, thereby ending what many hoped was an anomalous validation of blatant racism by a part of the Israeli public. The decision was passed in 1986 and then appealed to the Israeli Supreme Court, which upheld the Knesset's decision in 1987. Kahane, however, was not finished. His ouster energized him even more, and his supporters viewed their plight as a stain on Israeli democracy even as, ironically, Kahane did not believe in Israeli democracy.

In 1987 much of Kahane's animus came to literary expression when his book *Uncomfortable Questions for Comfortable Jews* was published. A scathing critique of liberalism, democracy in Israel, Israeli leadership, and Zionism more generally, the book in many ways was payback for those who had assured his removal from the Knesset. Published in English, this polemical work was the third part of a trilogy that began with his more optimistic *Our Challenge* and continued with his revisionist rendering of Zionist history in *Listen World, Listen Jew*. It is in *Uncomfortable Questions* that Kahane's Zionism really unravels, where he accuses every existing political expression of Zionism not only of failure but of racism and denigration of Judaism.

A number of themes in *Uncomfortable Questions* are rehearsed elsewhere in Kahane's earlier writings but grow more emphatic in this sweeping critique of Zionism. Perhaps most prominent is the notion of normalcy, which we have already discussed. More generally, Kahane's critique of Israel in *Uncomfortable Questions* in the 1980s largely mirrors his critique of American Judaism in the 1960s and early 1970s. America was the last diasporic hope for rebuilding the Diaspora Jew as a proud Jew with a fist; but it failed. Assimilation was too strong and liberalism dominated the cultural landscape in the aftermath of Vietnam. Israel was thus the final hope for a renewed Jew who could reinstate Jewish power without guilt and without aping the gentile. By the mid-1980s Kahane believed this had failed as well, and for very similar reasons. Israel had simply become a political and cultural mirror of America.

In *Uncomfortable Questions* Kahane also targets the concept and practice of democracy itself. Democracy arguably served as the political spine of the modern Zionist movement just as socialism was its prevalent economic theory early on. Yet the oft-repeated description of Israel as a "Jewish and democratic" state was not part of its original Declaration of Independence. Rather, "democratic" was added in a later amendment to the Basic Laws passed in 1985 (Amendment 9, clause 7A). This may be why Kahane spent so much time on democracy in *Uncomfortable Questions* (1987): he viewed this amendment as undermining Israel's "Jewish" character as codified in the 1948 Declaration of Independence.

The nature of Israel's democracy is a complex issue that has been debated in Israel for years.[66] While the term "ethnic democracy" was not in vogue when Kahane was writing, he likely would have scoffed at it as a useless attempt to defend the indefensible. For Kahane contemporary Israel cannot be a democracy if it takes its Jewish character seriously, and Arabs within its territory should never be allowed to have the vote. Even if they are accorded the franchise, the most perceptive among them will understand it as a sham.[67] The Arab, Kahane claims, "knows that a Jewish State cannot be a democratic one, in the western sense of the word, a concept that gives all people, regardless of nationality, equal rights. Democracies are not modified by adjectives. There is no *Jewish* or *Arab* democracy. There is *democracy*. Or a *Jewish State*. Or an *Arab one*."[68]

As the title suggests, in *Uncomfortable Questions* Kahane sees himself posing blunt, honest queries that make his hypocritical Jewish adversaries squirm. One rhetorical question posed early on in this book, which strikes "terror in the heart of the Jew," is: *"Do the Arabs in Israel have a right to quietly, peacefully, democratically equally, and liberally become the majority*?"[69] If not, Kahane contends, Israel cannot call itself a democracy.[70]

> Not only is there a clear intellectual, ideological, and philosophical contradiction between Zionism and western democracy, but the Declaration of Independence of Israel, a mindboggling example of schizophrenia, proceeds to institutionalize the contradiction unto all generations. The Declaration does not only passingly mention a "Jewish State." It fairly *wallows* in it. Paragraph after paragraph speaks of the *Jewish* people, Jewish history, *Jewish* rights. *Jewishness* permeates the very fiber of the document. . . . Is there, could there be, a clearer more uncompromising definition of the identity of Israel as a Zionist, Jewish State? . . . Consider now the inexplicable schizophrenia of this remarkable Declaration and the even more remarkable people who wrote it. . . . The Declaration of Independence . . . goes on to pledge, promise and guarantee "equal *political* and social rights to all its citizens regardless of religion or nationality" . . . of course any advocate or believer in western democracy would agree that Arabs have an absolute and inalienable right to the same political aspirations as the Jews.[71]

This assertion of an essential incompatibility between Israel's Jewish character and its democratic pretensions is shared, oddly, by critics of Israel from the radical secular left. Kahane's critique of Israel's hypocrisy mirrors the left's claim that the structure of the Israeli system cannot truly be democratic. As

Kahane put it, "For it is *not democratic* to demand that one become a Jew to benefit from the Law of Return. And it is certainly not democratic to define Israel as a Jewish State with the implication that one cannot allow non-Jews to become a majority. And this is the real tragedy and dilemma for the poor secular Herzogs and Zionists and A-Z Establishment types. They would dearly love to present Zionism as a paragon of democracy and equality. They cannot."[72] To religious anti-Zionists on the Jewish right such as the Satmar Hasidim and the Neturei Karta sect, Kahane would presumably say, "Your critique of Zionist secularism is correct but your *Judaism* is mistaken. The divine mandate is not to wait until redemption by divine fiat but to enact power though force to conquer the land." Their difference is on the nature of the messianic.[73] To the Jewish radical left, Kahane would presumably say, "Your critique of Israeli democracy is correct but your understanding of *Jewish* is mistaken. Jewishness is neither a secular, racial, nor ethnic category, nor even a category of peoplehood, but refers only to fidelity to God's Torah. It is not that Israel as the nation-state of the Jewish people *isn't* democratic; it is that it cannot *be* democratic." Only moderate Zionist secularists, mired as they are in the schizophrenia of "Jewish and democratic," think it can be; religious anti-Zionists and radical leftists know it is impossible.[74]

Given his antidemocratic stance, Kahane's policy prescriptions—voiced from the early 1970s onward—in favor of separation of Jew and Arab in Israel make perfect sense. As we have seen, even as early as 1974 he maintained that the best partial solution, the most humane in the long run, and the safest for Jews would be to separate the Arab minority from the Jewish majority through a planned and well-funded emigration of Arabs from Israel. As he noted then, "I speak here of the idea of an urgent creation of an Emigration Fund for Peace and I immediately point out that I refer only to a voluntary one, through the free choice and determination of individual Arabs."[75] He bases these views on a fairly conventional Orthodox theological understanding of the telos of Judaism, that of separation of Jew from non-Jew, or even good Jew from bad Jew. In Kahane's mind the Arabs represented "evil" not in any intrinsic way but in a pragmatic way; they threatened Jewish sovereignty.

Good and evil must be made separate, and indeed the very first act of the Almighty was to separate light and darkness since, in the words of the commentator Rashi, "G-d saw that it was not good that the two serve together."[76] "This notion of separation, as the midrash says, 'Holy—hallowed and sanctified, separated from the nations of the world and their abomination,' indeed serves as a cornerstone of the rabbinic understanding of Israel and the nations."[77] If the state of Israel aspires to be an exemplar of Torah, even if it may not be able to be a full-blown theocracy, it must abide by the fundamental precept of separation between Jew and non-Jew.[78] Thus, as mentioned earlier, one of Kahane's first orders of business when he arrived in Israel in the early 1970s was to call for the legal prohibition of intermarriage (or even interethnic dating) between Jew and Arab in Israel, even outside the rabbinate's authority.[79]

Kahane wanted to make such a prohibition a matter of civil law punishable through the legal system; he wanted to make it a Zionist principle. He noted that, in a 1985 article in the Israeli women's magazine *Olam ha-Isha*, Labor Knesset member Ra'anan Cohen had written, "Mixed marriages have become a practical problem since Kahane was elected to the Knesset. Before this, no one dealt with it, despite the fact that it is not a new phenomenon."[80] The problem for Kahane is not intermarriage per se, at least in Israel; there is little threat of Jews disappearing as a result, which was the fear in America. Rather, intermarriage in Israel is not a symptom of assimilation but of the Hellenization of the Zionist project.

Kook and Kahane

Although I touched on differences between Kahane's and Kook's views above, a closer look is merited in part because after Kahane's death, the neo-Kahanist movement that remained increasingly viewed itself as in accordance with a Kookean vision. I maintain that in many ways Kahane's and Kook's visions are diametrically opposed, even as they may share common cause on the ground. While a much more detailed comparison is a desideratum, here I want to point to a few distinctions that help clarify Kahane's Zionism more generally. Religious Zionism today, especially as it has taken root in the settlements, appears to be an odd amalgam of Kookean romanticism and Kahanist pragmatism. And this, I suggest, extends far beyond the small number of people who still identify as Kahanists.

If we look a bit more carefully, we can see that Kahanism and Kookism are in many ways incompatible, and their synthesis in contemporary Israel is more a product of present-day settler Zionism than how either Kook or Kahane understood the Zionist project. Kahane notably almost never mentions either Abraham Isaac Kook or his son Zvi Yehuda in his writings. We have one photograph of Kahane and Zvi Yehuda Kook taken sometime in the early 1970s when Kahane was visiting his son who was studying at the Mercaz Harav

Yeshiva (founded in 1924 by Abraham Isaac Kook) in Jerusalem. Otherwise Kahane's Zionism seems void of Kookean influence. Both Kooks openly opposed the use of violence, the father even more than the son, and both held strong romantic visions of living on the cusp of the messianic era that would unfold and resolve the conflicts facing Israeli society.

Kahane rejected the Kookean view that conflict would be resolved by divine fiat or that the reunion of Israel with its ancestral land would somehow transcend the reality of perennial hatred or bring about some kind of collective repentance (*teshuva*). Kahane exhibited none of the romanticism of the Kookean school, instead presenting the position of a hard-nosed political pragmatist founded on theological premises. As mentioned above, according to Kahane, the right of Jews to be on the land is divinely conferred. Nevertheless, that right will not result in any coexistence with the non-Jew residing in the land—or even any utopian redemptive outcome—but rather perennial conflict that must be managed through force. Just as he believed that anti-Semitism in America could never be eradicated, only managed, the conflict with the Arabs in Israel could never be resolved, only managed. The Arabs would never recognize Israel's right to the land, and Kahane did not think they necessarily should. Thus attempts at reconciliation were futile. Kahane counters the Kookean idea of Zionism as transvaluation with Zionism as zero-sum game.

Another crucial difference between Kahane and the Kooks concerns secularism. Abraham Isaac Kook, who died in 1935 before statehood, viewed the secular national project as a vehicle for his redemptive vision, and his son Zvi Yehuda viewed the state, even in its secular guise, as "holy," an embodiment of divine revelation,[81] and the best way to realize his ultimate vision of sovereignty over the totality of the land of Israel. This sanctification of the state and its apparatus led Zvi Yehuda to deem military service a mitzvah and democracy as the best, albeit not ultimate, vehicle for Israel's fulfillment as redemption unfolded.[82] The tolerance of both Kooks was founded on a belief that they were living on the cusp of redemption and the conflict with the Arabs would be resolved by divine fiat. History for both, whether the Balfour Declaration or the Six-Day War, was the material disclosure of messianic metaphysics.

While Abraham Isaac and Zvi Yehuda Kook may have viewed Israel's connection to the land and its sovereignty as theologically anchored, neither rejected the secular foundations of the Zionist project or, in the case of Zvi Yehuda, the secular state as a legitimate manifestation of Israel's destiny.[83] Both Kooks, to different degrees, based themselves on a theological romanticism according to which the transformative process of divine disclosure was underway and would facilitate the necessary correctives to the Zionist project. Both Kooks exhibited an optimism that the end-time was near, and this is arguably the basis of their religious-Zionist vision.[84]

Kahane's Zionism, by contrast, was imagined purely as an exercise in power; religion served only to validate claims of abnormality that subverted any alternative claims of Arab nationalism, even though he fully understood that such nationalism would not disappear. Kahane, too, believed that the state of Israel presented the Jews with the conditions for the end-time, but its fulfillment would be arbitrated only by force and violence. In some sense, then, one way to parse the differences between Kahane and the Kooks is on the question of human agency. What role do Jews play in the unfolding redemptive drama? Are Jews handmaidens of divine disclosure or soldiers who push the envelope by instantiating divine will by force? Although, in some way, the neo-Kahanism that emerged in the 1990s and 2000s deftly combines both visions, the visions remain quite disparate.

Even more strongly, Kahane's political platform in his early work *Our Challenge* diametrically opposes the established religious-Zionist framework that had been developing from the works of Zvi Yehuda Kook and his disciples who, in the early 1970s, were just beginning to coalesce as a movement (e.g., the settler organization Gush Emunim was founded in 1974, the year *Our Challenge* appeared).[85] The Kookeans were using the secular state as their template for messianic politics.[86] Kahane argued that "the time has come to isolate the psychopathic leftists and pseudo-intellectuals whose hatred of religion so effectively mirrors their own self-disgust."[87] He accorded no legitimacy to the secular state, and, as noted, his critique of rightist politician Geula Cohen could be just as harsh as his critique of leftist politician Yossi Sarid.[88]

Whereas the Kookeans spent little time criticizing secular nationalism and its architects, Kahane's *Our Challenge* discusses the period of secular nationalism and criticizes its founders at great length. In the 1980s Kahane goes much further to say, taking an almost anti-Zionist position, "Secular nationalism is selfish, foolish, and racist. Unlike other nations, the Jewish People were created not for mere nationalism, but for a holy purpose, to accept the yoke of heaven and submit to G-d and His Mitzvot."[89]

This is because whereas the Kookeans are invested in the state with a deeply held belief in its transvaluation, some viewing it as the penultimate messiah or "Messiah ben Joseph," Kahane approaches Zionism as a revolutionary liberation movement committed to undermining the secular foundations of the state in order to save it from the clutches of normalization.[90] From a religious and theological perspective, there can be little tolerance for secular nationalism when it means Zionism is not founded on a belief in imminent divine intervention.[91]

The amalgam of Kookean and Kahanist thinking in contemporary Israel belies a deep rift between the two ideological positions. Ironically, the messianic ideology of transvaluation now too often has a materialist-activist component that arguably undermines the spiritual optimism Abraham Isaac Kook embodied. In part it may be because the messianic optimism is waning, giving way to a more militant and radical alternative still dressed in Kookean attire.

Violence

On February 25, 1994, the Jewish holiday of Purim, Baruch Goldstein, a physician who lived in the West Bank Jewish settlement of Kiryat Arba, woke up before dawn, calmly got dressed in his IDF reserve uniform and, with a supply of firearms, traveled the short distance to the mosque at the Cave of the Patriarchs in Hebron where hundreds of Muslims were engaged in morning prayer. He entered the mosque, took out his automatic weapon, opened fire, and murdered twenty-nine men and boys before he was beaten to death by surviving worshippers. The event shook the foundations of Israeli society.

While much of Israeli society shunned Goldstein's murderous act, a small but vocal group of Jewish extremists influenced by Kahane viewed him as a hero and his massacre as a sanctification of God's name or *Kiddush ha-Shem*, a term that (as we will see) was central to Kahane. Goldstein himself had a relationship with Kahane and viewed himself as part of his circle of disciples.[92] The continued sanctification of Goldstein, small as it is, is evident in numerous places in contemporary Israel. For example, his tombstone at his grave in Kiryat Arba, which some view as a holy site, bears the inscription, "He gave his life for the people of Israel, its Torah and land"; the grave is located, not accidentally, adjacent to Kahane Park. A book praising his alleged heroism, *Barukh ha-Gever* (Baruch the Hero), a play on a verse from Jeremiah 17:7, was published in his memory in 1995.[93]

What theory underlay Goldstein's act of terror and his supporters' celebration of it? While Goldstein's act may be singular, the attitude that motivated it is not.[94] The idea of violence as sanctification is part of the modern eschatology of the later work of Goldstein's mentor Kahane, appearing especially in a 1982 book entitled *Forty Years* that he wrote in Ramle Prison in Israel where he faced charges of sedition and of playing a role in a plot to blow up the Dome of the Rock.[95] The violence called for in Kahane's modern eschatological vision is not only, or exclusively, directed against the Arab enemy but against anyone who desecrates God's name (*Hillul ha-Shem*).[96]

There is a notable difference between Kahane's early views while living in America and the positions he takes in his later work after his initial incursion into Israeli politics had failed. Missing from Kahane's previous perspectives on violence was any overt theological underpinning or eschatological resonance. His early work, as exemplified in *Never Again!* and *The Story of the Jewish Defense League*, rarely speaks about messianism or divine violence, even when the topic is Zionism.[97] As we have noted, Zionism, for the early Kahane, was not much more than an act of Jewish self-assertion, an opportunity to nationalize Jewish power, and a path out of the exilic mentality of weakness and passivity. Arguing that anti-Semitism was a kind of colonialism, trapping the Jew in a state of powerlessness and subjugation even as Jews in America may have prospered economically, Kahane offered a notion of violence as a liberating force.[98]

In Israel Kahane's views changed, as seen in the eschatology espoused in *Forty Years*.[99] Basing his newly evolved outlook on a selective reading of prophetic texts, in particular the book of Ezekiel, Kahane becomes a self-appointed prophet of doom who foresees the destruction of the Zionist project—unless he and his political allies attain the power required to stop it. Yossi Klein Halevi captures this turn: "In speeches and articles Kahane's brilliant sarcasm lost its perfect timing. He rambled and threatened, strongly hinting that he was a prophet sent by God to warn of the coming destruction: a holocaust in the Diaspora 'far worse' than Auschwitz, with an assault against Israel culminating in an international army marching on Jerusalem, just as the biblical prophets had foreseen."[100] Increasingly Kahane held sway over a more radicalized audience, including young disenfranchised Mizrachi men and devoted followers from America who had moved to Israel with him.[101]

In *Forty Years*, violence is not an act of self-defense or identity formation but a holy act that brings about the renewal of God's promise to destroy the enemies of Israel, external and internal. While Kahane's other works sometimes cite biblical texts to illustrate a point (much less so in his earlier American writings), *Forty Years* is unique in being structured around biblical citations that are applied to the present. It presents a prophecy not of peace and reconciliation but of divine retribution and violence. Jews in Israel become the means to fulfill the first stages of this prophecy.[102]

It is worth pausing momentarily to contrast this view with that of a better-known variety of religious Zionism that emerged from the works of Rabbi

Abraham Isaac Kook and Rabbi Zvi Yehuda Kook. Both Kooks, *père* and *fils*, believed that the establishment of the Jewish state was an act of God and the final unfolding of cosmic history. This was interpreted differently, in line with two competing messianic theories in the classical tradition: some viewed it as consolation for the Holocaust, a highly contested notion, while others saw it as the natural progress of redemption "in its time" as opposed to redemption "due to Israel's merit."[103] Neither Abraham Isaac nor Zvi Yehuda Kook, however, promoted proactive violence as a necessary prelude to the eschatological divine violence that underlies Kahane's later theory .[104]

Kahane understands the emergence of the Jewish state quite differently. For the Kahane of *Forty Years*, Israel's establishment represents the beginning of God's punishment of the gentile, which needs to be aided and abetted by the Jewish population.[105] "And so, a Jewish state rose from the crematoria and ashes, not because we deserved it, but because the gentile did. Because the punishment and awesome wrath of God were being prepared for a world that had mocked and humiliated the Name of the Lord, God of Israel."[106] Modern Israel is both a blessing and a reward for the Jews, and a divine punishment *against* the gentile. Kahane cites Ezekiel 36:22–23: "I do not do this for your sake, O house of Israel, but for My holy name which has been profaned among the nations. . . . And the nations shall know that I am the Lord when I shall be sanctified through you before their eyes."[107] As he understood these verses, that sanctification must be accomplished by Israel as it does God's bidding in acts of revenge against God's enemies as the first stage of the redemptive process.[108] In *The Jewish Idea* Kahane writes in the same vein that "whoever relents from revenge against Israel's enemies is giving up on avenging G-d, for whoever attacks the people of Israel is actually attacking to the G-d of Israel by showing that he does not fear Divine retribution."[109]

For Kahane Israel is clearly a miracle, a sanctification of God's name (*Kiddush ha-Shem*), but its miraculous nature is realized only if it functions to eradicate the desecration of God's name threatened by the non-Jewish nations. In an unpublished pamphlet Kahane produced in 1976 and distributed among his students entitled *Hillul ha-Shem*, he wrote, "A sovereign Jewish State which provided the Jew a home, majority status, land of its own, a military of its own and a victory over the defeated Gentile in the battlefield—*is exactly the opposite* [of a *Hillul ha-Shem*; it is a] *Kiddush ha-Shem*."[110] In *They Must Go*, published in 1981 (two years before *Forty Years*), Kahane makes it clear that the gentiles he has in mind are primarily the Arabs: "The Arabs of Israel represent a *Hillul ha-Shem* in its starkest form. . . . Far from fearing what the gentile will do if we do such a thing, let the Jew tremble as he considers the anger of the Almighty *if we do not*. . . . Tragedy will be ours *if we do not* move the Arabs out."[111] Violence against the enemy—and here the enemy becomes all who oppose the Jewish state—is a holy act that propels a divine retribution that in turn ushers in a final redemption. As Adam and Gedaliah Afterman note in their essay on Kahane and revenge, "The modern Jewish state in the historical land of Israel is an instrument for activating the redemptive process, rather than a result or sign of such a process."[112] By deploying prophetic verses from Ezekiel among other prophets in *Forty Years*, Kahane argues that this activation occurs *through* the divine violence promised by the prophets toward the enemies of God, both external and internal.

Who exactly is the enemy for Kahane that deserves violence as a sanctification of God's name in order to activate the return of divine violence and complete the redemptive process? That is, who or what embodies *Hillul ha-Shem*? Certainly the Arab who will not, and according to Kahane, cannot ever recognize Jewish sovereignty in the land of Israel. The Arabs, he argued, were just as nationalistic as the Jews, and thus justifiably could never accept a Jewish state. But Kahane's targets are not limited to the Arabs. He also appears to have "the West" in his crosshairs for having desecrated the Jew, and thus God, for millennia. And in addition, Jewish liberals both in the Diaspora and in Israel who have absorbed and adopted the attitudes of the gentile. For Kahane the true lessons of the long exile have been lost on such Jews: "For the exile was thrust upon the Jew by his God as a divine punishment in the hope that it would bring him to penitence and repentance. But what happens when, despite the exile, or worse, because of it, the Jew does not become more believing, but less so? . . . In a word, what happens when the Jew, through a lifetime of un-Jewishness, reaches the point of literally losing the ability to choose between Torah truth and non-Torah falsehood, between good and evil, between life and death?"[113]

Because of such Jews, exile has become "the personification of Jewish weakness."[114] And Jewish weakness is a *Hillul ha-Shem*. Here exile is envisaged not as a physical space but as a mental state perpetuated by "Hellenized" (secularized) Jews who cannot grasp Balaam's proclamation in the book of Numbers (23:9) that the Jews are "a nation that dwells alone." This phrase is the signpost of Kahane's New Jew. "The values of Judaism," he writes,

> are, in so many areas, and so overwhelmingly, different from those of western-gentilized Hellenism. . . . A nation rejects its special, distinctive holiness for the common, the universal profane . . . the worst opiates are

> the gentilized ideas that the intellectuals of Hellenism, the artists of gentilization, dance about as some Calf of Dross shouting, "These are your Gods O Hellenes of Israel. . . ." We reap the poisonous, noxious seeds of secular Zionism, a dream of Jewish gentiles which sought to cut away Judaism from Jewish nationalism and who, thus, guaranteed the death of the latter. Secular Zionism is bankrupt . . . [it] became one more form of vapid, empty, meaningless, ugly, secular nationalism. It died the day it was born.[115]

Kahane lumps into his enemies list not only secular Zionists but also religious Zionists, since the latter are no more inclined than the former to see themselves as the vehicle of divine violence against the Arab and the West. Neither the secular nor the religious Zionists were willing to "remove the Ishmaelite cancer and desecration of the land of Israel."[116] For Kahane this was more of a religious imperative than a security issue. As he states in *They Must Go*, "*It is a religious issue, a religious obligation, a commandment to erase Hillul Ha-Shem.* Far from fearing what the Gentiles will do if we do such a thing, let the Jew tremble as he considers the anger of the Almighty *if we do not*."[117] This inclusion of both secular and religious Zionists in the enemy category is a sign of Kahane's abandonment of any conventional understanding of Zionism in favor of a militant form of eschatological post-Zionism.[118] Zionists have addressed the "Arab question" in various ways over the generations, but Kahane's theological absolutism was arguably unprecedented in Zionist history, extending beyond even the most maximalist Revisionists and representing a break with the Zionist tradition. He intentionally used the more classic term Ishmaelite (he also uses the term Pharoists) instead of "Arab" to drive home his eschatological point. [119]

This militant post-Zionist turn against Jewish enemies places Kahane squarely in the tradition of Ezekiel and Jeremiah, who turn inward to blame the sinning Israelites for their own tragic fate. This move also aligns him with ultra-Orthodox anti-Zionism, for example, the Satmar Rebbe, Yoel Teitelbaum, who also used absolutist and even eschatological language to accuse the secular Zionists, as well as the religious Zionists, of desecrating God's name. (Teitelbaum, however, adopted a pacifist stance of awaiting a solution by divine fiat.)[120]

The notion of *Kiddush ha-Shem* has a long history in classical Jewish literature; an early articulation occurs in the story of the martyrdom of the seven sons in 2 Maccabees 7. The idea appears once again in the aftermath of the Jewish-Roman wars in the first century, in which many Jews gave their lives rather than abandon their Judaism. In later rabbinic and medieval Jewish writing, *Kiddush ha-Shem* became associated with what was seen as the quintessential devotional act of choosing death over being defiled physically or spiritually. The Talmud legally codifies *Kiddush ha-Shem* through its obligation of martyrdom in response to the forced performance of three acts: murder, idolatry, and forbidden sexual unions, and it became liturgically codified with the inclusion of the Ten Martyrs of the first century in the Yom Kippur liturgy. The early second-century rabbinic sage Akiva, who was tortured and burned to death by the Romans for refusing to stop teaching Torah, became a martyr and heroic model for *Kiddush ha-Shem* memorialized in Jewish liturgy into the modern era.

Modern Zionism replaced Akiva as the exemplary Jewish martyr with Bar Kokhba, the legendary leader of the last, failed Jewish uprising against Roman rule in Palestine. (Early Zionist organizations often evoked his memory in their names; the Bar Kokhba Society in Cairo and the Bar Kokhba Association in Prague are but two examples.)[121] Postwar Zionists, building on this celebration of active resistance, similarly held up as moral exemplars the Warsaw Ghetto fighters, who persisted in a suicidal mission to the end. In the Zionist tradition, violence as self-defense became the equivalent of Jewish fidelity to divine will, and the notion of *Kiddush Ha-Shem* became associated with active resistance rather than principled martyrdom à la Rabbi Akiva.

Kahane emerges downstream from these Zionist innovations. But by the 1980s he took *Kiddush Ha-Shem* in an even more radical direction, glorifying violence beyond that which is needed for self-defense. Self-defense morphs into self-assertive and proactive violence for God's sake. Citing Ezekiel 3:17, "Son of man, I have made thee a watchman unto the house of Israel: therefore hear the word at my mouth, and give them warning from me," Kahane comments, "And a world that refuses to know Him must crumble and be shattered. And a Jewish people, chosen with love from all the other nations to be hallowed and elevated with its unique Divine form, must cleave to its destiny or suffer the agony of Divine punishment. That is the reality and there is no escape from it."[122] Those who refuse to know God must crumble, and here their crumbling is said to come about by the agency of Jews. Those who refuse to take the needed violent action—who remain wedded to older understandings of *Kiddush ha-Shem* as either passive acquiescence or violence limited to self-defense—are fated to be on the receiving end of divine violence. Divine violence will return as part of the redemptive process; where it is directed depends on the Jews' willingness to do God's bidding as a prelude to divine intervention.

For Kahane in later publications such as *Forty Years* and *The Jewish Idea*, the stakes are very high; either the Jews do God's bidding by destroying the gentile, or God will destroy the Jews. "Showing mercy to the cruel only leads to cruelty being shown to Israel."[123] In this stark conceptual universe, nonviolence becomes an act of desecration, a *Hillul ha-Shem*. As I mentioned above, for Kahane "exile is the personification of Jewish weakness." Early on this referred to not fighting back against the anti-Semite. Now it seems to refer to enacting Ezekiel's prophecy about proactive destruction. Exile and nonviolence have merged to become different iterations of *Hillul ha-Shem*. Extending a traditional motif beyond Zionism's own subversion can also be seen in Kahane's notion of the New Jew.

In *The Jewish Idea* Kahane also associates *Hillul ha-Shem* with the gentile's lack of recognition of Jewish superiority, that is, their covenant with God (Israel being its prime exemplar), and with Jewish unwillingness to see the divinely ordained modern establishment of a Jewish state as the definitive end of exile and of the exilic mentality. If the gentiles refuse to recognize Israel, their *Hillul ha-Shem* will be met by divine wrath. If the Jews refuse to heed the divine directive to establish a *Kiddush ha-Shem* by using the Jewish state to separate themselves from the foreign culture of the gentile (which includes secular Zionism), God will wield violence against them. These are both instantiations of the "birth pangs of the messiah" (*hevlei moshiah*), each expressed through divine violence against either the gentiles or the Jews. If the Jews establish a *Kiddush ha-Shem* by acting against the *Hillul ha-Shem* of the gentile who does not recognize the holiness of the Jew, the Jews will deflect divine wrath against them. If they succumb to the foreign culture of the gentile, perpetuating their own *Hillul ha-Shem*, they too will be the victims of divine violence.[124]

In *Forty Years* we see Kahane's increasing opposition to secular Zionism:

> A secular Zionist, be he the most strident and maximalist? Judaism recognizes no such thing. Love of people or love of land is meaningless and ultimately absurd without the basis of the uniqueness and specialness of that people and land because of the foundation of God. To embrace the Jewish people and fight for the Jewish land has meaning only if both are special. That uniqueness comes only through God and His law. One who does not understand that, understands nothing. He has no answers. He is irrelevant to the destiny of the Jew. Both secular hawk and dove are ideologically plucked of Jewish feathers.[125]

The secular Israeli Jew for Kahane is nothing more than the internalization of the assimilationist Diaspora Jew, both of whom advocate for a false right of self-determination. This is because the conceptual framework of secularism is antithetical to Zionism and should not be tolerated for its temporary efficacy but rejected because of its impurity and the danger it poses. "The adoption of foreign, gentilized concepts by a Jewish state invites the vomiting out of a people, opens the doors to a national tragedy." It is not coincidental that such a comment could have easily been uttered by an ultra-Orthodox anti-Zionist. Kahane's radical eschatological Zionism founded on a catastrophic model that draws from the prophetic tradition turns into anti-Zionism for which conventional Zionism is what needs to be overcome.

For Kahane the best the Jewish people could hope for in the Diaspora was to live a sovereign life protected from anti-Semitism by having the power to manage it rather than be managed by it. This power was achieved by instilling fear and was maintained by the threat of violence. All the rest would be worked out in the messianic days.

Once Kahane settled in Israel, his attitude toward violence changed for at least three reasons. First, he was now living in a state with a Jewish majority, with an army and the state infrastructure to ensure the protection of its Jewish citizens. Second, his Israeli life exhibited a sharp turn toward religious doctrine and ideology; in short, like many other new immigrants, he "finds religion" in his ancestral home and this increasingly takes the form of messianism. It does not result in insular piety but rather a political activism that is now largely expressed in theological and increasingly eschatological terms. Third, the liberal Jewish establishment he fought against in America was now the Zionist government itself; Kahane's Zionism was a battle against the state.

This all shows, in my view, that Kahane's Americanness remains throughout his Israeli career. It is true that his conception of violence shifts from defense, self-fashioning, and deterrence in America to a kind of apocalyptic "forcing the end" in Israel. But his belief that violence potentially has a role to play in Israel's fate is something he had already developed in America (for that matter, Baruch Goldstein was born and raised in the Modern Orthodox community of Brooklyn). As I mentioned earlier, even as Kahane fashions himself after prestate Jewish terrorist groups such as the Irgun and the Stern Gang, it seems more likely that his militancy stems from the violent groups in the American race wars of the later 1960s.

By the mid-1980s, even before his election to and subsequent ouster from the Knesset, Kahane's writings became increasingly more apocalyptic. This stays with Kahane after he is expelled from the Knesset and informs the remainder of his life. He became an increasingly rejected prophet with a dwindling yet still devoted audience. His voice seems to periodically find a new audience when messianic romanticism sours or history seems to resist its anticipated redemptive conclusion. In those moments Kahane's militant (post-) Zionism remains there for the taking.

6

Militant Post-Zionist Apocalypticism

KAHANE'S *THE JEWISH IDEA*

"Everyone wants to change the world, but no one wants to change themselves."

LEO TOLSTOY

THIS FINAL CHAPTER is unlike those that precede it in that it is devoted to an analysis of a single book: Kahane's final work, *The Jewish Idea*. Published in Hebrew and then in English, with over six hundred pages in Hebrew and over a thousand in English, it is arguably the most widely read and popular of Kahane's works, certainly in Israel. *The Jewish Idea* leaves behind all of the criticisms of contemporary figures and events that occupy Kahane's previous books and focuses on presenting his Torah-based vision of Israel's future through a myriad of rabbinic sources. Below I argue that what we see in *The Jewish Idea* is an attempt to write a musar text for the Jewish collective and that it is rooted in Kahane's thirteen years of study in the Mir Yeshiva in Brooklyn.

Why conclude with *The Jewish Idea*? *The Jewish Idea* in some way is the book Kahane always wanted to write, certainly after emigrating to Israel, but could never find the time to finish. It was likely woven together from collections of notes and from classes he gave over the course of many years. One aspect of *The Jewish Idea* is that while it claims to be a rabbinic work, it presents a distinctly antirabbinic worldview. The rabbis, in complicated ways, developed a religion for the Diaspora.[1] There is much in rabbinic literature that valorizes the land of Israel and even imagines a triumphant return, but this literature offers a mostly antiapocalyptic approach to exile and redemption.[2] The rabbinic hero is Rabbi Akiva, the martyr, and not Bar Kokhba, the warrior. In some sense, then, the rabbinic corpus can be described as counterbiblical; the glorious imperial Israelite past has morphed into a devotional life framed in a divine decree of exile.

Kahane tries to use this rabbinic tradition against itself by choosing to analyze rabbinic dicta that promote an activist and militaristic agenda of (re)conquest, especially as Israel enters the final phase of its redemptive history. In this way *The Jewish Idea* reads the rabbis through a biblical lens; Kahane follows a trajectory of other religious and even secular Zionists who argued similarly. There is good reason why David Ben-Gurion held that the Hebrew Bible, and not the rabbinic tradition, was the best exemplar of modern Israel.[3] The rabbinic sources for conquest and domination that Kahane deploys certainly exist, and he cleverly uses them to his advantage. But the underlying premise he gleans from these sources that the sages, far from quiescent arbiters in "waiting," were promoting a proactive endeavor of achieving redemption by human agency does not bear rhetorical or interpretive weight.

Many other works, such as Rabbis Elizur-Hershkowitz and Shapira's *Torat ha-Melekeh*, which is primarily a halakhic work, make similar arguments and rabbinic scholars can argue their merits.[4] My argument in this chapter is that Kahane overlays a kind of neobiblical apocalyptic template on his rabbinic sources that yields a normative picture whereby the rabbis would support his proactive and militaristic messianism.

In addition, *The Jewish Idea* is framed as a musar text, a guide to self-perfection through altering modes of thinking and religious behavior. Kahane's implied "musar" claim is that the modern Jew has deviated from an unbridled and guilt-free stance of Jewish chauvinism and exceptionalism that would legitimize, even promote, militaristic behavior to assure Jewish survival. Whereas many musar texts view deviance as a product of human weakness and succumbing to the desires of the flesh, Kahane maintains that deviance also results from a liberal mindset that views Israel as a responsible actor on the world stage and the arbiter of equality and freedom for the non-Jew in its midst. That is, for Kahane musar becomes a legitimization of exceptionalism. This is certainly an interesting adaptation of musar, although I will argue that far from cultivating an ethical personality, it creates an angry collective that seeks revenge on those who stand in its path of domination.

Thus in some way *The Jewish Idea* culminates the success and tragedy of Kahane's entire career. It propounds a revision of Judaism in a way that collapses tradition upon itself. As he does throughout his career, Kahane takes what is often a legitimate critique, in this case concerning the liberal view that rabbinic Judaism is a source of pluralism and tolerance, and overextends himself to use the rabbis to promote a neobiblical ethos of conquest and domination. Musar, a theory of self-perfection used to enhance a person's sensitivity and gratitude, becomes a template for conquest as an exercise in superiority.

Kahane's Summa: Contextualizing *The Jewish Idea*

By the mid-1980s Kahane had been living in Israel for over a decade. He had spent considerable time in Israeli prisons on a variety of charges related to his militant activism. Yet even given his quasi-outlaw status, or perhaps because of it, his popularity continued to rise in certain sectors of Israeli society such as the Mizrachim who felt increasingly alienated from the Ashkenazi political class, and some religious Zionists who felt newly empowered by the Likud government's right-wing policies with Begin's election in 1977.

By the mid-1980s Israeli society had changed considerably since Kahane's immigration in 1971. Begin made settlement expansion official government policy. Gush Emunim, founded in 1974, had grown to become a major political and ideological force in Israel. The conflict with the Palestinians remained ongoing and messianic Zionists' expectation of redemption after 1967 had not quite materialized. The Yom Kippur War was a decade old and yet its impact on Israel's sense of invincibility was still being felt. In 1978 Peace Now had emerged as the first real collective resistance to the occupation. In September 1978 the Camp David Accords had stipulated Israel's first territorial withdrawal. And in 1982 the First Lebanon War had resulted in many casualties and destabilized Israel's northern border.

In addition, Israel was moving further away from its agrarian roots in the kibbutzim, and urban centers like Tel Aviv and Haifa were blossoming and becoming more prosperous. Jerusalem was becoming more *haredi*. The collectivist secular-Zionist ideology upon which the country was founded was slowly being replaced by two trends: urban secularism that was now beginning to look beyond Israel's borders for economic opportunities in technology and global commerce, and religious Zionism that was cultivating its own form of Zionist ideology founded on Kookean idealism, which was being generated by growing settlements and a burgeoning religious-Zionist school system.[5]

The trajectory of Kahane's career moved from being a social critic of, and activist against, liberalism and what it produced in America, to a religious ideologue and apocalyptic thinker in Israel.

Finding his place in the rapidly changing Israel of the 1980s was Kahane's challenge. Even though he viewed himself as a disciple of Jabotinsky, he never had much sympathy for secular Zionism and certainly not in its new bourgeois iteration. He was certainly sympathetic to the Kookean project but found its romanticism and its tolerance of secularism largely unappealing.

While Kahane continued to write to and for American Jews after emigrating to Israel, by the early 1980s he turned his attention to a new constituency: religious-Zionist youth. But his later writings, specifically *The Jewish Idea*, espoused a very different redemptive ideology than the Kookean thinking popular in those circles. Whereas Kook's writings were drawn from Jewish mystical literature, Kahane's was a pragmatic ideology culled from his reading of the Hebrew Bible and the classical tradition through the lens of musar. Musar, often referring more broadly to pietistic or devotional Jewish literature, has a long history extending back into the Middle Ages. I use the term here to refer to what is known as the modern musar movement, with its focus on self-perfection through devotional practices and acts of behavior modification through the lens of the Jewish tradition. Whereas Kook's thought is founded on a dialectic whereby the secular will be sanctified, Kahane lived in a bifurcated world of good and evil. For him, evil had to be eradicated, not transformed.

By this time writing almost exclusively in Hebrew, Kahane posited a militant religious ideology that was not only an alternative to the Kookean model but in many ways contradicted it. His later writing from the mid- to late 1980s until his death became infused with the apocalyptic urgency of a writer desperate to convince his readers of the failure of the Zionist project and the need to create an entirely new template of Jewish life in the land of Israel so as to prepare for the impending end-time. I call this Kahane's program of national correction; it constitutes a nationalized vision of the musar tradition he learned as a young man in the Mir Yeshiva.

During the 1980s Kahane became more immersed in the study of Torah and more influential in the right-wing religious community. This community arose under the influence of Gush Emunim and Zvi Yehuda Kook and his colleagues, who cultivated a national-religious ideology of land conquest and political domination combined with a romanticized messianism.[6] While Kahane never seemed taken by Abraham Isaac Kook's romantic vision of redemption nor his mystical dialectics, he knew that the young yeshiva students from the nationalist camp were now his natural constituency. This became even more pronounced after the return of Sinai including the settlement of Yamit in 1982 as part of the peace treaty with Egypt, when many in the nationalist camp began to feel disenchanted by the apparent reversal of their expansionist program.[7] During those years Kahane taught on and off in various yeshivot, including the Ateret Cohanim Yeshiva in the Muslim Quarter of the Old City of Jerusalem. It was in those institutions that *The Jewish Idea* (*Ha-Ra'ayon ha-Yehudi*) really began to take form, although Kahane was likely working on notes and collecting sources for years. *The Jewish Idea* stands in stark opposition to Kook's ideology of a convergence of the sacred and the profane.

It is not exactly clear when Kahane began writing this book, but by the late 1980s he decided he needed to publish a "short version" while he kept working on a much longer version that was published only posthumously.[8] Perhaps he thought he would not live to finish what is now considered his magnum opus. *The Jewish Idea* consists of thirty-nine chapters filled with hundreds of primary sources accompanied by Kahane's often brief comments and extrapolations. As opposed to his other works where he often offers long and often tangential asides, in *The Jewish Idea* he lets the sources do most of the talking, citing them in rapid succession to make his case for Jewish chauvinism and divine election. Also unlike his many other works, *The Jewish Idea* is mostly void of contemporary events or figures; all references to the present are general and schematic. This is because it was meant to be a *sefer*, a traditional Jewish book that could be studied outside the orbit of its own context. One question that needs first to be addressed is: What kind of *sefer* is it?

Kahane and Musar: The Mir Yeshiva

An often overlooked fact of Kahane's life is that as a young man he studied for thirteen years in the Mir Yeshiva (sometimes spelled Mirrer Yeshiva). The Mir Yeshiva has a long history and remains one of the great yeshivot in nineteenth-century Eastern Europe.[9] It was originally established in Mir, Belarus, in 1815; after World War I it moved to the Ukraine and then back to Mir in 1921. After World War II most of the yeshiva's survivors emigrated to Mandatory Palestine or the US. In Jerusalem, "the Mir" (as it is often called) was reestablished in the Beit Yisrael neighborhood where it stands to this day, and in the US, the transplanted version of the yeshiva moved various times but ended up in the middle-class Jewish neighborhood of Flatbush, Brooklyn, in 1946.

The Mir Yeshiva in America began with the financial support of a few American Jews, Charles (Yechezkel) Kahane, Meir's father, being one of them.[10] The honorary president of the yeshiva's New York branch was Rabbi Abraham Kalmanowitz (1887–1964). Rabbi Kalmanowitz was born in Minsk Province, Belarus and began his studies at the Telz Yeshiva in Lithuania; in 1905 he transferred to the Musar Yeshiva in Slobodka, Russia. He was elected honorary president of the Mir Yeshiva in 1926 and subsequently relocated to the United States during the war. For our purposes Rabbi Kalmanowitz's importance is threefold. First, he studied as a young man in the yeshiva of Rabbi Noson Zvi Finkel (the Alter of Slobodka), one of the most celebrated musar teachers of his generation.[11] Second, Rabbi Kalmanowitz stood out in the yeshiva world for his tireless efforts to help save Jews in Europe during the war and was also instrumental in providing Jews living in Arab lands with assistance and relief. Finally, he was a close mentor of Kahane, ordaining him as a rabbi as well as officiating at his wedding.[12] Regarding Rabbi Kalmanowitz's personal impact on Kahane, Libby Kahane writes, "Meir was influenced by his family, his schooling, and the youth groups he joined. But most of all, he was influenced by the Mirrer Yeshiva. The yeshiva provided the foundation for the direction he took in his life."[13]

Understanding Rabbi Kalmanowitz's musar background and the Mir Yeshiva in America more generally sheds crucial light on Kahane's posthumous *The Jewish Idea* as a nationalized musar project. The structure and approach of this book emerge from Kahane's thirteen years at the yeshiva studying with Rabbi Kalmanowitz and others. Whereas classic musar ideology normally focuses on the individual, Kahane's advocacy of national militancy, drawn from his more general sense of redemptive politics, breaks with modern musar. As Kahane reads it, musar's main message of *tikkun ha-midot* (individual self-perfection and ethical behavior) should apply to the Jewish people as a collective body and not only to the Jewish individual.

In those years Kahane was one of the few home-grown Americans in the yeshiva, which was made up mostly of immigrants from Europe. Through his family he also had ties to Modern Orthodoxy. Often shunned by the Mir's more traditional and strident student body, Kahane traveled to Manhattan to hear the lectures of the Modern Orthodox rabbi Joseph Soloveitchik at Yeshiva University, something few Mir students did in those days.[14]

Only much later, in the mid- to late 1980s, does Kahane seem to return to those early years in the 1950s when he spent his days in Torah study. But instead of entering the apolitical world of the *beit midrash* (place of religious study), he used Torah as a tool to build a national-religious ideology founded on the basic principles of musar, which he nationalized; he turned musar's focus on *tikkun ha-midot* into a template for national rejuvenation, fulfillment, and correction.

The Modern Musar Movement: A Prelude to Kahane's *The Jewish Idea*

As I mentioned above, the term "musar" often refers to Jewish literature that focuses on personal behavior, ethical practices, and self-perfection. While many of these topics are dispersed throughout the rabbinic canon, some have suggested that the Mishnah tractate *Ethics of the Fathers* and the later work *The Fathers According to Rabbi Nathan* offer perhaps the most sustained and focused discussion of rabbinic musar.[15] The Middle Ages produced numerous works of musar, both philosophical and mystical. From the sixteenth century to the eighteenth century, pious asceticism becomes even more prevalent as an ideal of Jewish behavior.

What is known as "modern musar," the movement initiated by Rabbi Israel Salanter in the nineteenth century and then continued by his students, presents a different mode of discourse. It is in this tradition that we see the foundations of Kahane's *The Jewish Idea*. Studying at the Mir Yeshiva would have given him a solid grounding in classical sources and a deep sense of the possibility of reconstructing the self through what he often described as "self-sacrifice" and fidelity to "Jewish ideas." This notion of self-sacrifice is a cornerstone of his thinking and the first step for a person in reaching completion. Very much in the spirit of musar, he writes, "When a Jew gives up something of himself, that is precisely when he becomes perfect and complete."[16] This principle of self-sacrifice is often used to advocate for a countercultural life that cuts through the pleasures of postwar America, the "Hellenistic" values of selfishness, and the liberal values that Kahane believed had poisoned both American Jews and Israel. In his estimation, self-sacrifice was only way the Jew could become a "true Jew" amid modernity.

The general themes of modern musar are set out succinctly by Dov Katz in the first volume of his five-volume *Tenu'at ha-Musar* (The musar movement).[17] Katz argues that the goal of modern musar is largely in concert with its premodern antecedents: the perfection of the human being, more specifically the Jew. The assumption is that fidelity to Torah and mitzvot, while a necessary condition for such perfection, is not a sufficient condition for its accomplishment. Something more is needed for the Jew to fully embrace and abide by the covenant.[18] This is in part because of human nature. We are more readily able to adhere to ceremonial and ritual obligations, musar teaches, than those that require us to conquer our natural tendencies and desires.

In his famous *Iggeret Musar* (Letter on Musar), Rabbi Salanter notes that while few observant Jews would eat bread without the required ritual washing of the hands, "people engage in speaking *lashon ha-ra* [derogatory words about others], which is far worse, without even a great desire to do so." In other words, pious Jews readily transgress such prohibitions without much thought. This point will become relevant for Kahane in *The Jewish Idea*. The notion of Zionism as a mitzvah is something he stresses in his assessment of the Zionist project. However, he believes that many, even many religious Zionists, completely ignore the subtler yet no less crucial aspects of this mitzvah, in particular, purity and separation from the gentile world and culture.

Zionism without this aspiration to purity and separation could be likened, for Kahane, to ritual hand washing while engaging in *lashon ha-ra*. In other words, one can do the mitzvah and undermine it at the same time. In addition, as we will see, for Kahane the mitzvah of Zionism becomes sullied and loses its divine mandate if it is not accompanied by a national corrective against the infiltration of "foreign culture" and the continued existence of the Arab enemy in its midst. Under those conditions it may not even be a mitzvah at all.[19] The famous rabbinic adage about "immersing in the mikvah while grasping a non-kosher animal [*sheretz*] in one's hand" is, for Kahane, an illustration of secular Zionism.[20] Regarding the defilement entailed by gentile culture, Kahane writes, "As a result, even Jews who mechanically keep the mitzvot and call themselves 'religious' are immersing in Torah water while grasping a contaminated animal—non-Jewish culture—in their hands."[21] *The Jewish Idea* maintains that such an assessment can be supported by both biblical and rabbinic sources.

Katz writes, "The modern musar movement is founded on three principles: the completion [*shleimut*] of Torah, the completion of human behavior, and the completion of the human being."[22] Kahane would add another layer: the completion of the collective, or the Jewish nation. Musar then is not simply about human perfection (*tikkun ha-midot*) but about the completion of Torah, which remains unfulfilled as long as its adherents are accustomed to ignoring the mandate that is built into the covenant and delineated through its ethical demands. This point will be developed by Kahane as well, except that in his case, as noted, the focus is on the collective rather than the individual. The enemy within from the standpoint of modern musar becomes for Kahane Western values that undermine Zionism as the opportunity for national redemption.

In *The Jewish Idea,* Kahane points to an opportunity for Jews to choose whether redemption will come "in haste" or "in its time"—whether Israel will bask in the triumphalism of redemption or reach the finish line wounded, damaged, and suffering. Without the national corrective he advocates, the road to redemption will come in any case because now is the time, but it will be paved with Jewish blood—not only because the gentile hates the Jew but because Jews themselves are unwilling to make the commitment to fulfill their destiny according to the mandates of tradition.

The Structure of *The Jewish Idea*

One way to view *The Jewish Idea* is as an Israeli companion to *Uncomfortable Questions for Comfortable Jews* (1987), which is Kahane's vicious critique of the Zionist establishment that had just rejected him. *The Jewish Idea* is written for a very different public. Constructed as a *sefer,* it speaks exclusively to a religious audience who accept the classical sources as authoritative directives for modern political statecraft. Yet Kahane, as we will see, maintained that many in the religious community, as a result of millennia of Diaspora life, held distorted values that they were trying to wed to their Torah convictions. As opposed to simply rejecting this amalgam as irredeemable, *The Jewish Idea* presents a "Torah argument" for Israel based on the premises of musar as a national corrective that can purify Torah from its diasporic defilement. Just as musar literature offers directives to amend individual character traits so that they will be more aligned with "Torah values," *The Jewish Idea* does the same for the Jewish collective body in Israel.

There is little difference here from many musar masters who focused on individual self-perfection. Kahane, however, believed those values could also be used to construct a modern Jewish nation-state. While he understood that the modern context might not allow a full-blown theocratic monarchy, he maintained the possibility, and posited a divine mandate, to achieve something as close to that as possible.

Like many musar books, *The Jewish Idea* is structured thematically. The themes can be divided into three basic categories: classic musar themes, nationalized musar themes, and themes revolving around redemption. Standard musar themes include The Yoke of Heaven, Humility, Submission and

Loneliness, *Ahavat ha-Shem* (Love of God), Mercy and Compassion, Faith and Trust, *Kedusha* (Holiness), and *Mesirat Nefesh* (Self-Sacrifice). Nationalized musar themes include The Non-Jew in Israel, The Chosen People, The Jewish Government, The Mitzvah to Live in Israel (note that he posits "Israel" and not "the land of Israel"), War and Peace, and Eretz Yisrael (the land of Israel). Themes of redemption include Time of Redemption, Elimination of the Exile, Hastened Redemption, God, Signs of the Redemption, Moshiah ben-Yosef, and The Majesty of Redemption Is in Our Hands. More specifically, the most recognizably Kahanist chapters related to one of those three categories include "Revenge," "The Nations' Punishment for the Persecution of the Jews," and "Haughtiness of the Nations."

While *The Jewish Idea* sets its sights on nationalizing musar, there are many instances where Kahane presents a classical musar position focused on the individual and resembling teachings in almost any modern musar text. One example is his discussion of accepting the yoke of heaven:

> G-d gave us the commandments and behavioral guidelines as decrees to fetter our ego. If today a Jew fulfills a given commandant because he intellectually and emotionally *agrees* with it, what will he do tomorrow when he encounters one that is *hard* for him to digest, that he cannot agree with? With our own eyes we see today the tragedy and devastation caused by those who have reinterpreted G-d's decrees as a mere vehicle to provide them with pleasure. . . . The truth is this: a mitzvah is conceived with a man's accepting the yoke of heaven and born when he fulfills it because he was commanded to.[23]

This conveys a classic musar polemic against *ta'amei ha-mitzvot* (reasons for the commandments) more generally, that is, tying obligation to convenience or coherence with one's moral inclinations. It finds one of its strongest expressions in the work of the Israeli public intellectual Yeshayahu Leibowitz (1903–1994), who viewed commandments as void of any intrinsic meaning other than pure obligation and submission to divine will.[24] For Leibowitz, ulterior motives for fulfilling mitzvot constituted a deviation from the act of submission that is the centerpiece of Jewish ethical practice. Kahane, in line with musar more generally, would not go as far as Leibowitz precisely because he believed mitzvot had intrinsic meaning and value; the question is whether we are always able to ascertain that meaning or value. At times such as ours, Kahane maintains (also in line with some standard musar teachings), Jews have become so blinded by the values of "foreign culture" that they often are unable to clearly understand the values the Torah is teaching. To confer "foreign culture" values on mitzvot is to sully and dilute their meaning and purpose. For Kahane *ta'amei ha-mitzvot* fails if the value system foisted on the mitzvot is a by-product of the influence of secularism.

Expressing similar opposition to mechanical ritual, Kahane argues that mistaken intention is not simply an error but a sin. "Mechanical ritual is not the main thing but the thought and motive behind it. If one's motive is evil, not only does one not fulfill a mitzvah but one commits a terrible sin, cloaked in a mitzvah."[25] Given Kahane's larger program, this appears to be a swipe at liberal Judaism including secular Zionism, where ideological commitments, in his view, stain the Judaism espoused and perhaps make it worse than not fulfilling the mitzvah at all.[26] In the case of Zionism, mistaken intention undermines rather than procures Zionism's redemptive potential. This is because for him Jewish secularism in general and secular Zionism in particular is an act of profanation, of *Hillul ha-Shem.*[27]

Kahane's worry, reflecting many musar writers before him, was that giving a rationale for mitzvot or interpreting them to conform to one's preconceived notion of what is right and true easily enables one to discard them when they do not express the meaning for which one intended them. He focused less on the intellectual rationale of *ta'amei ha-mitzvot* and more on the banal relaxation of religious practice because that was more ubiquitous in his time, certainly in his experience as a rabbi in postwar America. If one does not embody self-sacrifice and submission to the structure of mitzvot as a response to divine command, many mitzvot will simply be too inconvenient or uncomfortable to fulfill. Sacrificing oneself to the framework gives one the strength to maintain fidelity amid difficult circumstances. Such an approach is certainly in concert with much of the musar tradition.

Kahane continues this line of thinking in numerous places. For example, in his chapter on "Trust," writing about the prophet Samuel chastising King Saul for attempting to appease the Philistines in Gilgal (1 Samuel 13:5–14), he states, "We learn an important, harsh lesson here: When God establishes a mitzvah for us, even if it is exceedingly difficult to fulfill it, and even if it appears unlikely and unrealistic that we will be able to do so, and even if in logical terms and *for the sake* of fulfilling the mitzvah, so to speak, it is better to alter or 'improve' it, a Jew should take hold of complete faith and trust in G-d that if he just obeys G-d's word without deviation and trusts in Him, that is the Torah way."[28] Here again, self-sacrifice and submission, even to that which appears outdated, is the "Torah way" to keep the system intact and achieve a sense of human perfection (*tikkun ha-midot*) through the very act of sacrifice, even if the specific object of sacrifice may seem superfluous.

One more example will suffice to give a sense of Kahane's musar approach that will then be deployed for collective and nationalistic ends. A few pages after the above quote, we read a comment on Rashi's note to Proverbs 28:14, "Happy is the man who fears always." Rashi states, "One should worry about punishment, thereby distancing himself from sin."

> Yet if G-d commands a person to do some deed and promises that if he does it no harm will befall him, that person must fulfill his mission without fear or second thoughts. This is not to say that he should not fear constantly or that he should not examine his deeds. Indeed, let him scrutinize himself constantly just as anyone must seek out ways to correct wrongdoings. Yet, he should not make this a reason not to carry out his mission. . . . A person should not allow himself constant worry lest it cause sin. Moreover, he should not become confused and twist his path with all kinds of thoughts such as "Perhaps I am unworthy"; or, "Perhaps the generation is not worthy of this." If our holy Torah requires us to do a particular mitzvah or deed, we should lift our feet and set out on our way.[29]

Here Kahane gently pushes back on Rashi's comment, which implies that one should constantly "worry" about whether one has correctly ascertained correct behavior, an idea that is often repeated in musar literature. While agreeing in principle, Kahane suggests that such introspection should not impede one's ability, or commitment, to act. Although the larger context is not explained in these passages, Kahane was keenly sensitive to the ideational conflicts between divine command and modern values, specifically but not exclusively regarding matters of Zionism and the state of Israel.

The conflict between the explicit divine mandate of the Jewish conquest of the land including the establishment of the Jewish state on the one hand, and Israel being a member of the community of nations committed to democracy on the other, was a central concern for Kahane. He viewed the conflict between being a Jewish state and being a democratic one as the greatest challenge for modern Israel.[30] Significantly, the biblical context he used here concerns the failure of King Saul to implement the divine command in regard to the Philistines, which would later help lead to Saul's political demise. Whereas classic musar texts would generally use such examples and then personalize them to refer to one's individual devotional life, Kahane here wants to keep the political context in sharp relief.

For Kahane liberalism and free thinking born from "science" provide a modern form of heresy that turns divine sanctity into blasphemy, making authentic worship that much more difficult. Although Kahane was not against science and made use of all it had to offer, he took issue with the sort of scientific mindset that pretends to offer a legitimate Judaism that is a *Hillul ha-Shem* cloaked in a *Kiddush ha-Shem*. The practical dimensions of science are not the problem for Kahane; what is destructive is science as a worldview, whereby it elevates the human to the stature of one who alone can ascertain truth. Here he shares much with other contemporaries such as Rabbi Menachem Mendel Schneerson of Lubavitch.[31]

Science and the secular remain complex categories in Kahane's writing. He was, after all, university-trained and lived a fully modern life. Closer to a *haredi* mindset that he increasingly adopted in the 1980s, and certainly within the orbit of musar, Kahane espoused the stance that science undermined our capacity to believe.[32] When modernity (specifically liberalism) becomes the lens through which Judaism is refracted, especially in regard to the national project of Zionism, it distorts the message and squanders the divinely given opportunity for redemption.[33] In fact, he links the rise of science to the very need for redemption.

> There is another reason for the redemption's beginning precisely in our generation, and it lies in the real, unprecedented changes that have recently taken place. The growth of science and technology, which has shrunken the world and united it in *Hilul Hashem*, has created—without any connection to the Jewish People—arrogance and a feeling of man being godlike and omnipotent. . . . Man's astonishing progress has sown in him seeds of rebellion which have moved him to mentally depose G-d from His throne of glory, to install his alien self in G-d's place . . . and to crown himself master of his fate and master of the universe. . . . Never in history has the world known so much lack of faith, so much blasphemy and heresy, as it does now.[34]

This fallen state of humanity does not quite cohere with Kahane's more general participation in, and attitude toward, the modern world. This is one instance among many where his later work, especially *Forty Years* and *The Jewish Idea*, begins to adopt a more ultra-Orthodox (or *haredi*) mindset that is absent from his earlier work. This is partly attributable to the increasingly eschatological mood that informed his work in Israel, especially after his ouster from the Knesset, and perhaps partly to the recognition that his audience in Israel was changing and much more sympathetic to that worldview than his American audience from the 1970s. The amalgam of national-religious Zionism and *haredism* that later coalesced in the movement known today as Hardal (*haredi–dati le'umi*, i.e., *haredi*–national religious) was in its infant stages when Kahane was alive. And yet *The Jewish Idea* begins to show this orientation.

To better understand what is going on in *The Jewish Idea*, I engage below with some specific themes where the musar approach becomes embedded in a kind of political theology of conquest and militarism as devotional acts—defined as *Kiddush ha-Shem*—aimed at procuring the success of Zionism as a redemptive project, as part of an opportunity for Jews to separate themselves from the diasporic experience of accommodationism that, in Kahane's view, has plagued Jewish history for millennia.

According to Kahane, the difficulty with achieving those collective goals in the Diaspora was largely due to two intersecting problems. First, the Jews were unable to separate themselves enough to achieve a unique status outside the orbit of foreign influence. Second, communities like the ultra-Orthodox who did protect themselves from foreign influence mistakenly adopted a quietistic messianic posture that opposed an activist attempt to fulfill the divine command of land conquest.[35]

For Kahane modern Israel provided the perfect context to correct the diasporic errors on both fronts and produce the kind of fully activist yet also separatist society that was necessary for redemption. "Removing the exile from Israel is ten times harder than removing Israel from the exile, and this is the reason that even in the Land of Israel a nation has arisen that trembles at flesh-and-blood gentiles, a nation lacking in trust in G-d."[36] His solution is a collective project facilitated through a nationalized musar, in effect a realignment of the collective self-identity, combined with the fearlessness and power that comes with political autonomy and confidence in the divine mandate of Zionism.

Purity and Separation

Purity and separation occupy a central place in musar literature. In general, the pious life of devotion to God and the attainment of purity require one to separate oneself from temptation and to seek a state of the soul that is not sullied by the material world. Purity is achieved by various means including fasting, sexual abstinence, and other forms of self-abnegation. While modern musar focuses less on the categorical division of body and soul and more on the psychological act of *tikkun ha-midot* (or behavior modification), there remains an ethos of separation even in these more integrative materials.

In general, this advocacy of ascetic behavior is not found in the Hebrew Bible, where social and political themes are more prevalent than pietistic ones. Yet the Bible is no stranger to the project of separation and purity, occasionally commanding the Israelites to separate themselves from those around them ("I have separated you from the nations," Leviticus 20:26), forbidding the practices of gentiles, and warning the Israelites against being influenced by their mores (e.g., Leviticus 18:3). The biblical prohibition against contact with the gentiles is tied to their inherently immoral culture and practices—and in particular to idol worship. The Bible exhibits an ostensible zero-sum intolerance toward such practices, demanding the Israelites not only avoid them but also violently destroy any man-made images, natural markers where worship takes place (trees, etc.), or houses of worship when they enter the land (e.g., Deuteronomy 12, 32). Rabbinic teaching excises the violent commandment to destroy these images but reiterates and expands the various prohibitions of using them, engaging with them, or benefiting from them. Much of rabbinic teaching on the subject is included in the Talmudic tractate *Avodah Zarah*.[37] The reasons given in the biblical tradition are twofold: first, these practices defile the land (and thus must be destroyed); and second, interacting with people who engage in such practices will result in absorbing their values and thus distract the Israelites from their exclusive fidelity to God. Throughout the Hebrew Bible, Israelite deviance is attributed in large part to engaging with and being influenced by surrounding societies.[38] The Hebrew Bible arguably advocates an insular political reality even though in practice this was never realized in ancient times, and its prohibitions certainly did not rule out foreign alliances even though such alliances were discouraged, as we see in the late Hasmonean period.[39]

Kahane was a serious reader of the Hebrew Bible, writing a Hebrew commentary to part of it entitled *Perush ha-Maccabee*. On the question of separation and piety, Kahane utilizes musar ideas of personal piety to promote a modern-day political theology of the nation-state that seeks to implement the biblical worldview of separation as an alternative to the liberal nation-state ideology of secular Zionism. Kahane views separation as a necessary corrective to avoid deviation from Israel's covenantal mandate.

Separation and purity are intertwined in the Hebrew Bible, and the laws of purity and impurity occupy the epicenter of the Levitical code that describes Israelite Temple-based practices.[40] For his part, Kahane, citing a passage from *Midrash Tanhuma* on Numbers about the arbitrariness of purity laws, presents a purely functional view of purity. In this midrash, Rabbi Yohanan ben Zakkai is asked by a convert about the purity ritual of using the ashes of a red heifer. Ben Zakkai provocatively responds, "As I live! The dead do not defile us, neither does the red heifer or water purify us, rather, G-d said, 'I have ordained an ordinance. I have decreed a decree. You are not entitled to violate it.'" On this Kahane adds, "In other words, G-d created and introduced into the world an artificial concept of purity and impurity so there would be concrete, physical elements paralleling the intellectual concepts of good and evil. In this way, man could sense, in practical terms, the severity of impurity, i.e. evil. Whoever violates these laws, would feel the punishment of impurity, so to speak. Man is incapable of feeling a concept as a reality. G-d therefore created symbols. This is the reason he invented impurity."[41] The description of impurity as a symbol or "artificial concept" to enable one to feel the prohibitive nature of "evil" suggests that for Kahane the purity laws have no ontological basis but function solely as symbolic markers of separation. Thus when God decrees the impurity of the nations, it is not a statement about some essential nature of the nations per se but a marker of separation in order for Israel to maintain its status as holy ("evil" and "unholy" being two iterations of the concept of the "other"). Purity is thus for Kahane simply about being differentiated, or chosen, nothing more. "Thus, *Erez Yisrael,* once Israel were chosen to be G-d's people, became the only holy place on earth, while all the other lands are impure."[42]

This raises an issue as to the roots of Kahane's thinking on these matters. One might suppose that given his predilection for separation, ethnocentrism, and even racism he would be more inclined to the model offered by Yehuda Halevi, whose book *The Kuzari* espoused an intrinsic, even ontological distinction between Israel and the nations, and between the land of Israel and all other lands. Halevi's view filtered through medieval Kabbalah, the MaHaRal of Prague (Rabbi Judah Loew), and became a crucial element in Kookean theology. And yet Kahane, especially here, also seems to lean more toward a Maimonidean view that holiness is not ontological but a product of divine command. For example, on Maimonides, Maimonides scholar Menachem Keller remarks, "According to his view holiness cannot be characterized as ontological or essentialism since holy places, persons, nations, and objects are in no objective way distinct from profane persons, nations, times, and objects; holiness is a status, not a quality or property. . . . This sort of holiness does not reflect objective reality, it helps constitute social reality."[43] Here Kahane's utter disinterest in mystical doctrine is in full view; he refuses to base Jewish difference on ontology—although he does make an ontological claim about anti-Semitism—and yet also eschews any semblance of Maimonidean universalism that may emerge from holiness simply being status and not quality. Thus for Kahane everything rests on a fairly straightforward belief in revelation and divine mandate.

In a very musar register, Kahane insists that the nations must be avoided because they serve as a distraction from God, separation being the requisite act of attentiveness to the holy. While this can be viewed through the lens of the individual, for Kahane it also speaks to the collective. "One who trusts in man automatically removes from his heart trust in G-d. Therefore, trust in G-d demands two things: (1) 'Cursed be he who trusts in man.' A Jew must cut himself off from reliance on the 'non-Jew,' and simultaneously, (2) 'Blessed be he who trusts in the Lord.' When one scorns the non-Jews' aid, this necessarily makes him trust in G-d. Conversely, as long as a Jew lifts his eyes in hope to the non-Jew and his aid, it is impossible that he will completely believe that G-d is all powerful."[44] There is an interesting move here from "man" to the "non-Jew" and from the individual to the collective. The psalmist's warning against trust in "man" does not designate Jew or non-Jew; the assumption is that trust in man is itself a distraction from trust in God. By shifting the emphasis from "man" to "non-Jew" and shifting the locution of "trust" to "aid," Kahane politicizes this pietistic adage as a warning to modern Israel. The modern Zionist idea of Israel as a nation among nations, in need of support and aid from foreign powers, prevents it from achieving its redemptive goal that requires complete faith in God. Kahane views this all as a zero-sum game. "Whoever hesitates, whoever fears the non-Jew, shows that he questions G-d's ability to help His people. It is doubtful whether he completely believes in G-d as an Omnipotent Supreme power."[45]

This is all deployed as a critique of Israel's unwillingness to recognize, or at least fully integrate, the opportunity that Zionism presents. "While G-d has afforded us the greatest most powerful miracles since the Hasmonean victories, we have remained that same exilic product, the same slave to the nations and slave to slaves, with that same base spirit which led G-d to decree what he decreed against our ancestors in the desert. . . . We must never forget the following principle: Whoever relies on the non-Jew and seeks his aid, repels the Messiah, pushes off the redemption, and brings us G-d's wrath and ire. Redemption will come only when Israel are alone, without any protection or help."[46] Elsewhere Kahane quotes Rabbi David Kimhi's (Radak) comment on Isaiah 30:2: "For a slave to seek dependence on a different master constitutes enormous rebellion against his first master."[47] As Kahane reads it, unless the Jews totally rebel against their first master, the gentiles, they can never take on their true master, God. For holiness to be an operational category for Israel it must separate itself from the unholy, and that requires not only removing the non-Jew from its soil, something Kahane advocated politically, but also releasing Israel from dependence on other nations as a spiritual exercise of purification.[48] There is, for Kahane, a decree of holiness and a fulfillment of holiness; the former is divinely ordained ("You are holy unto Me"), the latter is enacted through separation ("I separate you from the nations").

Unlike even most religious Zionists, who understand the need, and efficacy, of foreign alliances as part of the necessary condition of modern statecraft, for Kahane Israel as a "nation alone" not only has no allies but *cannot* have any allies. This is the very condition of redemption, as only this will secure Israel's full trust in God. Thus the purpose of separation is not only to minimize foreign influence but also to cultivate a piety of dependence on God that for Kahane is impossible as long as alliances and dependencies exist. "G-d longs for this trust in Him, which will lead Israel to isolation and to relying only on G-d. This, in turn, will open the gates of *Kiddush Hashem*."[49] If exile itself is a state of defilement, a *Hillul ha-Shem*, then the establishment of a state is a gift of holiness, a *Kiddush ha-Shem*, but only on the condition of severing ties to the nations.[50] The very nature of such dependencies merely recalibrates a diasporic kind of servitude, even if is now being enacted in a state of sovereignty.

Whereas radical secular Zionists such as Yosef Hayyim Brenner or Micha Yosef Berdyczewski viewed Zionism as liberating the Jew from the Diaspora, including the Judaism it produced, Kahane saw the project of emancipation from exile as involving a recommitment to Judaism via a cleansing of an exilic mentality that had seeped into Judaism. The mandate of Zionism is not to become "like all the nations," which is false diasporic rhetoric in Kahane's view, but just the opposite: to create a sovereign nation-state to prove "both to the nations *and to Israel* that G-d is omnipotent, and that the entire universe is under His control."[51] Commenting on Rabbi Shimon bar Yochai's worry about Torah being forgotten in Israel, Kahane writes, "We, too, due to the exile we have endured for close to two thousand years as a Jewish minority unavoidably influenced by non-Jewish culture, concepts and values, have mixed together alien ideas with our Jewish beliefs. These ideas have distorted Torah and created a conceptually taboo combination that has caused the pure truth of G-d's Torah to be forgotten. As a result, even Jews who mechanically keep the mitzvot and call themselves 'religious' are immersing in Torah waters while grasping a non-kosher animal—non-Jewish culture in their hands."[52] Secular Zionists such as Brenner and groups such as the Canaanites saw Zionism as a way to overcome Judaism; Kahane saw it as a way to purify a contaminated Judaism.[53] This purification process required a radical severance of any dependence on the outside world and the removal of Arabs, not only because they were an enemy that could never accept Jewish sovereignty (as Kahane had argued in previously published work) but also because of the mandate of separation—or as Kahane put it, "The real reason for the prohibition against a non-Jew living in a city is not at all a matter of holiness but of separation."[54]

As musar masters taught, holiness (*kedusha*) and purity (*taharah*) are achieved through separation (*havdalah*). To support his claim, Kahane quotes Rabbi Obadiah Sforno's comment to Deuteronomy 23:15, "Your camp must be holy": "He, therefore, decreed separation from the nations and from the profane, because without it, *kedusha* is impossible, as it states explicitly, *You shall be holy unto Me, for I, the L-rd am holy, and I have separated you from the nations to be Mine* (Leviticus 20:26)."[55] For Kahane separation must have both an internal and an external aspect: separating the polity from foreign dependence and purifying the land from non-Jewish influence. "There are two components to this separation. On the one hand, Israel must leave the exile and live only in their special land, lest they be influenced by the nations and their culture. On the other hand, even in *Erez Yisrael* itself Israel must separate themselves from that evil culture."[56] Leaving the Diaspora, the raison d'être of Zionism, was not itself an *act* of purification but only a *condition* of purification. The Jewish state came into being only to erase the scourge of *Hillul ha-Shem*: "*When they came unto the nations . . . they profaned My holy name.*"[57] The fulfillment of separation grows only from the purification from gentile influence that Kahane claimed both the religious community and Zionism failed to achieve.

The Betrayal of the Torah Scholars

The mandate that the Israelites must separate themselves from the surrounding peoples is a central tenet of the Hebrew Bible and later Judaism, manifest in both Jewish law and custom.[58] This prohibition is intrinsically tied to the perceived immoral culture and practices of the other nations. The biblical context has to do with image-worship that is associated with immoral behavior and social deviance. The Bible exhibits an ostensible zero-sum intolerance toward such practices, demanding the Israelites not only avoid them but also violently destroy any man-made images, natural markers where worship takes place (trees, etc.), or houses of worship when they entered the land (e.g.,

Deuteronomy 12, 32). Rabbinic teaching excises the violent commandment to destroy these images but reiterates and expands the various prohibitions of using them, engaging with them, or benefiting from them. The reasons given in the biblical tradition are twofold: first, these practices defile the land (thus they must be destroyed); and second, interacting with people who engage in such practices will result in absorbing their values and thus distract the Israelites from their exclusive fidelity to God. Rabbinic teaching expands the latter category while largely minimizing the former one.

The Jewish experience of exile and the construction of a new form of collective life in the Diaspora shifted the perception of Jewish-gentile interaction considerably. In some parts of the religious tradition, the land itself was considered defiled because of the abovementioned practices and the absence of a Temple, while in other parts of the tradition the land retained its full sanctity even without a Temple or Jewish collective residency.[59] Interaction with surrounding cultures in the Diaspora was inevitable and even necessary, even if halakhah sought to curtail it as much as possible.[60] The question for jurists was not *whether* their constituents would be influenced by surrounding cultures but *how much* influence was permissible and under what conditions.[61] But for Kahane the very existence of exile is a defiled state, in part because the infiltration of foreign culture and ideas was inevitable.

Kahane goes even further, calling exile a *Hillul ha-Shem*; and thus the best the Jews can do is to protect Judaism through attenuated practice until such time as they can return to the land and purify Judaism from its foreign influence. "Only if Israel enter the Land do they receive G-d as their L-rd and Master. Outside the Land, they live under the nations and their harmful cultural influence. This involved *Hillul ha-Shem*, because when we live among the nations, under their rule, the nations' gods and culture enjoy superiority. Moreover, the Torah is adulterated by alien, non-Jewish ideas."[62] Kahane argued throughout his later writings that the Judaism of the Diaspora is tainted by the exilic experience and its having absorbed "alien culture." For example: "Today, people have risen up to destroy us who are smitten with the alien culture. Tragically, these include even Torah scholars and learned Jews who have pronounced that, halakhically speaking, there is no state of war between us and the Arabs in our land, hence we are forbidden to treat them as enemies."[63] He further states that anyone who renders a halakhic ruling that Jews are obligated to treat the Arab mercifully is a *rodef* (one who attacks with the intent to kill) "who collaborates with the gentile in the killing of Jews."

Kahane does not spare even Torah scholars from the *rodef* epithet. As products of a diasporic community irredeemably tainted by a surrounding alien culture, these traditionalists may think they are exhibiting Torah values, but in Kahane's estimation they are teaching a distorted or false form of Judaism. Kahane's call to remove this contamination is the musar teaching at the very core of *The Jewish Idea*.

This enterprise requires him to reframe traditional Jewish understandings of mercy. Kahane begins by referring to a Talmudic dictum in the tractate Shabbat, 151b: "Whoever shows mercy to his fellow man shall be shown mercy by G-d, and whoever does not show mercy to his fellow man shall not be shown mercy by G-d." This passage has often been used as a signpost for Judaism's merciful tendency. But Kahane sees that reading as decontextualized and thus mistaken.

> Let the reader understand that our sages learned this principle from a verse quoted immediately following the command to burn and destroy the apostate city (Deuteronomy 13:18): *God shall make you merciful and have mercy on you.* Precisely this indicates a Divine decree. It shows that the definition of mercy and love of Israel are what G-d defines them to be, and not the mercy of fools enslaved to alien culture. Together with the mitzvah of bestowing love and mercy on our fellow Jew, it is also a mitzvah to hate the Jew who has cast off his yoke. Our sages therefore labeled such persons "enemies of Israel."[64]

For Kahane the rabbinic view that Jews with power are obligated to show "mercy" to the Arab has been tainted by "Western" values that do not cohere with the divine decree. Compassion and mercy, for him, are mandates defined solely in the classical literature (albeit in the texts he chooses) and not as interpreted through the lens of liberal values.

Zionism and the state of Israel create for him the possibility of correcting these distortions, thereby purifying the land from its defilement, but only if Torah authorities are willing to acknowledge the inevitable distortion that has taken place over time: "Hence, if such a non-Jew performed a hostile act against a Jew, he most certainly deserves to die. Let us pay no heed to assimilated Hellenists influenced by alien culture, who show compassion to cruel individuals who in the future will show cruelty to merciful sons of merciful fathers."[65] It is not, for Kahane, that the Arab who acts in a hostile manner "deserves to die" simply as a matter of security; rather, it is, for him, part of the divine mandate that Jews once again have the ability to enact these imperatives. Just as the Bible warned the Israelites that they would be led astray if they commingled with the surrounding peoples, Kahane argued that the Diaspora made that inevitable and thus a return to sovereignty required a collective correction of *tikkun ha-midot* to return to the biblical mandate.

Here as elsewhere we see that Kahane's project has a kind of antirabbinic resonance in two senses. First, he advocates a return to the biblical model of conquest as he understands it, one that he believed should be reactivated once the Jews were again sovereign in their land. Second, while part of the rabbinic project is arguably to reread the Bible through its own (exilic/diasporic) lenses, Kahane proposes the reverse. Returning to the Bible, for him, does not mean marginalizing the rabbis but rather constitutes a rereading of them *through* the Bible as opposed to the rabbinic project of reading the Bible through the rabbis.[66] The Bible is turned into the lens through which the rabbis can now be revised and purified from foreign influence.[67] Kahane sees himself championing a resurgence of biblical ideas of conquest, revenge, and purification—ideas that the rabbis of exilic times denuded, softened, and contextualized.

For example, speaking against the disease of secularism, Kahane draws on some biblical motifs to explain the reality he faces:

> The leprosy of our time is the penetration of alien, non-Jewish culture into our holy camp. Such infiltrations are like the idols brought into the Temple sanctuary, where only the Ark of Testimony was permitted. . . . Countless myriads of Jews have been taken captive intellectually by the defective ideas of foreign culture. . . . Indeed, this is the root of evil in our day; there is no greater, more important or essential task than to eradicate that root, blighted with gall and wormwood. Unless we halt the penetration of foreign culture, then all the false, distorted, alien thought and the dreadful hodgepodge which have infiltrated our midst will remain in the Torah.[68]

As opposed to the romantic notion of transforming the profane into the holy, common in the religious-Zionist Kookean school, Kahane's musar approach advocates both separation from and, more stridently, destruction of those forces that distort the tradition as it emerges from a dormant state of Diaspora. For example, soon after his immigration to Israel, Kahane advocated uprooting churches in Jerusalem, claiming that they transgressed the biblical mandate against idolatry in the land. The comparison to idolatry made here and elsewhere is suggestive of the Bible's stark intolerance toward such phenomena and its mandate to destroy, and not only avoid, such influence. This is the basic template of Kahane's *The Jewish Idea*: a return to the biblical mandate with the return to power. The rabbinic sages, in eliminating the violent call for the destruction of idolatry and for mercilessness toward the surrounding peoples, may have been influenced by their own exilic and powerless state. But for Kahane the sovereign return to the land renewed the possibility of fulfilling Jewish life on neobiblical terms.[69]

Democracy and Equality

Uncomfortable Question for Comfortable Jews contains two long chapters on democracy: "A Jewish State versus Western Democracy" and "Judaism versus Western Democracy." Each is marked by what is arguably Kahane's most sarcastic, caustic, and vicious prose defending himself against the secular-Zionist enterprise that was trying to eject him from government.[70] Later in the book, Kahane's critique of Israeli democracy (as we have seen, he maintained that if Israel was *truly* democratic it could not be *Jewish*) moves from a political argument to a theological one:

> The liberal west speaks of the rule of democracy, of the authority of the majority, while Judaism speaks of the Divine truth that is immutable and not subject to the ballot box, or to majority error. The liberal west speaks of the absolute equality of all peoples while Judaism speaks of a spiritual *status*, of the chosenness of the Jews from and above all other people, of the special and exclusive relationship between G-d and Israel. The liberal west speaks of subjective truth, of no one being able to claim or know what is absolute truth, while Judaism speaks of objective, eternal truth that is known, having been given by G-d at Sinai. . . . But above all else, Judaism differs from liberal *and non-liberal* western values in that the foundation upon which it rests is that of "*the yoke of Heaven*," the acceptance of G-d's law and values and concept of truth, without testing them in the fires of one's own knowledge, choice, desire, and acceptance.[71]

For Kahane the very nature of democracy undermines the possibility of a return of the Jews to their land to set up a sovereign Torah-style state in preparation for redemption. The political unviability of democracy to ensure Jewish sovereignty stands at the center of his political critique; the use of democracy as the political model of modern Israel stands at the center of his theological critique. The return to *Judaism* that in his mind is Israel's raison d'être, at least in the latter part of his career, can never take place as long as democracy reigns. He makes this quite clear in his conclusion:

> The State of Israel which rose up in the year 1948, I am convinced, is the beginning, not only of redemption, but of the grace period granted us. In the very marrow of my bones I feel the Almighty, in His infinite mercy and goodness, gives the final beseeching opportunity to turn needless suffering into glorious and instant redemption. . . . For make no mistake. The magnificent miracle of return and rise of a Jewish State is surely the beginning of the Final Redemption, but hardly the end. The true finality, the magnificent era of the Messiah, comes to fruition gloriously and majestically and breathtakingly only if we cleave to the great axiom, "if you walk in my statutes . . . I will give peace unto the land" (Leviticus 26). This is the immutable law of the People of Israel. There is no escaping it. [72]

In addition to the political and theological critique of democracy in *Uncomfortable Questions*, there is a third critique that emerges only in *The Jewish Idea*. Whereas in *Uncomfortable Questions* democracy is considered incommensurate with Torah generally, in *The Jewish Idea* it is treated as a foreign implant, likened to the golden calf or idolatry: "This principle of forcing goodness on the public invokes another area in which Torah ideals fundamentally contradict the alien culture of the nations; namely, the issue of democracy and following the majority in every matter. According to that alien culture, there is no deity more lofty, no calf more golden, than democracy before which every non-Jewish knee must genuflect and every informer's tongue must swear. Democracy has given approval to abominable sins and transformed the world from the exclusive holding of Hashem, its master, into the private property of lowly man."[73] Kahane supports his position by citing a Talmudic passage, Sanhedrin 26a, about the controversy between King Hezekiah and Shevna the Scribe during Sennacherib's siege of Jerusalem. Arguing about the benefits and dangers of surrender, Hezekiah says, "Perhaps God favors the majority, and since they would surrender, perhaps we should too," at which point a prophet appears and says, "Do not treat as a coalition that which this people calls a coalition." The Talmud continues, "Shevna's coalition was evil, and such a coalition does not count." I assume Kahane doesn't address majority rule in halakhic literature because that would not correlate with democratic majority rule where the criterion for inclusion is simply citizenship. He notes that in the tradition, majority rule does not apply to those who do not abide by the commandments and certainly not to non-Jews.

"Democracy was given to societies and countries lacking the truth."[74] It is not simply antithetical to a Jewish state; for Kahane it undermines the special status of the Jews more generally.[75] As a political entity Israel must remain "abnormal" for it to fulfill its destiny. This is why liberal-democratic principles function for him as idolatry, drawing Israel away from its divine purpose. "A thick wall divides Israel from the nations, a divine partition which separates the sacred from the profane, between Israel and the nations. Indeed, holiness and separateness descended upon us from heaven as a beloved pair, bound to one another by Divine decree."[76]

Although Kahane's audience here was mostly convinced of the theological and messianic implications of the state, many remained somewhat uncertain about how the state and theological destiny merged. Zvi Yehuda Kook, building on his father's outlook, offered a dialectical model of transvaluation, involving the irony that redemption is initiated by those who don't quite believe in it. But the unfolding of events, he surmised, would eventually lead many of them to return to their roots and more clearly see the cosmic import of their early behavior.[77] In *The Jewish Idea* Kahane offered a different template. For him the process of redemption had begun, and a ticking clock was counting down the years in which Israel would have to purify itself from foreign influence to prepare for redemption. He develops this notion in detail in *Forty Years*. If those conditions are not met, redemption will come anyway, but as discussed above it will come through Jewish blood and not the blood of Israel's enemies.

Unlike the Kooks, Kahane did not trust any process of transvaluation of the secular. Rather, Jews had to purify the body and polity of Israel, excising those foreign elements before time ran out. While this is a pillar of his program to expel the Arabs, it is also the engine that generates his critique of secular Zionism and the foreign elements it brought into Israel. Building a true Jewish polity requires an act of purification within and without, and there is no real difference for Kahane between the threat of the Arabs and the threat of democracy. Each prevents the process of purification required for the coming end-time. In Kahane's estimation democracy is the best form of government for a "normal" country but not for Israel, which needs to embrace its "abnormality" to fulfill its destiny. Here he twists the anti-Semitic trope of Jews being abnormal by conceding the point and then using it to justify why Israel could not be a democracy. One sees in Kahane a kind of Möbius strip of political and theological considerations involving Arabs and democracy, normalization and isolation. Although each can be discussed separately, they constitute a single political theology.

Revenge and Redemption

One of the best-known aspects of Kahane's theo-political platform is the importance he accords to revenge. *Nekama* in Hebrew, revenge is a term that appears frequently in biblical literature, less so in rabbinic literature, and even less so in musar literature.[78] And yet revenge becomes a central tenet of Kahane's program for national correction. Messiah and redemption are of course central motifs both in classical Judaism and Zionism, specifically religious Zionism, but they appear less frequently in Kahane's early writings. Belief in the messiah is of course implied, but it is not the driving force behind Kahane's writings in the 1970s. In *The Jewish Idea,* however, the final twelve chapters, comprising more than two hundred pages, are devoted to messianic themes and revenge plays a role in almost every one.

That God is a vengeful God in the Hebrew Bible is fairly clear ("The Lord is a zealous and avenging God" [Nahum 1:2], "God of vengeance" [Psalms 94:1], "With a strong hand and an outstretched arm, and with overflowing fury" [Ezekiel 20:34]).[79] At issue for Kahane is the extent to which the notion of revenge functions as an obligation for Jews (and not only God) in relation to those around them. And furthermore, what is the correlation between revenge and redemption? That God can and does take revenge on Israel's enemies is a precept of Torah and comes through very forcefully in the prophets and in Psalms. And this notion has been popularized in the liturgy. For example, one traditionally responds to human violent tragedy by stating, "May God avenge their blood." When, how, and under what conditions are *Jews* allowed or even obligated to take revenge on their enemies is another matter.

Kahane asserts that divine vengeance is not simply an act of divine punishment but a necessary prelude to redemption: "Hashem is not just a 'God of vengeance,' a 'zealous and avenging God,' at present. The complete redemption as well, will come about through God's rising in His fury to avenge the profanation of His name and the spilt blood of his servants."[80] If all Kahane did was offer a plethora of biblical and rabbinic sources on divine revenge, there would be nothing new here or even provocative. While more modern or liberal versions of Judaism often seek to suppress, contextualize, or interpret many of these instances, the idea that God will take revenge against God's (and Israel's) enemies is impossible to conceal. It is, for example, one of the pillars of the book of Psalms.[81] But Kahane goes much further than this. He views the relationship between God and Israel as covenantal not only in the sense that there is mutual responsibility and obligation, but that both partners are implicated in the other such that an attack on one is an attack on both. An attack on Israel, that is, is an attack on God. Put otherwise, an attack on Israel, for whatever reason, is a *Hillul ha-Shem* that warrants divine revenge, even if that revenge is meted out by Israel. Quoting the midrash *Mekhilta d'Rebbe Ishmael*, "Whoever attacks Israel is treated as having attacked God," he writes, "Hence God must rise up and take revenge against those who attack Israel, for they attack God Himself."[82]

This idea comes through in Kahane's reading of the midrash *Sifri* on Numbers 31:1–3, which states, "God spoke to Moses, saying, 'Take revenge for the children of Israel against the Midianites.' . . . Moses spoke to the people saying, 'Detach men for armed service against Midian, so that God's revenge can be taken against the Midianites'."[83] Kahane notes that the midrash calls this "God's revenge" so as "to inform us that the two are the same."[84] That is, when Israel is commanded to take revenge, they are doing so at God's behest. When does such a command apply if it is not explicitly given as in Numbers 31? Kahane held that it applies whenever Israel is attacked or in danger, because that very act constitutes an attack against God.[85] Thus acting in revenge against an enemy of Israel is acting to prevent the erasure of God—which is the consequence of a *Hillul ha-Shem*—from the world. In some sense, then, acting against Israel is a manifestation of impurity that needs to be extirpated to the extent that the desecration is linked to the laws of purity.[86]

The covenantal agreement, according to Kahane, includes Israel's right, even obligation, to "resurrect God" though revenge. "Great is revenge for it resurrects G-d, proves His existence, and humbles the arrogant sinner so that the righteous and the world joyously declare, *Verily there is a reward for the righteous; verily there is a G-d who judges on earth* (Psalms 58:12)." Alternatively, one who forgoes the obligation of revenge, for reasons that Kahane claims are the influence of liberalism or "Hellenism" ("assimilationist devotees of an alien culture"), in essence acts against God and will thus become subject to divine wrath.

Here Kahane cites Ahab's failure to take revenge in 1 Kings 20. "In response to this indulgence, this foolish mercy on Ahab's part, one of the prophets—some say Micha—says to him, *Thus says the L-rd, Because you have released this man who incurred a death sentence your life shall go for his life, and your people for his people* (1 Kings 20:42)."[87] To forgo revenge is to enable and empower the erasure of God, which in the end-time will be eradicated through violence against Israel's enemies and all those who aid and abet their war against God. "It follows that the redemption will come in the wake of G-d's desire to take His revenge, thereby sanctifying His great and awesome Name."[88]

Even as Kahane basically viewed revenge as a mitzvah like any other, no different from Sabbath laws or dietary restrictions, the distinctiveness of the mitzvah of revenge is that it is quite difficult to enact devoid of emotion, as the very obligation arises from an act, threat, or violence against oneself or one's people. Taking a musar approach, Kahane addresses this problem through a lengthy reading of commentaries on the avenging of Dina in Shechem, the classic narrative case of revenge in the Pentateuch (Genesis 34). The story concludes with Jacob's apparent anger at Simeon and Levi, the two who instigated the violent revenge against the people of Shechem. After a long series of citations, Kahane states:

> To conclude, Jacob did not, G-d forbid, curse Simeon and Levi, but their *rage*, the evil cause of their sin. It therefore says, "Cursed be their rage, for it is fierce," and our sages comment (Bamidbar Raba 99:6), "He only cursed their rage." We also find (Lekach Tov to Genesis 49:7), "Cursed be their rage for it is fierce": "May their rage be deferred and diminished. May their anger be lessened." Zealotry and vengefulness are crucial attributes. But only if exercised for the sake of heaven. As done by Phineas and Elijah, and others like them. If vengeful acts are motivated by sinful anger, however, that anger must be condemned. [89]

Revenge is a tricky mitzvah and yet it is essential to the process of purification required for redemption. In fact, for Kahane revenge itself serves as a purifying force: "Revenge is zeal for a good cause. By switching the order of the letters, לקנאות—*lekan'ot*, to be zealous, becomes לנקות—*lenakot*, to cleanse. Whoever is zealous on G-d's behalf cleanses the evildoer through his revenge. Until he does so, the evildoer remains unclean."[90]

However, much of what appears as a justification for revenge as an act of purification, if done without the rage of Simeon and Levi, is undermined in Kahane's chapters "The Nations' Punishment for the Persecution of the Jews" and "The Haughtiness of the Nations" toward the end of *The Jewish Idea*. In those chapters, and in his final chapters on redemption and messianism more generally, Kahane exhibits anger and vitriol that hardly conforms with his view of revenge as a mitzvah "for the sake of heaven." The lofty ideal of disinterested revenge never takes root. In fact, it arguably undermines the entire musar teaching *The Jewish Idea* tries to convey.

Kahane's view of the role of the state of Israel in the redemptive process is quite straightforward. Israel came into existence to erase *Hillul ha-Shem* from the world; that is its raison d'être. In this sense it is the political arm of Jewish civilization more generally that has been mired in impurity for millennia and thus unable to procure its own salvation. For Kahane Israel is an opportunity, not in itself the inauguration of redemption; political sovereignty created that possibility. In addition, it has to prevail in an external war against God's enemies (who for him are identical to the Jews' enemies), with the Arabs as only the proximate players; its military capabilities created that possibility.

Kahane does not shy away from using the term "war" against those Jews who act against the trajectory of redemption. Basing himself on a stark comment about the *erev rav* (mixed multitude, Exodus 12:38) by Rabbi Elijah of Vilna (the Vilna Gaon or GRA) cited in Hillel Rivlin's *Kol ha-Tor,* Kahane notes, "The *erev rav* is that part of the Jewish People intent on war against G-d and against the truth and credibility of Torah. With them we face an uncompromising battle to the finish, and the GRA emphasized this in his call to holy war against them."[91] The GRA, as cited by Rivlin, viewed the *erev rav* as the group of Jews who seek to separate the two messiahs (Messiah son of Joseph and Messiah son of David) by mating Esau and Ishmael.[92] This is done by the GRA through Armelius, who parenthetically is the Antichrist figure in *Sefer Zerubbabel.*[93]

Kahane's point here is much more prosaic and has little need for the mythology extant in the GRA's comment: "I have elaborated on this in order to make clear to the nation smitten with insanity, blindness, and mental confusion just how great redemption 'in haste' can be if we are just worthy of it. . . . It will not come as long as Israel profanes G-d's name by their refusal to expel from *Erez Yisrael* the Ishmaelites, who revile and profane G-d's name, as long as the Temple Mount remains a den of alien Ishmaelite foxes who come near yet are neither killed nor banished. . . . No redemption based on *Kiddush ha-Shem* can arrive while Israel concedes regarding *Hillul ha-Shem.*"[94] Channeling Ezekiel, Kahane proclaims that divine fury will appear. Who will be its target remains largely dependent on how much of a correction the Jews are able to accomplish before it arrives.

Conclusion

The last line in the text cited above, "No redemption based on *Kiddush ha-Shem* can arrive while Israel concedes regarding *Hillul ha-Shem,*" captures Kahane's entire binary analysis of Zionism. Kahane viewed his time as the great opportunity for divine purification and national correction. This required the act of severing, even violently, Israel from the exile. "The whole *liquidation* of the exile is for Israel's good, so they do not assimilate among the nations" (emphasis added). Israel was also required to engage in two related endeavors: first, to isolate itself as an act of purification; second, to enact revenge against God's enemies, violently if necessary, to erase *Hillul ha-Shem* until God entered and completed the program.[95]

For Kahane this is not a matter of "yes" or "no" regarding redemption: Israel's existence signals that the end-time is upon us. The question is only if it will happen "in haste," that is, triumphantly, or in travail, that is, "in its time." Given the millennia of exile and the deep foreign influences on Jews and Judaism, the way to procure redemption "in haste" is through purification of the Jewish mind and body from those influences and return to the biblical mandate of conquest, isolation, and revenge against the enemies of God (who are by definition also the enemies of Israel).

The template for all this is musar's notion of *tikkun ha-midot*, the correction of moral character as a desideratum of true Torah observance. Kahane's approach to the question of musar in *The Jewish Idea* is twofold. First, he nationalizes the musar project to make it the foundation of a national redemptive religiosity and theo-politics. Second, he returns to the biblical mandate as he understands it and asks his readers to reread the Bible as a program for national *correction*.

He errs, in my view, in staking his claim on rabbinic literature and building his program as a form of nationalized musar. Kahane is essentially a neobiblical, and in many ways an antirabbinic, thinker and perhaps his ties to Orthodoxy and normative Judaism prevent him from making that overt. His select use of rabbinic sources belies a much more imperialistic neobiblical frame. In terms of musar, his advocacy of revenge and blatant antihumanism were too emotionally charged to enable his followers to act in dispassionate ways or cultivate a personality sensitized to suffering. In fact, his program promoted a kind of warrior personality, not only against the *yezer ha-ra* (evil inclination) but against other human beings.

It is worth considering here yet another way in which Kahane's vision breaks with the Kookean school and its view of the end-time. The Kookean rendering of the approaching end-time is cosmological in nature and regards the Jews as part of a larger process about which they are aware to differing degrees. The Jews certainly have a role to play, but that role is largely in settling and populating the land of Israel and ensuring that religious practice, now wedded with living on the land, continues to flourish. In Abraham Isaac Kook's aspirational vision, this new society—one that did not yet exist—would embrace what he called "musar elyon," read by some of his more liberal readers as a heightened state of humanistic values that are in accord with his romantic vision of Torah values. Kook's romantic-cosmological approach allows for tolerance of the nonobservant Jews who dwell in the land as part of a larger seismic shift that will eventually result in collective *teshuva* following a realization that their secular project is bound up with redemptive history. In addition, democracy is tolerated in the Kookean schema as the best possible political mandate at present, a way station that will evolve as redemption nears.[96]

The Kahane of the mid- to late 1980s, by contrast, deployed musar's focus on self-correction and its view of Torah as a map for self-perfection to support his program of a radical revision of Judaism itself—from a religion infected with the disease of foreign influence to one that would unabashedly enact its original purpose: eradicating *Hillul ha-Shem* so as to prepare for God's reentry into history. It is an uncompromisingly Manichean vision filled with binaries of good vs. evil and requiring self-sacrifice as an act of purification for the sake of national restoration. Rather than early Zionism's self-sacrifice of working the land on behalf of the collective common good, Kahane proposes an overcoming of one's (liberal) inclinations to engage in the messy and violent work of national purification. Kahane's later views encapsulated in *The Jewish Idea* owe more to an eschatology of conquest that is better expressed by the prophet Ezekiel than by Ze'ev Jabotinsky.

The biblical and rabbinic tradition serves Kahane's goals of presenting a Jewish political theology founded on divine election, and the requirement of separation from the gentile as a condition of political and spiritual sovereignty. The Bible and the rabbis often differ on the implementation of such separation including the role of violence in it, but Kahane argues that the basic rubrics of separation and purity remained intact as the Jews moved from territorial control to the Diaspora with the hope of a renewed conquest.[97] In addition, he claims that rabbinic ambivalence about the use of power is in part the necessary consequence of the Jews' historical situation but also, and more importantly, illustrates the corrosive way in which dispersion distanced the rabbis from the biblical mandate. This is what I mean by maintaining that *The Jewish Idea* is a neobiblical work, an attempt to reconstruct the biblical mandate now refracted through rabbinic lenses at a time when the conditions were ripe as a result of Zionism.

Moving past Kahane to the decades after his death, where is *The Jewish Idea* in right-wing Zionism today? Although it remains his most widely read book, in some sense the contemporary settler movement, very complex in its makeup, is still dominated by Kookean influence and in some circles has become a kind of amalgam of Kookean mystical romanticism and Kahane's materialist militarism (even among those who are not neo-Kahanists). Thus the sentiment implied in "Kahane was right" ("Kahane tzadak"), a graffito that dots the Israeli landscape, is a popular rendering of how some Israelis view the unending conflict with the Palestinians. While not necessarily acceding to Kahane's militaristic solutions, many still maintain that his diagnosis of the problem was essentially correct. This is why when we think about Kahane's influence today, we need to draw a much wider circle than one that would include only open Kahanists. There is a much more extensive orbit of influence of those who believe he was essentially right even as his tactics may have been mistaken, as illustrated in the anecdote that begins the introduction to this study.

This is why more generally the question of violence remains a crucial issue in the contemporary settler movement; is it justified and if so, on what grounds?[98] That is, if one thinks Kahane was "right," why were his solutions wrong? In some way, Kookean romanticism in part holds back Kahane's militarism. As long as people believe divine fiat is still operational, human agency can be held in check. But as I noted at the end of chapter 5, once history seems to be moving in a different direction, militarism is there for the taking.[99]

Both the Kooks and the later Kahane were driven by a belief in the coming end-time. And each envisioned a return to full sovereignty through conquest. They differed on the role of the Jews as well as the tactics necessary to achieve that end.[100] To some degree, however, Kahane's musar approach in *The Jewish Idea* and the mystical romanticism in the elder and younger Kooks' writings have produced a strange brew whose influence is still being felt. Completed at a time just before the Oslo Accords in 1993 when it seemed Kahane's project for the militant transvaluation of (post-) Zionism had collapsed, *The Jewish Idea* is Kahane's final word on Judaism, Jewishness, and what he viewed as the last phase before redemption. His redemptive dream was silenced by the assassin's bullet in November 1990. Or was it? Apparently, his proactive redemptive politics lives on. And *The Jewish Idea* is its testament.

Conclusion

THIS BOOK ARGUES that while Kahane left America in 1971, America never left Kahane. As a member of Betar Youth, he was reared with the revolutionary politics of the Zionist Revisionists amid fantasies of the Irgun fighters and a newly conquered land. He was also raised in postwar American Orthodoxy in Brooklyn, a world traumatized by the Holocaust and reluctant to make waves, living what Kahane called "*Shah-schtil* Judaism." Finally, he came into his own as the New Left was radicalizing America's youth, as the race wars shook American cities, and as the Six-Day War suddenly put Israel on the radar for many American Jews. Kahane absorbed identity politics and made it central to his program to instill pride in Jews through power and, if necessary, violence.

The combination of radical Zionism, in which Kahane did not directly take part, New Left radicalism that he witnessed from a distance, the race wars, which were closer to home, and Israel's new muscle triumphalism after 1967 formed Kahane's public persona. He adeptly used the tactics of the far left for the purposes of the reactionary right. He channeled the passion of the antiwar movement, which he opposed, into the movement for Soviet Jewry, which for a short time he ostensibly led. He made being a Jewish radical chic for a generation of young Jews looking beyond the quiescence of their parents. He moved to Israel in 1971 but never shed his American mindset. In Israel his political agenda of separation, chauvinism, pride, and violence in many ways mirrored his program to save the Diaspora Jew in America. As noted in the introduction, we often look at Kahane's career backward, from his more well-known political life in Israel to his ur-career in America. This book reverses that trajectory. Understanding Kahane is understanding Kahane as an American Jew. That is what he was, and that is what he remained. It is for this reason, I argue, that while he may have aroused the angst and anger of a disenfranchised Israeli population, his political program failed miserably. It is only in the afterlife of Kahane, with the rise of a homegrown neo-Kahanism, that his Israeli influence is more deeply felt.

Spurned by the Israeli establishment, by the late 1980s Kahane was largely living the life of an ideological vagabond. When he was removed from the Knesset through the "Racism Law," his new home had effectively rejected him (even though he retained his Israeli citizenship) while he had largely rejected America, his country of birth. He continued his work, both in Israel and America, but became increasingly marginal. Kahane had become a persona non grata in many American venues where he had often spoken before. There were still places that welcomed him, such as Brooklyn College, Yeshiva University, some Orthodox synagogues, and a few Hillel centers, but the invitations declined over time.[1] His manner became more erratic, his rhetoric more volatile, and his demeanor more cynical and bitter. He was an outlaw with a diminishing audience yet his ideas continued to resonate.

One of his last appearances before his assassination was at Brandeis University in November 1990, where I was a graduate student at the time. There, four days before he was murdered in Manhattan, he faced a very contentious crowd. Kahane's vitriol was on full display.[2] For his ardent followers, the then-mounting optimism about a possible compromise in Israel/Palestine had only exacerbated their anxiety. Kahane remained for them an important voice of impending doom.

On the evening of November 5, 1990, Kahane gave a speech to a group of mostly Orthodox Jews at the Marriott Hotel in Manhattan. After the speech he was approached by a man disguised as an Orthodox Jew who pulled out a .357-caliber pistol and shot him in the neck. Soon after Kahane died of his wounds. The assassin, El Sayyid Nosair, an Egyptian-born American citizen living in New Jersey, fled the hotel and was later arrested by a police officer. Claiming innocence, Nosair was acquitted of the crime but was found guilty of other charges that resulted in a twenty-two-year sentence. He was later found guilty in connection to the first World Trade Center bombing in 1993 and around that time confessed to murdering Kahane.[3] It was later revealed that Nosair was a member of a terrorist cell connected to Omar Abdul-Rahman, the mastermind of the first World Trade Center bombing who also had ties to Al Qaeda. Kahane may thus have been the first American assassinated by someone connected to Al Qaeda.[4]

Despite his pariah status in Israel after his expulsion from the Knesset, his funeral was one of the largest in the country's history, attended by almost 150,000 people. He was eulogized by many respected figures of the time such as Rabbi Moshe Tendler of Yeshiva University, the Sephardic chief rabbi Mordechai Eliyahu, and popular singer Shlomo Carlebach. This occurred well after he was deemed racist by the Israeli government and his political party declared illegal.[5]

All this only speaks to the ubiquity and complexity of this iconoclastic figure. In many ways Kahane was the underbelly of American Orthodoxy and American Jewry more generally. He countered the liberal American establishment with a mix of identity politics, radicalism, and religion, offering the younger generation a way to absorb and respond to the aftermath of the Holocaust and to question their ostensibly safe situation in America. While American Jewry during the period of Kahane's activism was to a large degree liberal in orientation and proud of its acculturation and success in American society, there remained a deep ambivalence about America, a sense of mistrust that remained from the proximate memory of the Holocaust and that was just beginning to find a voice in the public square in the 1960s as Kahane was emerging as a public figure.

Kahane felt that Jews were being threatened from opposite ends: in the race wars of the 1960s they were considered "whitey" by blacks and thus targets for attack, while they were seen as pariahs by WASP America and thus vulnerable to Christian anti-Semitism. Being stuck between two warring factions was an all too familiar position for Jews. But America was supposed to be different. When the race wars positioned Jews once again in the middle, vulnerable from both sides, Kahane surmised that Jews could not escape their diasporic fate. American would not be the "new promised land" many immigrants had envisioned.[6]

Kahane expressed a sentiment that shared much with what would later become known as neoconservatism. He certainly read *Commentary*, mentioning the magazine a number of times, and even submitted a few articles to them, none of which were accepted for publication. But for the most part the so-called New York Intellectuals seemed uninterested in him.[7] In some way this was a class issue. Kahane catered to a population of young first-generation immigrants whose parents were survivors and who lived on the edges of, or mostly below, the middle class. Kahane viewed himself as a radical and modeled his movement after the Black Nationalists and other radical student groups on campuses, albeit with an exclusively Jewish agenda. He readily adopted "Jewish Power" as a moniker. The New York Intellectuals, by contrast, were mostly immigrants and children of immigrants from broadly leftist—and in some cases socialist and Trotskyite—backgrounds, and they clustered in enclaves such as City College in the 1940s.[8] Many of the New York Intellectuals were from Western or Central Europe. Some, like Lucy Dawidowicz, were Eastern European and more traditional, but they were the exception to the rule.[9] Thus during those formative postwar years there were two reactionary movements against Jewish liberalism only a subway ride apart and yet mostly disconnected from each other. As Norman Podhoretz wrote in 1967, "One of the longest journeys in the world is the journey from Brooklyn to Manhattan—or at least from certain neighborhoods in Brooklyn to certain parts of Manhattan."[10]

The New York Intellectuals largely responded to the political and cultural upheaval of the 1960s and the birth of the New Left by turning rightward. Kahane, never a liberal to begin with, responded to the radicalism of that era by cultivating a Jewish radicalism to counter the radical left, sharing the tactics and the rebellious orientation of other radical movements yet fixating on an exclusively Jewish rather than universal cause. Kahane would have been, for the New York Intellectuals, part of what Lionel Trilling called the "adversary culture," the enemy of their attempt to recapture the American dream.[11] Kahane left America too early to witness the rise of neoconservatism, which he would have likely both supported and criticized at the same time; he would have favored its attack on liberalism and denigrated its secularism or even perfunctory religiosity.

Kahane's transition to Israel was difficult and largely unsuccessful in terms of his personal career. He brought with him the identity politics of the late 1960s, the consequences of the race wars and anti-Semitism, and an antiliberal mindset that had no organic roots in Israel. When Kahane emigrated to Israel in 1971, the country's now robust religious right was nowhere in sight; it would emerge soon after the Yom Kippur War in 1973 with the founding of Gush Emunim. At the time Israel was largely a left-leaning social-democratic society struggling to come to terms with occupying a large Palestinian population after 1967. What radical movements existed in the country were almost all of the left.[12]

Although Kahane, like most American Jews who immigrated to it at that time, romanticized Israel, it is apparent from the outset that he did not settle there to integrate into the country that existed but rather to transform it. His intention was to found an international JDL in Jerusalem that never materialized. His contentious political aspirations emerged almost immediately after his arrival and his first arrest came less than a year later. He took the radical politics of the American streets in a more religious direction, developing in his final years an apocalyptic, militant political theology targeting not only Arab

Israelis but all of secular Israel. His new constituency in Israel was made up of two indigenous groups. The first were disenfranchised Mizrachi Jews, mostly poor and from development towns, who oddly viewed this American new immigrant as a champion of their cause against the Ashkenazi elite. The second comprised young religious-Zionist yeshiva students schooled in the Zionism of Rabbi Abraham Isaac Kook and his son Zvi Yehuda but drawn to Kahane's activist theology of revenge. A third, smaller circle of followers was composed of Jewish immigrants from the Soviet Union who knew of him because of his involvement in the Soviet Jewry movement. Kahane's initial electoral success seemed to rest on what Ehud Sprinzak called "the increasing polarization of Israeli society along ethnic, social, and political lines" in the early 1980s.[13] Mounting anti-Arab sentiment in the poor development towns and the marginal yet growing desire for activism among some young yeshiva students helped drive whatever electoral success Kahane had.

He was murdered at the age of fifty-eight, and it is hard to imagine what would have become of him had he lived into an old age. Yet it seems clear that his larger worldview of perennial anti-Semitism, alongside his call for the Jews to prepare themselves for the fight for physical survival, remains evergreen in Jewish communities around the world.

The afterlife of Kahane is a story deserving of its own study, and one that can only be touched on here. Although America doesn't really have anything like a Kahanist movement today, many staunchly pro-Israel American Jews, especially in the Orthodox community, share certain Kahanist views without following his call to violence. And many American Jews support Kahane's right-wing solutions for Israel albeit not in Kahane's nomenclature.

In Israel it is a different story. There Kahane built an ideational infrastructure that outlived the now-outlawed Kahanist organizations. We see the effects of this neo-Kahanism to this day among settler youth who go by various names: "price-taggers," "hilltop youth," the Lahava (Prevention of Assimilation in Israel) movement, the Derech Chaim movement (following the vision of Rabbi Yitzchak Ginsburgh), and the Jewish Leadership movement, although the last is indeed an indigenous Israeli phenomenon with deep roots in the Israeli experience including Kookean theology.[14]

Israeli Jewish aficionados of neo-Kahanism do not share the experience of living in the Diaspora that fed his militancy. As we have seen, in *Our Challenge* he even criticizes sabras (native-born Israelis) for their inability to understand the dangers of living as a minority because of their lack of Diaspora experience. Yet this does not put off Kahane's most ardent followers, both in America and

Israel, who claim his legacy has been distorted and his teachings misunderstood. For example, in 2016, twenty-six years after Kahane's death, Shlomo Moriah published an article in the *Jewish Press* entitled "Thirty-Six Little-Known Admirers of Rabbi Meir Kahane" that featured personal testimonies from leading mainstream figures in the Jewish world who had spoken highly of Kahane, including chief rabbis of Israel, prominent *haredi* jurists, Zvi Yehuda Kook, and Modern Orthodox rabbis in the US and Israel.[15] It is not insignificant that this article was published in America, the place where Kahane's base in Brooklyn remains intact.

Today, as when Kahane was alive, his support largely comes from the Orthodox world, as Moriah's list of thirty-six "secret" admirers shows. While his Orthodox supporters express an affinity with the worldview propounded in Kahane's summa, *The Jewish Idea*, in his early years he had many secular American followers as well, a ragtag coterie of countercultural Jews alongside middle-aged lawyers like Bertram Zweibon, who cofounded the JDL, and Irv Rubin, who succeeded Kahane at the JDL.

Religion did not constitute the backbone of Kahane's American career but it increasingly did in Israel. A shift emerges from an early identarian Kahane in America to a later apocalyptic Kahane in Israel. But even here the shift is less extreme than we may think; the seeds of Kahane's later apocalypticism can already be felt in the identarian focus of his American career. It is simply that in Israel the stakes were much higher and the messianism that penetrated religious Zionism more generally was increasingly absorbed by Kahane in his later years. It is this very apocalypticism that leads Kahane out of Zionism to something darker and more pernicious.

Whereas the early Kahane mostly used religion as a source of identity politics, in Israel religion became the basis of his critique of secular Zionism and the centerpiece of his apocalypticism. And yet there are continuities in his public career, including in particular the role of religion in his thinking. Oddly, as I showed in chapter 6, his early yeshiva background was essential to his later thought, even as it was somewhat concealed in his earlier writings. In some sense the religious messianic Zionism that emerges just as Kahane is getting settled in Israel in 1971 makes religion both more relevant and more palpable.

That is not to say religion was central to Kahane's early American writings. A search of his early books and *Jewish Press* articles for Torah sources will reveal very few. His aim at the time was actually quite secular in orientation: survival and the cultivation of *hadar*, Jewish pride, through Jewish force and the unmasking of anti-Semitism. He knew that religion alone would not achieve his goals. His street activism was not about religion but about self-defense and about identity. Kahane held a starkly materialist view of Jews and Judaism, which is why he had such little interest in the Kooks, father and son, even later on in Israel. This is not true of the Israeli-born neo-Kahanists whose ideology is an amalgam of Kookism and Kahanism.

The Meir Kahane who is respected, even venerated, in Israel and America today is neither the cultural critic and ideologue for Jewish power and identity of his earlier phase, nor the critic of liberalism and the American Jewish establishment. Instead, for many reasons, he has become a martyr for the cause of Torah, the Jewish people, and the land of Israel. First, the 1960s identity politics that emerged from the race wars of that decade is no longer relevant in the same way. Multiculturalism and the resurgence of religion (e.g., the Tea Party, evangelical Christianity, and the rise of Jewish Orthodoxy) changed the playing field by placing religion more at the center of political and cultural debates. Second, the militancy of his tactics has fallen out of style. Third, the liberal American Jewish establishment, the target of his reactionary attacks, has been influenced by neoconservatism. This establishment has become more conservative and while certainly not Kahanist, has absorbed some of his early ideas about Jewish identity and pride. Radicalism became less necessary when some of the radical ideas seeped into the political and cultural mainstream. We can see this conservative turn in the resistance to Jewish progressivism in certain Jewish institutions. The rise and influence of AIPAC or of the Zionist Organization of America (admittedly much less influential) are but two examples.

Fourth, in Israel the Mizrachi animus against the Ashkenazi establishment has waned, though it is still operative and has produced Mizrachi groups like Shas to do much of its work. In short, in almost every sector where Kahane's influence was felt, conditions have changed enough to make such direct influence obsolete. The exception is the realm of religion, where Kahanism can still operate but only if his worldview and tactics are embedded in the romantic, messianic Zionism of Kookism. Thus for a variety of reasons having nothing to do with Kahanism, Kahanism's home today is within certain sectors of religion.

The irony here is that while Kookism, which today still dominates religious Zionism, and Kahanism are diametrically opposed in many ways as I illustrated in chapter 5, today they often work in tandem. There is enough that they share—a reified notion of the Jewish people, an expectation of the imminent end-time, a belief in the sanctity and Jewish ownership of the land, and a constitutive mistrust of liberalism—that enable them to function in tandem and productive tension.[16] This is partly because romanticism can easily become seduced by, and strengthened through, power.

Whereas in America it is not uncommon to encounter Jews who, when asked about Kahane, respond, "I believe in his ideas but not his tactics," as in my anecdote about my bat mitzvah interlocutor, in Israel one is more likely to encounter supporters of both his ideas *and* his tactics. As we move more than a century from that hopeful moment of the Balfour Declaration when Abraham Isaac Kook was inspired to believe that the end-time was coming and Herzl was the "Messiah son of Joseph," and more than half a century after that moment in 1967 when it seemed to Zvi Yehuda Kook and his followers that the end-time had arrived, those romantic visions have become jaded after the Camp David Accords, Oslo (beginning in 1993), and the two intifadas (beginning in 1987 and 2000, respectively). The disappointment that ensued made the activist approach of "pushing the end" appear more reasonable, and the Kahanism of *The Jewish Idea* provided a valuable resource for that purpose.

Kahane was never interested in waiting for divine fiat. For him, as a materialist, human agency was everything. God only redeems the Jewish people when Jews redeem the Jewish people. There is something transgressive about such a view, almost blasphemous, and yet one can see the attraction of it for a people still reeling from genocide. After the Holocaust, who could argue with it, especially those whose faith was shattered in the memory of "burning children."[17]

What about Kahane's afterlife in the Diaspora? I limit myself here to the Jewish communities in North America, where I see three approaches to Kahane that remain. The first is an utter and reflexive dismissal of him, espoused by many in the liberal Jewish community who view him as nothing more than a "thug," a "racist," and an "embarrassment to the Jewish people." Most of these opinions refer to Kahane's Israeli career with only a cursory understanding of the impact he had on American Jewry in the 1960s and 1970s. People who hold this attitude find it odd and troubling that I would devote a study to the development and trajectory of his thought. As one colleague told me, "Kahane has no thought!"

The second response comes mostly from the Orthodox world, those Jews who share Kahane's reflexive disdain for secularism even as they are deeply part of the secular world, and believe that he was "right" about most things but his expression and tactics undermined his message. This stance is embodied in many of the thirty-six figures presented in Moriah's article mentioned above. In a sense, for this group, who certainly hold a minority view, Kahane was mostly a mirror reflecting their own anxieties of living in America, or in secular Israel, and feeling under siege by the liberal society that refuses to understand the rabbinic idiom "Esau hates Jacob," that is, anti-Semitism is endemic to human civilization and the only way to fight it is through deterrence. While most in this group would not promote violence as a proactive tactic, Kahane's assertiveness is something they continue to respect.

The third response is much subtler. It is proffered by some on the center-right of the Jewish political spectrum. Over the course of my research for this book I have often been surprised by how much Kahane's general approach in the 1960s and 1970s, albeit not his tactics, has been absorbed and echoed by institutional American Jewry.[18] We can argue that the return to Jewish pride, assertiveness, and a sense of renewed Jewish identity in America is the result of the multiculturalism of the 1980s, which in many ways is true. American Jewry owes a tremendous debt to multiculturalism, which offered it the opportunity to find its identarian footing in a changing world.

Here, though, Kahane was in one sense ahead of his time, and in another, very much a product of it. The first aspect marked his success; the second, his failure. His critique of what he viewed as the assimilationist American Jewish establishment concerned its unwillingness and inability to contest the erasure of identity with a strong and robust expression of pride and responsibility of one Jew for another. This is the thrust of his book *Why Be Jewish?* based on the 1972 sitcom *Bridget Loves Bernie*, the first television show about intermarriage between a Christian and a Jew. Kahane, for his part, refers to the Jewish establishment as proffering "Berniesim." Here he was merely echoing Orthodoxy's long-standing view that the liberalism of the left is more dangerous to Jews than the right.[19]

But Kahane also plugged into the changing affiliations of many young Jews who, radicalized by the 1960s, were alienated from the New Left after 1966 and began reconsidering their Jewishness. This resulted in, among other things, the *havurah* movement, the *Jewish Catalogs*, and the popularization of the Soviet Jewry movement. Kahane both understood and capitalized on the radicalism of this youth culture, speaking to their anxieties and desire to renew their Jewish identities. While few became acolytes, many expressed tepid sympathy for the project, especially as it became manifest in Kahane's activism for Soviet Jewry from late 1969 through 1973. Soviet Jewry was the magnet that brought the Jewish left and the Jewish right in America together. For a short time, Kahane stood at the center.

On the reactionary front, Kahane's political conservatism predated the rise of neoconservatism. Largely secular in orientation, and not specifically focused on Jewish identity per se, neoconservatism in some way supported

Kahane's earlier political views. A link to this connection is Kahane's childhood friend and later partner Joseph Churba, who became a figure of some renown in the Republican Party in the 1980s. He and Kahane were engaged in reactionary political activity in the 1960s, and Churba was very much part of the Republican establishment in the 1970s and 1980s.

Kahane combined a radicalism drawn from the left's critique of liberalism with a reactionary political orientation to form a Jewish identarian movement in a time of turmoil and transition in American history and Jewish history as well. This was an era before and then after the Six-Day War, a time when New Left Jews were being marginalized from the movement by Black Power's alliance with the Palestinian cause, and also a time of rising intermarriage rates.

Kahane's failure to capitalize on these trends was largely the consequence of his militarism and his inability to seize the opportunities that presented themselves to him. Two examples were the Brussels Soviet Jewry conference, which made him an international figure, and the March 1971 Washington rally a few months later that catapulted him to the main stage of advocacy for Soviet Jewry. But violence continued to plague him and his movement, and the Sol Hurok bombing ended any goodwill that came his way. He was simply a product of this time yet could not transition out of it. His failure was that he was never able to abandon that militancy even as it was abandoned by other radical groups by the mid-1970s. The JDL simply became anachronistic in its approach and methods, ultimately a street gang rather than a movement. That may have been partly because Kahane exited the scene by emigrating to Israel in 1971 and essentially losing interest in the JDL.[20]

And yet Kahane's demise did not erase his legacy. In America he left three things behind that have to some degree merged in the first decades of the twenty-first century: an assertive expression of Jewish identity that was bolstered by multiculturalism, a deep mistrust of liberalism that was bolstered by Jewish neoconservatism, and a belief in the omnipresence of anti-Semitism that made American Jews wonder whether American democracy would, or could, ultimately protect them. We can see this in everything from the ADL to the Jewish anxiety about Black Lives Matter and the anti-Israel sentiment in some progressive circles. In my view, these three aspects are Kahane's legacy in American Jewry, and many who espouse one or more of these attitudes are part of Kahane's legacy even as they utterly reject him as a historical figure.

Kahane was often uncannily able to discern critical aspects of a situation and evoke the emotions and anxieties of his readers. But he also consistently overreached, thereby undermining his often incisive observations. He was a tortured figure with many demons, was deeply insecure, spent time living a double life, and had an incessant need to be relevant. In almost every case, his often astute diagnosis yielded a disastrous result. And yet much of that influence remains, right and left, often no longer tethered to his name.

To return once more to the Modern Orthodox man I encountered at the buffet table in 2018, it is not at all clear to me that he quite understood the man he largely agreed with. By that time Kahane had become either a fallen prophet or a tragic heretic. In some way he represented a dark shadow of the tradition, but one that brought comfort to those who feel under siege by the complexity of everything, from the fear of assimilation to "wokeness," from leftist anti-Israelism to pro-Israel white anti-Semitism. Kahane's world could easily be simplified as "Esau hates Jacob." But as I hope I have shown, it is far more complicated than that.

Meir Kahane was a quintessential American Jew. He was also a sharp critic of the society that gave him the opportunity to be who he became. He advocated taking Judaism to the streets before there was a Jewish social-justice movement. For Kahane, American Jewish bourgeois religiosity was a sham. Jewish liberalism was a sham. Jewish quiescence and accommodation was a sham. He claimed Jews were selling their birthright for a house in the gilded suburbs and membership in the clubs that used to exclude them. But he also desired all of those things, even using the pseudonym Michael King to blend into gentile society.

In response, Kahane constructed his own countercultural Judaism. He failed because he could not overcome his anger and his hatred. He often said, "I don't hate Arabs, I love Jews." But that was not true; in some macabre sense, he hated both. He was his own worst enemy, but his influence remains. Here I have tried to figure out this vexing, disturbing, and compelling product of postwar America: Meir Kahane, an American Jewish radical.

NOTES

Introduction: Why Kahane?

1. For a recent reassessment of the strike in relation to anti-Semitism, see Ferguson, "Ocean Hill-Brownsville."

2. This is of course not the first study of Kahane but, I hope, the most extensive study of his thought and its influence.

3. On Soviet Jewry, see Beckerman, *When They Come for Us*. On Kahane's role in the movement, see Weiss, *Open Up the Iron Door*.

4. To give two other examples, Diner's *Jews of the United States*, 340–43, discusses Kahane as well as the JDL, and M. Goodman's *History of Judaism*, a study of Judaism from its beginnings to the present, discusses Kahane at 507–8.

5. Breslauer, *Meir Kahane*. The difference between a "fanatic" and a "radical" is important. Fanatics are usually those whose actions, while they may be informed by ideas deemed radical, often act out of impulse and irrational motives. Radicals, right and left, are often those whose ideas call for substantive change yet whose actions conform, more or less, to their radical commitments. I consider Kahane more of a radical than a fanatic, though late in his life his actions leaned more toward the fanatical in his despondence over his rejection by the Israeli government.

6. I discuss the term "radical" and why it applies to Kahane in chapter 2.

7. L Kahane, *Rabbi Meir Kahane*; Breslauer, *Meir Kahane*; Kotler, *Heil Kahane*; Friedman, *False Prophet*.

8. This arguably speaks to the nature of radicalism more generally. Radical movements are often short-lived, in part because they upset the system and often implode under the weight of their own shortcomings and their call for radical change that is suffocated by the conventions of a society seeking to maintain the status quo. And yet, these "failed" movements often have much longer afterlives that infiltrate conventions and begin to alter them from within. One can see this in our day in the Occupy movement, which lasted merely a few months and yet helped change the American discourse about socialism and progressivism. This is true, I think, of Kahanism as well, as illustrated by the anecdote that begins this introduction.

9. This point is lost on many studies of Kahane in Israel, which do not see his American career as the very foundation of his Israeli political life.

10. I develop this idea in my *American Post-Judaism*, 186–232.

11. Dolgin's *Jewish Identity* begins to move in this direction but given when it was published it does not offer a systemic gender critique.

12. On masculinity in America more generally, see Kimmel, *Manhood in America.*

13. Imhoff, *Masculinity*, 1–21 and 217.

14. Yet Imhoff notes that "Jewish norms of masculinity did not directly mirror their Protestant counterparts." *Masculinity*, 16.

15. For examples of polemics against Kahane, see Friedman, *False Prophet*, and Kotler, *Heil Kahane*. Breslauer in *Meir Kahane* offers a more balanced if also very critical view. None of these books delves very far into his life and work with accompanying archival material and thoroughgoing analysis of the social and political context of his life. Kotler spends more time on his Israeli career, while Breslauer and Friedman focus more on his American career.

16. See Scholem, *Sabbatai Zevi*. A new edition, with an important introductory essay on the history of the book by Yaacob Dweck, was published in 2019. On the pervasiveness of Sabbatai Zevi in modern Judaism, see Liebes, "Status of Sabbateanism," 41–51.

Chapter 1. Liberalism

1. The details of the strike and its importance will be discussed at length in chapter 3.

2. See, for example, Apply, *Liberalism and Republicanism.*

3. See Harding, *Martin Luther King*, 1–22.

4. As noted later in this volume, in 1977 Kahane wrote an entire book about intermarriage, *Why Be Jewish?*, that was based on the sitcom *Bridget Loves Bernie*. For a discussion, see Breslauer, *Meir Kahane*, 113–30.

5. On those challenges, see Kranson, *Ambivalent Embrace.*

6. See W. Goodman, "Rabbi Kahane Says." The relationship between reactionary Jewish-nationalist programs and the countries in which they take root has a history. For example, Jabotinsky's Revisionist movement in Poland showed extreme signs of patriotism toward Poland. As Daniel Kupfert Heller notes, "Despite agreeing there was something 'Polish' about Revisionist Zionism, Betar's members and leaders frequently debated what it meant for a Zionist to 'act Polish' or what functions these performances of 'Polishness' could serve. . . . Some Betar members viewed the Polish national struggle as an inspiration but simultaneously insisted that they felt no connection to the Polish state and were foreigners en route to their distant homeland. Others felt that every Jew bore the responsibility to make sacrifices for their 'two fatherlands'; the land of Israel and Poland"; Heller, *Jabotinsky's Children*, 18. This was also the case regarding the JDL. Kahane himself began his career trying to save the American dream for Jews. And when he decided in 1971 that the JDL should switch its mandate to mass *aliyah*, he encountered significant resistance from many leaders in the movement who remained steadfast in their belief that the JDL existed to protect Jews in the Diaspora. Of course, as I will argue, Kahane adopted much from militant groups such as the Black Panthers but not as much from right-wing fascist groups in the US the way Betar did in Poland. Heller shows how Menachem Begin, for example, was close to certain Polish fascist groups, and Jabotinsky himself, whose liberal ideas were much more complicated, had ties to right-wing groups in Italy.

7. See Gitlin, *The Sixties*; Elbaum, *Revolution.*

8. It is worth noting that for both the far left and Kahane's reactionary right, liberalism was viewed as a "malaise" of sorts. The sociologist Charles Liebman noted that Jewish liberalism in

America largely grew out of Jewish marginality, the product of an unfinished emancipation. As Jews felt more "American," liberalism would become less necessary. In this sense the New Jews and Kahane shared a sense of comfort in America their predecessors did not. Liebman, *Ambivalent American Jew*; Feingold, *American Jewish Political Culture*, 76–77. For a study of the relationship between upward mobility and American Jewish liberalism, see Kranson, *Ambivalent Embrace*, 44–67.

9. Kahane's book against intermarriage *Why Be Jewish?* makes this case. The structures and nature of postwar American liberalism are, of course, much more nuanced than Kahane makes them out to be. See, for example, Self, *All in the Family*; Connolly, "Strange Career."

10. Afterman and Afterman are correct when they note about Kahane's later career, "Some might argue that Kahane is a political thinker using religious arguments to justify his ideological outlook rather than an essentially religious thinker who deals in politics." Afterman and Afterman, "Meir Kahane," 202.

11. See, for example, Taylor, *White Identity*.

12. Fine, "New Jewish Politics," 34. See also Dollinger, *"Is It Good for the Jews?"* The published version of that book is Dollinger, *Black Power*.

13. Liebman, *Ambivalent American Jew*, 159.

14. See, for example, in Breslauer, *Meir Kahane*, 98–99.

15. See my review of the film in "'I'm Crazy but I'm Normal.'"

16. On radical Jews, see Michels, *Jewish Radicals*. On Goldman, see E. Goldman, *Living My Life*. On Landauer, see Mendes-Flohr and Mali, *Gustav Landauer*. On Buber, see his *Paths in Utopia*, a book that was popular among many New Leftists including SDS members. Books like Porter and Dreier's *Jewish Radicalism* with essays by countercultural Jews, and essays like Kaye/Kantrowitz, "To Be a Jewish Radical," illustrate the way many in the counterculture took the term "radical" as a badge of pride.

17. For a rendering of the revolutionary components in Zionism, see Fisch, *Zionist Revolution*.

18. Ziegler, "Jewish Defense League," 35.

19. Michels, *Jewish Radicals*. Curiously, Michels never really defines the term "radical" in this book.

20. See, for example, in Da. Bell, *Marxian Socialism*, esp. 55–116.

21. W. Goodman, "Rabbi Kahane Says," 122.

22. G. Ross, "Zionism," 310.

23. Anarchism in its myriad forms was quite popular among early twentieth-century Jews in Germany. Gershom Scholem, the renowned scholar of Jewish mysticism and a lifelong Zionist, defined himself as a "religious anarchist" and also critically described Martin Buber as an anarchist. See Scholem, "Interview with Muki Zur," 1–48.

24. For example, see Robinson, *Black Marxism*, 175–240.

25. See Kahane, "To the Young," 330; Kahane, "Karl Marx," 45–50.

26. Here see Glazer, "Exposed American Jew," 25–30.

27. Halpern, *Blacks and Jews*, 96.

28. See Halpern, 99; Balint, *Running Commentary*, 79–96.

29. In chapter 4 below I argue that Kahane's main enemy was communism with its anti-Semitism and unwillingness to allow Jews to exercise their Jewish identities.

30. In terms of an economic theory, in a 1987 interview with Raphael Mergui and Philippe Simonnot originally published in French and later in English in numerous places, Kahane does offer a very boilerplate economic theory of the state of Israel that amounts to a basic liberal position. The government should not own the land, it should be privately owned; the country should be open to private investment by Jews in the Diaspora, etc. When Mergui and Simonnot ask him afterward, "So as far as economics are concerned, then, you are a liberal?" Kahane responds, "Yes." See Mergui and Simonnot, "G-d's Law," 389–90.

31. See M. Kaufman, "Jewish Activists," *New York Times*, May 25, 1970.

32. Here see Breslauer, *Meir Kahane*, 97–112.

33. On Kahane in Allenwood Federal Prison, see "Kahane Ordered to a U.S. Prison." On the Kahane-Rackman exchange, see Kahane, "Fight for Jewishness."

34. In the section on his theory of violence in chapter 5, I argue that for Kahane violence was not only a tool of self-defense but, in Fanonian terms, a tool of self-fashioning.

35. His first book on Israel *Our Challenge*, published in English in 1974, presented a coherent if also unrealistic vision of Israel that attempted to wed his radical program with Realpolitik. By the 1980s his rhetoric became more violent, as in his 1981 book *They Must Go*.

36. On this in detail, see chapters 5 and 6.

37. Sleeper, "Case for Religious Radicalism," 51, 53. Similarly, Rothman and Lichter write, "The New Left was implicitly revolutionary from the beginning, despite an initial reliance on liberal rhetoric. Their patronage of the oppressed stemmed from a strong hostility toward American society, and particularly toward the middle-class world they sought to escape." Rothman and Lichter, *Roots of Radicalism*, 13. On the New Jews' challenge to liberalism, see Staub, *Torn at the Roots*.

38. Waskow has a slightly different formulation than Sleeper: "That is why for some young Jews in this generation of our history, Judaism itself requires us to be revolutionary. Not that what the Jewish tradition requires is always revolutionary. It is not. Under most circumstances the law of the kingdom is law. *Din malchut din*." Waskow, *The Bush Is Burning!*, 133. Waskow notes three crises facing Jews in the 1960s, concerning: the "American Empire"; whether the Diaspora is intrinsically good; and liberation: "Of ourselves to be ourselves. Of humanity to be itself." These three crises—involving, that is, imperialism in the Vietnam War; Zionism and Diaspora; and global injustice—dictate for Waskow that Judaism be turned into a revolutionary movement or at least become part of the larger revolutionary movement that is transpiring among the radical left. On Waskow, see Feldman, *Shadow over Palestine*, 137–45.

39. And King's speech "Beyond Vietnam: A Time to Break Silence," delivered at the Riverside Church in Manhattan on April 4, 1967, explicitly drew the connection between racial equality and the war in Vietnam.

40. Kahane, *Our Challenge*.

41. Porter and Dreier, "Roots," xvi–xvii. On this see Rubin, "New Jewish Ethics," 13: "Jewish youth had not abandoned liberalism, they simply redirected it to a new target—Judaism. . . . Instead of confronting white racists they took aim at the 'Jewish establishment.'" Cf. Dollinger, *"Is It Good for the Jews?"*, 175.

42. Interestingly, Jack Newfield argues that Waskow was one of the "humanist liberals," a moderate sector of the New Left that was deeply affected by the new radicalism but remained somewhat on the margins. See Newfield, *Prophetic Minority*, 133.

43. As we will see below, Porter and Dreier's *Jewish Radicalism* devotes an entire section to responses to the JDL but the group is viewed as outside the orbit of the Jewish radicals of the time.

44. Newfield notes that "the New Radicals are the first products of liberal affluence. They have grown up in the sterile suburbs, urban complexes bereft of community, impersonal universities. They are the children of economic surplus and spiritual starvation" (*Prophetic Minority*, 23). But see Clawar, "Neo-Vigilantism," 169–87, 293–94, who shows that many of the early JDL supporters were from middle- and upper-middle-income families. Cf. Halevi, *Memoirs*.

45. Kahane, "Jewish Vigilantes."

46. Russ, "'Zionist Hooligans,'" 19. I want to thank Menachem Butler for providing me with a copy of this important study.

47. See, for example, Rosen, "Jewish Neighborhoods."

48. *Jerusalem Post*, "The JDL."

49. See Self, "Black Panther Party," 39.

50. See Newfield, *Prophetic Minority*, 81.

51. I borrowed the term "frontier" in this context from the term "urban frontier areas" in Clawar's "Neo-Vigilantism," 132.

52. It should be noted that many prominent JDLers such as Bertram Zweibon, who co-founded the JDL with Kahane, were middle-aged and upper-middle-class Jews; Zweibon in particular was a lawyer. But the main body that comprised the young members of the organization largely fit the portrait I am giving. For an extended essay on Zweibon, see Okon, "'Never Again!'"

53. See, for example, H. Epstein, *Children of the Holocaust*.

54. Bongartz, "Superjew."

55. See Novick, *Holocaust in American Life*, 63–84.

56. Halevi, *Memoirs*, 136–37.

57. Halevi.

58. See Williams, *Negroes with Guns*. See also Cobb, *How Guns Made the Civil Rights Movement Possible*.

59. Malcolm cogently captured the Third Worldism of Black Nationalism when he said in 1964, "It is not a Negro problem, nor an American problem. This is a world problem; a problem for humanity. It is not a problem of civil rights but a problem of human rights" (Malcolm X, "Appeal," 85). This attitude was not limited to Black Nationalists. For example, in a *New York Times* interview in July 1979, Jimmy Carter compared the Palestinian issue to "the civil rights movement here in the United States"; Silk, "Carter." Lior Sternfeld is presently working on a book on Third-Worldism in the Middle East.

60. See Loeffler, *Rooted Cosmopolitanism*, 262.

61. A classic example of this is Minor, *Third World Round-Up*, a pamphlet published in August 1967 by the Student Nonviolent Coordinating Committee. As Keith Feldman notes about this influential document, "SNCC's article was part of a broad swath of post-civil rights cultural production, one that animated the Black freedom struggle's international horizon through a complex and sustained engagement with Palestine. I call this Black Power's Palestine." Feldman, *Shadow over Palestine*, 60.

62. See, for example, Kahane, "Radical Left's Battle."

63. King [Kahane] and Churba, *Jewish Stake in Vietnam*. This work will be discussed in chapter 4.

64. Kahane often used the term "establishment"; it was common among New Leftists in the 1960s, indicating Kahane's absorption of New Left rhetoric. For a critique of the term "establishment," see Fairlie, "Evolution," 173ff.; Alter, "Revolt," 11–13.

65. Kahane, *Never Again!*, 98.

66. Cited in Kempton, "What a Problem!"

67. Newfield, *Prophetic Minority*, 93.

68. W. Goodman, "Rabbi Kahane Says."

69. Baumel, "Kahane in America," 312.

70. See, for example, in Braiterman, "Jewish Defense League," 3–15, esp. 5.

71. See on this Beckerman, *When They Come for Us*, 212; and Burack, "Emergence of the Jewish Defense League," 206.

72. See Breslauer, *Meir Kahane*, 79–96; Beckerman, *When They Come for Us*, 150–72.

73. Quoted in Anti-Defamation League, *Research Report*, cited in Burack, "Emergence of the Jewish Defense League," 209n93.

74. Kahane, *Never Again!*, 52–72.

75. Kahane, 34–51.

76. See Russ, "'Zionist Hooligans,'" 51: "Although a fringe group, the JDL never posed a threat to the social order of American society. Quite the opposite, its values were very conservative; rather than an advocate of change, JDL represented the status quo of 'law and order.'" This is certainly true, but regarding American Jewish society Kahane's program was as radical as that of the Black Panthers; he wanted to totally reconfigure the American Jew.

77. Kahane often wrote about Jews in Arab lands, mostly to chastise the Jewish liberal establishment for ignoring their plight. See, for example, Kahane, "Innocent Victims."

78. See, for example, a JDL letter to the rabbinic community in Philadelphia about "Arab Jewry," signed by Edward Ramov, president of the ADL's New England chapter, April 20, 1972 (in JDL Collection, Box 1, Folder 7, American Jewish Historical Society Archives, New York).

79. See, for example, M. Kaplan, "Kahane and Colombo." In "Jewish Defense League: Aims and Purposes," we read: "JDL is prepared at all times to work with all groups, both Jewish and non-Jewish." Kahane wasn't the first reactionary American Jew to have ties with the Italian Mafia. In the 1940s Alexander Refaeli and Hillel Kook, two members of the American Irgun Delegation, made contacts with the Jewish Mafia figure Mickey Cohen, and they had a connection to notorious Mafia chief Lucky Luciano. See Baumel, *"Bergson Boys"*, 277. Cf. Kotler, *Heil Kahane*, 46–52.

80. Kahane gives the rationale for his relationship with Colombo in W. Goodman, "Rabbi Kahane Says." See Russ, "'Zionist Hooligans,'" 20. Russ rightly notes that Kahane's interest in these other ethnic organizations was mostly tactical and did not stem from any sincere interest in their well-being or their struggle.

81. See "Kahane Defends Alliance." New York. Yossi Klein Halevi notes on the Kahane-Colombo alliance, "Kahane's charisma came from his willingness to violate every limit; and in that sense, the Mafia alliance enhanced his appeal." Kahane claimed he had allied with Colombo because he viewed the Italian American community's situation as similar to that of the Jewish community in terms of black violence as well as violence from what he referred to as "ethnic

whites" and WASPS. Halevi, *Memoirs*, 150. Kahane also tells of his relationship with Colombo in his interview to Mergui and Simonnot, "G-d's Law," 401–2.

82. Mergui and Simonnot, "G-d's Law," 402.

83. For a reaction to Kahane's claim that the JDL was out to save the American dream in regard to the event at Temple Emanu-El in Manhattan, see the editorial "Dream or Nightmare?," *New York Times*, June 25, 1969.

84. "Jewish Defense League: Aims and Purposes," 4. Elsewhere Kahane says, "The dream that is America, that saw the eager eyes of millions in the Old World turn to it, is in immense danger today and all the citizens of these United States face the consequences of the collapse of that dream." In Pride, "We'll Riot," 5.

85. There was considerable resistance to the ad in the press. See, for example, the JTA article from October 14, 1969, "Defense League Ad Created Furor," in which former Supreme Court justice Arthur Goldberg denounced the ad as well as Kahane's campaign against Mayor John Lindsay. Cf. A. Goldberg, "Goldberg Backs Lindsay," in which Goldberg, then president of the American Jewish Committee, denounced the JDL, the ad, and the subsequent campaign against Lindsay. See also "Jewish Defense League Advertisement, Tactics Denounced"; Russ, "'Zionist Hooligans,'" 128.

86. See Kahane, *Never Again!*, 34–52. In his book *Time to Go Home* Kahane describes America as the greatest and most tolerant democratic country in history and as the best for the Jews in the Diaspora. His claim that Jews had no future in the Diaspora, *even* in America, stemmed from his view that no diasporic context could ensure that Jews would survive and flourish.

87. W. Goodman, "Rabbi Kahane Says."

88. Kahane, *Manifesto*; L. Kahane, *Rabbi Meir Kahane*, vol. 1, 95.

89. The document "Jewish Defense League: Aims and Purposes" states, "We believe that Jewish power is something which should be utilized in the best possible democratic sense."

90. While Kahane refused to acknowledge any non-anti-Semitic anti-Zionism because he believed that gentiles in general were anti-Semitic, there were cases to be made in the early 1970s that anti-Zionism and anti-Semitism had become fused, not because all anti-Zionists were anti-Semites but because by that time Jewish interests had become so grounded in the state of Israel that any anti-Israel sentiment was by definition against a main Jewish interest. This was argued by Glazer in "Jewish Interests," 158. Stokely Carmichael, who as a leader of the Black Nationalist movement came out against Israel after 1967 (earlier he had referred to Black Nationalism as "Black Zionism"), often made the case that his rejection of Israel was not a rejection of Jews. More than the Six-Day War and the Palestinian dilemma, what seemed to turn Carmichael against Israel was its growing alignment with apartheid South Africa. See Carmichael and Thelwell, *Ready for Revolution*, 557–58.

91. Newfield, *Prophetic Minority*, 33. See also 22 where he defines New Radicalism as embodying "anarchism, pacifism, and socialism."

92. Reprinted in Porter and Dreier, *Jewish Radicalism*, 279.

93. "Jewish Defense League: Aims and Purposes," 2. Cf. Clawar, "Neo-Vigilantism," 93.

94. See Clawar, 93.

95. See, for example, in Kahane, *Story*, 120. The JDL was less like the Black Panthers than Kahane might have imagined. The Panthers were committed to urban reform and poverty relief as much as militarism. They instituted free breakfast programs in urban venues like Oakland

and established schools to train young Panthers. They were far more organized than the JDL ever was, and more adept at using the political system. In addition, they had prominent female leaders. For an informative documentary, see Nelson, dir., *Black Panthers*.

96. See Russ, "'Zionist Hooligans,'" viii. Cf. W. Goodman, "Rabbi Kahane Says," where Goodman asks Kahane, "So your tactics have been influenced by the successes of the black militants," to which Kahane replies, "Of course. And it's a tragedy that the government lets us push them around." He also says in the same interview, "We are links in a chain with the Irgun, the Maccabees, with all the Jewish groups that used violence for a Jewish cause." On maximalist Zionism Revisionism, see Shavit, *Jabotinsky*. On Revisionism in the US, see Medoff, *Militant Zionism*.

97. Kahane's relationship to Zionism is complex and multilayered; I will discuss it in greater detail in subsequent chapters. For his quite radical revision of Zionism, see his *Listen World*. Judith Tyler Baumel suggests that Kahane's interpretation of Revisionist ideology was "more radical than the original" because it was infused with religious-nationalist content. See Baumel, *"Bergson Boys"*, 274.

98. Kahane, "Communism vs. Judaism," November 3, 1967.

99. There was a motion to change the name of the Jewish Defense League to the Jewish Defense Corps. Kahane told the *Newark Star Ledger* in an interview published on August 8, 1968, "Corps might be construed as too militant and we are totally dedicated to legal means." This would change by 1969 when the JDL, in their Soviet Jewry activism, began to engage in arms smuggling and bomb making. Much of this began in preparation for the second summer of Camp Jedel, 1970, where Kahane wanted more gun training and this required smuggling guns from out of state. See Russ, "'Zionist Hooligans,'" 193–210.

100. Russ, 46. One could also add the Ku Klux Klan to this story as they too engaged in militant activity for reactionary causes. The Klan, however, represented the Protestant majority and often were tacitly supported by law enforcement as opposed to blacks and Jews in America.

101. Interview to *Playboy*, October 1972, 70.

102. Kristol, "Why Jews Turn Conservative." Interestingly, the photo that accompanies this article is of JDL members holding up a "Never Again!" sign at a protest.

103. Officially launched in 1962 with the Port Huron Statement, SDS had a slow start. By 1964 it had only a few hundred members. By 1968, however, it claimed 80,000 to 100,000 members on several hundred college campuses.

104. On the New Left, see Rothman and Lichter, "Rise and Fall." For more on the history of the roots of Jewish radicalism, see Waskow, *The Bush Is Burning!*, 11–46.

105. I deal with the strike and its implications in depth in chapter 3.

106. Kahane had particular disdain for Eisendrath, who epitomized the Jewish establishment for him. On Eisendrath, see Shulman, *Biography of Rabbi Maurice Eisendrath*. Forman, who served as executive secretary of the Student Nonviolent Coordinating Committee from 1961 to 1966, is an interesting figure here. Against the SNCC leadership, Forman was very reluctant to take a pro-Arab stand on the Arab-Israeli conflict even though he realized that most American blacks were inclined toward such a position. In the mid-1960s he acted as a moderating force in black-Jewish relations.

107. This was not the only case of JDLers barring a black militant from speaking in a synagogue. The *Jerusalem Post* in "The JDL" describes another instance in Philadelphia where black

militant Muhammad Kenyatta spoke at the Main Line Reform Temple, demanding reparations. He claimed that he would return that coming Friday, and JDLers warned him when he left that it might not be safe to do so. Cf. Braiterman, "Jewish Defense League," 9.

108. Interestingly, this phrase seems to have been adopted by some radical Jewish leftists as well. For example, the Brooklyn Bridge Collective, a radical-left non-Zionist group, published an article in their newspaper entitled "We Are Coming Home" that asserted, "Jewish philanthropy no longer aids Jews who need it; Jewish education tones down our own people's historic fight to survive and teaches us to be 'nice Jewish boys and girls.'" This group, though antithetical to Kahane's right-wing JDL, shared much of its revolutionary tenor.

109. See Shelly, "Is This Any Way?"

110. While this may have been largely true at that time, not without important exceptions, the rise of multiculturalism, and of Jewish progressivism in light of multiculturalism, has proved this thesis wrong. Progressive Jewish organizations such as the Jewish World Service, T'ruah, Tikkun Community, and many others are founded on Jewish practice and a positive Jewish identity that remains focused on global issues of injustice. This was also true of Waskow's group Jews for Urban Justice. I maintain only that Kahane served as an illustration of the New Left's criticism of Jews.

111. Greenberg, "Self-Hatred."

112. See Glazer, "Jewish Interests," 163.

113. See, for example, Neuberger, "Black Zionism." Cf. Magid, "Zionism," December 12, 2018, https://www.tabletmag.com/sections/arts-letters/articles/zionism-pan-africanism-and-white-nationalism.

114. Kahane, *Story*, 97.

115. One sees this among New Jew radicals as well, called the "*Shah-schtil* pattern." See Cantor Zuckoff, "Oppression of Amerika's Jews."

116. Interview to *Playboy*, 74.

117. See Clawar, "Neo-Vigilantism," 118n13.

118. W. Goodman, "Rabbi Kahane Says."

119. In *Time to Go Home* Kahane argued that Jews had no future in America. However, his goodbye to American Jewry didn't last long; for the remainder of his life he spent about half his time in America and continued to write books in English for American Jews. As Clawar notes, "Between 1968–1970 numerous subjects [JDL members] said, 'if getting tough in Israel was necessary, maybe Jews in the U.S. need to do a little of the same.'" "Neo-Vigilantism in America," 58. Cf. Burack, "Emergence of the Jewish Defense League," 163.

120. Kahane, "Galut in Israel," in *Beyond Words*, vol. 1, 210–13.

121. On Revisionists and their use of national and fascist movements in Europe, see Heller, *Jabotinsky's Children*.

122. Wieseltier, "Demons of the Jews," 24. Kahane devotes a passage at the end of his 1987 book *Uncomfortable Questions for Comfortable Jews* to attacking Wieseltier's essay; see 316–17.

123. The issue of Jewish masculinity in American Jewry is a complex story recently told by Imhoff in *Masculinity*.

124. Kahane develops this lineage in *Listen World*.

125. Kahane, *Story*, 227–73.

126. Mike James quoted in "Extent of Subversion of the New Left," hearings by the Committee on the Judiciary in the US Senate, 1970. Cited in Rothman and Lichter, *Roots of Radicalism*, 39.

127. On the move to obtain a bomb, see Russ, "'Zionist Hooligans,'" 222ff.

128. See Mittleman, *Does Judaism Condone Violence?*; R. Eisen, *Peace and Violence*.

129. Interview to *Playboy*, 70. Kahane often referred to the story of Moses killing the Egyptian as essentially the first Jewish act. One could push it back even further to the midrashic telling of Abraham smashing his father's idols.

130. Kahane, *Never Again!*, 136.

131. Kahane, *Story*, 134.

132. See, for example, in my *American Post-Judaism*, 209–19.

133. See *Jewish Press*, September 6, 1968, cited in Baumel, "Kahane in America," 322. Citing Kahane, Mel Ziegler wrote, "A Nazi is a Nazi whether he's in brown shirt or black skin. How long are we going to be pansies!" Ziegler, "Jewish Defense League," 30.

134. Kahane, "Commentary," September 30, 1968; Burack, "Emergence of the Jewish Defense League."

135. Kahane, "Story behind the Abdication ," cited in Burack, "Emergence of the Jewish Defense League," 108.

136. For an example, see Halevi, *Memoirs*, 134.

137. See a similar formulation in Waskow, *The Bush Is Burning!*, 11–29.

138. On his developing theories of violence, see chapter 5.

139. See Watts, *Mr. Playboy*.

140. In June 1967 Rubenstein was invited to participate in a *Playboy* symposium entitled "Religion and the New Morality," and his essay "Judaism and the Death of God" appeared in the July 1967 issue.

141. Interview to *Playboy*, 74.

142. Interview to *Playboy*. For a longer essay on Conservative Judaism, see Kahane, "And Then There Is, Conservative Judaism," March 1997, in *In His Own Words*, vol. 2, 463–74.

143. See Kahane, *Story*, 80–83.

144. Elsewhere Kahane notes, "A Reform temple may have an organ and a Conservative one mixed pews. That is not what sets them apart from true Judaism. That is merely a manifestation, a *symptom* of the difference. The real difference lies in the Jew who suits Torah to his own code versus the Jew who knows G-d and accepts upon himself the yoke of the heavenly kingdom." *Listen World*, 45.

145. See Ziegler, "Jewish Defense League," 30.

146. For Jabotinsky, who coined the term *hadar*, the idea was not merely about pride but an act of submission to the general will, so as to become true soldiers of the Jewish people. Jabotinsky stressed that this included becoming a "true gentleman," one others would look to as a model of decency and honor. This certainly did not describe the ragtag qualities of the JDL. On Jabotinsky and *hadar*, see E. Kaplan, *Jewish Radical Right*, 26–27.

147. See Kahane, "The Miracle of Howard Beach" (1960), in *Beyond Words*, vol. 1, 3–8. Of course Kahane is not the only one to do this in his time and afterward. It has become a cottage industry in neoconservative circles to make similar arguments. See, for example, Wisse, *If I Am Not for Myself*, and later Wisse, *Jews and Power*.

148. See Kahane, *Listen World*, 38, 44. "We live in a world that revels in 'freedom'; in the right to do what we wish. Rights and freedom . . . grow like some cancerous disease into license and moral anarchy. For the Jew there can be no such thing. For the Jew there can only be the heavenly kingdom."

149. Cited in Brick, *Daniel Bell*, 176

150. Interview to *Playboy*, 76. Cf. W. Goodman, "Rabbi Kahane Says": "Be proud you are a Jew. Identify with it. It's not saying that you should be an Orthodox Jew. Not at all. What it is saying is, 'Study and see what made your ancestors such stubborn people who refused to give up.'" Cf. also Kahane, *Story*, 80: "The JDL is not a religious organization and is open to all Jews. But one need not be a religious Jew to understand that the pride of a Jew is irrevocably tied to the greatness of Jewish culture and tradition." Cf. also Breslauer, *Meir Kahane*, 61–64.

151. See Ziegler, "Jewish Defense League," 36.

152. See Mergui and Simonnot, *Israel's Ayatollahs*, 43.

153. More generally see the discussion in Staub, "Liberal Judaism Is a Contradiction in Terms: Antiracist Zionists, Prophetic Jews, and Their Critics," in his *Torn at the Roots*, 45–75.

154. Yitzchok Brandriss makes the case that, in fact, Kahane's program is anti-Orthodox. See Brandriss, "Kahanism Is Not Orthodoxy," *Jewish Week*, March 18, 1994.

155. Dolgin, *Jewish Identity*, 72.

156. Dolgin, 65–99. The comparison, of course, is somewhat flawed. We read in Deuteronomy that Moses blessed the tribes of Yissachar and Zevulun: "Be joyful Zevulun in your going forth, and Yissachar in your tents" (33:18). On this verse Rashi explains, "Zevulun and Yissachar made a partnership between them. Zevulun would dwell at the harbor and deal in business with ships, thereby sustaining Yissachar who would study Torah. Therefore, the verse mentions Zevulun before Yissachar, because the Torah of Yissachar came through Zevulun." In Kahane's scholar-*chaya* relationship, the *chaya* enacts the precepts that are developed by the scholar. Both embody the "New Jew," each playing his role in the proliferation of Jewish pride according to his abilities.

157. See, for example, in Kahane, *Our Challenge*, 112–55; *Uncomfortable Questions*, 243–74; and in *Forty Years*.

158. Porter and Dreier, *Jewish Radicalism*, xxxii.

159. Mandel, "Radical Zionist's Critique," 299.

160. See "Kahane Defends Alliance."

161. B. Novak, "Failure of Jewish Radicalism," 308–9.

162. On this phenomenon as a form of American Jewish civil religion, see Woocher, *Sacred Survival*.

163. Waskow, *The Bush Is Burning!*, 100. On his use of "multi-particularism," see ibid., 20.

164. See "Kahane Would Ship All U.S. Jews to Israel."

165. "Kahane Would Ship All U.S. Jews to Israel," 309.

166. W. Goodman, "Rabbi Kahane Says."

167. Reprinted in Porter and Dreier, *Jewish Radicalism*, 277–87. The quote is from 279–80.

168. See Feingold, *American Jewish Political Culture*, 78–79, where he maintains that by 1970 one could discern three forms of Jewish liberalism that were at play with, and against, one another: "The older survivors were associated with the prewar Jewish labor movement. . . . They are followed and sometimes overlap with a group of slightly younger citizens that became

identified with the New Deal. Finally, there are the new liberals composed of middle-class, formally educated secular citizens, many mobilized during the civil rights struggle of the sixties, who are reenergized by the systemic economic crisis that began in 2008."

Chapter 2. Radicalism

1. The play on the Purim story is not unique to Kahane. For example, the Student Struggle for Soviet Jewry created a Purim Megillah entitled "The Megillah of Anatoly Sharansky," with Brezhnev playing the role of Haman. "The Megillah of Anatoly Sharansky" was actually performed in 1981. A mimeograph of "Megillat Heyman" begins with the following: "The Jewish Defense League has been picketing the offices of George C. Heyman Jr. to protest the lack of concern shown by the Federation of Jewish Philanthropies in their neglect of Jewish Education, protection of Jewish neighborhoods and Soviet Jewry" (in JDL Collection, Box 1, Folder 10, American Jewish Historical Society Archives, New York).

2. Kahane, *Story*, 160–62.

3. Kahane was certainly aware of this group and even wrote an essay about Hoffman after his death. See Kahane, *Beyond Words*, vol. 6, 418–22. In this caustic eulogy Kahane makes Hoffman an example of the Jew who is the enemy of the Jews. He writes, "Abbie Hoffman was never a person so much as he was a concept. He personified the lost, truly lost young American Jew [who] belonged to the generation of young Jews that was murdered by parents and temples."

4. At the conclusion of his feature essay on the JDL in *New York* in April 1971, Ziegler wrote, "Jewish-oriented radical, leftist, socialist, Zionist groups are beginning to spring up here and there. Other than a general sense of consciousness and defense, all that these groups share with the JDL—no matter how much Kahane is trying to change it—is a common distaste for the Jewish establishment." Ziegler, "Jewish Defense League," 36. This chapter argues that those ties are far more complex than Ziegler suggests.

5. Advertisement for the Baltimore-Washington Union of Jewish Students, *Doreinu* 2, no. 7 (April 1971): 11. See Kranson, *Ambivalent Embrace*, 138.

6. Braiterman, "Jewish Defense League," 3–15.

7. On New Deal liberalism, see Cowie, *New Deal*, 35–62, 123–52. The term "New Jews" was coined in the book edited by Sleeper and Mintz, *New Jews*. It is interesting that the term "New Negro" was used in the Harlem Renaissance in the 1920s. See, for example, in Locke, *New Negro*; Gordon and Franklin, *Story of Marcus Garvey*, 35. I do not know whether the creators of the New Jews knew of this connection, or, even more ironically, whether Kahane, who coined his own New Jew moniker, knew of the New Negroes. I use the term "American Jewish establishment" to refer to mostly liberal Jewish organizations in the 1950s and 1960s that became the target of the radical left and the reactionary right represented here by Kahane. Kahane used the term "American Jewish establishment" often in his writings, describing them as his main adversary. For an important and widely read book that laments the New Left and yearns for a return to the Old Left, all through the lens of the Jewish immigration to the US, see Howe's *World of Our Fathers*. For an important early study of these New Jews, see the ethnography of the *havurah* movement by Prell, *Havurah in American Judaism*.

8. See Russ, "'Zionist Hooligans,'" 35.

9. B. Ross, "'Jewish Radicals,'" 53.

10. Another difference between the New Jews whom Kahane was espousing and the New Jews of the radical left was that the latter were in many cases cultivating a new kind of diasporic existence, Arthur Waskow calling them "celebrants of the New Diaspora." They were interested in a new Jewish assertiveness but not necessarily in the form of reflexive Zionism. See Waskow, "Judaism and Revolution Today," in Porter and Dreier, *Jewish Radicalism*, 22.

11. Kahane, "A Decade Ends."

12. Kahane.

13. In "A Spoonful of Sugar," Kahane notes on the question of the race wars that "Bnai Brith and the American Jewish Congress along with their non-Jewish counterparts that comprise the liberal establishment have little or no comprehension of the radical mind and less of the thinking of the masses. It is this ignorance that has proven them wrong on almost every major foreign policy issue and which is causing them to lead us astray in the racial crisis that could mean destruction for the country and for the Jews."

14. This group of New Jews is discussed in numerous places. For example, see Kaye/Kantrowitz, "Jews in the Civil Rights Movement," 105–122; Forman, *Blacks in the Jewish Mind*, 135–92; Staub, *Torn at the Roots*, 194–240; Mendes, *Jews and the Left*, 261–65. Both Forman and Staub offer excellent insights into these New Jews. Forman focuses mostly on these groups' relationship to issues of black America; Staub expands this analysis to discuss radicalism more generally, largely in regard to the changing attitudes toward Israel after 1967. Both also touch on Kahane and the JDL, Staub more so than Forman. In this context I argue that Kahane and his radical antiliberalism played a more central role than either Forman or Staub suggests. The overlap between Kahane and many in the New "Jewish" Left is radicalism as a political and cultural posture, one that seeks to undermine a system through proactive means that include disruption and even violence. More generally see Matelpunkt, *Israel in the American Mind*.

15. See "Symposium: Chicago's 'Black Caucus,'" 99.

16. B. Novak, "Failure," 305–7.

17. Plaut, "My Evolution as a Jew."

18. One example that I will mention in the last section of this chapter is the three-volume *The Jewish Catalog*, edited by Michael Strassfeld, Sharon Strassfeld, and Richard Siegel. Vol. 3, subtitled *Creating Community*, contains a long section on Israel and Zionism, 318–88; there are only scattered references to Israel in vols. 1 and 2, and it not clear why. Vol. 1 is devoted to a "do it yourself" Judaism, vol. 2 to *Sources and Resources*. Perhaps the topic of community, as in vol. 3, provided the best place for Israel's role in the American Jewish collective consciousness.

19. Russ, "'Zionist Hooligans,'" 26. On this see Mi. Himmelfarb, " 'Never Again!'."

20. Waskow, *The Bush Is Burning!*, 26.

21. The 1968 school strike will be discussed at length in chapter 3. For a recent study of the impact of the Ocean Hill–Brownsville strike on the JDL, see Dorman, "Dreams Defended." The JDL was not the first such organization. In 1965 in Crown Heights, Brooklyn, a small organization known as the Maccabees was founded by a local rabbi to patrol the neighborhood and protect Jews. It was often thought, incorrectly, that Kahane was behind this group, though the JDL may have been in part modeled after it. See Littman, "Jewish Militancy," 292. On the Maccabees, see Aronowitz, "Maccabees Ride Again"; and Dawidowicz, "Civil Rights," 188–90. Cf. Duker, "Negro-Jewish Relations," 24; Moore, *Jewish New York*, 292. In addition, Dory Schary

notes in a letter to the editor on Mel Ziegler's April 19, 1971, article on the JDL in *New York* that when he was growing up in Newark, there was a group that called themselves the Happy Ramblers who would respond to calls about harassment of Jews, mostly at that time perpetrated by Poles, and respond in kind. In some neighborhoods, such as Boro Park, Brooklyn, the JDL patrols did not gain popularity. In their place, Jews in that neighborhood established the Boro Park Auxiliary Police, which worked with the NYPD to train civilians to carry out civil patrols in their own neighborhoods.

22. See Moore, *Jewish New York*, 295.

23. "Jewish Defense League: Aims and Purposes," 2.

24. See in JDL Collection, Box 1, folder 8, American Jewish Historical Society Archives, New York.

25. For Jewish organizations that rejected the JDL, see Anti-Defamation League, *The JDL*; "Progressive Jewish Leaders Condemn JDL"; and "The JDL Is a Menace." A statement by the Jewish War Veterans dated October 21, 1971, reads: "Jeremy Cohen, National Director of the Jewish War Veterans of the U.S.A today declared that the cause of 'freeing' Jewry from the grip of Soviet repression is being severely damaged by the escalating violence and over-heated rhetoric of some extremist groups." The letter then cites Kahane and the JDL specifically ("JWV Commander Condemns Violence"). While the ADL, for its part, did provide valuable information to the FBI about the JDL, they also released a resolution in 1971 by National Chairman Seymour Graubard that the ADL unequivocally rejected FBI surveillance of the JDL or any other such organization. The resolution reads, in part: "We will continue to denounce the JDL so long as it continues to use violence and other tactics. But we will likewise denounce the actions of the Attorney General of the U.S. in employing wiretapping not authorized by a court of law" (JDL Collection, Box 47, Folder 47.3, YIVO Archives, New York). See also "ADL Deplores Wiretapping on the JDL." A debate between ADL member Dore Schary and Kahane aired on television's popular *David Frost Show* on July 9, 1971.

26. See, for example, Ziegler, "Jewish Defense League," 28–36; for the Rackman quote see 32. Cf. Clawar, "Neo-Vigilantism," 291. Clawar further notes on 317, "In general the findings indicate that many Jews do, indeed share the concerns of the JDL. However, there is a clear distinction, in most cases, between those types who support the ideology and those who support the ideology and tactics (as well as those who reject both)."

27. Kelner, "American Mobilization to Free Soviet Jewry," 4.

28. Cited in Kelner, 17.

29. Kelner, "Bureaucratization," 362.

30. The Lubavitcher Rebbe, Menachem Mendel Schneerson, whose role in this Jewish turn is now being explored, openly criticized this adage in one of his talks (*sihot*). More generally, see Miller, *A Biography of the Rebbe*. See also Wexler and Rubin, *The Lubavitcher Rebbe's Transformative Paradigm*; and my review "Another Side of the Lubavitcher Rebbe," https://www.tabletmag.com/jewish-news-and-politics/287321/another-side-of-the-lubavitcher-rebbe.

31. Waskow, "Radical Haggadah," cited in Staub, *Torn at the Roots*, 167.

32. Waskow's sentiment later became a template for the *havurah* and Jewish Renewal movements and, even more broadly, for large swaths of American Judaism. For example, there are now many Jewish rituals such as the Tu Bishvat Seder, a largely forgotten kabbalistic ceremony

likely originating with Sabbateans in the seventeenth century, that are dedicated to ecology and environmentalism.

33. Waskow, *The Bush Is Burning!*, 20.

34. See the transcript of Kahane's lecture in Folder 48A, Religious Zionist Archives, Bar-Ilan University, and cited in L. Kahane, *Rabbi Meir Kahane*, vol. 1, 290–91.

35. See *Jewish Defense League Newsletter* 1, no. 7.

36. See Aharoni, "Now, Greater than Life," http://articles.latimes.com/1990-11-07/local/me-3531_1_meir-kahane. I am not sure whether Hoffman knew it but his locution comes quite close, albeit the inverse, to something Martin Luther King said. Speaking about his disappointment regarding southern Jews, he remarked, "I have almost reached the regrettable conclusion that the Negroes' greatest stumbling block in the stride toward freedom is not the White Citizen's Councilor or the Klu Klux Klan, but the white moderate who . . . constantly says, 'I agree with you on the goal you seek, but I can't agree with your methods.'" Cited in Dollinger, *Jews and Liberalism*, 168.

37. Brandriss, "Kahanism."

38. "Jewish Defense League: Aims and Purposes," 2. On the other hand, Kahane said, "The Radical Left is a problem for Jews and a danger to the Jewish people." See *Jerusalem Post*, "The JDL."

39. See "JDL Denounces Jewish Anti-War Groups."

40. See "Hillel vs. the Elders," 118. This comment supports the issue raised in Harris's *Ocean Hill-Brownsville Conflict* that many in the black community perceived that Jews were at least in part invested in black rights for self-interested reasons.

41. Elkins, "Negro-Jewish Relations," 22.

42. Russ, "'Zionist Hooligans,'" 101. Cf. Bongartz, "Superjew" on Kahane in *Esquire*, August 1970. Comparisons, or lack thereof, between the Jewish history and the black history of oppression were common in the late 1960s; Kahane's comment is likely responding to this. One well-known spokesperson who wrote about this issue was celebrated author Ralph Ellison, who argued that black oppression trumped the oppression of the Jews. See, for example, in "A Very Stern Discipline," 234.

43. Rosenberg, "My Evolution as a Jew," 53.

44. Staub, *Torn at the Roots*, 196.

45. Staub.

46. See Waskow, *The Bush Is Burning!*, 13, 14.

47. See Breslauer, *Meir Kahane*, 69–70.

48. *New York Times*, May 18, 1969. For a description of the incident, see Russ, "'Zionist Hooligans,'" 99–106.

49. The role of summer camps in the youth protests of the late 1960s and early 1970s is analyzed in Prell, "Jewish Summer Camping." I worked at Camp Ramah-Palmer in 1989, the year Ray Arzt returned as a guest director, and we had numerous conversations about the summer of 1969.

50. "Radical Zionist Manifesto," in Staub, *Jewish 1960s*, 246–47.

51. "Radical Zionist Manifesto."

52. See Isaac and Isaac, "Rabbis of Breira"; Staub, *Torn at the Roots*, 280–308. For some new illuminating features of Breira, see Levin, "Another Nation," 219–42. There were numerous other

pro-Palestinian groups among American Jews at that time, including American Jewish Alternatives to Zionism (AJAZ), established by one of the founders of the anti-Zionist American Council for Judaism, Elmer Berger, and the Committee on New Alternatives for the Middle East (CONAME), established by Noam Chomsky. Kahane does not mention either of these although he likely knew of their existence.

53. *Brooklyn Bridge* 1, no. 4 (June 1972), cited in Staub, *Torn at the Roots*, 239–40. Any comparison of injustice toward blacks and Nazism was sure to stir controversy. See, for example, Baldwin and Katz, "Of Angela Davis," 3–10.

54. Rudd, "Why Were So Many Jews in SDS?"

55. Porter and Dreier, *Jewish Radicalism*, xxii.

56. See Kahane, *Listen World*, Appendix A to the 1980 reprint edition (Jerusalem: Institute for the Jewish Idea), 202–15. Focusing on intermarriage and the 1970s sitcom *Bridget Loves Bernie*, Kahane discusses the American bar mitzvah at length. See also Breslauer, *Meir Kahane*, 30–32.

57. See the discussion in Kranson, *Ambivalent Embrace*, 159.

58. Thanks go to Naomi Seidman for that reference.

59. Waskow, *The Bush Is Burning!*, 99.

60. Kahane, *Never Again!*, 114–15.

61. Kahane was not alone in this. In " Radical-Zionist Strategy," Tsvi Bisk railed against "the disgusting orientation of Jewish bar mitzvahs and weddings," claiming they were void of Jewish content. In an article "The Oppression and Liberation of the Jewish People in America," published by Jews for Urban Justice in *Response*, Fall 1971, we read of the "desanctified family-competition scene typified by the Super Bar Mitzvah." Both articles are reprinted in Porter and Dreier, *Jewish Radicalism*, 87–99 and 323–46.

62. Interestingly, the bar mitzvah was also used in the Soviet Jewry movement through the practice of bar-mitzvah twinning in the mid-1970s, in which an American boy or girl twinned with a Soviet boy or girl. See Kelner, "Bureaucratization," 383.

63. See "800 Protesters."

64. Cited in Dolgin, *Jewish Identity*, 122. Dolgin offers a compelling Lacanian interpretation of Kahane's reinvention of the bar mitzvah. I take it in a slightly different direction but have learned much from her reading.

65. It is interesting that today in many American Jewish communities the bar mitzvah includes "mitzvah projects" that consist of social action initiatives, helping the poor, getting involved in Israel advocacy, etc. It would be worth exploring whether this notion of the nonsynagogue bar-mitzvah act that augments its synagogue-based ritual actually began with Kahane's notion of the bar mitzvah of the street protest for Jewish causes.

66. Dolgin, *Jewish Identity*, 123.

67. Kahane actually rejected the concept of the New Jew even though in some way he adopted it. He wrote, "[The JDL] was truly a revolution but, ironically, not one that was meant to create a 'new' Jew but rather to recreate the old one." Kahane, *Story*, 74. This is developed further is his retelling of the history of Zionism in *Listen World*. This pushback on the New Jew may have been his response to Max Nordau's New Jew as a secular muscle Zionist who had abandoned his commitment to the Jewish past; Kahane wanted to revive the militancy of the Jewish past and thus "recreate" the Old Jew. Yet Kahane wavers on this New Jew–Old Jew

dichotomy. For example, a JTA article from July 12, 1971, "Kahane: JDL Would Use Dynamite 'If Necessary,'" quotes him as saying that "the JDL represents 'a new kind of Jew.'"

68. Both of these documents can be found in Staub, *Jewish 1960s*. Cantor Zuckoff's essay appears earlier in Porter and Dreier, *Jewish Radicalism*, 28–49. For a very different view, see Kristol, "Kind Words for Uncle Tom," https://harpers.org/archive/1965/02/a-few-kind-words-for-uncle-tom/.

69. I discuss this in chapter 5.

70. Staub, *Jewish 1960s*, 249. The question of black anti-Semitism draws much scholarly attention. See in Hentoff, *Black Anti-Semitism*, 3–14. I discuss this at length in chapter 3.

71. See Raab, "Black Revolution," 20.

72. See Forman, *Blacks in the Jewish Mind*, 248. The notion of the ghetto as a kind of black colony in America was a topic of debate at that time. See, for example, Blauner, "Internal Colonialism," 393–408; Denton, *American Apartheid*, 67, 85–87; Forman, 138.

73. See "Behavior: The Black and the Jew," http://content.time.com/time/magazine/article/0,9171,841586,00.html.

74. Cantor Zuckoff, "Oppression," 255.

75. By 1972 Kahane seems to have lost all hope for American Jewry and was strongly advocating mass *aliyah*. See especially in *Time to Go Home*, 61–142.

76. Here I would also add a much more recent assessment in contemporary Jewish neoconservatism; see Wisse's *Jews and Power*.

77. On Rubenstein in this context, see Forman, *Blacks in the Jewish Mind*, 201–2.

78. Even though Kahane became known for "Jewish Power," it wasn't only Rubenstein before him who wrote about it. Conservative rabbi Jacob Chinitz, in a newspaper article quite early, called for "Jewish Power which would include Jewish Studies courses in both high school and university, distinctive Jewish dress," and wearing a kippah. Cited in Dollinger, "*Is It Good for the Jews?*," 155. For an early rendering of Kahane and Jewish power, see Applebaum, "Jewish, Irish, and Italian Power."

79. Another example of this is Bisk, "Uncle Jake, Come Home." Bisk moved to Israel, and his approach is even closer to Kahane's and thus in some way less relevant to my argument.

80. Rosenberg, "Self-Destruction." See Kranson, *Ambivalent Embrace*, 152.

81. Rosenberg, "To Jewish Uncle Toms," in Staub, *Jewish 1960s*, 232. A slightly altered version of this article appeared as "To Uncle Tom and Other Such Jews" in *Jewish Defense League Newsletter*. It is indeed interesting that the JDL would reprint Rosenberg's essay as Rosenberg, even given his newly discovered Jewishness, was still very much a part of the Jewish left.

82. In Staub, *Jewish 1960s*, 232–33. This is, of course, not true; American Jews such as Nathan Glazer, Charles Liebman, and others had written against the melting pot years before. But like Kahane, Rosenberg is not that deeply informed. His point is rhetorical—to illustrate what American Jews can learn from Black Nationalism and how they haven't done so.

83. Kahane, *Why Be Jewish?*, 27. Kahane cites from Rosenberg's article "To Uncle Toms and Other Such Jews."

84. Kahane said something quite similar in a television interview in 1970: "We [the JDL] believe, after six million dead Jews, that before you have love you must have respect. And one does not have respect unless one has self-respect. And that means that just as other ethnic groups say 'this or that is beautiful,' well, that beautiful—black is beautiful for blacks. That's

great. Well, Jewish is beautiful and primarily, for Jews." Cited in Dorman, "Dreams Defended," 428. On the phrase "Jewish is beautiful," see the list of demands of a group of high school students in Minneapolis in 1969 that appeared in the *Jewish Morning Journal*, January 9, 1969 (reprinted in J. Kaufman, *Broken Alliance*, 202–3). The list of demands ended with "Curly hair is beautiful, we are Jewish, therefore we are wonderful, Being Jewish is beautiful."

85. Rosenberg, "To Jewish Uncle Toms," 233–34.

86. Rosenberg, 235.

87. Rosenberg, "My Evolution as a Jew," 53. Cf. Staub, *Torn at the Roots*, 289.

88. The extent to which there may be an incongruity among those who support groups like Black Lives Matter and yet refuse to criticize Israel's treatment of Palestinians is examined in my "Is It Right to Compare Ferguson to Gaza? Reflections from a Jewish Protester," http://www.tikkun.org/nextgen/is-it-right-to-compare-ferguson-to-gaza-reflections-from-a-jewish-protester.

89. Fuller, *Understanding Unchurched America*. There is a plethora of literature on this turn in American religion in the 1970s. For a more retrospective history going back to the nineteenth century, see Leigh Schmidt, *Making of American Spirituality*. This transition happens slowly and we can see its roots in the late 1950s and 1960s as well in the popularization of Buddhism and Hinduism through the Beatles, the Esalen Institute, founded in 1962, and later Woodstock in 1969.

90. Strassfeld and Strassfeld, *Third Jewish Catalog*, 318–87. The *Jewish Catalogs* actually began as a master's thesis by Richard Siegal and George Savran at Brandeis University. Siegal stayed on for the second volume but not the third. Savran did not continue after the first published volume; he became a professor of Hebrew Bible, first at Indiana University and then at the Schechter Institute in Jerusalem where he taught until his retirement. On the importance of the *Jewish Catalogs*, see Diner, *Jews of the United States*, 347–48.

91. There are many critiques of the New Left and the New Jews by Jewish liberals moving more toward the center on the path to neoconservatism." For one salient example, see Nathan Glazer, "Jews, Israel," 32-37.

Chapter 3. Race and Racism

1. See Wilderson, *Red, White, and Black*); Wilderson, *Afropessimism*.

2. See, for example, "After the Elections," www.jta.org/1984/07/30/archive/after-the-elections-fear-and-apprehension-over-kahanes-election-to-the-knesset. Cf. Segev, *Seventh Million*, 405–10.

3. Kahane's book *They Must Go* is the first sustained articulation of his plan for "transfer" as the only viable way to salvage Israel's Jewish character. He ran, and lost, on this platform twice before getting elected in 1984.

4. Right before the 1984 elections in which Kahane won a seat, an Israeli satirist wrote, "Kahane is the AIDS virus in the weary body of Israeli society. . . . He undermines what remains of its immune system. We will not die from Kahane himself, but he makes it much easier for the fatal illness to develop." Cited in Cromer, *War of Words*, 100.

5. *Maariv*, May 29, 1981.

6. Kahane's mission to expel the Arabs became a major part of his platform and continued even after he was removed from the Knesset; I will deal with this topic in chapter 5. See Sprinzak, *Brother against Brother*, 193–200.

7. See *Jerusalem Post*, August 1, 1985; and Anti-Defamation League, *Research Report*. For a classic text Kahane often used, see Maimonides, *Mishneh Torah*, "Laws of Idolatry," 5:6: "When Israel is strong in the land, it is forbidden for them to allow non-Jews [literally "idolaters"] to live amongst them [in the land]."

8. See Pedahzur, *Israeli Response*, 53. Pedahzur notes that there were numerous attempts over the years to use this law to disqualify parties from elections; all were denied.

9. For a discussion of Kahane's departure from Zionism, see chapter 5.

10. In 1987 Kahane would publish his book in English *Uncomfortable Questions for Comfortable Jews*, part of which responds to the "Racism Law" and, I argue, essentially gives up on Zionism as a hopeless "Hellenistic" project. Kahane's repudiation of Zionism comes through in his book *Forty Years* as well, a work written in Hebrew while he was in Ramle Prison in 1982 and then later translated into English, well before his political demise.

11. While black anti-Semitism did emerge from the 1968 strike, it had already showed up some years earlier in New York. In 1965 a Jewish police officer named Sheldon Liebowitz shot an unarmed black man in Brooklyn; he was acquitted in court. This incident sparked a series of anti-Semitic articles by Eddie Ellis, who would also be a founding member of the New York Black Panther Party, in the Black Nationalist magazine *Liberator*. See Ellis, "Semitism." On the tensions between Jews and blacks in Harlem in the mid-1960s, see Baldwin and Davis, "Anti-Semitism and Black Power," 77.

12. The first real action, which received less attention, involved fifteen JDL members picketing NYU and demanding the dismissal of Professor John Hackett, who had published an essay "The Phenomenon of the Anti-Black Jews and the Black Anglo-Saxon" in the November/December edition of *Forum*, the official newspaper of the AATA (African American Teachers Association). See Kahane, *Story*, 91–92.

13. Kahane himself refers to reverse racism; see his "Commentary" in the *Jewish Week*, October 25, 1968.

14. Quoted in *Jerusalem Post*, "The JDL."

15. Feldman, *Shadow over Palestine*, 66.

16. While to my knowledge Kahane never mentioned Baldwin's essay, given its prominence and Kahane's voracious reading it is likely he was aware of it. Much of Kahane's initial popularity, before he dove into the Soviet Jewry movement in 1970, was as a protector of Jews at risk from violent black crime. Baldwin's essay was originally published in 1967, and he apparently took the title from a 1967 *New York Times* article "Negroes Are Anti-Semitic Because They're White" that originated in a study by the ADL. See Spiegel, "Jews Troubled over Negro Ties"; Dorman, "Dreams Defended," 422. Baldwin's essay was reprinted many times; see in Hentoff, *Black Anti-Semitism*, 3–14. Also see Baldwin, *The Fire Next Time*; and his earlier essay "Harlem Ghetto," which in many ways presages his 1967 essay.

17. I use the term Negro here because it was the operative term during this period. Dore Schary, then president of the ADL, "cautioned the American Jewish community not to exaggerate fears of Negro anti-Semitism" even in the context of the 1968 Ocean Hill–Brownsville

school strike; Kahane, *Story*, 106. On Kahane's debate with Schary on the *David Frost Show*, see Bemnrome, "Rabbi Meir Kahane Wrestles with Dore Schary," 10–11.

18. Kahane, "I Hate Racism," March 1987, in *Beyond Words*, vol. 5, 226–29.

19. Kahane, *Story*, 64.

20. White leadership in the NAACP did not go uncontested. For example, Black Panther Eldridge Cleaver penned a scathing critique of the NAACP in his "Old Toms Never Die Unless They're Blown Away." Cited in Glaude, *James Baldwin's America*, 87.

21. The influence went both ways. For example, Yasser Arafat parroted Malcolm X when he said in 1969, "The liberation of our fatherland *by any means necessary*" (emphasis added). Cited in Sundquist, *Blacks, Jews, Post-Holocaust America*, 330.

22. See Carmichael, "What We Want," 269. The Harlem uprising in 1964 and the Watts riots in 1965 ravaged many Jewish businesses and manifested frustration felt by many black ghetto dwellers toward white business owners referred to as "Goldbergs."

23. Kahane, *Story*, 65. Bayard Rustin published an article "The Anatomy of Frustration" in the *Jewish Press*, a paper Kahane edited, that addressed the problem of Negro anti-Semitism in the black ghetto. Rustin came out very strongly against Dick Gregory and other prominent Black Nationalists who were voicing hatred of Jews. He urged his Jewish leaders to stay the course of Jewish liberal causes, asserting that "the issue never was, and never can be, simply a problem of Jew and gentile, or black and white. The problem is man's inhumanity to man and must be fought from that basic principle regardless of race or creed." The phrase "man's inhumanity to man" was used to describe the Holocaust.

24. On the deterioration more generally, see "Behavior: The Black and the Jew," 55–59. Cf. J. Kaufman, *Broken Alliance*, 267–80. On earlier periods of black-Jewish tension, see Diner, *American Jews and Blacks 1915–1935*; Clark, "Candor about Negro-Jewish Relations"; Drake and Clayton, *Black Metropolis*, 432n.

25. Rustin, "From Protest to Politics" (repr., League for Industrial Democracy, *Looking Forward*, no. 1 in a Series of Occasional Papers). Although it was originally published in *Commentary*, I am using the reprint of this essay; the web version contains no page numbers.

26. Rustin.

27. Rustin.

28. For a different view, see Shulweis, "Voice of Esau," 7–8. Shulweis argued that Jews should take their businesses out of the black ghettos as it was simply immoral to profit from the poverty of others.

29. See, for example, "Black Power, Jewish Power," in Sundquist, *Blacks, Jews, Post-Holocaust America*, 311–80. On the JDL as "Jewish Panthers," see Kahane, *Story*, 120.

30. Speech in Boston, *Patriot Leader*. In an article in the *Philadelphia Enquirer* on August 30, 1970, Philadelphia-chapter JDL leader Rabbi Harold Novoseller was quoted as saying, "The JDL came into existence to defend Jews. If to some people this means that we're storm troopers, or Jewish Panthers or all those other things, well, then, call us what you want."

31. Baldwin, *Notes of a Native Son*, 139.

32. On this see Kranson, *Ambivalent Embrace*.

33. See Halpern, *Blacks and Jews*, 104.

34. On Kahane's long-term affair with Gloria Jean D'Argenio aka Estelle Donna Evans, see Friedman, *False Prophet*, 71–75. Kahane even set up a foundation in her name after her suicide

in August 1966 (74–75). There were numerous articles about the affair in addition to what Friedman cites. See, for example, M. Kaufman, "Complex Life of Meir Kahane," and Kaufman, "Remembering Kahane." Most recently see Weinman, "Woman on the Bridge," https://www.thecut.com/2020/04/the-woman-on-the-bridge.html?fbclid=IwARoRIGQdfw-NoNgK1pGnlj_QWlTCC7qFoQNKHBGhSNFc-_TeDiiRLyvE-JU.

35. See especially Goldstein, *Jews, Race, and American Identity*. On the upward mobility of postwar America Jews, see Kranson, *Ambivalent Embrace*, 44–67.

36. See Dollinger, *"Is It Good for the Jews?,"* 83. Even setting aside the vexing question of Jews and "whiteness," it is pretty uncontestable that by the 1960s Jews were part of white society. See, for example, in Seligman, "Negro-Jewish Relations," 73.

37. Danzig, "In Defense of Black Power."

38. In describing anti-Semitism in late nineteenth- and early twentieth-century France, Chad Alan Goldberg uses the categories of "reactionary anti-Semitism" vs. "radical anti-Semitism." The first, which stemmed from the antirevolutionaries and the Catholic Church, argued that Jews were inextricably tied to the French Revolution, modernity, and the dismantling of French juridical and ecclesiastical authority; the second stemmed from the revolutionaries, who claimed that the Jews were primitive, backward, and antimodern. In America these two categories functioned similarly, the reactionaries being the white nationalists who viewed the Jews as subversive (and often communists), while the radicals viewed the Jews as "whitey" and colonialists regarding Israel. See Goldberg, *Modernity*, 27–42.

39. For an important discussion of the complex nature of the whiteness of the Jews, especially in regard to anti-Semitism, see Schraub, "White Jews," 379–407.

40. Cruse, *Crisis of the Negro Intellectual*, 100. Kahane would agree with such an assessment and remarks similarly when writing about Jewish assimilation. Cruse also writes, "But the Negro intelligentsia cannot give cultural leadership on these questions because they have sold out their own birthright for an illusion called Racial Integration," 111.

41. Wilderson, *Red, White, and Black*, 58.

42. Wilderson, 38. For a similar kind of comment by Malcolm X, quoted from a rally in New York City in 1965, see P. Goldman, *Death and Life of Malcolm X*, 14–15.

43. Wilderson, *Afropessimism*, 102.

44. See Frazier discussed in Raboteau, *Slave Religion*, 52.

45. Wistrich, *A Lethal Obsession*.

46. This point requires a much broader discussion of the psychic impact of anti-Semitism, which I hope to pursue in the future.

47. For a recent reassessment of the 1968 Ocean–Hill Brownsville school strike, see the podcast *School Colors*, episode 3, "Third Strike." Thanks to Susannah Heschel for the reference. See also Ferguson, "Ocean Hill-Brownsville." Thanks to Lila Corwin-Berman for the reference.

48. For example, see Isaacs, *Inside Ocean Hill-Brownsville*; Podair, *Strike That Changed New York*; Harris, *The Ocean Hill-Brownsville Conflict*. Also relevant is Brooks, "Tragedy at Ocean Hill." Dorman's "Dreams Defended" deals directly with the strike and its influence on Kahane. Dorman's work has informed my analysis here.

49. See, for example, Krebs, "Bernstein Incurs JDL's Wrath."

50. There is some irony in the fact that Brownsville–East New York, by the 1960s a predominantly black and Hispanic neighborhood, was in the earlier part of the century the largest Jewish

community in New York City and had one of the highest Jewish population densities in the US. See Landsman, *Brownsville*, 82–102.

51. Rickford, *We Are an African People*, 30. Cf. De. Bell, "Integration," 7. Decentralization was an issue raised in Jewish circles as well. See, for example, Murray, "Decentralization." The establishment of community councils began in Harlem in 1966 as part of a response to riots there in 1964. See Gurock, *Jews of Harlem*, 214–16.

52. See Kahane, "School Decentralization."

53. Podair, *Strike That Changed New York*, 4.

54. The question as to whether the teachers were "fired" or would indeed be assigned to other schools is a matter of debate.

55. See Dorman, "Dreams Defended," 417; Brooks, "Tragedy," 33–35; Podair, *Strike That Changed New York*, 103–22; Harris, *Ocean Hill-Brownsville Conflict*, 136–44.

56. J. Epstein, "Real McCoy."

57. See Gitlin, "Will Science Support Ocean Hill-Brownsville?," cited in Dorman, "Dreams Defended," 421. See also Ferguson, "Ocean Hill-Brownsville."

58. Cited in Dorman, "Dreams Defended," 417.

59. The full poem can be found in Ferretti, "New York's Black Anti-Semitism Scare." On Lester's journey to Judaism, see Lester, *Becoming a Jew*. Kahane hounded Campbell many times and focused on him as the epitome of the Black Nationalist anti-Semite. See, for example, "Jewish Activists Face Campbell"; Jewish Group Pickets Racist."

60. Kahane wrote numerous articles about the WBAI incident in the *Jewish Press*. See, for example, "Commentary," February 7, 1969; "Spotlight on Extremism." Kahane also wrote there on Lester: "Julius Lester's New Book." On the JDL protest of the radio studio, see "Jewish Activists in N.Y."

61. See the review of the exhibit by Kramer, "Politicizing the Metropolitan Museum." See also Kahane, *Story*, 110–12; Gurock, *Jews of Harlem*, 216–17.

62. See Frydl, *G.I. Bill*, 222–62, 303–51. Cf. Coates, *We Were Eight Years in Power*, 187.

63. While the issue of reparations was certainly a contentious one in the late 1960s, by 1983 an organization called the National Coalition of Blacks for Reparations in America (N'COBRA) had formed, and the NAACP endorsed reparations in 1993. See Bittker, *Case for Black Reparations*. Jewish groups also weighed in on this issue. See, for example, "Black Manifestos and Jewish Response," a document issued by Jews for Urban Justice in the late 1960s that maintains Jews should support reparations to American blacks for the racism and wrongs done to them throughout American history.

64. Kahane, *Story*, 101. It is not clear what massacre he is referring to that Luther perpetrated. In fact, Israel and West Germany signed the Reparations Agreement on September 10, 1952. There was a vehement debate in Israel and some who shared some of Kahane's political views, such as Menachem Begin, spoke out strongly against accepting any reparations from Germany. In the end Israel accepted 3.5 billion Deutsche Marks; see Segev, *Seventh Million*, 189–254. It is also worth noting that very few Germans in the 1950s thought the Jews were entitled to anything; they used Kahane's logic by saying, "We were not Nazis, it was the Nazis who perpetrated this act." See, for example, Coates, "Case for Reparations," in *We Were Eight Years in Power*, 203.

65. Kahane often borrowed from Malcolm X's playbook. When asked about the JDL protest in front of the WBAI studios after Lester Campbell read out the anti-Semitic poem by a young

black female student, Kahane said he would use "all means necessary" to ensure that Julius Lester, the show's host, would be forced to cancel the show. WBAI, as noted, eventually apologized but the show was not canceled. See "Jewish Activists in N.Y.," 3.

66. Kahane, *Story*, 100. See also "Forman Challenged by JDL." In the article a JDL member said they had come armed because "after CCNY [students at City College of New York having been beaten by armed extremists] we are not prepared to be unarmed again."

67. Stephen Whitfield wrote about Senator Joseph McCarthy, "No politician of his time was craftier at exploiting the habits of the press for his own self-aggrandizing ends." See Whitfield, *Culture of the Cold War*, 163. One could say the same about Kahane; he was a master of press attention and using the press as a vehicle for his own agenda.

68. Kahane, *Story*, 105.

69. Kahane.

70. There is much literature on Jews and slavery in the antebellum period. See, for example, Korn, *American Jewry and the Civil War*, 15–31; Silverman, "Antebellum Jews."

71. There were between 50,000 and 100,000 Jews in America in 1850; by 1920 there were 3.3 million; see http://www.jewishvirtuallibrary.org/jewish-population-in-the-united-states-nationally.

72. Coates, "Case for Reparations," 180, 184.

73. Kahane, *Time to Go Home*, 18.

74. Kahane, 92–93.

75. In a different take on this, Jodi Eichler-Levine argues that "in their commemorations of the civil rights movement, Ashkenazi Jews get to have it all, racially speaking. On the one hand, their 'white' (or white enough) identity is solidified because they are allies. They are portrayed as able to assist black Americans, who were, in this telling, less economically privileged, more circumscribed in their civil rights, and in greater physical risk." Eichler-Levine, "American Judaism and Race," 195. For a recent analysis of Jewish whiteness, see Schraub, "White Jews," 379–407.

76. Kahane, *Time to Go Home*, 100.

77. On this Harold Cruse notes, "But it was from the Jewish shopkeeper and trader that the Southern Negro got his latent anti-Semitism. Down through the years, Negroes learned to differentiate between whites and Jewish whites in trade, by the designation 'Jew store,' as oppose to other kinds of stores." Cruse, *Crisis of the Negro Intellectual*, 477.

78. This trope has a long history in Jewish literature. See G. D. Cohen, "Esau as Symbol."

79. The 1966 "Position Paper: The Basis of Black Power" spends a great deal of time explaining the movement's relationship to white liberals and makes a case as to why blacks need to take ownership of the movement. It is much less strident than the words of Malcolm X, Stokely Carmichael, or H. Rap Brown among others. It acknowledges the positive role whites have played in civil rights and explains why the next phase of the movement needs to be black only. On Jews as "colonial exploiters," see "Behavior: The Black and the Jew."

80. As Marc Dollinger notes, "[By the 1960s] for the first time in modern American history, Jews appeared to resemble the white majority more than they did an ethnic minority." See Dollinger, *"Is it Good for the Jews?"*, 99. Cf. Goldstein, *Jews, Race, and American Identity*, 194–201; Cruse, *Crisis of the Negro Intellectual*, 476–97.

81. See H. Cohen, *Jewish View of the Black Revolution*, 118.

82. See the essays in Hentoff, *Black Anti-Semitism*.

83. "Never Again . . . to Us."

84. See Kahane, "Hosea," in *Beyond Words*, vol. 2, 542. I borrow this term "grammar" from the film theorist Frank Wilderson III who writes, "Semiotics and linguistics teach us that when we speak, our grammar goes unspoken. Our grammar is assumed. It is the structure through which the labor of speech is possible." Wilderson, *Red, White, and Black*, 5.

85. See Ungar, "Phenomenon Called Kahane," 109. On Kahane as a racist, see Ravitzky, *Roots of Kahanism*, 28.

86. Wilderson, *Red, White, and Black*, 5.

87. The Black Panthers also viewed their use of violence as acts of self-defense. See Newton, "In Defense of Self-Defense."

88. "Jewish Defense League: Aims and Purposes," 3, 5.

89. *Beyond Words*, vol. 1, 148.

90. On Afrikanity, see Carter, *Race*, 126.

91. Kahane, "I Hate Racism," in *Beyond Words*, vol. 5, 226–29.

92. I discuss Kahane's theology in the final two chapters of this book. Suffice it to say here that Kahane uses "divine election" as a political tool to argue for the Jews' exclusive rights to the land of Israel.

93. This is a notion that comes close to the one offered by D. Novak in *Zionism and Judaism*. I draw out some of these parallels in my "Politics and Precedent."

94. Kahane, *Uncomfortable Questions*, 227.

95. Kahane, 228. It is significant to note that intermarriage was arguably one of the main factors behind Kahane's abandonment of American Jewry. Gerald Cromer notes that for Kahane "going home" to Israel was the only viable solution to the problem of intermarriage in the Diaspora. Only there, he argued, could Jews "preserve and create their own specific tradition and way of life, free of the spiritual and social assimilation of a foreign and abrasive culture." See Cromer, *War of Words*, 90; Kahane, *They Must Go*, 55.

96. Kahane, *Uncomfortable Questions*, 229.

97. Kahane, 229. Legally prohibiting intermarriage between Jew and non-Jews in Israel was part of Kahane's 1982 political platform. In reality, intermarriage is not formally illegal in Israel but is practically impossible because marriages are officially conducted by the Israeli rabbinate, which forbids such unions. On the question of intermarriage and "racism," see Darcy, "Are Your Views on Jewish Intermarriage Racist?," https://forward.com/scribe/381835/are-your-jewish-views-on-intermarriage-racist/. Cf. "Problems of Intermarriage in America Discussed in Israel."

98. *Uncomfortable Questions*, 55–56.

99. Afterman and Afterman rightly note that "Kahane does not perceive the concept of the 'chosen people' as 'racist.' Instead, he argues that the interpretation of this concept as racist stems from the infiltration of foreign culture into Judaism, leading the Jews to be ashamed of their superiority over gentiles." Afterman and Afterman, "Meir Kahane," 205.

100. Kahane, *Uncomfortable Questions*, 58.

101. On this see Yancy, *Backlash*.

102. See, for example, Harkov, "'Black Panther,'" http://www.tabletmag.com/scroll/256186/black-panther-is-a-great-zionist-movie; Munayyer, "Black Panther Is Not about Zionism," https://forward.com/opinion/395519/sorry-black-panther-is-not-about-zionism/.

103. Woocher, *Sacred Survival.*

104. Woocher, "Jewish Survivalism," 291–92.

105. Liebman, "Integration and Survival," in Liebman, *Ambivalent American Jew*, 23. A more recent assessment of this issue from a different perspective can be found in C. A. Goldberg, *Modernity*, esp. 76–103. Goldberg examines the Chicago School of sociology on the question of the Jews in America and their identification with the "marginal man," an idea common in social thought regarding the urbanization of postwar America.

106. Lester quoted in Complaint of United Federation of Teachers.

107. Arendt, "Reflections," 47.

108. Wilderson, *Afropessimism*, 42.

109. The question of integration fostered a major rift in African American activism of that period. For example, while generally a supporter of Black Power, James Baldwin was dead set against separatism. As Glaude notes, for Baldwin "no matter what happened we were, and would always be, American. The future of black people in this country resided not in some fantastical elsewhere but here. Baldwin never changed his mind about that." Glaude, *James Baldwin's America*, 92.

110. See, for example, in S. Goldman's *Zeal for Zion*, 270–308.

111. On the Israeli Black Panthers, see Cromer, "Creation of Others," 283; Pedahzur and Perliger, *Jewish Terrorism*, 79–80; Fischbach, *Black Power and Palestine*, 131–67.

112. See Herschthal, "Israel's Black Panthers Remembered."

113. See Chetrit, *Intra-Jewish Conflict*, 114.

114. Chetrit.

115. Fischbach, *Black Power and Palestine*, 136.

Chapter 4. Communism

1. On Churba's colorful life, see Friedman, *False Prophet*, 58–65. See his obituary, "Joseph Churba, Intelligence Aid." Cf. Yerushalmi, "Dr. Joseph Churba." Hayim Yerushalmi was one of the pseudonyms Kahane used in his *Jewish Press* articles. I want to thank Menachem Butler for this reference.

2. The story of Kahane's relationship with the FBI is complicated. Robert Friedman notes that he was told by an FBI agent that Kahane never worked for them. But a senior Justice Department official said that "he and the Bureau were well acquainted." See Friedman, *False Prophet*, 61–62; Kotler, *Heil Kahane*, 24–30.

3. See Friedman, *False Prophet*, 63. Libby Kahane notes that she tried unsuccessfully to locate Churba's papers after he died; she was notified by Sol Sanders, Churba's associate, that Churba had destroyed most of his files. See L. Kahane, *Rabbi Meir Kahane*, vol. 1, 587n20.

4. An advertisement in New York's *Herald Tribune* on June 29, 1965, announced the Fourth of July Movement under the names of Joseph Churba and Michael King (aka Meir Kahane).

5. King [Kahane] and Churba, *Jewish Stake in Vietnam*. The book is dedicated to "the enslaved Jews of Russia with fervent prayer for redemption."

6. L. Kahane, *Rabbi Meir Kahane*, vol. 1, 82–83.

7. Actually the PLO was officially founded in 1959 by Yasser Arafat, Salah Khalaf, and Khalil al-Wazir, all students who were living in Kuwait. In 1964, however, it became an activist movement.

8. Kahane, "Jewish Stake in Vietnam." The phrase "Because never before have so many known so little about so much" seems to be a paraphrase of British science historian and television producer James Burke, who said, "Never before have so many people understood so little about so much."

9. Kahane, "How the Extreme Left Reacted."

10. Kahane.

11. Personal communication with Michael Walzer, June 2018. Julius Lester, then field secretary of the SNCC, said, "Any Jew who does not question *Israel's existence* nullifies any meaning his opposition to the war in Vietnam may have." Cited in Feldman, *Shadow over Palestine*, 129. On the relationship between anti–Vietnam War activity and Zionist exceptionalism, see Feldman, 127.

12. Kahane, "Communism vs. Judaism: Israel and Vietnam—Are They Different?"

13. On the identity of religion and nationalism for Kahane, see *Listen World*, where he argues that nationalism is nothing more than an age-old expression of Judaism. I will examine this book, and its claim, more closely in chapter 5.

14. See Gitlin, *The Sixties*, 245.

15. Kahane, "Communism vs. Judaism," August 4, 1967. This segment of the series of articles "Communism vs. Judaism" is devoted to the Israeli Communist Party.

16. King [Kahane] Kahane and Churba, *Jewish Stake in Vietnam*, 21. Note that this was a year before the Six-Day War.

17. Kahane, "How the Extreme Left Reacted." *Renmin Ribao* was the official newspaper of the Chinese Communist Party and was published worldwide.

18. Kahane, "Communism vs. Judaism," June 23, 1967, 42.

19. Kahane, 29–30.

20. Kahane, 89–90.

21. Kahane, 52.

22. Kahane, 55.

23. Kahane, 55.

24. *The Jewish Week* of New York may have had a larger circulation than the *Jewish Press* at that time.

25. "Hearings before the Committee of Un-American Activities, House of Representatives, Ninetieth Congress, July 19, 1968," 2202.

26. He cites a letter by the famous rabbi Yisrael Meir Kagen Hakohen (the Hafetz Haim), written from Poland in 1929 about Russian Jewry after the revolution.

27. "Hearings," 2227. He also mentions the Soviet oppression of Catholics, 2232.

28. "Hearings," 2228.

29. See Gerson, "Kahane Tried to Sell Jewry on Vietnam." Gerson notes that left-wing Knesset member Uri Avneri was vocally critical of Golda Meir for supporting Nixon's war effort. Meir responded, "It is in our vital interest that our ties with the U.S. be as friendly as possible."

30. "Hearings," 2232.

31. See Halloran, "Blast Damages Soviet Building.

32. Kahane, *Story*, 29.

33. See Russ, "'Zionist Hooligans,'" 411.

34. Kahane, *Story*, 49.

35. See Weinraub, "Meeting"; "Brussels Declaration on Soviet Jews."

36. Kahane, *Story*, 56.

37. See "Kahane Uproar Stymies Brussels."

38. Beckerman, *When They Come for Us*, 226.

39. See Eytan, "Rabbi Kahane Came, Caused a Storm"; L. Kahane, *Rabbi Meir Kahane*, vol. 1, 187. Cf. Ginger, "Kahane Barred by Party." The *Times* reported that while Preminger disagreed with Kahane, he thought that "to throw him out was undemocratic and un-American."

40. L. Kahane, *Rabbi Meir Kahane*, vol. 1, 187.

41. Beckerman, *When They Come for Us*, 228.

42. Cited in Russ, "'Zionist Hooligans,'" 418.

43. Cited in Russ, 427.

44. "800 Arrested at Soviet Jewry Rally."

45. Kahane, "A Remarkable Event."

46. The JDL disrupted a performance of the Soviet choreographer Igor Moiseyev in Chicago in September 1970. An article in the *Morning Freiheit*, "Jewish Klansman," September 6, 1970, stated, "The JDL sails under false colors, Klansmen have no place in the Jewish community."

47. See Ledbetter, "Fire Bomb Kills Woman"; "Outrage upon Outrage."

48. Kahane published an essay "To Baruch on His Bar Mitzvah" in the *Jewish Press* on January 28, 1972.

49. "Kahane Calls It an Insane Act."

50. On the Bernsteins and the Black Panthers, see Wolfe, *Radical Chic*.

51. In JDL Collection, Box 1, Folder 7, American Jewish Historical Society Archives, New York.

52. See Kahane, *Story*, 6.

53. L. Kahane, *Rabbi Meir Kahane*, vol. 1, 282.

54. By "the same mistake" I mean that, although Kahane was presented with opportunities whereby he could rise to prominence, he could not transcend his anger and his inability to strategize in a way that would maximize his impact. He somehow could not transition out of a radical position to one that would implement radical ideas in a constructive way. In that regard he failed even as a radical compared to someone like Fanon, who had a vision of what would arise from his revolution against colonialism, what he called a "new humanism." Kahane had no such vision; it seemed that for him power was the essence.

Chapter 5. Zionism

1. The question of Israel and democracy among religious Zionists is an old one, much debated in the early years of the state. See, for example, in Kaye, *Invention of Jewish Theocracy*; Yedidya, *Halakha*.

2. This idea is taken up in a different way by Penslar in "Normalization," 223–49. Penslar convincingly argues that politically, socially, and existentially, the state of Israel in many ways mirrors the Diaspora mentality of Jews throughout history and is not a radical exception to it. Julie Cooper offers a similar analysis in her essay about Ben-Gurion's adaptation of Dubnowian diasporic historical narratives. See Cooper, "Reflections on Diasporic Jewish History," 254–84.

3. L. Kahane, *Rabbi Meir Kahane*, vol. 1, 22.

4. L. Kahane, 25.

5. On radical Revisionism in Israel, see most recently in English E. Kaplan, *Jewish Radical Right*. On American Revisionism, see Medoff, *Militant Zionism*. In America, see also Baumel, *"Bergson Boys."* The last two works are crucial to understanding Kahane's sense of Zionism in his youth that then coincides with the militarism of the 1960s.

6. Kahane was not alone in ignoring Jabotinsky's liberal side. Many of Jabotinsky's followers, sometimes called maximal Revisionists, ignored his liberalism; some examples are Abba Ahimeir, Yehoshua Heschel Yeivin, Uri Zvi Greenberg, and Benzion Netanyahu. See Shavit, *Jabotinsky*; E. Kaplan, *Jewish Radical Right*; and, in America, Medoff, *Militant Zionism*.

7. The term Zionism is, of course, highly contested ("What kind of Zionism, what kind of Zionist?"), and while I will here explore various strains, this chapter does not delve into the intricacies of defining Zionism and its boundaries. Still one of the best and most economical overviews of Zionism in English can be found in Hertzberg's long introduction to *The Zionist Idea*. Cf. Shapira and Reinharz, *Essential Papers*.

8. Kahane, "G-d and Zionism," in *Beyond Words*, vol. 1, 196.

9. Kahane, *Listen World*, 187.

10. This is not as provocative a notion as we think. Zionist historian Chaim Ganz calls it "proprietary Zionism, the belief that the Jews own the entire land in perpetuity," though Ganz, unlike Kahane, suggests this exists even without biblical mandate. See Ganz, *A Just Zionism*, 25–52. See also my "Bibi's Bad History."

11. See Kahane, *Our Challenge*, 60.

12. See, for example, Kahane, "Can Israel Go Under?," in *Beyond Words*, vol. 2, 364.

13. Guilt became a very important trait for Kahane as it epitomized the tainted state of Judaism's experience in exile. It represented the loss of self-worth, confidence, well-being; it was the product of a sick society. See Kahane, *Uncomfortable Questions*, 243–53.

14. Kahane, 243.

15. Here Kahane's rhetoric sounds quite similar to the contention in Oswald Spengler's *Decline of the West* that liberalism and pacifism are only a sign of civilization's decay. Although I am quite confident Kahane never read Spengler (I have not seen any reference to him in Kahane's corpus), Spengler's approach, which was taken up later by the Nazis, resonates in Kahane's writings against the Zionist establishment.

16. See, for example, Kahane, "Can Israel Go Under?," 364.

17. See in L. Kahane, *Rabbi Meir Kahane*, vol. 1, 211.

18. See Podhoretz, "My Negro Problem."

19. Telegram from Nash to Kahane, June 16, 1971 (in Folder ARC 4-1478, JNUL [Jewish National and University] Archives, Jerusalem), cited in L. Kahane, *Rabbi Meir Kahane*, vol. 1, 629n9.

20. Kahane, *Never Again!*, 159.

21. Kahane, 163. Interestingly, the Wikipedia entry for Ben-Yosef cites the JDL and the KACH movement as having revered him. Kahane writes more about him in *Listen World*, 128–29.

22. See Saidel, "Yitzhak Shamir," https://www.timesofisrael.com/yitzhak-shamir-why-we-killed-lord-moyne/. Moyne was also said to be involved in the sale of Jews for trucks in Hungary during World War II; see Bauer, *Jews for Sale?*

23. Kahane, *Never Again!*, 158. Linking Zionism to the biblical era, the days of Joshua, and so on was also a common motif among some maximalist Revisionists such as Abba Ahimeir. See,

for example, in E. Kaplan, *Jewish Radical Right*, 37–38. Kahane often speaks about Jabotinsky but rarely about the more radical Revisionists such as Ahimeir or Yehoshua Heschel Yeivin who were actually closer to his own political inclinations than Jabotinsky; it is not at all clear how much he knew about them. The idea that Jews never gave up on the land is not special to Kahane. For example, we find a similar passage in Abraham Joshua Heschel's *Israel: An Echo in Eternity*, 58–59: "Forced to leave their ancient country [the Jews] never abandoned . . . the Holy Land; the Jewish people never ceased to be passionate about Zion. It has always lived in a dialogue with the Holy Land." Heschel does not extend this to say that "Zionism" is effectively an ancient category, but he does maintain that Jews throughout history yearned and aspired to return. The story, of course, is a bit more complex and the attitude toward the land in Jewish literature is not as unequivocal as either Kahane or Heschel maintains. See, for example, Saperstein, "Land of Israel."

24. Later, in *Listen World*, Kahane will argue that this New Jew was the Old Jew lost in centuries of exile but revived through this national liberation movement. See further below.

25. His daughter Tova, thirteen, and son Baruch, twelve, had emigrated in July 1971 to prepare for the upcoming school year. Kahane had been invited to address the Zionist Organization of America on September 2, 1971, and stayed behind for the lecture, leaving New York on September 12.

26. Motti Inbari claims the settlement movement was in fact a response to the depression and humiliation of the Yom Kippur War rather than the optimism of the 1967 war. See Inbari, *Messianic Religious Zionism*, 11 and 15–35 where he differs with Ravitzky.

27. Kahane, *Our Challenge*, 32–33. The irony of Kahane's statement here is that most of his ideas about Israel are imported from the Galut.

28. Kahane, 137.

29. Kahane, 129.

30. This point is developed later in this chapter.

31. Kahane, *Our Challenge*, 108.

32. Kahane, *Listen World*, 159.

33. Kahane, "Isolated—but Not Alone," November 22, 1974, in *Beyond Words*, vol. 2, 71–74.

34. Kahane, *Our Challenge*, 62.

35. Kahane, 62; see also 97–98: "The Jew can teach his truths to man, but only when it [the Jew] stands aside, separate and chosen." Cf. Breslauer, *Meir Kahane*, 34–35.

36. Kahane, *Our Challenge*, 42–43. For a position that seems to support to some degree Kahane's understanding, see Yiftachel, *Ethnocracy*, 11–50.

37. Later on Kahane became more focused on messianism as the vehicle of Zionism. See, for example, in *The Jewish Idea*, vol. 2, 779: "G-d has inaugurated the final era. The redemption has begun. The Messiah's footsteps can be heard, and G-d's 'knocking' at the door." See also 791: "Only the blind and those who refuse to see will fail to understand that today we are right at the very heart of the Ikveta Demeshika, 'the footsteps of the messiah,' the beginning of the redemption." More apocalyptic writing on the end-time can be found in *Forty Years*. This messianic turn made a merger with Kookean thinking much easier in Kahanism after Kahane's death. *Our Challenge*, 46.

38. Kahane, 39–40. On the question of whether there is any real reconciliation between the Jews and the Arabs, Ben-Gurion shared Kahane's general assessment when he wrote, "There is no solution to the question of relations between the Arabs and the Jews. . . . And we must

recognize this situation. . . . We as a nation want this country to be ours; the Arabs as a nation want this country to be theirs." Cited in Lustick, *Paradigm Lost*, 4.

39. Here, ironically, Kahane would generally agree with Edward Said's remarks in *The Question of Palestine*, 56–114.

40. See Jabotinsky, "Iron Wall."

41. See Jabotinsky, "After Establishing the Border Corps," in *Collected Works*, vol. 10, 303.

42. Kahane, *Our Challenge*, 28.

43. "There is not now, and there never will be such a thing as a 'Palestinian' people or state." *Our Challenge*, 21. Cf. *Our Challenge*, 109: "There has never been a Palestine or Palestinian people and never will be."

44. This, as mentioned earlier in these notes, is close to the position of David Novak in *Zionism and Judaism*; see the discussion in my "Politics and Precedent."

45. In Kahane, *Our Challenge*, 23, we read: "The Land of Israel is the land of the Jewish people, whose claim to sovereignty over it—*all of it*—is clear and as ancient as G-d's decision to grant that sovereignty." This notion of "proprietary Zionism," a term coined by Gans in *A Just Zionism*, stands at the center of much of Zionist ideology. Kahane views it solely from the perspective of divine sanction.

46. Kahane, 15–16.

47. See Breslauer, *Meir Kahane*, 64: "Kahane's Zionism is fundamentally religious: the return to Zion is a religious imperative and the return must be a religious one characterized by the practice of Jewish law." I agree with this but would add that Kahane's Zionism, while religious, does not constitute any existing paradigm of religious Zionism. A comparison to Kookean Zionism illustrates that; see below and also my discussion in the concluding chapter.

48. See, for example, Aran, *M'Zionut Datit le'Day Zionit*; and Schwartz, *Etgar u'Mashber*, 209–19.

49. See BT Sanhedrin 98a. The relationship between the Holocaust and the state of Israel is the subject of an ongoing robust debate. For one of the latest iterations, see D. Novak, *Zionism and Judaism*, 225–50. Zvi Yehuda Kook viewed the Holocaust as a necessary prelude to the establishment of the state; see his *Sihot ha-Rav*, 281–83; Aviner, *Orot m'Ofel*, 48ff. *Our Challenge* was first published by Chilton Books in Pennsylvania in 1974. Kahane was already living in Israel at the time.

50. Kahane, *Our Challenge*, 177.

51. L. Kahane, *Rabbi Meir Kahane*, vol. 2, 113.

52. The book was printed twice more, in 1995 and a corrected version in 2011, both under the auspices of the Institute for the Publication of the Writings of Meir Kahane in Jerusalem.

53. For an overview, see Schwartz, *Religious Zionism*.

54. There is a literal library of work on Abraham Isaac Kook's thinking. In English see Ish-Shalom, *Rav Avraham Itzhak HaCohen Kook*; and Mirsky, *Rav Kook*.

55. Kahane, *Listen World*, 191.

56. See Lebel, *Politics of Memory*.

57. Kahane, *Listen World*, 25.

58. On the exilic mentality of the Babylonian Talmud, see Boyarin, *Babylonian Talmud as Diaspora*.

59. See Medoff, *Militant Zionism*, 45–72.

60. Ruth Wisse offers a similar, though much more nuanced, assessment of emancipation in her *Jews and Power*.

61. Kahane, *Listen World*, 85–95.

62. Kahane, 195.

63. See Kahane, "There Is No Palestine," in *Beyond Words*, vol. 2, 79–82.

64. See Kotler, *Heil Kahane*, 108–9.

65. Kotler, 110.

66. See, for example, Smooha, " Model of Ethnic Democracy"; Yiftachel, *Ethnocracy*; Ghanem and Khatib, "Nationalisation." Cf. Magid and Magid, "Ethnic Democracy." On democracy among religious Zionists, see Kaye, *Invention of Jewish Theocracy*, 33–44, 75–80.

67. It would be interesting to know whether Kahane was aware of the rabbinic debates about democracy and halakhah that were taking place a few decades earlier, for example, in the works of Chief Rabbi Isaac Herzog or earlier in the writings of Rabbi Chaim Hirschensohn. On Herzog, see Kaye, *Invention of Jewish Theocracy*, 99–121; on Hirschensohn, see Schweid, *Democracy and Halakhah*.

68. Kahane, *Uncomfortable Questions*, 83.

69. Kahane, 47.

70. Kahane quotes liberal Zionist Dan Ben-Amotz from an article in the Israeli paper *Hadashot*, February 15, 1985: "I don't understand something. If all our citizens are really equal before the law with no difference in religion, nationality, sex, or race, as stated in the Declaration of Independence, and if this is really a democratic state, perhaps you can explain to me why a Jewish citizen cannot sell his private land to a citizen whose mother is, by chance, not-Jewish." Cited in *Uncomfortable Questions*, 144.

71. Kahane, *Uncomfortable Questions*, 47–48.

72. Kahane, 58.

73. Here Arnold Eisen's comments about Zionism and Orthodoxy are relevant: "Either the Torah's legislation was intended *lekhatchilah*, a priori, and so contained a model to which any Jewish state at any time must conform, or it represented a code enacted *bedi'avad*, ex post facto, in accord with particular circumstances prevailing at one time but no longer. If the former, Neturei Karta in Israel and non-Zionists abroad such as the Satmar Hasidim are correct. Zionism is illegitimate; the Jewish state can have no religious meaning, and in fact violates God's laws. If the latter, a revision of halakha is needed commensurate with the revision of Jewish history accomplished by Zionism." See Eisen, "Concept of the Land of Israel," 288. Kahane's position here is much closer to the anti-Zionists than the Orthodox Zionists.

74. In a 1985 debate with Alan Dershowitz, Kahane asks Dershowitz, "Do you want your daughter to marry a Jew?" Dershowitz replies, "Yes." "Is it because of halakhah?" Kahane asks, to which Dershowitz replies, "No." "Then, Professor Dershowitz," Kahane replies, "you are a racist." The debate in Boston on March 25, 1985, can be seen on YouTube at: "Alan Dershowitz vs. Meir Kahane (1985 Debate)," https://www.youtube.com/watch?v=2ykrwmaKrLg.

75. Kahane, *Our Challenge*, 46. Ironically, what Kahane derisively regarded as liberalism's cynicism about buying off the Arabs is precisely what he is suggesting here: that the Palestinian can be enticed to give up his or her land for a good price. A bit later he writes, "Labor wants to get rid of the Arabs by giving them Jewish land; we want to try to keep Eretz Yisroel and find some means to convince the Arabs to leave," 49. In the 1980s in *They Must Go* and *Thorn in Our*

Sides, Kahane makes a more forceful argument for mandatory transfer of the Arab population; a transfer was something Jabotinsky opposed. See Jabotinsky, "Al Kir ha-Barzel," 253.

76. Jabotinsky, 258.

77. Kahane, *The Jewish Idea*, vol. 2, 735–36. See also Gellman, "Jewish Chosenness."

78. Rabbi Isaac Herzog, who was a strong advocate of theocracy in Israel, did not think a theocracy required the legal exclusion of the non-Jew. See Kaye, *Invention of Jewish Theocracy*, 76–79.

79. His book *Why Be Jewish?* (1977) is an extended assault on intermarriage in America as a natural by-product of the liberalization of Judaism. Kahane saw the intermingling of Arabs and Jews in Israel as indicating that Israel was simply becoming another form of Jewish Diasporism except that now Jews were the majority and had the power of legislation and policing.

80. Kahane, *Uncomfortable Questions*, 185.

81. See Z. Y. Kook, *Le-Hilkhot Zibbur*; Ravitzky, *Messianism*, 83–85, 136. For Abraham Isaac Kook, the secular-Zionist impulse manifested an unconscious drive to return to the authentic Jewish self. This is discussed in many places in his writings. See, for example, in Kook, *Orot ha-Teshuva*, 111–24. On Zvi Yehuda, see Schwartz, *Etgar u'Mashber*, 23–71; Ravitzky, *Messianism*, 79–145; Inbari, *Messianic Religious Zionism*, 15–36. On Abraham Isaac Kook more generally, see Mirsky, *Rav Kook*.

82. Thus when the state acts against those aspirations, the settler movement is thrown into crisis. See, for example, in Fischer, "State Crisis," 60–97; Fischer, "Neo-Hasidut"; Ravitzky, *Messianism*, 82–85; Ravitzky, "Radical Religious Zionism."

83. Inbari argues that after the evacuation of Yamit in 1978 and the relinquishing of the Sinai Peninsula in the Camp David Accords, Zvi Yehuda began to back away from his fidelity to the state. See Inbari, *Messianic Religious Zionism*, 32–36.

84. On this in detail, see Fischer, "Self-Expression," esp. 215–69.

85. On the circle of Zvi Yehuda Kook and its influence, see Schwartz, *Etgar u'Mashber*, 207–306.

86. See, for example, in Ravitzky, *Messianism*, 79–145. This changes in later iterations of religious-Zionist thinking where the state becomes more of an impediment rather than a vehicle for redemption. This is in part due to the influence of Rabbi Yitzchak Ginsburgh, whose Chabad-inflected theology does not share the transvaluative romanticism of Kookean thinking. Ginsburgh opposes Zionism and the secular state of Israel, in some ways similarly, though with marked differences, to Kahane. See, for example, in Katsman, "Reactions," esp. 281–84.

87. Kahane, *Our Challenge*, 165.

88. Yossi Sarid (1940–2015) was an Israeli Knesset member and cabinet minister from 1974 to 2006 and member of secular-left parties. He was indeed an avid secularist and defender of secular rights in Israel. He was often a target for Kahane, for whom he embodied the values Kahane saw as auguring the demise of the state.

89. See Kahane, *Or Hara'ayon: The Jewish Idea*, vol. 2 (in English), 725.

90. See Rosenak, *Sedakim*; Aran, "Kookisms"; Harel, "Beyond Gush Emunim," 131–33.The notion of secular Zionism as the penultimate Messiah ben Joseph is given credence by Abraham Isaac Kook's eulogy for Theodor Herzl where he refers to Herzl by that name. See Kook, "Eulogy," 94–99. For an English translation, see "The Lamentation in Jerusalem." See also Ravitzky, *Messianism*, 99, for an abbreviated translation of the relevant passage.

91. Later on Kahane became more focused on messianism as the vehicle of Zionism. See, for example, in *The Jewish Idea*, vol. 2, 779: "G-d has inaugurated the final era. The redemption

has begun. The Messiah's footsteps can be heard, and G-d's 'knocking' at the door." See also 791: "Only the blind and those who refuse to see will fail to understand that today we are right at the very heart of the Ikveta Demeshika, 'the footsteps of the messiah,' the beginning of the redemption." More apocalyptic writing on the end-time can be found in *Forty Years*. This messianic turn made a merger with Kookean thinking much easier in Kahanism after Kahane's death.

92. There are many articles about Goldstein and his relationship to Kahane. For one example, see Blumenfeld, "A Time to Kill," https://www.washingtonpost.com/archive/lifestyle/1994/03/20/a-time-to-kill/8ff1f7d1-ad8a-4c30-8720-ad8062501fd4/?utm_term=.1cd341741c6d. See also Sprinzak, *Brother against Brother*; Cromer, *Narratives of Violence*.

93. See Ben-Chorin, *Baruch ha-Gever*.

94. This is also the underlying thesis of the 2019 film *Incitement*, which deals with the Rabin assassination from the perspective of the assassin Yigal Amir.

95. As noted earlier, Kahane was in prison in Ramle in the early 1980s for his role in planning to blow up Haram al-Sharif, the Dome of the Rock. While in prison he wrote furiously, completing two books in Hebrew, *Thorns in Their Eyes* and *On Redemption and Faith*, and a shorter book also in Hebrew, *Forty Years*; all were later translated into English. In 1973, a couple of years after immigrating to Israel, Kahane wrote two essays in Hebrew, "Israel's Eternity and Victory" and "Numbers 23:9," that begin to set out the agenda that would form the basis of his work in Ramle Prison.

96. In fact, in 1976 Kahane wrote a pamphlet *Hillul ha-Shem* that was never made public and was circulated only among his students. In it he laid out his political theology of *Hillul ha-Shem* and retributive violence. On this see Sprinzak, *Brother against Brother*, 180; Afterman and Afterman, "Meir Kahane," 193–215.

97. Although *Story of the Jewish Defense League* was published in 1975, four years after Kahane immigrated to Israel, the book is really a reflection on his career in America.

98. Kahane's use of the language of colonialism in describing anti-Semitism mirrors the use of the term to describe racism in America. See, for example, Blauner, *Racial Oppression*; O'Dell, "Special Variety of Colonialism"; Kwaem Ture [Stokely Carmichael] and Hamilton, *Back Power*, 5.

99. I discuss this in some detail in my essay "Anti-Semitism as Colonialism."

100. Halevi, *Memoirs*, 259.

101. On Kahane's students who took over after he was killed, see Pedahzur and Perliger, *Jewish Terrorism*, 69–97.

102. Kahane returns to the themes of *Forty Years* a few years later in *The Jewish Idea*, vol. 2, 867–69.

103. See BT Sanhedrin 98a. The relationship between the Holocaust and the state of Israel is the subject of an ongoing robust debate. For one of the latest iterations, see D. Novak, *Zionism and Judaism*, 225–50. Zvi Yehuda Kook viewed the Holocaust as a necessary prelude to the establishment of the state; see his *Sihot ha-Rav*, 281–83; Aviner, *Orot m'Ofel*, 48ff.

104. The merging of Kookean ideas and Kahanist ideas occurred after Kahane's death; on this see my "Kahane Won." I agree with Pedahzur and Perlinger that Kahane and his followers "were antithetical to the Gush Emunim movement from almost every perspective, and they can be in fact viewed as a separate counterculture." Pedahzur and Perlinger, *Jewish Terrorism*, 74. See also Afterman and Afterman, "Meir Kahane," 208; they argue that Kahane's theology of revenge is a major departure from Kookean Zionism, which is founded on the notion that the state is part of a messianic process initiated by God that will lead Israel to redemption.

105. See Kahane, *The Jewish Idea*, vol. 2, 935–51.

106. Kahane, *Forty Years*, 16. An earlier iteration of this appears in Kahane, *Listen World*, 169: "The State of Israel came into being not because the Jew deserved it, but because the gentile did. It came into being not because the Jew was worthy of it but because the Name of G-d had reached its full humiliation and desecration." Cf. Kahane, *The Jewish Idea*, vol. 2, 867.

107. Kahane, *Forty Years*, 103.

108. Sprinzak, *Brother against Brother*, 49.

109. Kahane, *The Jewish Idea*, vol. 1, 276. See also vol. 1, 355, and vol. 2 , 801: "It follows that Israel's power, exaltation and victory over their own enemies and the blasphemous enemies of G-d is a *Kiddush Hashem*." See also vol. 1, 282: "Passing up the opportunity to carry out zealous, Halakhically mandated revenge is such a terrible sin that whoever refuses to do so deserves annihilation." See also Kahane's reading of the midrash *Sifri*, Beha'alotkha, 84, on Numbers 10:35: "Rather, the verse informs us that if someone hates the Jewish people, it is as though he hates God."

110. See also *The Jewish Idea*, vol. 2, 795.

111. Kahane, *They Must Go*, 275.

112. Afterman and Afterman, "Meir Kahane," 203.

113. Kahane, introduction *to Forty Years* (end). There is no pagination to this introduction.

114. Kahane, *Forty Years*, 37.

115. Kahane, 56–59. This sentiment persists in the radical-right Jewish Leadership movement of Motti Karpel and others today. According to Karpel, as stated by Motti Inbari, "Modern anti-Semitism rests on this same basis: anti-Semitism, according to Karpel, is a result of the cosmic rage of the nations of the world because Zionism is not fulfilling its role, offering instead pathetic, cheap imitation of gentile culture." See Inbari, "Post-Zionism." I want to thank Motti Inbari for sharing this essay before its publication.

116. Kahane, 68.

117. Kahane, *They Must Go*, 275–76. See also Cromer, *War of Words*, 89–103.

118. See Shavit, *Jabotinsky*, 203–309; E. Kaplan, *Jewish Radical Right*, 3–30; Sprinzak, *Brother against Brother*, 52.

119. Kahane, *Forty Years*, 82.

120. I explore the ideational relationship between the later Kahane and Teitelbaum in my "Politics and Precedent."

121. See, for example, Čapková, "Bar Kokhba Association." On the Bar Kokhba Society in Cairo, see Kimche, "Bar Kokhba Society (Cairo)."

122. Kahane, *Forty Years*, 28.

123. Kahane, *The Jewish Idea*, vol. 1, 339, citing 2 Kings 13:17.

124. See *The Jewish Idea*, vol. 2, 812–25.

125. Kahane, *Forty Years*, 91–92.

Chapter 6. Militant Post-Zionist Apocalypticism

1. For one example, see Boyarin, *Babylonian Talmud as Diaspora*.

2. There is much written about the rabbinic relationship to the land and redemption. See, for example, Primus, "Borders of Judaism"; Sarason, "Significance"; Saperstein, "Land of Israel."

3. Ben-Gurion famously organized a Bible-study group at his home in Sde Boker in 1958 that included some of the great Israeli luminaries of the time. See, for example, Shapira, "Ben-Gurion and the Bible"; Ben-Gurion, *Ben-Gurion Looks at the Bible.*

4. Elizur-Hershkowitz and Shapira, *Torat ha-Melekh.* See also von Mutius, "Positions of Jews and Non-Jews."

5. On the rise of the move toward globalization and multinational corporate prosperity, see Senor and Singer, *Start-Up Nation.* On the prominence of the settlers during this period, see Sprinzak, *Ascendance*; Gorenberg, *Accidental Empire.*

6. There is much written on this phenomenon. One of the most concise studies in English is still Ravitzky, *Messianism*, 79–144. Cf. Inbari, *Messianic Religious Zionism.*

7. See Inbari, *Messianic Religious Zionism*, 37–58, 107–32.

8. See the preface to vol. 1 of *The Jewish Idea*, 9.

9. The musar movement has a variegated history. On the modern musar movement, see Etkes, *R. Yisrael Salanter*, and more recently Claussen, *Sharing the Burden.* For a fresh new approach to the trajectory of musar literature going back to early modernity, see Koch, *Human Self-Perfection.*

10. See L. Kahane, *Rabbi Meir Kahane*, vol. 1, 6.

11. On the Slobodka school of musar, especially in regard to its ethos and practice, see Englander, "'Jewish Knight' of Slobodka."

12. For a hagiographical study of Kalmanowitz, see Birnbaum, *R. Avrohom Kalmanowitz.*

13. See L. Kahane, *Rabbi Meir Kahane*, vol. 1, 34.

14. On the advice of his father, who was a Yeshiva University alumnus, Kahane applied and was admitted to Yeshiva University for the term beginning September 1951. However, he decided to remain in the Mir Yeshiva and complete his undergraduate coursework at Brooklyn College instead. See L. Kahane, *Rabbi Meir Kahane*, vol. 1, 576n18. On the differences between these two communities, see Shapiro, *Between the Yeshiva World and Modern Orthodoxy* .

15. See Schofer, *Making of a Sage*; Diamond, *Fasting and Asceticism.*

16. Kahane, *The Jewish Idea*, vol. 1, 176.

17. Katz, *Tenu'at Musar.*

18. See my "Autonomous Self in the Musar Tradition."

19. In these and other ways Kahane, as pointed out earlier in these notes, comes quite close to the anti-Zionism of Rabbi Yoel Teitelbaum of Satmar, albeit from a different perspective. On the comparison between the two, see my "Politics and Precedent."

20. See B. Talmud Ta'anit 16a. See also Kahane, *Uncomfortable Questions*, 196: "This is the reality of secular Zionism: these are its victims. Children of Zion suddenly find Jesus in Tel Aviv and pagan Indian idols in Jerusalem, whose sick soul of ignorance seeks refuge in cults and strange gods of stranger lands far beyond the seas."

21. Kahane, *The Jewish Idea*, vol. 1, 101.

22. Katz, *Tenu'at Musar*, vol. 1, 73, 77.

23. Kahane, *The Jewish Idea*, vol. 1, 83.

24. Leibowitz, *Judaism*, 3–29, 61–78.

25. Kahane, *The Jewish Idea*, vol. 1, 161.

26. Interestingly, this seems to mirror Paul's critique of the Pharisees. See, for example, Gager, *Jewish Lives of the Apostle Paul*, 37–52; Gaston, *Paul and the Torah*, 135–50.

27. Although he does not quote this text, he could have cited Bamidbar Rabbah 17:6, which states to Israel that it embodies holiness in the performance of the mitzvot. If the people do not perform the mitzvot, they become *m'hollelim*, profane or unholy.

28. Kahane, *The Jewish Idea*, vol. 1, 469.

29. *The Jewish Idea*, vol. 1, 474.

30. The question of democracy was one that many early religious Zionists grappled with intensively. Many rabbinic figures pondered and wrote about the extent to which democracy could square with a religious-Zionist worldview. One instructive example is Eliezer Schweid's study of Rabbi Chaim Hirschenson in his *Democracy and Halakah*. Hirschensohn was one of the earliest Zionist rabbis to advocate for a symbiosis between halakhah and democracy. His early career was in Safed, Palestine, and later he became a rabbi in Hoboken, New Jersey.

31. See in Wexler and Rubin, *Social Vision*, 201–10.

32. For a Jewish scientist's take on this issue, see Pollack, *Faith*.

33. For an example of one *haredi* response, see my "Modernity as Heresy."

34. Kahane, *The Jewish Idea*, vol. 2, 821.

35. See, for example, my "Is There an American Jewish Fundamentalism?"

36. Kahane, *The Jewish Idea*, vol. 1, 504. See also vol. 2, 870–75.

37. See Wasserman, *The Talmud after the Humanities*. On idolatry in Judaism more generally, see Margalit and Halbertal, *Idolatry*; Goshen-Gottstein, *Same God, Other God*; Sommer, *Bodies of God*. On the construction of the gentile as "goy" in rabbinic teaching, which also speaks to the question at hand, see Rosen-Zvi and Ofir, *Israel's Other*.

38. The tolerance or lack thereof of "other gods" in the Hebrew Bible is a continued matter of scholarly debate. See, for example, Sommer, *Bodies of God*, 145-174; Goshen-Gottstein, *Same God, Other God*, 22–46. This also concerns the *erev rav* or mixed multitude, which the tradition often views as instigating Israelite sin. On this, see my "Politics of (un) Conversion."

39. On the political nature of the Bible's vision, see Walzer et al., *Jewish Political Tradition*, vol. 2, *Membership*; Halbertal, *Power*. In certain instances there was resistance to foreign alliances, for example, the later Maccabean reinstitution of the covenant with Sparta after the Maccabean Revolt.

40. See, for example, Douglas, *Leviticus*, esp. 87–103; Neusner, *Idea of Purity*.

41. Kahane, *The Jewish Idea*, vol. 1, 125. See *Midrash Tanhuma* on the weekly Torah portion Hukat, 8.

42. *The Jewish Idea*, vol. 2, 545. On holiness more generally see Dan, *Kedusha*; Mittleman, *Does Judaism Condone Violence?*, 23–88.

43. Kellner, *Maimonides' Confrontation with Mysticism*, 28. For a discussion on this, see Mittleman, *Does Judaism Condone Violence?*, 59–71; and on the dichotomy of Halevi and Maimonides, see Hartman, *Israelis and the Jewish Tradition*, 26–87. On the holiness of the land in Kabbalah, see Idel, "Land of Israel."

44. *The Jewish Idea*, vol. 1, 461. This is not an uncommon trope in some modern Jewish exegesis. See, for example, Rabbi Yaakov Moshe Charlap in his commentary to Psalms in *Mei Marom*, 64.

45. Kahane, *The Jewish Idea*, vol. 1, 461.

46. *The Jewish Idea*, vol. 1, 509.

47. *The Jewish Idea*, vol. 1, 483.

48. Kahane devotes two books, *They Must Go* and *A Thorn in Our Sides*, to his theory of the expulsion of the non-Jew from Israel.

49. Kahane, *The Jewish Idea*, vol. 2, 992. Cf. vol. 2, 534: "As long as Israel live among [the gentiles], they will be tightly bound to the foreign culture. Only separation, only isolation, can protect the Chosen People from the poisonous influence of that culture."

50. *The Jewish Idea*, vol. 2, 719.

51. *The Jewish Idea*, vol. 2, 874.

52. *The Jewish Idea*, vol. 1, 100–101. See BT Shabbat 138b.

53. On the Canaanites and the overcoming of Judaism, see Diamond, *Homeland or Holy Land?*, 9–23, 49–75, 125–36.

54. Kahane, *The Jewish Idea*, vol. 2, 614.

55. The method of separation differs in different biblical texts. For example, in Deuteronomy 7:1–2 we find a command to annihilate the inhabitants of the land, and in Exodus 23:27–30 we find a more tempered act of separation. And then in Judges 3 we find that at least some of the inhabitants remained in the land even after the Israelite conquest.

56. Kahane, *The Jewish Idea*, vol. 2, 546.

57. *The Jewish Idea*, vol. 2, 795.

58. Interestingly, Martin Buber's Zionism, built on the foundation of Hebrew Humanism (sometimes called Biblical Humanism), is also based on the notion of a biblical mandate—one, however, that seeks to create "a Jewish commonwealth that will promote the construction of a 'genuine human community' (*Gemeinshaft*) in accordance with the people of Israel's founding biblical mandate." See Mendes-Flohr, *Martin Buber*, 189. What stands between Buber and Kahane on this question is how each understands the mandate of the Bible, but both reject the more mundane notion of Zionism as simply about creating a political reality as a safe haven for Jews, a secular country like all others. That is, both reject the purely political motives of Zionism.

59. On this see Firestone, *Holy War*, 238–44. See also Lifshitz, "Holiness."

60. For an interesting rendering of this phenomenon, see G. Cohen, "Blessing of Assimilation." For recent analysis of this seminal essay, see the essays in *Jewish Quarterly Review* 106, no. 4 (Fall 2016).

61. On this more generally, see G. Cohen, "Blessing of Assimilation," 145–56.

62. Kahane, *The Jewish Idea*, vol. 2, 550–51. There is a well-known dispute between Maimonides and Nahmanides on whether there is a formal obligation to live in the land of Israel. See Maimonides, *Sefer ha-Mitzvot*, Positive Mitzvah 4. Nahmanides's gloss to *Sefer ha-Mitzvot* is discussed in *The Jewish Idea*, vol. 2, 562. This issue was of major concern to Rabbi Yoel Teitelbaum, the Satmar Rebbe, who argues with Maimonides that there is no positive mitzvah to live in the land, developing that theme in his essay "Yishuv Eretz Yisrael." One of the consequences of this would be whether a war to conquer the land in modern times constitutes an "obligatory war." Here Kahane argues with Nahmanides that it does; *The Jewish Idea*, vol. 2, 566. For a much longer discussion of this matter, which became a major issue in contemporary halakhic literature, see Myers, "'Commanded War.'"

63. Kahane, *The Jewish Idea*, vol. 1, 319.

64. *The Jewish Idea*, vol. 1, 179–80. See also 223–24, where Kahane cites Rashi's comment to Rabbi Nahman bar Yitzhak, who says in BT Ta'anit 7b, "It is permissible to hate the insolent." Rashi writes, "[It is permissible to hate him] even though it says, *Love your neighbor as yourself*."

65. *The Jewish Idea*, vol. 2, 630.

66. See, for example, Talmage, "The Bible in Medieval Jewish Scholarship."

67. This is an illustration of the term "reversing the gaze" used in S. Heschel's *Abraham Geiger*, 1–22, where she discusses Jewish attitudes toward Christianity.

68. Kahane, *The Jewish Idea*, vol. 1, 18.

69. I say "neo" here because he did not advocate sacrifices nor many of the other biblical mandates, arguing that those are Temple-dependent and thus cannot be reinstituted without a Jerusalem Temple. Rather, it was a return to the biblical in regard to purification and the relationship to the gentile.

70. Kahane, *Uncomfortable Questions*, 45–86, 155–242.

71. Kahane, 158–59.

72. Kahane, 323.

73. Kahane, *The Jewish Idea*, vol. 1, 135.

74. *The Jewish Idea*, vol. 1, 136.

75. Here we find many post-Kahanists such as Yitzchak Ginsburgh who share this view regarding democracy, although Kahane is usually not cited. See, for example, in Katsman, "Reactions," 277.

76. Kahane, *The Jewish Idea*, vol. 2, 719.

77. In detail, see Rosenak, *Sedakim*.

78. See, for example, Numbers 31:2–3; Judges 11:36; 2 Samuel 4:8; Jeremiah 50:15, 51:11; Ezekiel 21:15, 25:17; Psalms 18:48, 79:10, 94:1, 149:7; Lamentations 3:60. See Seeman, "Violence, Ethics, and Divine Honor."

79. The Bible is also replete with portrayals of God as a merciful God. In most though not all cases, that mercy is directed toward Israel. One verse, "The Lord your God is merciful and forgiving even though we have rebelled against Him" (Daniel 9:9), indicates divine mercy even in light of blatant rebellion. See also Psalms 86:5, 145:9.

80. Kahane, *The Jewish Idea*, vol. 1, 290.

81. See, for example, Zenger, *Understanding the Psalms of Divine Wrath*.

82. *Mekhilta*, tractate d'Shira, quoted in Kahane, *The Jewish Idea*, vol. 1, 308.

83. The midrash *Sifri* on Numbers, weekly Torah portion Matot, 157.

84. Kahane, *The Jewish Idea*, vol. 1, 276.

85. This is not uncommon. For a proximate example, see Charlap's commentary to Psalms in *Mei Marom*, Psalm 117:13, 77.

86. On this see Mittleman, *Does Judaism Condone Violence?*, 158–59.

87. Kahane, *The Jewish Idea*, vol. 1, 280.

88. *The Jewish Idea*, vol. 1, 294.

89. *The Jewish Idea*, vol. 1, 288.

90. *The Jewish Idea*, vol. 1, 281.

91. *The Jewish Idea*, vol. 1, 922. The GRA's comment can be found in Rabbi Hillel Rivlin of Skhlov, *Kol ha-Tor*, ch. 2:2. This work deals with redemption and often cites the GRA, Rivlin's teacher. On *Kol ha-Tor* see M. Cohen, "Introducing *Humash Kol Ha-Tor*," https://zeramim.org/current-issue/volume-iii-issue-3-spring-summer-2019-5779/introducing-ḥumash-kol-ha-tor-and-mgillot-kol-ha-tor-some-preliminary-considerations-martin-s-cohen/. Kahane is fond of *Kol ha-Tor* and cites it often in *The Jewish Idea*.

92. In the GRA's vision, Messiah ben Joseph destroys Esau and Messiah ben David destroys Ishmael. "Mating Esau and Ishmael" makes the job of each messiah impossible.

93. On Armelius and *Sefer Zerubbabel*, see Ma. Himmelfarb, *Jewish Messiahs.*

94. Kahane, *The Jewish Idea*, vol. 2, 927.

95. *The Jewish Idea*, vol. 2, 892.

96. There are many studies that treat Kook in depth. For an example in English, see Mirsky, *Rav Kook.* David Novak, in a sympathetic nod to Kook, argues that there is no biblical mandate for any particular political framework and thus democracy can be applied since it offers the best political system to maximize human flourishing in the land of Israel. See D. Novak, *Zionism and Judaism*, 153–96.

97. The move from biblical to rabbinic notions of violence is discussed in Mittleman, *Does Judaism Condone Violence?*, 154–92. Curiously there is no discussion of Kahane's theory of violence, which would have added another later of analysis to this interesting work.

98. See, for some examples, Sprinzak, *Brother against Brother*, 286-306; and Weisburd, *Jewish Settler Violence.*

99. See, for example, Sackett, "From Hebron to Pittsburgh," www.jewishisrael.org/from-hebron-to-pittsburgh-by-shmuel-sackett/.

100. It should be noted that in the settler community other voices such as the late Rabbi Shimon Gershon Rosenberg (Rav Shagar) and the later Rabbi Menachem Froman have offered critical revisions of Kookean thinking and rejected Kahane out of hand. Thus far their influence is nominal.

Conclusion

1. In his correspondence with Rabbi Avi Weiss, a friend and onetime follower of Kahane, by the mid-1980s we see Kahane asking repeatedly if Weiss can find him synagogues where he could speak. The letters become more laconic, and more desperate, as they move into the late 1980s. I want to thank Avi Weiss and Dov Weiss for sharing this correspondence with me.

2. Kahane's final raucous appearance at Brandeis is available for viewing at https://www.youtube.com/watch?v=82-hydVZWBY.

3. See "25th Anniversary of Rabbi Kahane's Assassination," *Jewish Press*, October 31, 2015.

4. See Kifner, "Meir Kahane."

5. In a similar case, the funeral of Rabbi Moshe Levinger in May 2015 was attended by over ten thousand people, and speakers included leading religious-Zionist figures. Levinger was a militant religious Zionist who settled illegally in Hebron in 1968. He was arrested more than ten times on charges of violence and was convicted in the death of an Arab shopkeeper in Hebron.

6. See Hasia Diner, *New Promised Land.*

7. On the New York intellectuals, see Howe, "New York Intellectuals," 29–51; Lederhendler, *New York Jews.*

8. See Balint, *Running Commentary*, 79–130.

9. See Sinkoff, *From Left to Right.*

10. Podhoretz, *Making It*, 3.

11. See Trilling, *Beyond Culture.*

12. See Greenstein, *Zionism.* On the role of the left in the emergence of the settler movement, see Gorenberg, *Accidental Empire*, 99–128.

13. Sprinzak, "Kach and Meir Kahane."

14. On this see Inbari, *Messianic Religious Zionism* , esp. 81–106, 13–150.

15. Moriah, "Thirty-Six Little-Known Admirers."

16. Here I am in full agreement with Hayim Katsman, who argues in regard to Rabbi Yitzchak Ginsburgh that although his Chabad-inflected mystical radicalism and advocacy of violence are in many ways opposed to the Kook-influenced religious Zionism, "a close analysis reveals similarities between Ginsburg's practical mode of action and declarations made by prominent Religious Zionist figures." See Katsman, "Reactions," 294.

17. The reference here is to Irving (Yitz) Greenberg's adage that one should not say anything (about the Holocaust) that one would not say in front of burning children.

18. In a recent article on the 1966 suicide of Estelle Evans, Kahane's mistress, Sarah Weinman mentions in passing that Kahane's influence remains far more pervasive than is often thought. See Weinman, "Woman on the Bridge."

19. See Stern, "Anti-Semitism and Orthodoxy," https://www.tabletmag.com/jewish-arts-and-culture/281547/anti-semitism-orthodoxy-trump.

20. Interestingly, in a 1978 *Jewish Press* article reflecting on the tenth anniversary of the JDL's founding, Kahane advocated for a nonviolent movement that could meet the needs of the present situation. See Kahane, "A Decade Ends," 51.

BIBLIOGRAPHY

Works by Meir Kahane

Books

The Jewish Stake in Vietnam. New York: Crossroads, 1967. (Coauthored by Michael King [Meir Kahane] and Joseph Churba.)

Never Again! New York: Pyramid Books, 1971.

Time to Go Home. New York: Nash, 1972.

Our Challenge: The Chosen Land. Radnor, PA: Chilton, 1974.

The Story of the Jewish Defense League. New York: Nash, 1975.

Why Be Jewish? Intermarriage, Assimilation, and Alienation. Tucson: Desert Ulpan Books, 1977.

Lesikim Be'nekhem [As thorns in your eyes]. Jerusalem: Hamachon Lara'ayon Hayehudi, 1981.

Listen World, Listen Jew. 1978. Reprint, Jerusalem: Institute for the Publication of the Writings of Rabbi Meir Kahane, 2011.

They Must Go. New York: Grosset & Dunlap, 1981.

Forty Years. Jerusalem: Institute for the Jewish Idea, 1983.

Uncomfortable Questions for Comfortable Jews. Secaucus, NJ: Lyle Stuart, 1986.

On Jews and Judaism: Selected Articles 1961–1990. Jerusalem: Institute for the Publication of the Writings of Rabbi Meir Kahane, 1993.

Perush ha-Maccabee [Commentary on the book of Exodus]. Jerusalem: Institute for the Publication of the Writings of Rabbi Meir Kahane, 1994.

Perush ha-Maccabee [Commentary on the book of Samuel and the early prophets]. Jerusalem: Institute for the Publication of the Writings of Rabbi Meir Kahane, 1995.

Or Hara'ayon: The Jewish Idea. 2 vols. in English, 1 vol. in Hebrew. Jerusalem: Institute for the Publication of the Writings of Rabbi Meir Kahane, 1996.

Beyond Words: Selected Writings 1960–1990. 7 vols. Jerusalem: Institute for the Publication of the Writings of Rabbi Meir Kahane, 2011.

Kahane, Meir, and Binyamin Kahane. *Kahane on the Parsha*. New York: Brenn Books, 2015.

Commentary of Exodus [translation of *Perush ha-Maccabi*]. Jerusalem: Institute of the Publication of the Writings of Rabbi Meir Kahane, 2017.*Hillul ha-Shem*. Privately published, n.d.

On Redemption and Faith. Privately published, n.d.

Articles and Other Short Works

"Dr. Joseph Churba." *Jewish Press*, March 19, 1965. (Published under the pseudonym Hayim Yerushalmi.)

"Communism vs. Judaism." *Jewish Press*, June 23, 1967.

"Communism vs. Judaism." *Jewish Press*, August 4, 1967.

"Communism vs. Judaism." *Jewish Press*, November 3, 1967.

"Communism vs. Judaism: Israel and Vietnam—Are They Different?" *Jewish Press*, July 14, 1967.

"How the Extreme Left Reacted to the Middle East Crisis." *Jewish Press*, June 23, 1967.

"The Innocent Victims of the New Holocaust." *Jewish Press*, July 7, 1967.

"The Jewish Stake in Vietnam." *Jewish Press*, May 19, 1967.

"Commentary." *Jewish Press*, September 30, 1968.

"Commentary." *Jewish Week*, October 25, 1968. "School Decentralization." *Jewish Week*, May 31, 1968.

"A Spoonful of Sugar." *Jewish Press*, December 27, 1968.

"The Story behind the Abdication of School Responsibility." *Jewish Press*, June 28, 1968.

"Commentary." *Jewish Press*, February 7, 1969.

"Jewish Activists Face Campbell." *Jewish Press*, January 24, 1969.

"Jewish Group Pickets Racist in Heart of Militant Area." *Jewish Press*, June 27, 1969.

"Julius Lester's New Book." *Jewish Press*, June 27, 1969.

A Manifesto. New York: JDL, 1969. In Folder 482. Archive of Religious Zionism, Bar-Ilan University, Israel.

"The Radical Left's Battle against Israel." *Jewish Press*, April 4, 1969.

Speech in Boston. *Patriot Leader*, December 2, 1969. In JDL Collection, Box 1, Folder 3. American Jewish Historical Society Archives, New York.

"Spotlight on Extremism." *Jewish Press*, February 7, 1969.

"JDL Liberation Seder." *Jewish Defense League Newsletter*, April–August 1970. Transcript.

"Jewish Vigilantes." January 12, 1970. In JDL Collection, Box 1, Folder 4. American Jewish Historical Society Archives, New York.

"A Remarkable Event." April 9, 1971. In *Beyond Words: Selected Writings 1960–1990*, vol. 1.

"To Baruch on His Bar Mitzvah." *Jewish Press*, January 28, 1972. In *Beyond Words: Selected Writings 1960–1990*, vol. 1.

"Karl Marx: A Study in Self-Hatred." In *Rabbi Meir Kahane: In His Own Words*, vol. 2.

"The Fight for Jewishness in Allenwood Federal Prison." *Jewish Week*, January 2, 1976.

"A Decade Ends—and Begins." *Jewish Press*, June 23, 1978.

"She Is a Daughter of Israel. Perhaps Your Sister, Your Daughter or Granddaughter." Advertisement. *Maariv*, May 29, 1981.

"To the Young: A Challenge." In *Rabbi Meir Kahane: In His Own Words*, vol. 1.

Secondary Literature

Afterman, Adam, and Gedaliah Afterman. "Meir Kahane and Contemporary Jewish Theology of Revenge." *Soundings* 98, no. 2 (2015).

Aharoni, Dov. "Now, Greater than Life: Meir Kahane: He was on the brink of becoming marginal. But with his murder, the legend of the martyr begins." *Los Angeles Times*, November 7, 1990.

Alter, Robert. "Revolt and the Democratic Society." In *The New Left and the Jews*. Edited by Mordecai Chertoff. New York: Pitman, 1971.

———. "Revolutionism and the Jews: 2. Appropriating the Religious Tradition." *Commentary*, February 1971.

Anti-Defamation League. *The JDL: Expositor of Fear*. February 1971. Peter Novik collection, Box 47, JDL folder. YIVO Archives, New York.

———. *Research Report: Extremism in the Name of Religion: The Violent Legacy of Meir Kahane*. New York: Anti-Defamation League, 1994.

Applebaum, Karl. "Jewish, Irish, and Italian Power: If Black Power, Why Not?" *Jewish Press*, January 31, 1969.

Apply, Joyce. *Liberalism and Republicanism in the Historical Imagination*. Cambridge, MA: Harvard University Press, 1992.

Aran, Gideon. "Kookisms: The Roots of Gush Emunim, the Settlers." [In Hebrew.] In Aran, *Culture, Zionist Theology, and Messianism in Our Age*. Jerusalem: Carmel, 2013.

———. "M'Zionut Datit le'Day Zionit: Reshit Gush Emunim k'Tenuah Datit." PhD diss., Hebrew University, 1987.

Arendt, Hannah. "Reflections on Little Rock." *Dissent*, Winter 1959.

Aronowitz, Alfred G. "The Maccabees Ride Again." *Saturday Evening Post*, June 27–July 4, 1964.

Aviner, Shlomo. *Orot m'Ofel*. Beit 'El: Hava Books, 2009.

Baldwin, James. *The Fire Next Time*. New York: Dial, 1963.

———. "Harlem Ghetto: Winter 1948, the Vicious Circle of Frustration and Pride." *Commentary*, February 1948.

———. "Negroes Are Anti-Semitic Because They're Anti-White." *New York Times*, April 9, 1967.

———. *Notes of a Native Son*. New York: Beacon, 1963.Baldwin, James, and Ossie Davis. "Readers' Forum: Anti-Semitism and Black Power." *Freedomways*, January 1967.

Baldwin, James, and Shlomo Katz. "Of Angela Davis and the 'Jewish Housewife Headed from Dachau': An Exchange." *Midstream*, June/July 1971.Balint, Benjamin. *Running Commentary: The Contentious Magazine That Transformed the Jewish Left into the Neoconservative Right*. New York: Public Affairs, 2010.

Bauer, Yehuda. *Jews for Sale? Nazi-Jewish Negotiations, 1933–1945*. New Haven, CT: Yale University Press, 1994.

Baumel, Judith Tydor. *The "Bergson Boys" and the Origins of Contemporary Zionist Militancy*. Translated by Dena Ordan. Syracuse, NY: Syracuse University Press, 2005.

———. "Kahane in America: An Exercise in Right-Wing Urban Terror." *Studies in Conflict and Terrorism* 22, no. 4 (1999).Beckerman, Gal. *When They Come for Us We Will Be Gone: The Epic Struggle to Save Soviet Jewry*. New York: Mariner Books, 2011.

Bell, Daniel. *Marxian Socialism in the United States*. Ithaca, NY: Cornell University Press, 1996.

Bell, Derrick. "Integration—It's a No-Win Educational Policy for Blacks." In *Federal Pre-School and Early Childhood Programs from a Black Perspective*. Edited by E. K. Moore. Washington, DC: National Policy Conference on Education for Blacks, 1972.

Bemnrome, David. "Rabbi Meir Kahane Wrestles with Dore Schary on David Frost Show." *The Hebrew Watchman*, July 22, 1971.

Ben-Chorin, Michael. *Baruch ha-Gever: Sefer Zicaron la'Kodesh Dr. Barukh Goldshtain*. Jerusalem: Shalom 'al Yisra'el, 1995.

Ben-Gurion, David. *Ben-Gurion Looks at the Bible*. Hebrew and English ed. Translated by J. Kolatch. New York: Jonathan David, 2015.

Berhan, Thea. Poem. In Fred Ferretti, "New York's Black Anti-Semitism Scare." *Columbia Journalism Review* 8, no. 3 (Fall 1969).

Birnbaum, Avrohom. *A Blazing Light in the Darkness: R. Avrohom Kalmanowitz*. New York: Artscroll, 2019.

Bisk, Tsvi. "A Radical-Zionist Strategy for the 1970s." *Jewish Liberation Journal*, December 1969.

———. "Uncle Jake, Come Home." *Jewish Liberation Journal*, May 1969.

Bittker, Boris. *The Case for Black Reparations*. Boston: Beacon, 1973.

Blauner, Robert. "Internal Colonialism and Ghetto Revolt." *Social Problems*, no. 16 (Spring 1969).

———. *Racial Oppression in America*. New York: Harper & Row, 1972.

Blumfeld, Laura. "Time to Kill." *Washington Post*, March 20, 1994.

Bongartz, Roy, "Superjew." *Esquire*, August 1, 1970.

Boyarin, Daniel. *A Traveling Homeland: The Babylonia Talmud as Diaspora*. Philadelphia: University of Pennsylvania Press, 2015.

Braiterman, Kenneth. "The Jewish Defense League: What Safety in Karate?" *Midstream*, April 1970.

Brandriss, Yitzchok. "Kahanism Is Not Orthodoxy." *Jewish Week*, March 18, 1994.

Breines, Paul. *Tough Jews: Political Fantasies and the Moral Dilemma of American Jewry*. New York: Basic Books, 1990.

Breslauer, Daniel S. *Meir Kahane: Ideologue, Hero, Thinker*. Lewiston, NY: Edwin Mellen, 1986.

Brick, Howard. *Daniel Bell and the Decline of Intellectual Radicalism*. Madison: University of Wisconsin Press, 1986.

Brickner, Balfour. "The Original Freedom Seder: Response to *Commentary*'s Attack." Letter to the Editor. *Commentary*, June 1971. https://theshalomcenter.org/node/1540.

Brooks, Thomas. "Tragedy at Ocean Hill." *Dissent*, February 1969.

Buber, Martin. *Paths in Utopia*. Reprint, Syracuse, NY: Syracuse University Press, 1996.

Burack, Emily. "'We Are Speaking of Jewish Survival': The Emergence of the Jewish Defense League." Honors thesis, Dartmouth College, 2017.

Cantor Zuckoff, Aviva. "The Oppression of Amerika's Jews." In *Jewish Radicalism*, edited by Jack Nusan Porter and Peter Dreier. New York: Grove, 1973. Reprint, in *The Jewish 1960s: An American Sourcebook*. Edited by Michael E. Staub. Hanover, NY: Brandeis University Press, 2004.

Čapková, Kateřina. "Bar Kokhba Association." *YIVO Encyclopedia of Eastern Europe*. http://www.yivoencyclopedia.org/article.aspx/Bar_Kochba_Association.

Carmichael, Stokeley. "What We Want." In *The Modern African American Political Thought Reader*. Edited by Angela Jones. Oxford: Routledge, 2013.

Carmichael, Stokeley, and Ekueme Michael Thelwell. *Ready for Revolution: The Life and Struggles of Stokeley Carmichael (Kwame Ture)*. New York: Scribner's, 2003.

Carter, J. Cameron. *Race: A Theological Account*. New York: Oxford University Press, 2008.

Charlap, R. Yaakov Moshe. *Mei Marom on Psalms and Proverbs*. Jerusalem: Beit Zevul, 1999.

Chetrit, Sami Shalom. *Intra-Jewish Conflict in Israel: White Jews, Black Jews*. New York: Routledge, 2013.

Churba, Joseph, and Michael King [Meir Kahane]. Advertisement for the Fourth of July Movement. *Herald Tribune*, June 29, 1965.

Clark, Kenneth. "Candor about Negro-Jewish Relations." *Commentary*, February 1946.

Claussen, Geoffrey. *Sharing the Burden: R. Simhah Zissel Ziv and the Path of Musar*. Albany, NY: SUNY Press, 2015.

Clawar, Stanley. "Neo-Vigilantism in America: An Analysis of the Jewish Defense League." PhD diss., Bryn Mawr College, 1976.

Cleaver, Eldridge. "Old Toms Never Die Unless They're Blown Away." Cited in Eddie S. Glaude Jr., *Begin Again: James Baldwin's America and Its Urgent Lessons for Our Own*. New York: Crown, 2020.

Coates, Ta-Nehisi. *We Were Eight Years in Power: An American Tragedy*. New York: One World, 2018.

Cobb, Charles E. *This Nonviolent Stuff'll Get You Killed: How Guns Made the Civil Rights Movement Possible*. Chapel Hill, NC: Duke University Press, 2015.

Cohen, Gerson D. "The Blessing of Assimilation in Jewish History." Reprinted in Cohen, *Jewish History and Jewish Destiny*. New York: JTS, 1997.

———. "Esau as Symbol in Early Medieval Thought." In *Jewish Medieval Renaissance Studies*. Edited by Alexander Altmann. Cambridge, MA: Harvard University Press, 1967.Cohen, Henry. *Justice, Justice: A Jewish View of the Black Revolution*. New York: Union of American Hebrew Congregations, 1968.

Cohen, Martin. "Introducing *Humash Kol Ha-Tor* and *M'gillot Ha-Tor*." *Zeramim*, August 6, 2019.

Connolly, Nate. "The Strange Career of American Liberalism." In *Shaped by the State: Toward a New Political History of the Twentieth Century*. Edited by Brent Cebul, Mason B. Williams, and Lily Geismer. Chicago: University of Chicago Press, 2019.

Cooper, Julie. "In Pursuit of Political Imagination: Reflections on Diasporic Jewish History." *Theoretical Inquiries* 21, no. 5 (2020).

Cowie, Jefferson. *The Great Exception: The New Deal and the Limits of American Politics*. Princeton, NJ: Princeton University Press, 2016.

Cromer, Gerald. "The Creation of Others: A Case Study of Meir Kahane and His Opponents." In *The Other in Jewish Thought and History: Constructions of Jewish Culture and Identity*. Edited by Laurence Silberstein and Robert Cohn. New York: NYU Press, 1994.

———. *Narratives of Violence*. New York: Routledge, 2017.

———. *A War of Words: Political Violence and Public Debate in Israel*. New York: Routledge, 2004; London: Frank Cass, 2004.

Cruse, Harold. *The Crisis of the Negro Intellectual*. New York: New York Review of Books, 2005.

Dan, Joseph. *Kedusha*. [In Hebrew.] Jerusalem: Magnes, 1998.

Danzig, David. "In Defense of Black Power." *Commentary*, September 1966.

Darcy, Allison. "Are Your Views on Jewish Intermarriage Racist?" *Forward*, September 11, 2017.

Dawidowicz, Lucy. "Civil Rights and Intergroup Tensions." *American Jewish Yearbook*, no. 66 (1965).

Denton, Nancy. *American Apartheid: Segregation and the Making of the Underclass*. Cambridge, MA: Harvard University Press, 1993.

Diamond, Eliezer. *Holy Men and Hunger Artists: Fasting and Asceticism in Rabbinic Culture*. New York: Oxford University Press, 2003.

Diamond, James S. *Homeland or Holy Land? The "Canaanite" Critique of Israel.* Bloomington: Indiana University Press, 1986.

Diner, Hasia. *In an Almost Promised Land: American Jews and Blacks 1915-193.* Reprint, Baltimore: Johns Hopkins University Press, 1995.

———. *The Jews of the United States 1654–2000.* Berkeley: University of California Press, 2004.

———. *A New Promised Land: A History of Jews in America.* New York: Oxford University Press, 2002.

Dolgin, Janet. *Jewish Identity and the JDL.* Princeton, NJ: Princeton University Press, 1977.

Dollinger, Marc. *Black Power, Jewish Politics: Reinventing the Alliance in the 1960s.* Hanover, NH: Brandeis University Press, 2018.

———. *"Is It Good for the Jews?" Black Power and the 1960s.* Unpublished manuscript, 2018.

———. *Quest for Inclusion: Jews and Liberalism in Modern America.* Princeton, NJ: Princeton University Press, 2000.

Dorman, Jacob. "Dreams Defended and Deferred: The Brooklyn Schools Crisis of 1968 and Black Power's Influence on Rabbi Meir Kahane." *American Jewish History* 100, no. 3 (July 2016).

Douglas, Mary. *Leviticus as Literature.* New York: Oxford University Press, 2001.

Drake, St. Clair, and Horace Clayton. *Black Metropolis: A Study of Negro Life in a Northern City.* Chicago: University of Chicago Press, 1993.

Duker, Abraham. "On Negro-Jewish Relations: A Contribution to a Discussion." *Jewish Social Studies* 27, no. 1 (January 1965).

Eichler-Levine, Jodi. "American Judaism and Race." In *Religion and Race in American History.* Edited by Kathryn Gin Lum and Paul Harvey. New York: Oxford University Press, 2018.

Eisen, Arnold. "Off Center: The Concept of the Land of Israel in Modern Jewish Thought." In *The Land of Israel: Jewish Perspectives.* Edited by Lawrence Hoffman. South Bend, IN: Notre Dame University Press, 1986.

Eisen, Robert. *The Peace and Violence in Judaism: From the Bible to Modern Zionism.* New York: Oxford University Press, 2011.

Elbaum, Max. *Revolution in the Air: Sixties Radicals Turn to Lenin, Mao, and Che.* London: Verso, 2002.

Elizur-Hershkowitz, Yosef, and Yitzhak Shapira. *Torat ha-Melekh: Dinei Nefashot bein Yisrael le-Akum.* Jerusalem: Ha-Machon ha-Torani sh-al-yad Yeshivat 'Od Yosef Chai, 2009.

Elkins, Dov Peretz. "Negro-Jewish Relations after the Kerner Report." *Reconstructionist* 34, no. 7 (May 1968).

Ellis, Eddie. "Semitism in the Black Ghetto." *Liberator*, February 1966; April 1966.

Englander, Yakir. "The 'Jewish Knight' of Slobodka: Honor, Culture, and the Image of the Body in an Ultra-Orthodox Jewish Context." *Religion* 46, no. 2 (2016).

Epstein, Helen. *Children of the Holocaust: Conversations with Sons and Daughters of Survivors.* New York: Putnam Books, 1979.

Epstein, Jason. "The Real McCoy." *New York Review of Books*, March 13, 1969.

Etkes, Immanuel. *R. Yisrael Salanter and the Beginning of the Musar Movement.* [In Hebrew.] Jerusalem: Magnes, 1984.

Eytan, Edwin. "Rabbi Kahane Came, Caused a Storm—and Was Ousted." [In Hebrew.] *Yediot Aharonot*, February 25, 1971.

Fairlie, Henry. "The Evolution of a Term." *The New Yorker*, October 18, 1968.

Fein, Leonard. "The New Jewish Politics." *Midstream*, October 1972.

Feingold, Henry. *American Jewish Political Culture and the Liberal Persuasion*. Syracuse, NY: Syracuse University Press, 2014.

Feldman, Keith. *A Shadow over Palestine: The Imperial Life of Race in America*. Minneapolis: University of Minnesota Press, 2015.

Ferguson, Leo. "Ocean Hill-Brownsville and the Myth of Black 'Antisemitism.'" *Jewish Currents*, February 12, 2020.

Firestone, Reuven. *Holy War in Judaism: The Rise and Fall of a Controversial Idea*. New York: Oxford University Press, 2012.

Fisch, Harold. *The Zionist Revolution: A New Perspective*. Worthing, UK: Littlehampton Books, 1978.

Fischbach, Michael. *Black Power and Palestine*. Stanford, CA: Stanford University Press, 2018.

Fischer, Shlomo. "Neo-Hasidut and Post-Kookism." In *Contemporary Uses and Forms of Hasidut*. Edited by Shlomo Zuckier. Jerusalem: Urim, forthcoming.

———. "Self-Expression and Democracy in Radical Religious Zionist Ideology." PhD diss., Hebrew University, 2007.

———. "The State Crisis and the Potential for Uncontrollable Violence in Israel-Palestine." In *Ploughshares into Swords: Reflections on Religion and Violence*. Edited by Robert W. Jensen and Eugene Korn. New Haven, CT: Yale University Press, 2014.

"Forman Challenged by JDL." *Jewish Press*, May 22, 1969.

Forman, Seth. *Blacks in the Jewish Mind: A Crisis of Liberalism*. New York: NYU Press, 1998.

Friedman, Robert. *The False Prophet*. London: Faber & Faber, 1990.

———. "Joseph Churba, Intelligence Aid Who Criticized General, Is Dead." *New York Times*, April 28, 1996.

Frydl, Kathleen J. *The G.I. Bill*. New York: Cambridge University Press, 2009.

Fuller, Robert. *Spiritual but Not Religious: Understanding Unchurched America*. New York: Oxford University Press, 2001.

Gager, John. *Who Made Early Christianity? The Jewish Lives of the Apostle Paul*. New York: Columbia University Press, 2015.

Gans, Chaim. *A Just Zionism: On the Morality of the Jewish State*. New York: Oxford University Press, 2011.

Gaston, Lloyd. *Paul and the Torah*. Eugene, OR: Wipf & Stock, 2006.

Gellman, Jerome. "Jewish Chosenness and Religious Diversity: A Contemporary Approach." In *Religious Perspectives on Religious Diversity*. Edited by Robert McKim. Leiden: Brill, 2016.

Gerson, Simon. "Kahane Tried to Sell Jewry on Vietnam." *Daily World*, January 21, 1971.

Ghanem, As'ad, and Ibrahim Khatib. "The Nationalisation of the Israeli Ethnocratic Regime and the Palestinian Minority's Shrinking Citizenship." *Citizenship Studies* 1, no. 14 (2017).

Ginger, Henry. "Kahane Barred by Party, Is Ousted from Belgium." *New York Times*, February 25, 1971.

Gitlin, Todd. *The Sixties: Years of Hope, Days of Rage*. Rev. ed. New York: Bantam Books, 1989.

Glaude Jr., Eddie S. *Begin Again: James Baldwin's America and Its Urgent Lessons for Our Own*. New York: Crown, 2020.

Glazer, Nathan. "The Exposed American Jew." *Commentary*, June 1975.

———. "Jewish Interests and the New Left." In *The New Left and the Jews*. Edited by Mordecai Chertoff. New York: Pitman, 1971.

———. "Jews, Israel, and the New Left." *Midstream*, January 1971.

Goldberg, Arthur. "Goldberg Backs Lindsay in Race." *New York Times*, October 10, 1969. Goldberg, Chad Alan. *Modernity and the Jews in Western Social Thought*. Chicago: University of Chicago Press, 2017.

Goldman, Emma. *Living My Life*. New York: Penguin Books, 2007.

Goldman, Peter. *The Death and Life of Malcolm X*. Champaign-Urbana: University of Illinois Press, 1973.

Goldman, Shalom. *Zeal for Zion: Christians, Jews, and the Idea of the Promised Land*. Chapel Hill: University of North Carolina Press, 2014.

Goldstein, Eric. *The Price of Whiteness: Jews, Race, and American Identity*. Princeton, NJ: Princeton University Press, 2006.

Goodman, Martin. *A History of Judaism*. Princeton, NJ: Princeton University Press, 2018.

Goodman, Walter. "Rabbi Kahane Says: 'I'd Love to See the J.D.L. Fold Up. But . . .'" *New York Times Magazine*, November 21, 1971.

Gordon, David E., and John Hope Franklin. *Black Moses: The Story of Marcus Garvey*. Madison: University of Wisconsin Press, 1960.

Gorenberg, Gershom. *Accidental Empire: Israel and the Birth of the Settlements, 1967–1977*. New York: New York Times Books, 2007.

Goshen-Gottstein, Alon. *Same God, Other God*. Cambridge: Palgrave, 2016.

Graubard, Seymour. ADL Resolution, 1971. In JDL Collection, Box 47, Folder 47.3. YIVO Archives, New York.

Greenberg, Clement. "Self-Hatred and Jewish Chauvinism: Some Reflections on 'Positive Jewishness.'" *Commentary*, November 1950.

Greenstein, Ran. *Zionism and Its Discontents: A Century of Radical Dissent in Israel/Palestine*. London: Pluto, 2014.

Griffith, Mark Winston, and Max Freedman, hosts. "Third Strike." *School Colors* (podcast). https://www.schoolcolorspodcast.com/episodes/episode-3-third-strike.

Gurock, Jeffrey S. *The Jews of Harlem: The Rise, Decline, and Revival of a Jewish Community*. New York: NYU Press, 2016.

Hackett, John. "The Phenomenon of the Anti-Black Jews and the Black Anglo-Saxon." *Forum*, November/December 1968.

Halbertal, Moshe. *The Beginning of Politics: Power in the Book of Samuel*. Princeton, NJ: Princeton University Press, 2019.

Halevi, Yossi Klein. *Memoirs of a Jewish Extremist: The Story of a Transformation*. Reprint, New York: Harper Perennial, 2014.

Halloran, Richard. "Blast Damages Soviet Building in Washington." *New York Times*, January 9, 1971.

Halpern, Ben. *Blacks and Jews: The Classic American Minorities*. New York: Herder & Herder, 1971.

Harding, Vincent. *Martin Luther King: The Inconvenient Hero*. New York: Orbis Books, 1996.

Harel, Assaf. "Beyond Gush Emunim: On Contemporary Forms of Messianism among Religiously Motivated Settlers in the West Bank." In *Normalizing Occupation: The Politics of*

Everyday Life in the West Bank Settlements. Edited by Marco Allegra, Ariel Handel, and Erez Maggor. Bloomington: Indiana University Press, 2019.

Harkov, Lahav. "'Black Panther' Is a Great Zionist Movie." Tablet, February 26, 2018.

Harris, Glen Anthony. *The Ocean Hill-Brownsville Conflict: Intellectual Struggles between Blacks and Jews at Mid-Century*. Lanham, MD: Lexington Books, 2012.

Hartman, David. *Israelis and the Jewish Tradition*. New Haven, CT: Yale University Press, 2000.

Heller, Daniel Kupfert. *Jabotinsky's Children: Polish Jews and the Rise of Right-Wing Zionism*. Princeton, NJ: Princeton University Press, 2017.

Hentoff, Nat, ed. *Black Anti-Semitism and Jewish Racism*. New York: Schocken Books, 1970.

Herschthal, Eric. "Israel's Black Panthers Remembered." *Jewish Week*, June 29, 2010.

Hertzberg, Arthur, ed. *The Zionist Idea: A Historical Analysis and Reader*. Philadelphia: Jewish Publication Society, 1997.

Heschel, Abraham Joshua. *Israel: An Echo in Eternity*. New York: Farrar, Straus & Giroux, 1969.

Heschel, Susannah. *Abraham Geiger and the Jewish Jesus*. Chicago: University of Chicago Press, 1998.

Himmelfarb, Martha. *Jewish Messiahs in a Christian Empire: A History of the Book of Zerubbabel*. Cambridge, MA: Harvard University Press, 2017.

Himmelfarb, Milton. "'Never Again!'" In *Jews and Gentiles*. Edited by Gertrude Himmelfarb. New York: Encounter Books, 2006.

Howe, Irving. "The New York Intellectuals: Chronicle and Critique." *Commentary*, October 1968.

———. *World of Our Fathers*. Reprint, New York: Galahad Books, 2001.

Idel, Moshe. "The Land of Israel in Medieval Kabbalah." In *The Land of Israel: Jewish Perspectives*. Edited by Lawrence Hoffman. South Bend, IN: Notre Dame University Press, 1986.

Imhoff, Sarah. *Masculinity and the Making of American Judaism*. Bloomington: Indiana University Press, 2017.

Inbari, Motti. *Messianic Religious Zionism Confronts Israeli Territorial Compromises*. New York: Cambridge University Press, 2012.

———. "Post-Zionism in the Religious Zionist Camp: The 'Jewish Leadership Movement.'" Unpublished manuscript.

Isaac, Rael Jean, and Erich Isaac. "The Rabbis of Breira." *Midstream*, April 1977.

Isaacs, Charles. *Inside Ocean Hill-Brownsville: A Teacher's Education, 1968–1969*. New York: Excelsior, 2014.

Ish-Shalom, Benjamin. *Rav Avraham Itzhak HaCohen Kook: Between Rationalism and Mysticism*. Albany, NY: SUNY Press, 1993.

Jabotinsky, Ze'ev. "Al Kir ha-Barzel" [The iron wall]. In Jabotinsky, *Ba-Derekh. la-Medinah*. Jerusalem: Eri Jabotinsky, 1959.

———. *Collected Works*. [In Hebrew.] Tel Aviv: Hotsa'at Sefarim, 1957–1958.

———. "The Iron Wall: We and the Arabs." [In Hebrew.] In *Eretz Yisrael*, vol. 1, *Writings*. Edited by Aryeh Naor. Tel Aviv: Menachem Begin Center, 2005.

Jewish Defense League. Letter to the rabbinic community in Philadelphia about "Arab Jewry," signed by Edward Ramov. April 20, 1972. In JDL Collection, Box 1, Folder 7. American Jewish Historical Society Archives, New York.

Jewish Defense League Newsletter 1, no. 7 (April–August 1970). In JDL Collection, Box 1, Folder 13. American Jewish Historical Society Archives, New York.

Jewish Telegraphic Agency. "Defense League Ad Created Furor." October 14, 1969. In JDL Collection, Box 1, Folder 3. American Jewish Historical Society Archives, New York.

Jews for Urban Justice. "Black Manifestos and Jewish Response." Jews for Urban Justice Collection. American Jewish Historical Society Archives, New York.

———. "The Oppression and Liberation of the Jewish People in America." *Response*, Fall 1971.

Kahane, Libby. *Rabbi Meir Kahane: His Life and Thought*. Vol. 1. *1932–1975*. Jerusalem: Institute for the Publication of the Writings of Meir Kahane, 2008.

Kahane, Libby. *Rabbi Meir Kahane: His Life and Thought*. Vol. 2. *1976–1985*. Jerusalem: Institute for the Publication of the Writings of Meir Kahane, 2008.

Kaplan, Eran. *The Jewish Radical Right: Revisionist Zionism and Its Ideological Legacy*. Madison: University of Wisconsin Press, 2005.

Kaplan, Morris. "Kahane and Colombo Join Forces to Fight US Harassment." *New York Times*, May 14, 1971.

Katsman, Hayim. "Reactions toward Jewish Radicalism: Rabbi Yitzchak Ginsburg and Religious Zionism." In *Jewish Radicals: Historical Perspectives on a Phenomenon of Global Modernity*. Edited by Frank Jacob and Sebastian Kunze. Oldenbourg, Germany: De Gruyter, 2019.

Katz, Dov. *Tenu'at ha-Musar*. Vol. 6. *Pulmos Musar*. Bnei Brak, Israel: Sefarit 2006 (vol. 6: Jerusalem, 2011).

Kaufman, Jonathan. *Broken Alliance: The Turbulent Times between Blacks and Jews in America*. New York: Scribner's, 1988.

Kaufman, Michael. "The Complex Life of Meir Kahane." *New York Times*, January 24, 1971.

———. "Jewish Activists See Ranks Growing." *New York Times*, May 25, 1970.

———. "Remembering Kahane, and the Woman on the Bridge." The Week in Review, *New York Times*, March 6, 1994.

Kaye, Alexander. *The Invention of Jewish Theocracy: The Struggle for Legal Authority in Modern Israel*. New York: Oxford University Press, 2020.

Kaye/Kantrowitz, Melanie. "Stayed on Freedom: Jews in the Civil Rights Movement and After." In *The Narrow Bridge: Jewish Views on Multiculturalism*. Edited by Marla Brettschneider. New Brunswick, NJ: Rutgers University Press, 2007.

———. "To Be a Jewish Radical in the Late Twentieth Century." In Kaye/Kantrowitz, *The Issue Is Power: Essays on Women, Jews, Violence and Resistance*. San Francisco: Aunt Lute, 1992.

Kellner, Menachem. *Maimonides' Confrontation with Mysticism*. Portland, OR: Littman Library of Jewish Civilization, 2011.

Kelner, Shaul. "The Bureaucratization of Ritual Innovation." *Jewish Cultural Studies*, no. 3 (2011).

———. "Ritualized Protest and Redemptive Politics: Cultural Consequences of the American Mobilization to Free Soviet Jewry." *Jewish Social Studies*, New Series, 14, no. 3 (2008).

Kempton, Murray. "What a Problem!" *New York Review of Books*, June 29, 1972.

Kifner, John. "Meir Kahane, 58, Israeli Militant and Founder of the Jewish Defense League." *New York Times*, November 6, 1990.

Kimche, Ruth. "Bar Kokhba Society (Cairo)." *Encyclopedia of Jews in the Islamic World*. https://referenceworks.brillonline.com/entries/encyclopedia-of-jews-in-the-islamic-world/bar-kokhba-society-cairo-SIM_0003150.

Kimmel, Michael. *Manhood in America: A Cultural History*. 4th ed. New York: Oxford University Press, 2017.

King Jr., Martin Luther. "Beyond Vietnam: A Time to Break Silence." Speech delivered at Riverside Church, New York, April 4, 1967. In King, *Time to Break the Silence: The Essential Works of Martin Luther King, Jr., for Students*. Boston: Beacon, 2013.

Koch, Patrick. *Human Self-Perfection: A Re-Assessment of Kabbalistic Musar-Literature of Sixteenth-Century Safed*. Los Angeles: Cherub, 2013.

Kook, Abraham Isaac Hakohen. "The Eulogy in Jerusalem." [In Hebrew.] In Kook, *Ma'amrei ha-Reiyah*. Jerusalem: Mossad HaRav Kook, 1984.

Kook, Abraham Isaac Hakohen, and Bezalel Naor. "The Lamentation in Jerusalem." In Kook and Naor, *When God Becomes History: Historical Essays of Rav Abraham Isaac Hakohen Kook*. New York: Kodesh, 2016.

Kook, Zvi Yehuda. *Le-Hilkhot Zibbur*. Jerusalem: Mossad HaRav Kook 1987.

———. *Orot ha-Teshuva*. Jerusalem: Mossad HaRav Kook, 1966.

———. *Sihot ha-Rav Zvi Yehuda Kook*. Edited by Shlomo Aviner. Jerusalem: Hava Books, 1993.

Korn, Bertram W. *American Jewry and the Civil War*. Philadelphia: JPS, 1951.

Kotler, Yair. *Heil Kahane*. New York: Adama Books, 1986.

Kramer, Hilton. "Politicizing the Metropolitan Museum." *New York Times*, January 26, 1969.

Kranson, Rachel. *Ambivalent Embrace: Jewish Upward Mobility in Postwar America*. Chapel Hill: University of North Carolina Press, 2017.

Krebs, Albin. "Bernstein Incurs JDL's Wrath." *New York Times*, May 27, 1971.

Kristol, Irving. "A Few Kind Words for Uncle Tom." *Harper's*, February 1965.

———. "Why Jews Turn Conservative." *Wall Street Journal*, September 14, 1972.

Landsman, Alter. *Brownsville: The Birth, Development and Passing of a Jewish Community in New York*. New York: Bloch, 1969.

Lebel, Udi. *Politics of Memory: The Israeli Underground's Struggle for Inclusion in the National Pantheon and Military Commemoralization*. London: Routledge, 2013.

Ledbetter, Les. "Fire Bomb Kills Woman, Hurts 13 in Hurok Office." *New York Times*, January 27, 1972.

Lederhendler, Eli. *New York Jews and the Decline of Urban Ethnicity, 1950–1970*. Syracuse, NY: Syracuse University Press, 2001.

Leibowitz, Yeshayahu. *Judaism, Human Values, and the Jewish State*. Cambridge, MA: Harvard University Press, 1995.

Lester, Julius. *Lovesong: Becoming a Jew*. New York: Arcade, 1988.

Levin, Geoffrey. "Another Nation: Israel, American Jews, and Palestinian Rights, 1948-1977." PhD diss., New York University, 2019.

Liebes, Yehuda. "The Status of Sabbateanism in the Religion of Israel." In Liebes, *Le'Zvi u' le'Gaon: From Sabbatai Zevi to the Gaon of Vilna*. Tel Aviv: Idra, 2017.

Liebman, Charles. *The Ambivalent American Jew: Politics, Religion and Family in American Jewish Life*. Philadelphia: JPS, 1973.

Lifshitz, Joseph Isaac. "Holiness and *Eretz Yisrael*." In *Holiness in Jewish Thought*. Edited by Alan Mittleman. New York: Oxford University Press, 2018.

Littman, Deborah. "Jewish Militancy in Perspective." *Otherstand*, February 24, 1971. Reprinted in Jack Nusan Porter and Peter Dreier, eds., *Jewish Radicalism: A Selected Anthology*. New York: Grove, 1973.

Locke, Alain, ed. *New Negro: Voices of the Harlem Renaissance*. Reprint, New York: Touchstone, 1999.

Loeffler, James. *Rooted Cosmopolitanism: Jewish and Human Rights in the Twentieth Century*. New Haven, CT: Yale University Press, 2018.

Lustick, Ian. *Paradigm Lost: From Two-State Solution to One-State Reality*. Philadelphia: University of Pennsylvania Press, 2019.

Magid, Shaul. *American Post-Judaism*. Bloomington: Indiana University Press, 2015.

———. "Another Side of the Lubavitcher Rebbe." Tablet, July 3, 2019.

———. "Anti-Semitism as Colonialism: Meir Kahane's 'Ethics of Violence.'" *Journal of Jewish Ethics* 1, no. 2 (Summer 2015).

———. "Bibi's Bad History: Benjamin Netanyahu's UN Speech." *Religion Dispatches*, October 7, 2013.

———. "'I'm Crazy but I'm Normal': The Banality of Baruch Marzel." *Tikkun*, August 16, 2017. http://www.tikkun.org/nextgen/im-crazy-but-im-normal-the-banality-of-baruch-marzel.

———. "Is There an American Jewish Fundamentalism? Part II. Satmar." In *Fundamentalism: Perspectives on a Contested History*. Edited by Simon A. Wood and David Harrington Watt. Charleston: University of South Carolina Press, 2014.

———. "Kahane Won." Tablet, March 15, 2019.

———. "Modernity as Heresy: The Introvertive Piety of Faith in R. Areleh Roth's *Shomer Emunim*." *Jewish Studies Quarterly* 3, no. 4 (1997).

———. "Politics and Precedent: David Novak, Meir Kahane, and Yoel Teitelbaum (the Satmar Rebbe) on *Zionism and Judaism*." In *Covenantal Thinking: Essays in Honor of David Novak*. Edited by Yaniv Feller and Paul Nahme. Toronto: University of Toronto Press, forthcoming.

———. "The Politics of (un) Conversion: The 'Mixed Multitude' (*erev rav*) as Conversos in Rabbi Hayyim Vital's *Etz Ha-Da'at Tov*." *Jewish Quarterly* 95, no. 4 (Fall 2005).

———. "The Road from Religious Law (*halakha*) to the Secular: Constructing the Autonomous Self in the Musar Tradition and Its Discontents." In *Jewish Spirituality and Social Transformation*. Edited by Philip Wexler. Chestnut Ridge, NY: Herder & Herder, 2019.

———. "Zionism, Pan-Africanism, and White Nationalism." Tablet, December 12, 2018.Magid, Shaul, and Yehuda Magid. "Ethnic Democracy and Ethnocracy in Israel Today." Public Seminar, New School for Social Research, Winter 2019.

Maimonides. *Mishneh Torah*. Standard edition.

———. *Sefer ha-Mitzvot*. Standard edition.

Malcolm X. "Appeal to African Heads of State." Quoted in *Malcolm X Speaks*, edited by George Breitman. New York: Grove, 1990.

Mandel, David. "A Radical Zionist's Critique of the Jewish Defense League." In Mandel, *Jewish Radicalism*. New York: Grove, 1973.

Margalit, Avishai, and Moshe Halbertal. *Idolatry*. Cambridge, MA: Harvard University Press, 1998.

Matelpunkt, Shaul. *Israel in the American Mind: The Cultural Politics of U.S.-Israel Relations*. New York: Cambridge University Press, 2018.

Medoff, Rafael. *Militant Zionism in America: The Rise and Impact of the Jabotinsky Movement in the United States 1928–1946*. Tuscaloosa: University of Alabama Press, 2006.

Mendes, Philip. *Jews and the Left: The Rise and Fall of a Political Alliance*. London: Palgrave, 2014.

Mendes-Flohr, Paul. *Martin Buber: A Life of Faith and Dissent*. New Haven, CT: Yale University Press, 2019.

Mendes-Flohr, Paul, and Anya Mali. *Gustav Landauer: Anarchist and Jew*. Berlin: de Gruyter, 2015.

Mergui, Raphael, and Philippe Simonnot. "G-d's Law: An Interview with Meir Kahane." In Kahane, *Beyond Words: Selected Writings 1960–1990*. 7 vols. Jerusalem: Institute for the Publication of the Writings of Rabbi Meir Kahane, 2011, vol. 5, 389–90. https://rabbikahane.wordpress.com/2010/08/25/rabbi-kahane-interview-with-raphael-mergui-and-philippe-simonnot.

———. *Israel's Ayatollahs: Meir Kahane and the Far Right in Israel*. London: Saqi Books, 1987.

Michels, Tony, ed. *Jewish Radicals: A Documentary History*. New York: NYU Press, 2012.

Miller, Chaim. *Turning Judaism Outward: A Biography of the Rebbe, Menachem Mendel Schneerson*. Brooklyn: KoL Menachem, 2014.

Minor, Ethel. *Third World Round-Up: The Palestine Problem: Test Your Knowledge*. Atlanta: Student Nonviolent Coordinating Committee, 1967.

Mirsky, Yehuda. *Rav Kook: Mystic in a Time of Revolution*. New Haven, CT: Yale University Press, 2014.

Mittleman, Alan. *Does Judaism Condone Violence?* Princeton, NJ: Princeton University Press, 2018.

Moore, Deborah Dash. *Jewish New York*. New York: NYU Press, 2017.

Moriah, Shlomo. "Thirty-Six Little-Known Admirers of Rabbi Meir Kahane," *Jewish Press*, November 18, 2016.

Munayyer, Yousef. "Sorry, Black Panther Is Not About Zionism." *Forward*, February 28, 2018.

Murray, Albert. "Decentralization: The Atomization of the New York Public School System." *Jewish Press*, November 22, 1968.

Myers, David. "'Commanded War': Three Chapters in the 'Military' History of Satmar Hasidim." *JAAR*, March 2013.

Nash, Edward L. Telegram to Meir Kahane, June 16, 1971. In Folder ARC 4-1748. JNUL (Jewish National and University) Archives, Jerusalem.

Nelson, Stanley, dir. *Black Panthers: Vanguard of the Revolution*. 2016.

Neuberger, Benjamin. "Black Zionism: The Return to Africa in Theory and Practice." *Transnationalism*, no. 19 (2009).

Neusner, Jacob. *The Idea of Purity in Ancient Israel*. Leiden: Brill, 1973.

Newfield, Jack. *A Prophetic Minority*. New York: New American Library, 1966.

Newton, Huey P. "In Defense of Self-Defense." *Black Panther International News Service*, June 1967.

Novak, Bill. "The Failure of Jewish Radicalism." In *Jewish Radicalism: A Selected Anthology*. Edited by Jack Nusan Porter and Peter Dreier. New York: Grove, 1973. (Originally published in *Genesis*, no. 2 [April 1971].)

Novak, David. *Zionism and Judaism: A New Theory*. New York: Cambridge University Press, 2016.

Novick, Peter. *The Holocaust in American Life*. New York: Mariner Books, 2000.

O'Dell, Jack. "A Special Variety of Colonialism." *Freedomways* 7, no. 1 (1967).

Okon, May. "'Never Again!': Slogan of the Jewish Defense League Is at Heart of Its Militant Activities." *New York Sunday News*, March 7, 1971.

Pedahzur, Ami. *The Israeli Response to Jewish Extremism and Violence: Defending Democracy*. Manchester: University of Manchester Press, 2002.

Pedahzur, Ami, and Arie Perliger. *Jewish Terrorism and Israel*. New York: Columbia University Press, 2011.

Penslar, Derek. "Normalization and Its Discontents: Israel as a Diaspora Jewish Community." In *Critical Issues in Israeli Society*. Edited by Alan Dowty. Westport, CT: Praeger, 2004.

Plaut, Steven. "My Evolution as a Jew." *Philadelphia Jewish Exponent*, January 15, 1971.

Podair, Jerald. *The Strike That Changed New York*. New Haven, CT: Yale University Press, 2002.

Podhoretz, Norman. *Making It*. New York: Random House, 1967.

———. "My Negro Problem—and Ours." *Commentary*, February 1963.

Pollack, Robert. *The Faith of Biology and the Biology of Faith*. New York: Columbia University Press, 2000.

Porter, Jack Nusan, and Peter Dreier. "The Roots of Jewish Radicalism." In *Jewish Radicalism: A Selected Anthology*. Edited by Jack Nusan Porter and Peter Dreier. New York: Grove, 1973.

Prell, Riv-Ellen. "Jewish Summer Camping and Civil Rights: How Summer Camps Launched a Transformation in American Jewish Culture." David W. Belin Lecture in American Jewish Affairs at the University of Michigan, Ann Arbor, vol. 13, 2006.

———. *Prayer and Community: The Havurah in American Judaism*. Detroit: Wayne State University Press, 1989.

Pride, Don. "We'll Riot If Necessary." *Manhattan Tribune*, March 15, 1969.

Primus, Charles. "The Borders of Judaism: The Land of Israel in Early Rabbinic Judaism." In *The Land of Israel: Jewish Perspectives*. Edited by Lawrence A. Hoffman. South Bend, IN: Notre Dame University Press, 1986.

Raab, Earl. "The Black Revolution and the Jewish Question." *Commentary*, January 1969.

Raboteau, Albert J. *Slave Religion: The "Invisible Institution" in the Antebellum South*. New York: Oxford University Press, 1980.

Ravitzky, Aviezer. *Messianism, Zionism, and Religious Jewish Radicalism*. Chicago: University of Chicago Press, 1996.

———. "Radical Religious Zionism from the Collective to the Individual." In *Kabbalah and Contemporary Spiritual Revival*. Edited by Boaz Huss. Beer Sheva, Israel: Ben-Gurion University Press, 2011.

———. *The Roots of Kahanism: Consciousness and Political Reality*. Jerusalem: Hebrew University, 1986.

Rickford, Russell J. *We Are an African People: Independent Education, Black Power, and the Radical Imagination*. New York: Oxford University Press, 2016.

Rivlin, Rabbi Hillel of Shklov. *Kol ha-Tor*. Jerusalem: Rabbi Menachem Mendel Kasher, 1968.

Robinson, Cedric. *Black Marxism: The Making of the Black Radical Tradition*. Chapel Hill: University of North Carolina Press, 2000.

Rosen, Elly S. "The Jewish Neighborhoods: Aftermath." *Jewish Press*, June 9, 1972.

Rosenak, Avinoam. *Sedakim: Al Achdut Hafakhim ha-Politi v'Talmidei ha-Rav Kook*. Tel Aviv: Resling, 2013.

Rosenberg, M. Jay. "My Evolution as a Jew." *Midstream*, August/September, 1970.

———. "The Self-Destruction of Judaism in the American 'Jewish' Community." *Doreinu* 2, no. 5 (January 1971).

———. "To Jewish Uncle Toms." In *The Jewish 1960s: An American Sourcebook*. Edited by Michael E. Staub. Hanover, NH: Brandeis University Press, 2004.

——— "To Uncle Tom and Other Such Jews." *Jewish Defense League Newsletter*, February 13, 1969.

Rosen-Zvi, Ishay, and Adi Ofir. *Goy: Israel's Other and the Birth of the Gentile*. Oxford: Oxford University Press, 2019.

Ross, Benjamin. "'Jewish Radicals' and the Jewish Community." *Midstream*, March 1970.

Ross, Gabriel. "Zionism and the Jewish Radical." In *Jewish Radicalism: A Selected Anthology*. Edited by Jack Nusan Porter and Peter Dreier. New York: Grove, 1973.

Rothman, Stanley, and S. Robert Lichter. *Roots of Radicalism: Jews, Christians, and the Left*. New Brunswick, NJ: Transaction, 1996.

Rubenstein, Richard. "Judaism and the Death of God." *Playboy*, July 1967.

Rubin, Ronald. "The New Jewish Ethics." *Tradition* 13, no. 3 (1973).

Rudd, Mark. "Why Were So Many Jews in SDS?" Lecture presented to the New Mexico Jewish Historical Society, October 2005.

Russ, Shlomo. "The 'Zionist Hooligans': The Jewish Defense League." PhD diss., City University of New York, 1981.

Rustin, Bayard. "The Anatomy of Frustration." *Jewish Press*, July 5, 1968.

———. "From Protest to Politics: The Future of the Civil Rights Movement." *Commentary*, February 1965. Reprinted in League for Industrial Democracy, *Looking Forward*. Series of Occasional Papers, no. 1.

Sackett, Shmuel. "From Hebron to Pittsburgh." *Manhigut Yehudit*, November 2, 2018.

Said, Edward. *The Question of Palestine*. Reissue ed. New York: Vintage, 1992.

Saidel, Joanna. "Yitzhak Shamir: Why We Killed Lord Moyne." *The Times of Israel*, July 5, 2012.

Saperstein, Marc. "The Land of Israel in Pre-Modern Jewish Thought: A History of Two Rabbinic Statements." In *The Land of Israel: Jewish Perspectives*. Edited by Lawrence Hoffman. South Bend, IN: Notre Dame University Press, 1986.

Sarason, Richard. "The Significance of the Land of Israel in the Mishnah." In *The Land of Israel: Jewish Perspectives*. Edited by Lawrence Hoffman. South Bend, IN: Notre Dame University Press, 1986.

Sarna, Jonathan. *American Judaism*. New Haven, CT: Yale University Press. 2005.

Schmidt, Leigh. *Restless Souls: The Making of American Spirituality*. Los Angeles: University of California Press, 2005.

Schofer, Jonathan. *The Making of a Sage: A Study in Rabbinic Ethics*. Madison: University of Wisconsin Press, 2005.

Scholem, Gershom. "Interview with Muki Zur." In Scholem, *On Jews and Judaism in Crisis*. New York: Schocken Books, 1976.

———. *Sabbatai Zevi: The Mystical Messiah*. Princeton, NJ: Princeton University Press, 1973.

Schraub, David. "White Jews: An Intersectional Approach." *AJS Review* 43, no. 2 (2019).

Schwartz, Dov. *Etgar u'Mashber b'Hug ha-Rav Kook*. Tel Aviv: Am Oved, 2001.

Schweid, Eliezer. *Democracy and Halakhah*. Lanham, MD: University Press of America, 1994.

Seeman, Don. "Violence, Ethics, and Divine Honor in Modern Jewish Thought." *Journal of the American Academy of Religion*, no. 73 (2005).

Segev, Tom. *The Seventh Million: The Israelis and the Holocaust*. New York: Henry Holt, 2008.

Self, Robert O. *All in the Family: The Realignment of American Democracy since the 1960s*. New York: Farrar, Straus & Giroux, 2013.

———. "The Black Panther Party and the Long Civil Rights Era." In *In Search of the Black Panther Party*. Edited by Jama Lazerow and Yohuru Williams. Durham, NC: Duke University Press, 2006.

Seligman, Ben. "Negro-Jewish Relations." *Midstream*, January 1966.

Senor, Dan, and Saul Singer. *Start-Up Nation: The Story of Israel's Economic Miracle*. New York: Twelve, 2009.

Shapira, Anita. "Ben-Gurion and the Bible: The Forging of an Historical Narrative." *Middle Eastern Studies* 33, no. 4 (1997).

Shapira, Anita, and Jehuda Reinharz, eds. *Essential Papers on Zionism*. New York: NYU Press, 1995.

Shapiro, Marc B. *Between the Yeshiva World and Modern Orthodoxy: The Life and Works of Rabbi Yehiel Jacob Weinberg, 1894–1966*. Portland, OR: Littman Library of Jewish Civilization, 2002.

Shavit, Yaakov. *Jabotinsky and the Revisionist Movement 1925–1948*. London: Frank Cass, 1988.

Shelly, Steve. "Is This Any Way for Nice Jewish Boys to Behave?" *Distant Drummer*, July 23, 1970. In JDL Collection, Box 1, Folder 14. American Jewish Historical Society Archives, New York.

Shulman, Avi. *Like a Raging Fire: A Biography of Rabbi Maurice Eisendrath*. New York: UAHC, 1993.

Silk, Leonard. "Carter Expects Rise in Joblessness: Believes G.O.P Will Pick Reagan." *New York Times*, August 1, 1979.

Silverman, Jonathan. "The Law of the Land Is the Law: Antebellum Jews, Slavery, and the Old South." In *Struggles in the Promised Land: Toward a History of Black-Jewish Relations in the United States*. Edited by Jack Salzman and Cornel West. New York: Oxford University Press, 1997.

Sinkoff, Nancy. *From Left to Right: Lucy S. Dawidowicz, the New York Intellectuals, and the Politics of History*. Detroit: Wayne State University Press, 2020.

Sleeper, James. "The Case for Religious Radicalism." In *The New Jews*. Edited by James Sleeper and Alan Mintz. New York: Vintage Books, 1971.

Smooha, Sammy. "The Model of Ethnic Democracy: Israel as a Jewish and Democratic State." ECMI Working Papers 13, European Centre for Minority Issues, Flensburg, Germany, October 2001.

Sommer, Benjamin E. *The Bodies of God and the World of Ancient Israel*. New York: Cambridge University Press, 2011.

Spengler, Oswald. *The Decline of the West*. Edited by Helmut Werner and Arthur Helps. Translated by Charles Francis Atkinson. New York: Vintage Books, 2006.

Spiegel, Irving. "Jews Troubled over Negro Ties: Long Civil Rights Support Strained by Antagonisms." *New York Times*, July 8, 1968.

Sprinzak, Ehud. *The Ascendance of Israel's Radical Right*. New York: Oxford University Press, 1991.

———. *Brother against Brother: Violence and Extremism in Israeli Society*. New York: Simon & Schuster, 1986.

———. "Kach and Meir Kahane: The Emergence of Jewish Quasi-Fascism II: Ideology and Politics." Taylor & Francis Online, May 28, 2010. https://doi.org/10.1080/0031322X.1985.9969834.

Staub, Michael E., ed. *The Jewish 1960s: An American Sourcebook*. Hanover, NH: Brandeis University Press, 2004.

———. *Torn at the Roots: The Crisis of Jewish Liberalism in Postwar America*. New York: Columbia University Press, 2002.

Stern, Eliyahu. "Anti-Semitism and Orthodoxy in the Age of Trump." Tablet, March 12, 2019.

Strassfeld, Michael, and Sharon Strassfeld, eds. *The Third Jewish Catalog: Creating Community*. Philadelphia: JPS, 1980.

Strassfeld, Michael, Sharon Strassfeld, and Richard Sigel, eds. *The Jewish Catalog*. Philadelphia: JPS, 1973–1975.

Sundquist, Eric. *Strangers in the Land: Blacks, Jews, Post-Holocaust America*. Cambridge, MA: Harvard University Press, 2005.

Talmage, Frank. "Keep Your Sons from Scripture: The Bible in Medieval Jewish Scholarship and Spirituality." In *Understanding Scripture*. Edited by Clemens Thoma and Michael Wyschogrod. Mahwah, NJ: Paulist Press, 1987.

Taylor, Jared. *White Identity: Racial Consciousness of the 21st Century*. Oakton, VA: New Century Books, 2011.

Teitelbaum, Yoel. "Ma'amar 'al Yishuv Eretz Yisrael." In Teitelbaum, *Vayoel Moshe*. Brooklyn: Beit Mikhsar ve Hoza'at Sefarim, 1961.

Trilling, Lionel. *Beyond Culture: Essays on Literature and Learning*. New York: Viking, 1965.

Ture, Kwame [Stokely Carmichael], and Charles V. Hamilton. *Black Power: The Politics of Liberation in America*. New York: Vintage Books, 1967.

Ungar, Andre. "A Phenomenon Called Kahane." *SHMA* 1, no. 14 (1972).

von Mutius, Hans-Georg. "The Positions of Jews and Non-Jews in the Rabbinic Law of Overreaching (*Ona'ah*)." In *The Three Religions*. Edited by Nil Cohen et al. Munich: Herbert Utz Verlag, 2002.

Walzer, Michael, Menachem Lorberbaum, Noam J. Zohar, and Ari Ackerman, eds. *The Jewish Political Tradition*. Vol. 2. *Membership*. New Haven, CT: Yale University Press, 2006.

Waskow, Arthur. *The Bush Is Burning! Radical Judaism Faces the Pharaohs of the Modern Superstate*. New York: Macmillan, 1971.

———. "A Radical Haggadah for Passover." *Ramparts*, no. 7, April 1969.

Wasserman, Mira Beth. *Jews, Gentiles, and Other Animals: The Talmud after the Humanities*. Philadelphia: University of Pennsylvania Press, 2017.

Watts, Steven. *Mr. Playboy: Hugh Hefner and the American Dream*. Hoboken, NJ: Wiley, 2008.

Weinman, Sarah. "The Woman on the Bridge." *The Cut*, April 12, 2020.

Weintraub, Bernard. "Meeting Appeals to Soviet Jews." *New York Times*, February 20, 1971.

Weisburd, David. *Jewish Settler Violence: Deviance as Social Reaction*. University Park: Pennsylvania State University Press, 1989.

Weiss, Avi. *Open Up the Iron Door: Memoirs of a Soviet Jewry Activist*. New York: Toby, 2015.

Wexler, Philip, and Eli Rubin. *A Social Vision: The Lubavitcher Rebbe's Transformative Paradigm for the World*. New York: Herder & Herder, 2019.

Whitfield, Stephen. *The Culture of the Cold War*. Baltimore: Johns Hopkins University Press, 1991.

Wieseltier, Leon. "The Demon of the Jews." *The New Republic*, November 11, 1985.

Wilderson, Frank III. *Afropessimism*. New York: W. W. Norton, 2020.

———. *Red, White, and Black: Cinema and the Structure of Antagonisms*. Durham, NC: Duke University Press, 2010.

Williams, Roger. *Negroes with Guns*. New York: Marzani & Munsell, 1962.

Wisse, Ruth. *If I Am Not for Myself: The Liberal Betrayal of the Jews*. Boston: Free Press, 1992.

———. *Jews and Power*. New York: Schocken Books, 2007.

Wistrich, Robert. *A Lethal Obsession: Anti-Semitism from Antiquity to the Global Jihad*. New York: Random House, 2009.

Wolfe, Tom. *Radical Chic and Mau-Mauing the Flak Catchers*. New York: Farrar, Straus & Giroux, 1970.

Woocher, Jonathan. "Jewish Survivalism as Communal Ideology: An Empirical Assessment." *Journal of Jewish Communal Service* 54, no. 4 (1983).

———. *Sacred Survival: The Civil Religion of American Jews*. Bloomington: Indiana University Press, 1986.

Yancy, George. *Backlash: What Happens When We Talk Honestly about Racism in America*. Lanham, MD: Roman & Littlefield, 2017.

Yedidya, Asaf. *Halakha and the Challenge of Israeli Sovereignty*. Lanham, MD: Lexington Books, 2019.

Yiftachel, Oren. *Ethnocracy: Land and Identity in Israel/Palestine*. Philadelphia: University of Pennsylvania Press, 2006.

Zenger, Erich. *A God of Vengeance? Understanding the Psalms of Divine Wrath*. Translated by Linda M. Maloney. Louisville, KY: John Knox, 1994.

Ziegler, Mel. "The Jewish Defense League and Its Invisible Constituency." *New York*, April 19, 1971.

Archival Material or Articles without Authorial Attribution

Student Nonviolent Coordinating Committee. "Position Paper: The Basis of Black Power" (1966). Reprint, The Sixties Project, 1993. http://www2.iath.virginia.edu/sixties/HTML_docs/Map.html.

"A Very Stern Discipline: An Interview with Ralph Ellison." *Harper's*, March 1967.

"Religion and the New Morality: A Symposium." *Playboy*, June 1967.

"Symposium: Chicago's 'Black Caucus.'" *Ramparts* 6, no. 4 (November 1967).

"Jewish Defense League: Aims and Purposes." YIVO Institute for Jewish Research, New York, 1968.

Interview with Meir Kahane. *Newark Star Ledger*, August 8, 1968.

"Behavior: The Black and the Jew: A Falling Out of Allies." *Time*, January 31, 1969. http://content.time.com/time/magazine/article/0,9171,841586,00.html.

Complaint of United Federation of Teachers, New York, N.Y. Concerning Station WBAI-FM, New York, N.Y., Fairness Doctrine, 17 F.C.C. 69-302 (1969).

"Hillel vs. the Elders." *Newsweek*, December 9, 1969.

"Jewish Activists in N.Y. March against Radio Station WBAI." *Jewish Press*, January 31, 1969.

"Jewish Defense League Advertisement, Tactics Denounced by New York Jewish Leaders."

Jewish Telegraphic Agency, October 10, 1969. https://www.jta.org/1969/10/10/archive/jewish-defense-league-advertisement-tactics-denounced-by-new-york-jewish-leaders.

"Problems of Intermarriage in America Discussed in Israel." *Jewish Press*, January 13, 1969.

"Jewish Klansman." *Morning Freiheit*, September 6, 1970.

"JDL Denounces Jewish Anti-War Groups as More Dangerous to Israel than Arabs." Jewish Telegraphic Agency, May 19, 1970. In JDL Collection, Box 1, Folder 11. American Jewish Historical Society Archives, New York.

Jerusalem Post. "The JDL: Heroes or Hooligans?" March 4, 1970. In JDL collection, Box 49, Folder 6. American Jewish Historical Society Archives, New York.

"Never Again . . . to Us." *Cambridge Phoenix*, February 5, 1970.

Novoseller, Harold. Article. *Philadelphia Enquirer*, August 30, 1970. In JDL Collection, Box 1, Folder 6. American Jewish Historical Society Archives, New York.

"ADL Deplores Wiretapping on the JDL." *Jewish Leader*, July 1, 1971.

Advertisement for the Baltimore-Washington Union of Jewish Students. *Doreinu* 2, no. 7 (April 1971).

"Brussels Declaration on Soviet Jews." *New York Times*, February 26, 1971.

"800 Arrested at Soviet Jewry Rally." *Jewish Press*, March 26, 1971.

"800 Protesters for Soviet Jews Arrested in Capital." *New York Times*, March 22, 1971.

Interview with Meir Kahane. *The Flame*, Winter 1971. Reprinted in Jack Nusan Porter and Peter Dreier, eds., *Jewish Radicalism: A Selected Anthology*. New York: Grove, 1973.

"Kahane Defends Alliance with Italian Group: Vows Harassment of Syrian, Iraqi Officials." Jewish Telegraphic Agency, April 1971. In JDL Collection, Box 1, Folder 12, American Jewish Historical Society Archives, New York.

"Kahane: JDL Would Use Dynamite If Necessary." Jewish Telegraphic Agency, July 12, 1971.

"Kahane Uproar Stymies Brussels." *Jewish Advocate*, February 25, 1971.

"Kahane Would Ship All U.S. Jews to Israel." *Jewish Post and Opinion*, May 7, 1971.

"Progressive Jewish Leaders Condemn JDL." *Morning Freiheit*, January 31, 1971. Interview with Meir Kahane. *Playboy*, October 1972.

"Kahane Calls It an Insane Act." *New York Times*, January 27, 1972.

"Outrage upon Outrage." *New York Times*, January 27, 1972.

"Kahane Ordered to a U.S. Prison." *New York Times*, November 27, 1975.

"After the Elections: Fear and Apprehension over Kahane's Election to the Knesset." Jewish Telegraphic Agency, July 30, 1984. https://www.jta.org/1984/07/30/archive/after-the-elections-fear-and-apprehension-over-kahanes-election-to-the-knesset.

"The JDL Is a Menace." *Torrington Register*, n.d. In JDL Collection, Box 1247, Folder 46. YIVO Archives, New York.

"JWV Commander Condemns Violence and JDL Threats." In JDL Collection, Box 47, Folder 47.4. YIVO Archives, New York.

The Megillah of Anatoly Sharansky, n.d. In JDL Collection, Box 1, Folder 10. American Jewish Historical Society Archives, New York.

INDEX

A NOTE ON THE TYPE

This book has been composed in Arno, an Old-style serif typeface in the classic Venetian tradition, designed by Robert Slimbach at Adobe.